T0320890

Monetary Policy in Low Financial Development Countries

Monetary Policy in Low Financial Development Countries

JUAN ANTONIO MORALES AND PAUL REDING

OXFORD
UNIVERSITY PRESS

OXFORD

UNIVERSITY PRESS

Great Clarendon Street, Oxford, OX2 6DP,
United Kingdom

Oxford University Press is a department of the University of Oxford.
It furthers the University's objective of excellence in research, scholarship,
and education by publishing worldwide. Oxford is a registered trade mark of
Oxford University Press in the UK and in certain other countries

First Edition published in 2021

Impression: 1

Published in the United States of America by Oxford University Press
198 Madison Avenue, New York, NY 10016, United States of America

British Library Cataloguing in Publication Data
Data available

Library of Congress Control Number: 2020952114

ISBN 978–0–19–885471–5

DOI: 10.1093/oso/9780198854715.001.0001

Printed and bound by
CPI Group (UK) Ltd, Croydon, CR0 4YY

*A Cécile et Geneviève
qui par leur soutien et leur patience ont permis la réalisation de ce livre*

Preface

The book is the outgrowth of the course 'Macroeconomic and structural adjustment: monetary and financial aspects' taught for many years by Paul Reding at the University of Namur in the Specialized Master in International and Development Economics. This programme is jointly organized by the University of Namur (UNamur) and the Catholic University of Louvain (UCLouvain), with the support of the Commission for Development Cooperation of the Belgian Académie de Recherche et d'Enseignement supérieur (ARES). Most of the students enrolled in the programme come from developing countries. Juan Antonio Morales participated as invited academic scholar over several years, teaching parts of the course and letting students benefit from his wide experience in policy-making, having served as President of the Central Bank of Bolivia for more than ten years.

Based on the experience with successive cohorts of students, both of us found it worthwhile to develop further the material prepared for the course and to extend it into a book. True to its pedagogical roots, the book is set at an intermediate level. When it refers to a theoretical analysis, top priority is given to economic intuition. It employs little mathematical formalization, without sacrificing rigour. It relies widely on empirical illustrations, and backs the discussion with case studies. We hope that this perspective, as well as the depth and width that we have endeavoured to give to the book, will be of interest to lecturers and students as well as to scholars, practitioners. and other readers, curious about the role and characteristics of monetary policy in developing countries, especially in those which face specific challenges because of their incomplete financial development.

Preparing the book has been an adventure for both of us. It was been shaped during many short-term visits by Juan Antonio to Namur, at the department of economics, and by Paul to La Paz, at the department of Maestrías para el Desarrollo of the Universidad Católica Boliviana (UCB). It is the fruit of numerous exchanges, face to face or over the internet, through which we have developed our analysis, drawing on our respective strengths and experiences, organized the discussion, and crafted the presentation of the issues this book is about. The book has also benefited from extended discussions with colleagues, in particular during seminars that we have respectively given in Namur and La Paz. Interactions with our students, which we were fortunate to experience over so many years, have been a very strong encouragement to complete the book. This valuable support from our colleagues and students from both universities is gratefully acknowledged.

Financial support by ARES of the Specialized Master in International and Development Economics allowed Juan Antonio to teach in the programme and, ultimately, triggered the book. This support is gratefully acknowledged, as well as the support of UNamur and of the Belgian Fonds National de la Recherche Scientifique (FNRS), which allowed Paul to make several research stays at UCB in La Paz. The Tinker Foundation and the IIE Scholar Rescue Fund gave Juan Antonio the opportunity to discuss his experiences and ideas with colleagues and students at the Institute of Latin American Studies at Columbia University in New York while he was a visiting professor.

Contents

List of Abbreviations

AD	aggregate demand
AE	advanced economy
ALP	autonomous liquidity position
BCEAO	Banque Centrale des États de l'Afrique de l'Ouest (Central Bank of WAEMU)
BEAC	Banque des États de l'Afrique Centrale (Central Bank of CEMAC)
CBDC	central bank digital currency
CBI	central bank independence
CEMAC	Communauté Économique et Monétaire de l'Afrique Centrale (Central African Economic and Monetary Community)
CEMLA	Centro de Estudios Monetarios Latino Americanos (Center for Latin American Monetary Studies)
CFA	Communauté Française d'Afrique (French African Community)
CIP	covered interest parity
CMI	Chiang Mai Initiative
CPI	consumer price index
DSGE	dynamic stochastic general equilibrium (model)
EAC	East African Community
ECB	European Central Bank
ECCU	Eastern Carribean Currency Union
ECOWAS	Economic Community of West African States
EME	emerging market economy
EMU	European Monetary Union
FD	financial development
FLAR	Fondo Latinoamericano de Reservas (Latin American Reserve Fund)
FPAS	forecasting and policy analysis system
FRB	Federal Reserve Board
FTPL	fiscal theory of the price level
FX	foreign exchange
GDP	gross domestic product
GIBC	government's intertemporal budget constraint
HI	high income
IMF	International Monetary Fund
IR	international reserves
IRF	impulse response function
IT	inflation targeting
LCR	liquidity coverage ratio
LFDC	low financial development country
LI	low income
LIC	Low income country

LM	lower middle income
LOLR	lender of last resort
M_1	money stock (narrow definition)
M_2, M_3	money stock (broad definitions)
MFI	micro-financial institutions
MPR	monetary policy rate
MTM	monetary transmission mechanism
MU	monetary union
NDA	net domestic assets
NFA	net foreign assets
NGO	non-governmental organization
NIR	net international reserves
NKPC	New Keynesian Phillips curve
NMFI	non-monetary financial intermediary
OCA	optimal currency area
OMO	open market operation
ONIR	overnight interbank rate
PCL	Precautionary Credit Line (IMF)
PLS	profit and loss sharing
PPI	producer price index
RCF	Rapid Credit Facility (IMF)
RE	rational expectations
REPO	repurchase operation
RTGS	real time gross settlement
SDR	special drawing right
SSA	sub-Saharan Africa
UIP	uncovered interest parity
UM	upper middle income
WDI	World Development Indicators (World Bank)
WAEMU	West African Economic and Monetary Union
WAMZ	West African Monetary Zone

List of Figures, Tables, and Boxes

Figures

Tables

Boxes

Introduction and overview

The aim of the book is to give a broad and rigorous overview of the main monetary policy issues and challenges faced by developing countries which have low domestic financial depth and are weakly integrated with the international capital market. Most of these countries—which we label 'low financial development countries' (LFDCs)—are in the low- or middle-income categories. Their monetary policy issues have attracted less attention than those of emerging market countries.

In our book we address the main aspects of monetary policy-making from the specific perspective of LFDCs. We take into account major differences in institutions and in economic and financial structures between LFDCs and other countries. These include shallowness of their financial markets, high exposure to external price shocks, extent of informal labour markets, low degree of financial inclusion, weak coordination between governments and central banks, and difficulties in establishing credibility of the monetary policy authorities in countries marked by a long history of inflationary derailments.

For the monetary policy issues we have selected, we take as starting point the academic and policy discussions of these issues in advanced and emerging market countries. We then go a step further and assess to what extent the broad lessons of these discussions need to be qualified when applied to a LFDC. With this purpose in mind, we draw on the many fine studies in academia or in research departments of international organizations published in recent years, specifically dealing with monetary policy issues in low-income countries., For each issue, we first present the concepts needed to grasp its essence, and survey the relevant research findings and their policy conclusions. Figures and tables illustrate the situation in LFDCs for the issue at hand, while case studies explore significant policy experiences.

The book is structured in seven chapters.

Chapter 1 gives a general overview of the nuts and bolts of monetary policy. It discusses, with some historical background, the special role of money in the financial system, the functions of central banks, the mandates society has entrusted them with, and the operating framework they use to achieve these goals. It also presents the main characteristics of the LFDCs. A synthetic financial development indicator is used to give an empirical content to our selection of countries.

Chapter 2 explores the monetary transmission mechanism in LFDCs, in turn discussing the interest rate, asset price, bank credit, balance sheet, exchange rate, expectations, and real balance channels. Each individual channel's strength and reliability is examined for the context of LFDCs and the available empirical evidence is surveyed. The specificities of the bank lending channel are discussed at some length, pointing to the challenges to its effectiveness posed by weak lending incentives, a high level of informal or semi-formal (microfinance) financial intermediation, and, in some countries, a duality between the conventional and Islamic banking systems. The chapter concludes with a global assessment of the effectiveness of the monetary transmission mechanism in LFDCs. Evidence points to a transmission mechanism that is active although not very strong, and possibly also more uncertain than in advanced and emerging market countries.

Chapter 3 presents and discusses the instruments of monetary policy that are used by LFDCs' central banks. Direct instruments, like exchange controls, are still common in LFDCs, but indirect instruments similar to those used in advanced economies are increasingly employed. The chapter surveys the particular features of each instrument, with a discussion of its purpose, its mechanisms, and the operational aspects and modalities of its use. The following instruments are examined: reserve requirements, refinancing and deposit facilities, open market operations, and foreign exchange interventions, as well as the instruments deployed by central banks to guarantee financial stability.

Chapter 4 focuses on two key aspects of the monetary policy process. First, on the trade-offs between the three goals that fall within the purview of central banks: price stability, output stabilization, and financial stability. Second, on the role of central bank credibility for the efficacy of monetary policy and the contributions of central bank independence and transparency in enhancing credibility. The emphasis is on how specific features of LFDCs impact the nature of the policy trade-offs, such as informality in the labour market for the inflation–output trade-off, or the high exposure to external shocks combined with a lack of financial depth for financial stability concerns. The effectiveness of central bank independence and transparency to help achieve monetary policy goals, particularly keeping a check on inflation, is also assessed.

Chapter 5 explores two significant challenges faced by central banks in LFDCs: fiscal dominance and exogenous shocks. Monetary policy can be dominated by governments which rely on seigniorage generated by the central bank or which impose other constraints, akin to financial repression, to facilitate the financing of persistent deficits. The chapter discusses and illustrates for several countries the concept of seigniorage, examines the mechanisms of fiscal dominance, and assesses its consequences. An appendix is devoted to the fiscal theory of the price level and its possible relevance for LFDCs. External oil and food price shocks also raise several monetary policy challenges. Using a theoretical approach, the chapter explores the trade-off between price and output stabilization that the central bank faces after an international commodity price shock, taking into account whether the country is a net exporter or a net importer of the commodity and whether it follows a fixed or a flexible exchange rate regime. The chapter discusses in particular the coordination issues between monetary and fiscal policies when windfall gains accrue to the government.

Chapter 6 evaluates the choice of a monetary anchor for LFDCs. Nominal anchors are a crucial part of an explicit monetary framework, even if not all LFDCs have a clearly spelled-out one. We focus on three main anchor types: exchange rates, monetary aggregates, and inflation targeting. For each nominal anchor, the advantages, drawbacks, prerequisites for its adoption and modalities of its implementation are discussed, without sidelining the salient observation that such processes are often pursued in a blurred and eclectic way in LFDCs. The chapter also examines in detail the special case of anchors in dollarized economies, i.e. in countries where foreign currency is used pervasively in functions of domestic currency. The chapter contains two appendixes. The first deals with international reserves and their international borrowing arrangements. The second is a case study of the West and Central African Economic and Monetary Unions.

This last chapter deals with the analytical approach developed by central banks with the use of various types of model, both for forecasting and for policy analysis. The chapter discusses the main characteristics of the models used, their strengths and limitations. It assesses how dynamic stochastic general equilibrium (DSGE) models are used for monetary policy analysis. Examples are provided on how they contribute to exploring fundamental, long-term policy issues specific to LFDCs. The chapter also discusses the contribution of small semi-structural models that, though less strongly theory-grounded than DSGE models, can be brought closer to the available data and are therefore possibly better suited to the context of LFDCs. Attention is also drawn to the key role of judgement as the indispensable complement, in monetary policy decision-making, to model-based policy analysis.

The book shows that monetary policy in LFDCs has to deal with many of the same issues faced by emerging market and advanced economies. But, though monetary policy issues may indeed be, in an abstract way, the same as in any other country, they have to be addressed differently in LFDCs. The challenges encountered by monetary policy in these countries are significantly more salient, and made more severe by the typical constraints that characterize them or are imposed on them. These include a difficult monetary policy transmission mechanism, high vulnerability to external shocks, weak institutional capacity, and poor capability to monitor the economy because of the paucity of data. Much progress has been made in recent years by LFDC central banks in improving their capacity to deal with these challenges. These remain huge, however, particularly since they are now compounded by the unprecedented shock of the corona virus pandemic. We briefly discuss this new challenge in our Afterword.

1

Money, Central Banks, and Low Financial Development Countries

1.1 Introduction

Of all aspects of economic policy, the issues addressed by monetary policy are probably among the most difficult to apprehend. Although money is in people's everyday life a familiar concept, the role it plays in the economy and the reasons why it should be monitored or controlled by some authority are far from self-evident. Understanding this fundamental question is particularly important when one realizes that central banks, the authorities in charge of monetary policy, are assigned in almost all countries, advanced or developing, a predominant role in the design of a country's economic policy.

Monetary policy is currently a well-established branch of economic policy. Together with fiscal, trade, industrial, educational, environmental policies and other branches of economic policy, it aims at influencing the behaviour of economic agents, households, firms, and organizations, so as to reach specific welfare-improving policy goals.

As a subdiscipline of macroeconomic policy, monetary policy is concerned with aggregate nominal and real variables which are of paramount importance for the well-being of a country's residents, like price and wage levels, employment, output, interest rates, and exchange rates.

In this chapter we first explore this question at a general level. We discuss in section 1.2 the various aspects that make money special in an economy: (i) how it is defined and shaped by people's attitude with regard to its fundamental characteristic, that of being a 'generally accepted means of payment'; (ii) how changes in its supply and demand impinge on the equilibrium of the financial system, in which it is deeply embedded; (iii) how the mechanisms through which it is supplied endows the central bank with the capacity to influence the financial system and thereby exert its monetary policy responsibilities. Section 1.3 is then devoted to the analysis of the central bank's monetary policy missions. Society nowadays entrusts central banks with a fundamental mission: 'anchoring' the country's price level by pursuing price stability as the principal monetary policy goal. Other important mandates are also given to central banks, like smoothing output business cycles and guaranteeing financial stability. To achieve their monetary policy

Monetary Policy in Low Financial Development Countries. Juan Antonio Morales and Paul Reding, Oxford University Press.
© Juan Antonio Morales and Paul Reding 2021. DOI: 10.1093/oso/9780198854715.003.0001

goals with maximum effectiveness, central banks put in place a specific monetary framework. The role of such a framework is to help them monitor the effects of their instruments on their ultimate goals, in the context of significant uncertainty about the environment in which the economy evolves. The choice of ultimate goals and the choice of specific intermediate and operating targets, as well as the set of available instruments, fully define the operational space in which the central bank implements its monetary policy. The framework's two main building blocks are intermediate targets and operating targets. For each of them, we discuss the alternatives among which central banks may choose.

Following this mostly general discussion of money and monetary policy, we devote section 1.4 to the specific case of the low financial development countries (LFDCs) which are the centre of this book. The aim is to offer a more thorough discussion of the main monetary policy issues relating to this special case. While we leave the in-depth discussion to the following chapters, in this section we present the main characteristics of LFDCs that are relevant for the design of monetary policy. We pay particular attention to the features of their economic and financial environment that condition the effects of central banks' interventions on the country's financial and real sectors, or that impose particular constraints on monetary policy. We then identify empirically the countries which we consider belong to our set of LFDCs. To this end, we develop a simple synthetic Financial Development Index and use it in the selection of LFDCs. Our set contains 112 countries, for which we provide the relevant characteristics.

1.2 Money and the financial system

Monetary policy is a very specific macroeconomic policy. It focuses on the mechanisms through which changes in the supply and demand of money affect the economy's nominal and real variables, having as key target variables aggregate output and the general price level. These mechanisms are embedded in the economy's financial system. Money is only one in a basket of many assets which people maintain as a store of value—though a very particular one.

Loosely speaking, the financial system organizes the ways in which agents can allocate their wealth among many different assets and can accumulate and transfer it across time. Money plays a key role in the financial system, and thus monetary policy necessarily operates in the heart of the broad financial environment. Changes in the supply and demand of money will alter the conditions that agents confront in their decisions on wealth allocation and accumulation. A telling example is the effect of money on the level of nominal interest rates.

We briefly discuss money, its definition and evolution, and its role in the financial system.

1.2.1 Money

Money can be defined in its more general sense as 'anything that is generally accepted in payment for goods and services or in the repayment of debts' (Mishkin 1995: 3). Money is a good different from other goods in the economy in that it does not generate utility directly. People use money primarily because it facilitates transactions. Because it is, by definition, a 'generally accepted means of payment', money saves on information and transaction costs, which enhances economic efficiency and improves people's welfare. The transition from barter to a monetary economy is one of mankind's very early instances of technical progress.

Money is what the public accepts as money, i.e. as means of payment. To be useful, money needs to display first and foremost its fundamental characteristic of general acceptability as a means of payment, currently as well as in the future. The good used as money needs to inspire full confidence that its value, expressed in terms of all the other goods and services, is stable over time. Money has to inspire unconditional trust to its users. Also, there are some technical requirements for a good to serve as money, like divisibility and easiness of storage. In its early history, the use of the 'money good' imposed itself on direct barter transactions because, in addition to being a means of exchange, it kept its own 'use' or intrinsic value. Gold and silver possessed this double characteristic.

Over time, fiat monies were introduced. Banknotes, or 'paper money', have no intrinsic value. They circulate on the basis of a general confidence in the issuer of the notes, and are used as long as such confidence is maintained. Banknotes now circulate as legal tender in almost all countries. With the development of commercial banks, the deposits people held with them evolved to become another generally accepted means of payments, scriptural money. The changes in form money has undergone have always been driven by society's efforts to minimize the cost of using and holding it for transaction purposes. Money's history is that of successive financial innovations in the technology of payments (see Box 1.1).

Despite the fact that money does not yield direct utility, nor in general carries a return as an asset, no modern economy would be viable without it. Indeed, money is a necessary institution for exchange. In the absence of money, transaction costs would be staggering and would paralyse the economy.[1] Beyond its mere existence,

---

[1] The breakdown of the chain of payments that frequently goes with a bank panic suggests what such paralysing effects could be. With the breakdown, transactions are conducted only in bills and coins, and in some extreme cases, recourse is made to barter. These primitive forms of exchange have on impact very large efficiency costs that cause significant drops in output. However, judging from historical experience, payments breakdowns are transitory, as the reconstitution and consolidation of banks, crucial agents in the payment system, are seen as a priority by the authorities and the public itself. The banks' recovery then proceeds rapidly.

Box 1.1. Money and technical progress in payments

Over the course of history money has experienced many changes and has been the object of significant technical progress. In the very beginning, goods like cattle, shells, salt bars, and jewels served as money, in addition to their other uses. Soon, precious metals that had the desirable characteristic of being high-value goods with respect to their weight, and that furthermore were divisible, were used in the form of coins. To enhance the acceptability of coins, they would often carry a seal given by the authorities. Minted coins were characterized by a standard weight of precious metal, fixed by the issuing authority. However, this official guarantee was often eroded by the seigneurs who tried to obtain more coinage with the same amount of precious metal. This was called 'debasement'. The net gain so achieved was called seigniorage. The first coins were issued in Lydia (Asia Minor) in the seventh century BC as well as in China at about the same period (Eagleton and Williams 2007: 23). Greek, Roman, and Chinese coins circulated in their respective zones of economic and cultural influence. Coinage later became widespread in Europe, Asia and North-Africa.

Paper currency appeared in Europe in the seventeenth century, first in Sweden, later in France and Britain. It was already circulating in China in the twelfth century, as exchange notes with no date limitation that were issued by the Imperial Treasury. During the Mongol Yuan dynasty, from the early thirteenth to mid -fourteenth century, it even circulated as the only means of payment, as the use of metallic coin money was not permitted (Eagleton and Williams 2007: 149). In Europe, paper currency was initially issued by banks set up as joint stock companies, often with close links to the sovereign. Bank exchange notes were a pledge granted by the issuing bank to convert on demand the paper notes into metallic monies, and were thus called 'fiat money'. Later, in the nineteenth century, a monopoly to issue paper money was given to a selected bank. The latter became the country's central bank, entrusted with missions of public interest. In the course of history, convertibility was not always assured, particularly in times of war or civil strife, yet often paper money continued circulating. The role of paper money as means of payment was further reinforced with the property of legal tender given to it. With legal tender creditors cannot, in principle, refuse payment in domestic paper money, unless agreed differently in a contract.

Bank notes were soon complemented by another form of money, *scriptural money*, that emerged with the advent of commercial banks. Their customers deposited paper currency and metallic monies with them, and were offered the facility to draw cheques against these deposits as well as make transfers to other people. A large part of the paper currency and metallic monies deposited by customers could then be lent by banks to other customers. This was done by crediting the amount of the loan to the deposit account of the borrower. The latter could then write cheques to make payments. The banks' lending created thereby money, the 'scriptural' form of it. This was an early step in dematerializing money. Developments in the payments technologies like electronic transfers and the extraordinary recent expansion of fintech (an amalgam of finance and digital technology) have further contributed to the dematerialization of money. Banknotes, while still used, represent a decreasing fraction of total transactions, both in industrialized and in developing countries.

it is the quality of money, i.e. its *general* acceptability as a means of exchange, that is the crucial determinant of its contribution to economic efficiency.

Money is used as a means of payment because it rests on a 'network externality'. People use and hold money because they know that everyone else in the country will accept it, now and in the future, as payment for goods and services and for the settlement of debts. As such, money is a social institution. Also, the organizations that issue, manage, and preserve it are of key importance. Money's defining quality, the *general* acceptability as a means of exchange, is usually taken for granted and may go unnoticed in tranquil times. However, in periods of economic and financial stress, the officially circulating money of a country can be contested by its users. Box 1.2 gives some examples that illustrate, by contrast, the qualities any means of payment needs to fulfil the role of money.[2]

Most fiat monies were and are issued by governments, or the authority delegated by them to this end, the central banks. They have a government backing and they are legal tender.[3] This obviously strengthens their general acceptability. Scriptural money is issued by private (and sometimes public) financial intermediaries. Its quality as a generally accepted means of payment rests on the confidence people have in the issuing banks and on the quality of the interbank payments

---

[2] Again, the key quality of money is to be a generally accepted means of payment in a given country, as a minimum within its borders. Thus, 'complementary currencies', also called 'local currencies' or 'community currencies', cannot be considered as 'money', despite their name, as they do not meet this fundamental characteristic of general acceptability. These 'alternative currencies' have been developed to foster social inclusion and community development. They aim at stimulating socioeconomic interactions among members and reciprocity in services through the use of a specific 'means of exchange'. Their network is geographically limited (a village, a city block, a region) or active in specific sectors (education, health care). While most complementary currency networks are deployed in advanced economy (AE) countries, some have also been set up in developing countries as part as a development strategy targeting the poorest (e.g. the Sarafu Network in Kenya).

[3] This does not preclude, of course, that contracts can be written with a settlement clause in a foreign currency. In heavily dollarized countries, settlement in foreign currency is the norm rather than the exception.

Box 1.2. Money in periods of economic and financial stress

That money is a social institution becomes particularly clear in times of economic and financial distress. It is in such circumstances that money's defining quality, of being accepted without question by the population at large as medium of exchange, is put to the test. We briefly discuss four examples of how people have reacted in times of economic duress to current or expected changes in the quality of the domestic money stock.

- *Currency substitution.* In many countries across the world, episodes of high inflation and hyperinflation have imposed large opportunity costs on the use of domestic money. Hanke and Krus (2012) provide a list of fifty-six hyperinflation episodes over 1945–2011. Among those, are Latin America countries in the 1980s (e.g. Argentina–1989, Bolivia–1984, Peru–1988, Nicaragua–1986) and, in the 1990s, countries from Africa (e.g. Angola–1994 and the Democratic Republic of Congo–1998) and Central Europe (e.g. Armenia–1993 and Georgia–1992), and, as recently as 2007, Zimbabwe.[4] With bouts of monthly inflation rates frequently above three digits during such episodes, people realized that the future purchasing power of current holdings of domestic currency was turning to nil. They turned to an available alternative currency, very often the US dollar, or to goods that could be stored. Dollar bills (or Deutschmarks or South African Rands) were used in day-to-day payments. (Note that the guarantor of dollar bills in circulation is the United States government and not the national government.) Soon, domestic banks started to issue foreign-currency sight deposits to accommodate the public's demand to make domestic payments in foreign currency for large amounts. Cash automats dispensing both foreign and domestic currency notes also became widely available. Through economic interest as well as by social convention, a foreign currency was now widely accepted as means of payment, even as domestic money continued circulating at the margin, with legal tender among its few remaining qualities. In due course, currency substitution was accompanied by asset and liability substitution, with banks offering attractive quasi-monetary foreign-currency deposits and granting credits in foreign currency. This happened with the agreement of the domestic regulatory authorities, and paved the way for

---

[4] Hanke and Krus (2012) define, following Cagan (1956), the start of a hyperinflation episode as the month during which consumer prices increased by at least 50% (p. 11). Venezuela in 2018 can be added to the list in the text, as the country's annual inflation rate reached that year 65,374%, according to IMF's World Economic Outlook April 2020 database.

financial dollarization which still persists in many of these countries. The initial rejection of domestic money by the public following the destruction of its quality by high-inflation episodes has thereby profoundly altered the nature of financial institutions, as well as monetary policy, in these countries.

- *Fiat currency without any government backing: the Kurd experience (1991–2003).* In the account by King (2004) and Varian (2004), two currencies circulated in Iraq during and after the Gulf War in 1991, corresponding to the de facto division of the country into two parts. The first currency, 'Saddam dinars', were issued by the Iraqi government and were legal tender. When these were first issued in 1993, a short period of time was given to change the old dinars for the new ones. Since people in Northern Iraq could not or were not willing to change old dinars, these continued to circulate there. These dinars had been printed by a British printer using Swiss plates, and this gave the name of 'Swiss dinars' to the old dinars. As the government of Saddam Hussein had to finance its various war ventures and as it was increasingly isolated, it could not borrow internationally or domestically, and had recourse to the printing press, unleashing high inflation. In contrast, the Swiss dinars were in fixed supply. The implicit exchange rate of the Saddam dinar against the Swiss dinar fell precipitously. The important point to underline is that Swiss dinars, with no government backing whatsoever, circulated as good money, on the belief that they would continue to be widely accepted and that a future monetary institution, at the end of the war, would recognize and guarantee the value of the Swiss dinar (King 2004: 13). These expectations proved right ultimately: in 2003, after the defeat of Saddam, a new Iraqi currency was issued. The conversion of both currencies into the new one implied an exchange rate of 1 Swiss dinar against 150 Saddam dinars.
- *Quasi-money to make up for a shortage of narrow money*: the Argentinian experience (2001–6). Argentina was from 1991 on a currency board with the US dollar. This stipulated a hard peg to the US dollar and that the monetary base needed to be 100% backed by US dollar reserves at the central bank.[5] The currency board came under stress in 2001, because difficulties in serving the external debt, the low rate of GDP growth, and overvaluation of the exchange rate weakened the credibility of the peso–dollar peg (de la Torre et al. 2003). Despite adjustment measures by the government, huge difficulties remained in financing the budget deficit,

---

[5] A fuller account of currency board arrangements can be found in section 6.2.4.2.

Continued

Box 1.2. *Continued*

both for the general government and for the provinces. Having exhausted the financing possibilities of domestic markets and faced with the limited possibility of turning to the central bank for monetary financing without violating the rules of the currency board, the government and the provinces proceeded to make payments (e.g. salaries of public employees) in various types of short-term interest-bearing bonds, issued in small denominations. People were forced to accept these quasi-monetary public liabilities (lecops, patacones, and others), in payment for delivered goods or services, or as transfers. At the same time there was a shortage of money due to the sharp contraction of its supply, the result of significant capital flight, and the imposition of limits of withdrawals of cash from banks (the 'corralito'). As a result, acceptance of these quasi-monies as a parallel medium of exchange became more widespread, as supermarkets and retail stores accepted them at par with the peso and up to 100% of purchases, and as they were made redeemable for tax payments. These quasi-monies were issued in large amounts, reaching 37.5% of total pesos in circulation by March 2002 after the end of the currency board (de la Torre et al. 2003). They were however considered as second-class money, a medium of exchange which failed the test of general acceptability, the key characteristic of money. They were a kind of 'necessity money', which people preferred to spend, holding on to their pesos which were still convertible in dollars.[6] As noted by de la Torre et al. (2010: p.2) 'pesos were precious at the time, and the "quasis" did the trick rather well, in a re-enactment of Gresham's law'.[7] When the economy recovered after the devaluation, the amount of quasi-money in circulation was progressively redeemed by its issuers against regular pesos.

- *Parallel markets for different forms of domestic currency.* Parallel markets for foreign currency are well known when the availability of foreign currency is curtailed by exchange controls. However, exchanging one form of money for another form of the same currency at an exchange rate

---

[6] The term 'necessity money' goes back to the 1921 German hyperinflation, when cities and large enterprises issued their own banknotes (*Notgeld*) because the central bank, the Reichsbank, was unable materially to keep up printing and distributing new banknotes, which needed to be issued in ever larger denominations.

[7] 'Gresham's law' refers to the principle that if two types of money circulate with the same official face value, the 'bad' money will progressively drive the 'good' one out of circulation, as the 'good' one will be hoarded. The law dates back to the period when money circulated in the form of gold or silver coins. New coins issued with an intrinsic value below their face value (a 'debasement' by the issuer) dominated the older coins, whose value as precious metal still coincided with their face value and which people therefore preferred to hoard.

different from one is clearly an oddity. An example is the case of the Democratic Republic of Congo from 1993 to 1997, a period characterized by very high inflation and the disruption of banks' payment system. As told by Beauregard (2003) and Lendele and Kamanda Kimona-Mbinga (2005), banks had difficulties in converting deposits to domestic cash, not being themselves able to get the cash from the central bank. As a result, a significant discount on sight deposits relative to currency notes emerged, at times reaching levels above 50% and lasting several years. Beauregard (2003) also notes that during this period, new notes issued by the central bank often were not fully accepted as money over the whole territory of the Republic. New Zaire (NZ) notes were boycotted in Kasai province, while later a high-denomination NZ note introduced in Katanga was boycotted in Kinshasa. In each case the less accepted notes traded on a parallel market at a discount relative to the more widely accepted ones. These discounts clearly illustrate the principle that money is what people consider as money, i.e. what they expect to be accepted unconditionally by others in payments.

infrastructure. Both a strengthened regulation of banks and the setting-up of deposit insurance have contributed in many countries to the development of scriptural money in the recent past.

Today, a country's money stock, as defined in its narrow function of means of payment, consists of banknotes issued by its central bank (fiat money) and of balances on current accounts with financial depository institutions (scriptural money) that are held by the country's residents. Balances on current accounts are also called checkable, sight, or demand deposits. This narrow monetary aggregate, the sum of currency and sight deposits held by resident households and firms, is usually labelled M_1. It is a key aggregate which is closely monitored by the country's monetary authorities. Because money is *the* means of payment, any changes in the supply of money or in the desired holdings of it by agents will therefore, in general, spill over, directly or indirectly, into changes in agents' spending and thereby ultimately affect the economy's real sector, its output, and its price level.

1.2.2 Quasi-money

Alongside money, there are other assets with monetary characteristics insofar as they can be converted easily into money, and on which there is an explicit nominal return. These quasi-money assets, like savings passbooks and savings and term deposits, need, however, to be converted into 'narrow' money to be used as means of payment. The liquidity of these quasi-monetary assets therefore depends on the ease of converting them into narrow money. Adding quasi-money assets to the narrow money aggregate M_1, one obtains broader monetary aggregates, M_2, M_3, and even sometimes M_4. Their definition is country-specific. These 'higher-order' monetary aggregates give a broader measure of the economy's liquidity. As their definition often varies from country to country, they need to be interpreted in the light of the degree of liquidity of the categories of quasi-monetary assets that are included.

Financial innovation alters the substitutability between money and quasi-monies. Debit cards erase the distinction between sight deposits and saving pass-books within certain limits. Also, some banks may pay a small return on sight deposits, while simultaneously charging fees on withdrawals and transfers.[8] In line with this decrease in the user cost of money balances, the general trend has been the dematerialization of money, i.e. an increasing preference for the use of the scriptural form of money. Despite the fact that currency is still preferred for transactions in many countries (if not in most), the ratio between the two forms of money, currency and sight deposits, has significantly decreased over time, though not in a uniform way. The situation varies across countries depending as much on cultural factors as on innovations in technology.

We illustrate this for two quite different developing countries, Paraguay and Kenya. Figure 1.1 shows currency ratios as well as the ratios of broad money aggregates, either M_2 or M_3, to narrow money M_1. For both countries, M_2 adds savings accounts and term deposits to M_1. M_3 moreover adds foreign currency deposits of residents.

Several observations can be made. First, it appears that currency is at present still very important in Paraguay, but the declining trend, from high levels, is also very noticeable. As late as 1995, currency in circulation represented twice the amount of balances in checking accounts. This is in stark contrast with the case of Kenya, where currency is now a relatively small fraction of current accounts. In this country, innovations in technology—the high penetration of smartphones and their use in making money transfers (mobile money)—have been instrumental in this outcome. Second, the case of Paraguay also illustrates the role played by the confidence of people in the domestic banking system in explaining their preference between currency and bank deposits. Indeed, Paraguay experienced in 1995–9 a severe banking crisis. A consequence of this crisis was that the preference for domestic banknotes and foreign currency deposits increased, relative to domestic currency bank deposits. The latter indeed decreased by 26% in real terms from 1995 to 1999, while currency in circulation in *guaraníes*—the

---

[8] With fiat money bearing a zero nominal interest rate and sight deposits with banks having user costs in excess of any positive nominal interest rate, money has in any case a yield below that of nominal non-monetary assets. If money is still held by agents, it is because this opportunity cost is fully compensated by the benefits provided by its use in facilitating transactions.

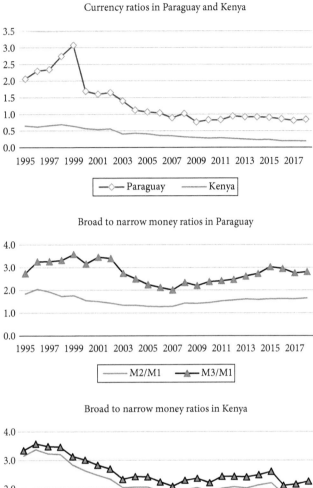

Figure 1.1. Currency and broad monetary aggregate ratios in Paraguay and Kenya

Notes: M_1 = currency + demand deposits in banks and (for Kenya) at non-bank financial institutions (NBFIs); $M_2 = M_1$ + savings and terms deposits in banks and (for Kenya) in NBFIs; $M_3 = M_2$ + foreign currency deposits of residents in domestic banks.

Sources: Paraguay: Banco Central del Paraguay (2019), Anexo Estadístico del Informe. Económico, www.bcp.gov.py/anexo-estadistico-del-informe-economico-i365; Kenya: Central bank of Kenya (2019), Monetary and Finance Statistics, www.centralbank.go.ke/statistics/monetary-finance-statistics/

domestic currency—increased by 10% and foreign currency deposits by 100%. Both the evolution of the currency ratio in Paraguay and the difference in evolution between M_2 and M_3 during this period reflect these temporary shifts in preferences.[9]

Finally, one observes that the ratios of M_2 to M_1 have been relatively stable in both countries during the last decade, which indicates that the substitutability between money and domestic currency quasi-money has not increased. The two countries differ, however, when foreign currency deposits are included in the liquidity aggregates. In Kenya, the difference between the M_3 and M_2 ratios is minimal and quite stable, reflecting the small role of foreign currency deposits in aggregate liquidity. On the contrary, in Paraguay, a more dollarized economy, the quasi-money in guaraníes is dominated by the quasi-money in foreign currency. In addition, sizeable changes in the dollarization ratio of quasi-money are observable over the period.

1.2.3 Money in the financial system

Money is deeply embedded in the financial system, both on its demand and its supply side. Money and non-monetary financial assets are substitutes in people's portfolio. This implies that any change in the demand for money affects the demand for other assets. Also, the supply of money is itself the result of the inter-action between the public, the central bank, and the commercial banking system. Equilibrium in the financial system is thus directly dependent on how equilibrium is reached between the demand and the supply of money.

1.2.3.1 The financial system: a quick overview
A country's domestic financial system encompasses the whole set of financial intermediaries and of financial markets through which households, firms, and the government can exchange funds—money—for other financial assets. The latter include quasi-money, bonds, and stocks. Financial intermediaries include commercial banks, non-bank depository institutions, mutual funds, pension funds, brokerage firms and insurance companies. The financial system offers agents who wish to spend less than their current income, postponing their consumption and other expenditures, the opportunity to do so in ways other than hoarding their money balances at home or in the acquisition of real assets (gold, real estate). They can put the money saved in interest-bearing deposits with banks, buy bonds issued by the government or by firms, or buy stocks issued by

---

[9] Strong interventions by the monetary authorities and the government succeeded in putting an end to the crisis. By 2000, confidence in the banking sector was restored, with 80% of banks' assets in foreign hands (Reinhart and Rogoff 2009: 377). Indeed, between the end of 1999 and the end of 2000, sight deposits in guaraníes increased by a hefty 78%!

the latter. Symmetrically, agents can finance current spending in excess of current income, not only out of accumulated cash or disinvesting real assets but with the help of the financial system. If the financial system is sufficiently developed, it allows them to sell their accumulated non-monetary assets on secondary markets or, as importantly, to resort to external finance. In the latter case, they can borrow from banks, e.g. through a mortgage or an investment loan. Also, firms as well as the government can issue their own interest-bearing debt in exchange for funds on the bond market. Firms can also tap the stock market.

Domestic financial markets can be more or less strongly integrated with the international financial markets. This allows residents to access a more diversified menu of assets for their portfolio investments, and increases their borrowing opportunities. When financial integration is weak, foreign exchange mostly facilitates the exchanges resulting from transactions recorded in the current account of the balance of payments. With increased international financial integration, the foreign exchange market is enlarged, as it also accommodates international capital flows, i.e. trade in domestic and foreign currency financial assets.

Financial intermediation thus revolves around money as a means of exchange, not only for goods and services but also for non-monetary financial assets, in domestic and foreign currency. The market for money and the markets for other assets are thus interdependent. Disequilibrium between supply and demand in the money market spills over to the other markets, unbalancing them. It is thus easy to understand that equilibrium between supply and demand in the money market will be a key component of global equilibrium in the domestic asset market and in the foreign exchange market. We briefly illustrate this in the following section.

1.2.3.2 Equilibrium in money and asset markets

Domestic money balances are held not only for the purpose of making transactions in goods and services but also as a store of value. The latter type of demand for money crucially depends on the yield of alternative available stores of value: savings or time deposits, bonds, stocks, or real assets. Changes in the demand for money thus spill over to the markets for those non-monetary assets. Consider for instance an increase in the demand for money for transactions purposes, holding the money supply fixed. The increase in money demand is necessarily accompanied in the agents' portfolio by a decrease of the same magnitude in demand for non-monetary assets. This results in an excess supply of those assets, which drives their price down and their expected yield up. Interest rates rise. This decreases the demand for money until it returns to its initial level. Equilibrium is restored both in the money market and in asset markets.

The portfolio reallocation following this increase of money demand can also spill over to the foreign exchange market if its counterpart is a decrease in the demand for foreign currency assets. In this case, the exchange rate—the price of foreign currency—will also be affected, if it is floating, and will decrease.[10] The same adjustment mechanism takes place when the initial excess demand for money is the result of a decrease in the money supply.

1.2.3.3 The central bank and the monetary base

This simplified explanation of the role of money within the financial system needs to be broadened. The money supply is not some fixed, exogenously given quantity, determined outside the financial system; rather, it is the result of the interaction between the central bank, which issues fiat money, the banks, which issue scriptural money, and the public. The latter's preferences between fiat and scriptural money, as well as between money and quasi-money, also matter.

The central bank issues the currency held by the public as well as the deposits that banks keep as reserves in the central bank's books. Frequently, though not always, governments also directly hold sight deposits with the central bank.

The sum of currency, held by the public and by the banks, and of sight deposits, held by the banks with the central bank, is called *central bank money* or *monetary base*. These sight liabilities issued by the central bank play an important role in the mechanisms of money and credit supply.[11] Banks' current account deposits at the central bank, as well as cash held in their tills, constitute their *reserves* in central bank money. Banks need these reserves to extend new credit or to buy interest-bearing treasury bills or bonds issued by the government or by firms. When banks add these assets to their balance sheet, they simultaneously issue new sight deposits for the benefit of the borrower or the seller of the assets. Most of the newly issued scriptural money will, however, not be kept as deposit with the issuing bank. Part of it will be withdrawn in cash, the more so the greater the public's preference for fiat money relative to scriptural money. Another part will flow out as soon as the borrower or the seller of the assets uses the new funds credited to his account to make a payment to people that have an account at another bank, or to the government that has an account at the central bank. The recipient commercial bank (or the central bank) will credit the account of the client (or of the government) who is the beneficiary of the payment. As counterparty to this, the recipient bank will register in its balance sheet a claim on the bank of origin, which will have to make a payment to the recipient bank to settle its debt. The bank of origin will then have to withdraw, from its reserves at the central bank, the cash needed to finance cash withdrawals from its depositors.

[10] If the central bank keeps the exchange rate fixed by buying the foreign currency sold by residents, the money supply will not remain constant as assumed in the discussion in the text. It will increase, and thus contribute to eliminate the initial excess demand for money and restore equilibrium in the money market.

[11] The theoretical analysis of the joint money and bank credit supply processes, and its implications for equilibrium in asset markets and for the transmission mechanism of monetary policy to the real sector, has been pioneered by Brunner and Meltzer (1968; 1972).

Such payments between financial intermediaries and with the central bank are necessarily and exclusively settled in central bank money. A bank may postpone using its reserves for settlement of its debt by temporarily borrowing from other banks on the interbank market. However, the bank will ultimately need to use its reserves to settle the debt. For this, the bank makes a transfer from its current account (reserve account) at the central bank to the account of its counterparty. If it does not have enough reserves available and is unable to borrow them on the market at reasonable conditions, it can borrow them directly from the central bank. The latter is therefore the actual *lender of last resort* of the financial system. This is the case in tranquil times, when a bank chooses to borrow from the central bank the liquidity needed to settle its debts against other financial intermediaries. The function of lender of last resort takes a particularly crucial turn when, in times of crisis, the central bank becomes the ultimate liquidity provider for the financial system as a whole (see section 1.3.2.6).

It is this function of lender of last resort that endows the central bank with the capacity to profoundly influence financial-sector equilibrium. The central bank manages the supply of banks' reserves by using its monetary policy instruments that determine the volume and the conditions under which it issues its monetary base.[12]

As discussed in detail in Chapter 3, a bank in need of additional reserves can borrow them at the central bank through its refinancing facilities, or sell assets by participating in the central bank's open-market operation. The interest rate at which the central bank lends to banks, and the amount of central bank liquidity granted, have a major influence on financial intermediaries and financial markets. The stronger this dependency of financial intermediaries on the central bank, through their need for reserves, the stronger will be the latter's capacity to carry out its monetary policy. Changes in the issuing conditions of its monetary base impact the financial intermediaries' asset and liability management, leading to portfolio adjustments by households and firms. This temporarily disturbs the equilibrium of financial markets, including the foreign exchange market. Equilibrium is restored through changes in asset prices and yields on the bond, stock, real asset, and foreign exchange market, as well as through adjustments in interest rates set by banks on their various types of loans and on the quasi-monetary deposits and securities they issue to the public. This equilibrium mechanism acting on financial markets transmits the monetary impulse initiated by the central bank to the real sector, as these changes in asset prices and yields will affect agents' decision to consume, invest, export, import...and ultimately change

---

[12] This is clearly the case in countries where the central bank intervenes mostly by using market-based monetary policy instruments, less so in the countries where the central bank still privileges direct control of banks' asset allocation and interest rate setting (see Ch. 3). The latter are declining in number.

the economy's aggregate output and its general price level. As discussed in Chapter 2, this transmission mechanism of the central bank's monetary policy impulses is thus clearly dependent on the structure of the country's financial sector. To understand how a country's monetary policy can achieve the output and the price level targets it pursues, it is therefore essential to take comprehensively into account the specificities of its financial system.

1.3 The central bank: repository of monetary policy responsibilities

1.3.1 The need for a nominal anchor

In order to live up to its key quality—general acceptability as medium of payment—money has to maintain its purchasing power across time. This implies *price stability*. The term refers to a situation where, over a given period of time—say a year—the average price, expressed in domestic currency units, of a country's representative basket of goods and services remains unchanged.

Inflation, i.e. continuous increase in the aggregate price level, hurts the use of money as a medium of exchange. The higher the rate of inflation, the higher the implied 'tax' on money holdings. This holds even when inflation is fully anticipated. Unanticipated inflation has additional costs, as it induces unwelcome redistributions of wealth, as discussed in Box 4.1. Higher inflation also means usually more variable inflation, and increasing uncertainty about future nominal and relative prices of goods and services. Economic decision-making is saddled with opacity, which leads to a global loss of efficiency. Prolonged high inflation is therefore detrimental to growth and development, as suggested by a large body of evidence (Fischer 1993). If unchecked, inflation dynamics can get out of hand. In a worst-case scenario it can evolve into hyperinflation, which deeply harms, if not destroys, the country's monetary and financial systems.

Symmetrically, deflation, i.e. a continuous decline in the general price level, is as pernicious. Not only does it divert money from its main medium of exchange function, as money is hoarded as an asset, but it threatens to precipitate the economy in a vicious 'debt deflation' loop, a term first coined by I. Fisher (1933). With deflation, the real value of nominal debt increases. To service the increased debt burden, borrowers have to sell assets. The ensuing general decrease in asset prices acts as an additional deflationary force, strengthening the decline in output and in the general price level and reinforcing the deflation dynamics. The upshot of these unattractive effects of both inflation and deflation is that price stability is a desirable goal that contributes to a society's welfare.

Price stability, a target of paramount importance for society, is thus to be pursued by the monetary authorities. Society entrusts them with the mission to 'anchor' the country's price level.

In complement to the consensus that acknowledges that price stability is a desirable goal of society, there is nowadays a large agreement about the role money can play in achieving this goal. The quantity theory of money, first formulated by classical economists such as David Hume or John Stuart Mill in the eighteenth century, holds that there is in the long run a strict proportionality between money and the general level of prices.[13] While there have been many questions raised about interpretations of this general rule and about the relevant conditions under which it applies, a large body of empirical evidence has made clear the important role of the growth of monetary aggregates in explaining the dynamics of inflation (see McCallum and Nelson 2010 for a thorough discussion of theoretical and empirical aspects).[14]

The role of money in the dynamics of inflation was popularized beyond the academic circles by M. Friedman: '*Inflation is always and everywhere a monetary phenomenon* in the sense that it is and can be produced only by a more rapid increase in the quantity of money than in output.' (Friedman 1970: 24, italics in original). Over time, the consensus about the monetary roots of inflation became widespread, to a point, as expressed by Mishkin (2011: 4), 'that central bankers came to recognize that keeping inflation under control was their responsibility'.

Actually, while strict price stability means zero inflation, it is usually not defined so narrowly for monetary policy purposes, and the accepted rate of inflation is somewhat higher. In the advanced economy countries (henceforth AEs), 2% per year average price increases is accepted as 'price stability'. In developing countries, inflation target rates are somewhat higher (see section 6.4).[15]

---

[13] This is the long-run property of 'neutrality of money'. In the long run, i.e. after all market adjustments have been effected, real variables will not depend on the level of nominal variables. Agents will be concerned only with the level of their real money balances. For a given level of these real balances a strict proportionality therefore exists between the nominal quantity of money and the price level (McCallum and Nelson 2010: section 2).

[14] There is little doubt of the tight relationship between the growth of monetary aggregates and high inflation. More controversial is the case of moderate or low inflation, for which the relationship is much less clear (De Grauwe and Polan 2005). In countries with diversified asset markets, mostly AEs, financial innovation and technological change can bring about large changes in the demand for money, altering the link between money growth and inflation. As we discuss in section 6.3, the shifting relationship between money growth and inflation has a profound effect on the choice of monetary procedures of central banks to achieve price stability. Whatever the policy procedures in use, central banks need to monitor any disequilibrium between money supply and demand, knowing that inflation cannot develop without, sooner or later, being accommodated, if not initiated, by increases in the supply of money.

[15] There are various reasons why inflation targets are positive. Price indices only measure inflation in an imperfect way. There is the risk that they overestimate actual inflation because they are based on overly rigid consumer baskets and do not therefore take into account substitutions that consumers make towards goods that are cheaper and of higher quality. Targeting an overly low inflation rate would risk opening the door to deflation. Also, a positive inflation rate is seen as 'greasing the wheels' of the economy when there are nominal rigidities, as it allows e.g. easier adjustments in real wages. In developing countries, inflation targets are higher, so as to give central banks additional flexibility to deal with external shocks. Inflation targets are usually also set as target ranges.

1.3.2 The central bank and its missions

Central banks have undergone major changes since their inception. The missions that have been or currently are part of the central banks' range of interventions reflect the situation, historically inherited, of the economic and financial system in which they were inserted. At various stages of their development, central banks have been called upon to improve the global performance of the economy and to address significant failures of the financial system so as to enhance its efficiency and its stability. Their missions have also been shaped by the evolution in the positive and normative economic thinking concerning the role of money and monetary policy.

1.3.2.1 Emergence of central banks

Central banks are a relatively recent institution. Only sixteen central banks were founded before 1900, and most of them are posterior to 1950 (Bordo and Siklos 2017: 33, 69). Nowadays practically all countries in the world have one. Central banks began, both in the advanced economies and in the developing countries, as purveyors of fiduciary money (bills and coins) whose issue was largely, although not uniquely, determined by fiscal needs. Initially, central bank were private banks which obtained from their sovereign the privilege of issuing notes backed with the prevailing metallic currency, gold or silver.[16] As counterpart to this privilege, banks financed government spending and helped place government debt with their clients. Early on, a monopoly was given to a single private bank to issue currency, thus putting an end to the system of competitive banking that had so far prevailed. This paved the way to the emergence of the country's central bank.

European countries exported this model to their colonies. They granted the privilege to issue colonial currency to private home country banks established in the colony. For example, the Indochina Bank operated in this way from 1875 in the French colonies of Cambodia, Laos and Vietnam. In 1921 Britain set up the British West African Currency Board for its West African colonies (now Nigeria, Ghana, Sierra Leone, and The Gambia). As noted by Guyer and Pallaver (2018: 10), reducing transactions costs between the colony and the home country as well as extracting seigniorage were important goals of introducing colonial currencies. When the Asian and African colonies gained independence, mostly in the 1960s, they established a national central bank to issue their own currency.[17]

---

[16] It is telling that some people and sometimes the press still refer to the Central Bank of Bolivia as Institute of Emission (Instituto Emisor in Spanish).

[17] In many cases the currency remained pegged to that of the former colonial metropole, although often only temporarily so, with the notable exception of French colonies in western and central Africa. For the latter, a strong link with France was kept through the creation of two monetary zones whose currency, the CFA (Communauté Française d'Afrique) franc was pegged to the French franc (Guyer

The Latin American countries gained independence much earlier from the Spanish and Portuguese colonial powers, most of them during the first half of the nineteenth century. However, central banks were only established about a century later. The five Andean countries—Bolivia, Chile, Ecuador, Colombia, and Peru—established their central bank in the 1920s, following the recommendations of the Kemmerer missions.[18]

New national central banks also surged in the 1990s and early 2000s in central and eastern Europe after the break-up of Yugoslavia and the USSR, founded by the former members of the respective federal states.

1.3.2.2 The bankers' bank

With the passing of time, central banks enlarged their functions beyond financing the sovereign and commercial business activities. Their position as sole issuer of notes put them in the position to concentrate the country's gold and silver reserves held in the private banks. This led the central banks to address the specific needs of the private banks (Bordo 2007). They offered discount windows and other refinancing facilities to the private banks that allowed them to settle their interbank operations and their operations with the government through accounts held with the central bank. Some central banks also offered clearance services of cheques for the banks. The functions clearly marked an important evolution of central banking and of the financial system, which evolved into a two-tier system, with the central bank as the first tier and banks as the second. Central banks became the bankers' bank for their day-to-day operations, but also the ultimate lender to any bank that experienced liquidity stress (see section 1.3.2.6). It is the position of issuer of legal tender notes, of banker to the government and of bankers' bank, that 'led Central Banks to develop their particular art of discretionary monetary management and overall support and responsibility for the health of the banking system at large' (Goodhart 1989a: 89).

1.3.2.3 Agent of economic development

With the state-led approach to economic development that prevailed until the 1970s, central banks were saddled, to varying degrees, with a multiplicity of functions well beyond monetary and financial stability. Some central banks in developing countries became intermediaries between the international lending agencies and the private banks. They undertook wholesale bank functions: the

---

and Pallaver 2018: 14–15). As further discussed in Appendix 6B, both zones are still operational and have grown into a monetary union, the West African Economic and Monetary Union (WAEMU), with 8 member countries, and the Central African Economic and Monetary Community (CEMAC) with 6 member countries. Both have their own common central bank. The CFA franc is now pegged to the Euro.

[18] Edwin Kemmerer, a Princeton academic later called the 'international money doctor', consistently recommended the establishment of a central bank to issue currency based on the gold standard as a remedy to pervasive financial instability (Seidel 1972: 525).

central bank would, on behalf of the government, receive the funds earmarked for specific lending projects, and lend them to a private bank, which would lend them further, to the ultimate recipients in the private or public sector.

Also, central banks in developing countries, and even in some advanced economies, were more inclined to satisfy the credit needs of the economy than to control the money supply. They attached great importance to the size and composition of the assets of the banking system, directing credit to priority sectors and nudging or forcing banks to make loans to the government. Central banks were less focused than nowadays in their mission to procure price stability; rather, they saw their priority as being active agents of economic development. For example, 'preserving a high level of employment', 'permitting the maximum use of the country's productive resources', or 'fostering appropriate conditions for an orderly and fast development of the economy' were key mandates of Latin American central banks from 1945 to the early 1990s (Jácome 2015: 20).

An extreme case of the state-led approach to economic development, focused on the real economy, could be observed after the Second World War in the countries that, in many parts of the world, implemented some home version of the command economy model. In these countries, particularly those under the sphere of influence of the Soviet Union and following its example, the financial system was nationalized and fully centralized around a unique State Bank. The latter exercised the functions of a central bank, issuing the currency, managing international reserves and the exchange rate, setting credit policy in line with the state's development strategy, etc., while simultaneously acting, directly or through its subsidiaries, as retail, commercial, investment, and development bank. The dismal performances of the command economies, as well as (for some countries) the break-up of their privileged trade and aid relationships with the former Soviet Union, led the authorities in these countries to reform their financial systems and to switch from a one-tier to a two-tier banking system. The state bank became the country's central bank, narrowing its operations to conventional monetary functions. Its other former financial intermediation functions were transferred to a new array of commercial banks and other financial intermediaries. This evolution of the state bank to a central bank happened, for example, in 1990 in Vietnam and in 1997 in Cuba. The transition to a two-tier banking system, however, did not necessarily imply that central banks forsook their role of assisting the state's development strategy, but this role became more subdued. In some countries, contribution to the state's development strategy is still part of the central bank's mandate.

1.3.2.4 Mandate for price stability

In the second half of the twentieth century and particularly after the high-inflation episodes of the 1980s, central banks delimited more clearly their functions as guardians of monetary stability, understood as maintaining the purchasing power of domestic money. This was influenced by two concurrent factors. First, significant additional space for central bank's discretionary policies arose with the abandonment of the gold standard in the early 1930s and of its softer version, the gold exchange standard, in 1971. The discipline involved by the nominal anchor of the peg to gold or to its substitute, the US dollar, had weakened over time and ceased to be the norm. Thereafter central banks regained full control over their domestic monetary conditions. Second, from the early 1960s, the monetary roots of inflation became increasingly acknowledged by central banks. It became a major duty for them to take control of the monetary conditions which caused inflation. Monetary aggregates featured prominently among the monetary conditions to monitor. This greater focus on price stability was reinforced in developing countries when the International Monetary Fund (IMF) progressively shifted the focus of its financial programmes which conditioned its lending, from the sustainability of the balance of payments, with emphasis on the current account, to the control of inflation. The fact that there were complementarities between a viable balance of payments and low inflation facilitated this transition.

As discussed in section 1.3.1, the focus on keeping inflation under control is now, in many developing countries as well as in AEs, the main objective, if not the only one, of monetary policy. To buttress their capacity to achieve price stability, central banks of AEs and, later, of developing economies gained legal independence from their country's executive branch. An essential reason for this drive towards greater central bank independence was recognition that inflation expectations held by forward-looking agents are a crucial determinant of the inflation process. Independence from government is seen as a key ingredient in the credibility of a central bank's commitment to low inflation. Independence reinforces the central bank's ability to 'anchor' inflationary expectations at its target level. We discuss at length in section 4.3 the salient characteristics of central bank independence and of its companion, stringent accountability, and explain their role in enhancing the credibility of monetary policy and thereby increasing its efficacy.

1.3.2.5 Mandate for stabilizing output

While price stability has become the key mission for central banks, the latter's concern for the real economy has not disappeared. Research on the role of money in the economy has indicated clearly that inflation is a monetary phenomenon. This has put onto central banks the burden of stabilizing the price level. The same research has also shown that monetary policy cannot permanently raise the level of employment. Sustained expansionary monetary policies will temporarily raise output and employment, but in the longer run will only result in higher inflation. This implies that monetary policies cannot be used as a permanent support for long-run development and growth strategies. However, it also indicates that monetary policy can be effective in stabilizing output in the short run in the face of exogenous shocks, provided—and this is a crucial caveat—that the central bank's commitment to price stability is perceived unconditionally as credible by economic agents. We discuss this at length in sections 4.2.1 and 4.3.1. The potential to use monetary policy to partly shield the real economy from the effects of exogenous shocks, even if this means accepting temporary deviations from the price stability goal, justifies (in the eyes of most central bankers) the additional mandate of stabilising output, i.e. limiting its volatility. Endeavouring to combine these two missions, price stability and output stabilization, in monetary policy-making is often referred to as 'flexible inflation targeting' (see e.g. Mishkin 2011: 32—see also our discussion in section 6.4).

1.3.2.6 Mandate for financial stability

Financial stability became a major concern of central banks worldwide, in light of the recurrence of banking crises during the twentieth and early twenty-first centuries, both in AEs and in developing countries. Central banks progressively took on the public responsibility of offering lender-of-last-resort (LOLR) support, not only in tranquil times to individual banks and on a case-by-case basis, but also to the whole banking system in times of crisis, when a bank run loomed large on the horizon. Central banks thus became insurers against systemic illiquidity for reasons of public policy. This public role was justified by the need to avoid the large costs to society entailed by full-fledged banking crises, as had repeatedly been observed in the wake of such crises. The LOLR support carries, however, like all types of insurance, a risk of moral hazard. Expecting to benefit from this support if needed, banks could have the incentive to engage in over-risky lending or in other imprudent speculative activities. To control for excessive risk-taking in the financial sector, countries set up a framework of regulation and supervision of the sector.[19] Depending on the institutional setup, these responsibilities were entrusted to the central bank or, in some countries, to a specific body, independent from the central bank. After the 2007–8 financial crisis, central banks in the AEs realized that the important progress towards price stability achieved over 1985–2006 had not prevented the emergence of the large imbalances in the financial sector that triggered the crisis.[20] LOLR interventions by central banks reached an unprecedented level during this crisis. In reaction, supervision was tightened across the world for banks and was extended to non-bank intermediaries. In the wake of the tightened regulation and supervision, central banks have in many countries been entrusted with additional responsibilities. Nowadays, according to

[19] An alternative, quite radical approach is to dispense with the LOLR so as to eliminate the implied risks of moral hazard and to restore a 'free' and competitive banking system. In such a system, banks would be, according to this line of thought, 'better incentivised to manage themselves prudently', as noted by Tucker (2014: 16), who goes on to show the fallacy of this type of argument.

[20] The period 1985–2006 has been called the Great Moderation, a period during which not only average inflation declined but also both inflation and output volatility were significantly lowered. Among the various factors that have been reported to explain this empirical observation, the role of a credible monetary policy pursuing price stability has particularly been stressed (see e.g. Bernanke 2004).

the 2011–12 World Bank Regulation and Supervision Survey, prudential policy is in the hands of central banks in more than 60% of the 143 countries surveyed (Čihák et al. 2012: 44). This percentage is even higher in developing countries and emerging market economies (henceforth EMEs), where 75% of central banks are also supervisory bodies.[21]

Financial stability has thus evolved in many countries into a full and important mandate for central banks. The mandate includes actual LOLR interventions to preserve the liquidity of the financial system when it is under stress, as well as the recourse to preventive prudential policies to head off any potential threat to financial stability.

Such a prominent role given to financial stability is not without controversy. It is indeed a huge challenge for central banks to establish adequate balance between the financial stability mandate and the other mandates with which it is entrusted , namely the price stability mandate and the mandate to stabilize short-term output volatility. Policy measures desirable to preserve financial stability may be detrimental to the other goals included in the central bank's remit. We discuss this more extensively in section 4.2.2. In this context of a 'dual' legal mandate of preserving both monetary and financial stability, it is to be noted that central banks in developing and emerging market economies are paying particular attention to the competitiveness and stabilization of the exchange rate, as well as to the stabilization of international capital inflows and outflows (see section 6.4.5.2).

1.3.2.7 Other missions

In addition to their missions of macroeconomic and financial stability, central banks in many countries provide crucial services to the financial sector like being pivots of the payments system, both for domestic and foreign transactions. Financial inclusion has in this context recently become an additional goal pursued by many central banks. Financial inclusion matters as part of a development strategy focused on growth and poverty reduction, but also because it directly impacts the financial environment in which monetary policy operates or because it may affect financial stability, either in a positive or in a negative way (Mehrota and Yetman 2015). Fostering financial inclusion implies, for instance, more flexible regulations for conventional banking to facilitate access for small firms and individuals to bank accounts and bank loans. But it also means that central banks need to take a proactive stance in addressing the challenges posed by new entrants in the financial sector, the fintechs (financial technology) firms. These non-bank operators are key actors in offering innovative financial services to a large part of

---

[21] Historical legacy matters in this respect. E.g. in Latin America the countries on the Pacific Rim and Bolivia established, following the recommendations of the Kemmerer mission in the 1920s, regulatory and supervisory bodies of the commercial banks, independent of the central banks. The countries on the Atlantic coast kept supervision and regulation within the central bank.

the population, particularly to the unbanked sector. They provide the appropriate software and the necessary infrastructures to facilitate payments, saving, and borrowing with the use of mobile phones. With the goal of financial inclusion in mind, several central banks are undertaking an active role in providing centralized payments infrastructure (the hard infrastructure) that enhances security and provides support to fintechs, complementing the private infrastructures set up by the sector.[22] Equally important, they are formulating rules and regulations (the soft infrastructure) to allow the smooth functioning of the new technologies both in banks and non-bank institutions (Bank of England 2019: 48). It is also up to the central banks to furnish the needed regulations to protect the users and shield the system from fraudulent financial activities. Finally, several central banks are assessing the pros and cons of issuing central bank digital currency (CBDC). A pilot study to test the technical aspect of a CBDC has successfully been carried out by the Central Bank of Uruguay in 2017–18. The E-peso was circulated as legal tender in limited amounts to mobile users, for payments in stores and peer-to-peer transfers (IMF 2019b: 16). Although the advantages of CBDCs in fostering financial inclusion through the reduction in transaction costs are evident, the implications of issuing them on a large scale need yet to be fully understood.

1.3.3 The structure of monetary policy

As discussed in section 1.3.2, central banks' mandates for implementing monetary policy may include several goals—price level stability, output stability, and financial stability. These goals are generally ordered hierarchically, with primacy given to price stability. Many countries now combine price and output stability mandates within a 'flexible inflation' strategy, while closely monitoring the impact of their policy on financial stability. We discuss more extensively in section 4.2 the challenges that central banks face in order to reach the proper balance between the different goals they are expected to pursue.

1.3.3.1 The monetary policy framework

To reach their monetary policy goals with maximum effectiveness, central banks operate with a specific monetary framework, which gives structure to their policy interventions. A monetary framework links four key monetary policy concepts: ultimate targets, intermediate targets, operating targets, and policy instruments.

---

[22] It is to be noted that many developing countries already have Real Time Gross Settlements (RTGS) platforms. These can be extended to open access to settlement accounts for new non-bank payment providers, following the example set by the Bank of England (Bank of England 2019: 47).

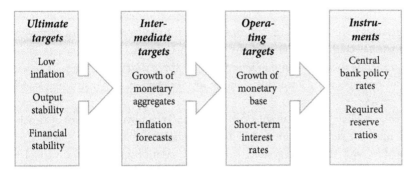

Ultimate targets	Inter-mediate targets	Opera-ting targets	Instru-ments
Low inflation	Growth of monetary aggregates	Growth of monetary base	Central bank policy rates
Output stability			Required reserve ratios
Financial stability	Inflation forecasts	Short-term interest rates	

Figure 1.2. The monetary policy framework

The sequence of monetary policy decisions is structured in the following way, at least in principle: the value, or the range of values, set for the ultimate targets (e.g. the inflation rate) implies the targets for the intermediate variables (e.g. the money supply); in turn, the latter determine the targets for the operating variables (e.g. the money base), which themselves are used for setting the policy instruments (e.g. the central bank refinancing rate).

Figure 1.2 illustrates schematically the relationship between these four concepts and indicates which specific variables are, for each of them, susceptible to be taken into consideration by central banks.

The need for such a sequence arises because central banks cannot directly and fully control the ultimate targets, the price level and output. Their policy interventions can only consist in changing the monetary policy instruments, over which they have full control. These actions will not, however, affect the final monetary policy goals instantly, but rather with long and variable delays. Also, the effects of these actions on the final goals cannot be known with certainty. In most instances the strength of economic agents' reaction to central banks' actions cannot be assessed very precisely in advance. In addition, many exogenous events may derail the intended effect of central banks' actions on their final goals. Waiting to see whether the final goals are achieved or not will then make it too late to take corrective action. Because of these lags and uncertainties, central banks monitor a set of variables that are available at short notice and that are known to affect the ultimate goal. These variables are called intermediate target variables. The daily implementation of monetary policy is itself guided by operating targets. The central bank has power over the latter—albeit not a direct handle but a tight indirect one through its policy instruments.

1.3.3.2 Intermediate targets
Observing the evolution of intermediate target variables provides central banks with the necessary information for forecasting the path of the ultimate goal

variables. They exploit the close relationship between intermediate and ultimate goal variables in order to set targets for the former in a way that is consistent with the targets selected for the latter. A divergence between an intermediate variable and its target is then a signal that a deviation of the ultimate goal from its target path can be expected. Corrective changes in monetary policy instruments will then be made.

An intermediate target variable should, beyond the obvious quality of timely and accurate measurability, meet the following two criteria: (i) a close, predictable relationship with the goal variable; (ii) a stable relationship with the variables chosen as operating targets by the central bank, so that the latter can effectively control the intermediate variable that is targeted and take the corrective measures when this variable is off-track (Bofinger 2001: 247).

Monetary aggregates in any of their various definitions $(M_1, M_2 ...)$, Net Domestic Credit, Net International Reserves, and long-term interest rates feature on the list of intermediate target variables, while short-term interest rates, the monetary base, banks' reserves, and exchange rates are operating target variables. In choosing their monetary policy framework, countries select the set of intermediate and operating targets and instruments, considering the stability of the relationships between these variables and the information they provide about the future evolution of the chosen final goals.

In practice, monetary policy frameworks are not necessarily designed in accordance with the stylized model discussed above. In the AEs, for instance, there has been an erosion of explicit intermediate targets since the end of the 1980s, when monetary aggregates failed to perform as expected. This failure has mainly been attributed to instability in the demand for money, brought about by successive rounds of financial innovation and deregulation. Also, many countries have adopted inflation targeting as their monetary framework. While this could be interpreted as dispensing of intermediate targets, a more appropriate view is probably to consider that these countries use inflation forecasts as an intermediate target, especially the central bank's own inflation forecast (King and Mancini-Griffoli 2018). In developing economies as well as in many EMEs, the traditional intermediate targets continue to be used more than in the AEs. Concomitantly, the shift away from explicit monetary targets has been less pronounced in the former than in the latter. We discuss these issues with more detail in Chapter 6.

1.3.3.3 Operating targets
Operating targets are key components of all monetary frameworks currently in use. In order to guarantee sufficient controllability of the operating target by the central bank's instruments, the relationship between the two sets of variables needs to be close and stable.

In AEs as well as in several EMEs, the choice of an operating target has been narrowed down to a short-term interest rate. As further discussed in section 6.4, the academic literature on monetary frameworks has pointed out that a rule-oriented approach for setting the short-term interest rate operating target can be a useful guideline for central banks, particularly for those which have opted for 'flexible inflation' targeting (Bofinger 2001: 268–9). According to such a feedback-type rule, known as 'the Taylor rule', the target set for the short-term interest rate should be a direct function of observed deviations of both inflation (or expected inflation) and output from their respective target values (Taylor 1993).

In developing economies and even in some EMEs, the shift towards short-term interest rate targeting has been less pronounced than in the more advanced economies. In a still significant number of developing countries, the volume of central bank liquidity continues to be used as operating target. Indeed, in many developing countries there is a close monitoring of the money base. For countries targeting the money base, the implicit assumption is that it has a reliable and predictable influence on the broader monetary aggregate chosen as intermediate target. This presumes that the money multiplier, which links the two variables, is stable. This framework is also conditional on the stability of the velocity of money, which links the monetary aggregate and nominal income, the final goal which combines the price level and real output targets. The multiplier depends on the public's preference for fiat currency and for quasi-monetary deposits, relative to sight deposits with banks, as well as on banks' holdings of central bank reserves, relative to their total deposits. Success of the monetary base/money supply aggregate framework hinges thus on the predictability of both the public's and banks' behaviour. The strategy can encounter difficulties if, for instance, banks unexpectedly decrease their excess reserves or if the public unexpectedly shifts from currency to sight deposits, as both reactions will move the multiplier as well as the associated monetary aggregate—the intermediate target—above their projected value. Similarly, following an unexpected fall in the demand for money, velocity rises above its expected value. This leads, if the target value for the intermediate target is maintained, to an excessive expansion of the money supply, with unintended effects on nominal income, the final target (see section 6.3.3).

Countries choosing the interest rate as operating target mostly select the overnight interest rate, which is determined in the interbank market for the settlement of balances. The reason for this preference is practical, as the overnight rate is usually the rate which the central bank can control most easily, given that it is the supplier of bank reserves and hence can directly affect their level (see section 3.2.2.2). In developing countries whose financial system lacks depth, central banks may prefer not to rely on these very short-term interest rate as operating targets. The structure and characteristics of the financial system may be such that the overnight rate plays no role or a very modest one in the structure of interest rates. To start with, often there is not a yield curve that makes much sense. Market interest rates tend to vary widely across banks for otherwise comparable operations. Also, they tend to fluctuate widely over time. On the other hand, if the stability conditions for pursuing the alternative strategy—the monetary base as operating target—are not fulfilled either, it could be advisable for the central bank to choose as operating target an interest rate with a longer maturity. It could choose interest rates with maturities going from one to three months, for instance those of treasury bills. Those interest rates, while still short-term, would seem to be more relevant to the market.

Finally, some developing countries choose the exchange rate as operating target when their domestic price level is strongly dependent on it, frequently because of a large share of imported goods in their consumption basket, as is for example the case for net food importers. Heavily dollarized economies may also make this choice, as large changes in the exchange rate may endanger the stability of their financial system (see section 6.5). Foreign-exchange interventions are in this framework the instrument of monetary policy which is preferred by central banks. Foreign-exchange interventions are of two types, unsterilized and sterilized. If only unsterilized interventions are considered, choosing the exchange rate as an operating target is de facto equivalent to targeting short-term interest rates. For instance, a sale of foreign currency by the central bank—an unsterilized foreign-exchange intervention designed to counteract a depreciation of the domestic currency—directly restricts central bank liquidity and raises short-term interest rates. Alternatively, had the central bank raised its operating target for the interest rate, the exchange rate would have reacted similarly, allowing the central bank to steer it to the desired level. When the central bank sterilizes its foreign-exchange interventions, it neutralizes the initial effects of its foreign-exchange sales (purchases) on the monetary base by simultaneously purchasing (selling) domestic currency bonds for an equivalent amount. It thereby leaves domestic interest rates unchanged. Sterilized interventions therefore provide, in principle, the opportunity to independently set the two operating targets. However, a necessary condition for this to hold is that domestic and foreign currency assets are imperfect substitutes. Indeed, sterilized interventions influence the exchange rate without affecting the domestic interest rate to the extent that they alter the risk premium investors require to hold domestic currency assets. Investors will require such a risk premium in countries where capital mobility is low, markets for local currency assets are thin, and exchange rate risk is high. Central banks in these countries can thus use sterilized interventions to specifically manage the exchange rate, while setting their short-term interest target separately, to some extent at least. We further discuss this issue in section 3.5.

To conclude this discussion about operating targets, it may be interesting to recall that interest rates (or exchange rates) on the one hand and the volume of central bank liquidity on the other cannot be set independently. If the money base is chosen as the operating target, the central bank has to let the market interest rate fluctuate. If the short-term interest rate is targeted, it is the central bank's supply-of-money base that needs to adjust to the demand-for-money base and fluctuate in response to liquidity shocks. This implies, for developing countries that target money or bank reserves aggregates that the interest rate will be subject to significant variations in reaction to exogenous shocks. The choice between reserve/money aggregate or interest targeting has obvious implications for the choice of instruments and for the conduct of monetary policy.

In a world of complete certainty, the choice between the money base and a short-term interest rate as the operating target would not matter. Targeting one or the other trivially yields the same equilibrium values for both. However, a more realistic setting is when there is uncertainty, i.e. when stochastic disturbances occur after the central bank has defined its operating targets and set its policy instruments in accordance with them. The optimal choice of the operating target will then depend on the nature of the shocks, especially on whether they are real or monetary. Poole (1970) argued, in his now classical analysis, that monetary authorities wishing to stabilize aggregate demand should select a money aggregate as operating target if the stochastic shock affecting the economy is real, i.e. originates in the demand for goods and services. In this case, the market-determined interest rate exerts a stabilizing influence on equilibrium aggregate demand. On the contrary, authorities should choose the interest rate if the shock is of monetary origin, either to the demand for money or to the money supply, if the latter can only be imperfectly controlled. Indeed, the transmission of the financial shock to aggregate demand is in this case fully suppressed.[23] However, things are in reality not that simple. The optimal choice becomes already more complex in Poole's model when both types of stochastic shocks are present simultaneously.[24] Walsh (2003: 436) notes, in addition, that Poole's simple model ignores inflation, expectations, and aggregate supply shocks, which all surely matter for choosing a framework. Also, extending the closed-economy model to an open economy would introduce additional stochastic shocks. The choice of an optimal operating target is therefore in reality a quite intricate question, as it depends on the nature of shocks, on the structural characteristics of the economy, and on the key parameters which define agents' behavioural functions that matter

---

[23] Under a money stock control policy, a given increase in liquidity preference (a positive shock to money demand) requires an increase in the interest rate to restore equilibrium on the money market. This increase will be larger if the demand for money is only weakly sensitive to the interest rate; the final effect of the shock on aggregate demand will, in addition, be larger when interest rates have a strong effect on aggregate demand, i.e. when the latter is very sensitive to interest rates. Under such a scenario, control of the money stock allows a positive shock to money demand to have strong negative effects on aggregate demand. Under an interest rate policy, the shock to money demand is simply reflected in an increase in the money supply. There is no transmission of the shock to the real sector.

[24] In this setting, interest targeting dominates money supply targeting when the variance of the financial shock is large, relative to that of the real shock, and when aggregate demand is quite sensitive to interest rates, while the demand for money is only weakly so.

for macroeconomic equilibrium. For this reason, central banks have to largely rely on their own experience, often informed by the results observed in countries similar to their own. Some are also in the process of developing fully-fledged quantitative economic models to help them tentatively simulate the effects of alternative operating targets on final goals (see Chapter 7).

1.4 Low financial development countries: general characteristics

Central banks exert their mandate in a monetary policy environment which varies from country to country. The economy's real and financial structure and, even more broadly, the quality of its institutions determine how monetary policy affects the economy's real and nominal variables. How strongly, how quickly, and how reliably inflation and output react to monetary policy impulses depends on factors such as the strength of the linkages between the real and the financial sector, the degree of international financial openness, and the central bank's institutional credibility. Indeed, central banks face various constraints from their country-specific environment, which may more or less severely affect their capacity to reach their goals. Huge exposure of the economy to external shocks, whether terms-of-trade shocks or swings in capital flows, or strong pressures from the fiscal authorities to finance the budget deficits make it much more difficult for the central bank to stabilize inflation and output.

A first step in discussing core monetary policy issues, such as the selection of a nominal anchor or the central bank's choice of instruments and policy procedures, is therefore to characterize the global environment in which policy is to be designed and implemented in a typical LFDC.

1.4.1 Characteristics of LFDCs: general aspects

The policy environment for low financial development countries, the focus of our analysis, is different in many ways, from that of industrialized countries and large EMEs. In what follows we will label Low Financial Development Countries (LFDCs) the set of countries that meet the following three conditions: (a) a relatively low per capita income; (b) a low degree of financial depth; (c) a weak integration with the international capital markets. It is important, from the outset, to underline that not all LFDCs are alike. There is wide heterogeneity among them with respect to each of the three characteristics we singled out. Some generalizations, while helpful for the clarity of exposition, may be somewhat arbitrary.

1.4.1.1 Low per capita income

Low per capita income is the result of low long-term GDP growth. Its causes are manifold, and have been amply studied in the literature since the 1940s. There are still many ongoing analyses. We will limit ourselves to mentioning those features that we think are more relevant for the design of monetary policy. We specifically point out the following unfavourable, mutually reinforcing obstacles that hamper, to a varying degree, the development process in these countries:

- undiversified exports, with a large share of the latter consisting of primary commodities, carrying great exposure to external shocks and high values at risk;
- an undeveloped manufacturing sector and a service sector of very low productivity;
- a tradable/non-tradable production structure with low elasticities of substitution, both in demand and supply, and largely biased toward the primary sector (agriculture and mining);
- a small tax base, that causes limited investment in education and in the infrastructures of public transport, information, and telecommunications;
- a high degree of informality in economic activities and in the labour market, and, in many developing countries, although not in all, a high dependence on aid and remittance inflows.

Even more importantly, weak institutions impair government effectiveness, give rise to uncertainty in the enforcement of contracts and property rights, and, more generally, lead to an environment and incentive structure that is not conducive to the development of sustained business activities.

1.4.1.2 Low financial depth

'Low financial depth' specifically refers to the underdevelopment of financial intermediation. Many households and domestic firms do not have access—or, when they do, have only a limited access—to the array of financial assets that could allow them to transfer, in an efficient and safe way, their current savings to future consumption. Moreover, they are often unable to borrow from financial intermediaries, or have to do so at costly terms, thereby being impeded from smoothing consumption or compelled to forgo profitable investment opportunities. In this setting, the economy faces strong impediments in achieving an efficient intertemporal allocation of resources, which hurts aggregate investment and growth. These effects are reinforced by the unavailability of accessible insurance products, which limits risk sharing and thereby decreases incentives to invest.[25]

---

[25] There is a huge theoretical and empirical literature analysing the link between the development of financial intermediation and growth performance. See e.g. Cecchetti and Kharroubi (2012).

1.4.1.2.1 Shallow domestic financial markets

With regard to the *domestic financial markets* we can make the point, using a broad generalization, that the bond and equity market, when they exist, are of little significance. Also, the financial infrastructures of support of capital markets are underdeveloped. Stock exchanges, brokerage houses, and dealers' institutions are painfully small and inadequate, except maybe in the larger, more populous developing countries.

1.4.1.2.2 Banks: an important role, a low performance

Banks are the backbone of the financial systems in LFDCs and their liabilities can be relatively large relative to GDP. However, deposits are often concentrated on a small number of large depositors, while the proportion of the unbanked adult population is high. This is the consequence of the lack of incentives for many households and small firms to hold deposits in the banking system. The poorest segments of the population, especially the rural, are unbanked and their payments are made mostly in cash. This is also true for the large urban informal workforce. Checkable accounts are used mainly by the few big enterprises, and payment for the purchase of consumer goods is rarely accepted in checks. However, debit and credit cards as well as electronic transfers, including mobile transactions, have witnessed a remarkable expansion in the recent past.

Banks tend to hold excess reserves and stick to their liquidity, hence the interbank market and the secondary market for securities are very thin.[26] In this particular setting, reinforced by the weak degree of integration with the world capital markets to which we refer in section 1.4.1.3, it can be expected that the usual channels of transmission of monetary policy work poorly.

LFDC banks are very conservative in granting credit to private borrowers, often preferring credit to the public sector. Credit to the private sector, especially to smaller firms, is often denied because of the lack of proper collateral.[27] Many potential borrowers never apply for bank loans because of lack of financial education or out of fear of being turned down. Also, they are discouraged by the complicated application procedures and the high interest rates. Small-scale firms, which contribute to a large part of global output in LFDCs, often finance their

---

[26] Banks structurally hold excess reserves out of a precautionary motive or because of high risk aversion in the face of risky investment opportunities. They may also be slow to adapt their lending to unexpected strong increases in their deposits. This happened in some LFDCs, when the export boom of 2003–14 led to a very rapid growth of domestic deposits: banks held then large excess reserves, well above the ratios required by the regulations.

[27] Problems with the design of prudential regulations may be the culprits in this state of affairs. Prudential regulations favour secured loans, very often requiring real estate collateral. Loan applications are then evaluated not on terms of their own merits but on the value of the collateral that is attached to them. This is a way to economize on information processing by the banks and by bank supervisors, but it punishes loan applicants with good ideas and projects. Innovative proposals often go unfunded because of lack of adequate collateral, as deemed by the banks' loan officers or, worse, by their lawyers.

expansion and working capital with retained earnings and loans from family and friends. There is scant recourse to external finance.

1.4.1.2.3 Informal finance

While the regulated and supervised financial markets are small, there is often alongside them a thriving informal financial market, the so-called 'curb' lending by traditional moneylenders.[28] Curb lending is a frequent, although diminishing, feature in many low-income countries. The interest rate that these moneylenders charge is high, and bears little connection to the rate charged in the formal markets.[29] However, they offer more flexible lending conditions.

Also among the myriad of arrangements of informal finance are tied trade credit and Rotating Credit and Savings Associations (ROSCAs), which are common throughout the rural communities of many developing countries. ROSCAs allow poor households to finance consumption expenditure, agricultural inputs, and small-scale investments. Such group lending, which implies joint liability of borrowers, has been developed in particular by microfinancial institutions (MFIs). Indeed, microfinance has over the last four decades greatly contributed, often with the help of international development agencies and non-governmental organizations (NGOs), to fostering financial inclusion for the poor. Relying on a revolving financing fund, MFIs give poor borrowers access to small credits at significantly better conditions than on the curb market. Some small MFIs continue to function in several countries as part of the informal financial sector, without a proper banking licence, and remain largely unregulated. However, in many LFDCs MFIs have also progressively evolved from informally organized, weakly regulated and subsidized institutions to regulated deposit-taking institutions.[30] Organized in a network, sharing a joint credit information system, and being supervised by a specific regulatory body, they now represent a specialized segment of the domestic financial sector, the *semi-formal financial system*. They cater to the financial needs of lower middle-class households and of micro- and small enterprises. Even if they can address some of the needs of the previously unbanked communities, they are however usually not in a position to provide long-term financing to small and medium-size enterprises. Also, unless they have upgraded to the status of a formal bank, they are not in the purview of the central bank and do not directly interact with it. Very often their payment operations with other financial intermediaries are not settled on the central bank books, as is the case

---

[28] The term 'curb markets' has often been used as synonym for parallel or informal financial markets (see e.g. Fry 1995: 128–30).

[29] Their risk premium is frequently variable and hence the interest rate they charge is quite immune to changes in the formal market and, a fortiori, to changes in the central bank policy rate.

[30] In some LFDCs, microfinance institutions have been at the forefront of innovations in payment technology, promoting the extensive use of mobiles.

with formal banks.[31] Yet these MFIs are not completely isolated from the traditional banks. They deposit their excess cash and, more importantly, they borrow from banks and other financial intermediaries, like pension funds, when they experience liquidity shortages. Moreover, banks are often second-tier institutions for the regulated microfinance operators.

Despite the positive trends in the regulation of MFIs, the weakly regulated or unregulated informal part of the financial system remains important in many LFDCs. While this does not necessarily pose major threats to the stability of a country's global financial system,[32] it nevertheless implies that the semi-formal and informal parts of the finance system are not yet ready to make up for the failure of the formal financial system to provide efficient financial intermediation.

Regarding monetary policy, the segmentation of the financial system in LFDCs poses a specific challenge. While regulated MFIs are linked to the banking system—though weakly so—the truly informal part of the financial sector is not connected at all with the formal financial sector. Monetary policy thus sees its outreach limited, given that the central bank mostly interacts with formal banks and operates in formal financial markets, tenuous as they may be. Some of the central bank's preferred instruments, especially interest rates, will only have a limited direct impact on savings, investments, or portfolio allocation decisions of agents who are clients of MFIs or of the informal financial sector (see section 2.3.3.3.2. The design of monetary policy, then, needs to take into account the indirect ways in which the central bank may be able to affect those agents' decisions, for example by increasing or decreasing global liquidity or global available credit. Monetary policy clearly has to adjust to the structural peculiarities of the country's financial sector as a whole.

Finally, the weak performance of organized financial intermediation also impacts on the financing of the government's budget, and vice versa. Often, LFDCs have a highly pro-cyclical fiscal policy in an environment where the domestic financial system is generally not capable of absorbing large amounts of debt financing. Moreover, because LFDCs have on average higher public-debt intolerance than in AEs, the monetary financing of public deficits is much more

---

[31] Most frequently, they do not participate in the Real Time Gross Settlements System (RTGS) which has become the norm for interbank settlements. However, this may change with the increasing attention paid to the advent of new technologies.

[32] When informal financial intermediaries are weakly interconnected, each dealing with a broad base of small depositors and small borrowers, concerns about their impact on global financial stability may be negligible. Indeed, microfinance institutions proved to be quite resilient during the banking crises in Latin America during the 1990s. Nevertheless, individual unauthorized informal financial intermediaries, semi-formal or formal, may fail as a result of mismanagement and lax lending policies. Also, straight Ponzi schemes can develop in the absence of proper regulation, with devastating effects for depositors (e.g. Albania in 1997, Lesotho in 2007, Jamaica 2008, Benin 2010: see Monroe et al. 2010 and IMF 2016b: 17). Both type of crisis undermine confidence in financial intermediation, and are significant drawbacks to a country's financial development.

likely in LFDCs. Also, financial repression, through which governments try to obtain loans on cheaper terms for themselves or for favoured sectors or enterprises, is still in place in many LFDCs, despite the move towards a more market-oriented monetary policy in the 1980s and 1990s.[33] Both the prevalence of monetary financing of the budget deficit and the continued resort to financial repression impinge upon the performance of organized financial intermediation, and hampers financial deepening.

1.4.1.3 A weak integration with international capital markets

This third characteristic of LFDCs is one of the most important factors shaping the policies implemented by their central banks. A weak link with the international capital market largely reflects the shallowness of their domestic financial markets. Notice that often the capital account of their balance of payments may even be de jure open but may de facto be pretty closed because of the country's rudimentary domestic financial structure. The significant items in the capital account of LFDCs' balance of payments are foreign direct investment and foreign aid. On the other hand, portfolio investment and cross-country bank loans are small in proportion to GDP, and they pale in comparison with EMEs and a fortiori with AEs. In fact, the amounts of financial cross-border operations are small or, in some countries, nonexistent. Even the local branches of international banks finance their domestic assets with deposits collected from domestic residents. LFDCs are in this respect in stark contrast with EMEs, which have a closer integration to international financial markets.

As a result, LFDCs do not benefit much from the various advantages international financial intermediation can offer to domestic agents. The more positive side of this is that LFDCs are not exposed to fluctuating inflows and outflows of capital of the magnitudes experienced in EMEs. They are largely isolated from these types of movement, or feel their effects only indirectly. Government funding from abroad in LFDCs is frequently (although not always) from official sources, bilateral or multilateral, on concessional terms.

Integration into international financial markets may be curtailed in some LFDCs by various types of exchange control put in place by authorities in order to avoid the devaluation of an overvalued exchange rate. In this case, access by private sector agents to foreign exchange on the official exchange market will be rationed, with variable intensity and duration. Almost inevitably, a parallel market for foreign currency emerges. The existence of such informal foreign exchange

---

[33] The concept of financial repression was introduced in the early 1970s, by McKinnon (1973) and Shaw (1973). The panoply of instruments of financial repression is varied: high minimum reserve requirements; rules for the allocation of credit to favoured sectors or enterprises, especially state-owned enterprises; ceilings on interest rates for credits and floors on interest rates on deposits; and, restrictions on foreign exchange. See section 3.2.

markets may greatly harm the implementation of monetary and exchange rate policies (see Box 6.1).

Finally, LFDCs often face a foreign-exchange constraint. Special care is thus reserved for the management of foreign assets, whose share in the economy's total financial assets is significantly higher than in AEs or EMEs. As a consequence, the exchange rate becomes a crucial variable, regardless of the monetary framework chosen. This features put an additional constraint on monetary policy.

While these characteristics of weak integration in international capital markets still apply to a typical LFDC, it is to be noted that several of them have taken steps to increase integration.

1.4.2 Characteristics of LFDCs: selected empirical aspects

To give an empirical content to the LFDCs' main characteristics, as described in section 1.4.1, we have employed for all AEs, EMEs and developing countries a simple Financial Development Index, based on four indicators of domestic financial depth and on one indicator measuring the degree of financial integration in international capital markets. The four financial depth indicators, taken from World Bank (2018), which reports data for 2016 for 187 countries, are the following: (1) *domestic credit to the private sector (% of GDP)*; (2) *financial system deposits (% of GDP)*; (3) *account holders at a formal financial institution (% of population aged 15 or more)*; and (4) *stock market capitalization (% of GDP)*.

In addition, we include a broad international financial integration indicator taken from Lane and Milesi-Ferretti (2017). This indicator, for which the most recent data are reported for 2015, provides information on the *sum of a country's total foreign assets and total foreign liabilities*, in % of its GDP. Total foreign assets and foreign liabilities include portfolio equity, foreign direct investment, debt, and financial derivatives. Foreign assets also include foreign-exchange reserves (gold excluded). We aggregate these five indicators into a synthetic Financial Development Indicator (FD) following the simple methodology used by the World Economic Forum (2012). Appendix 1A details this methodology. The indicator ranges from 1 to 7, from the lowest to the highest degree of financial development. We use this indicator to guide our selection of LFDCs, to reflect as closely as possible their three defining characteristics, already stated above: low per capita income; low degree of financial depth; and weak integration with the international capital markets.[34] Therefore, we apply the following criteria to

---

[34] A more sophisticated Financial Development Index was developed in an IMF publication in 2016. It is based on 20 indicators, observed over 1980–2013, that measure depth, access, and efficiency of financial institutions and financial markets (Svirydzenka 2016). The aggregation of the individual indicators in a synthetic Financial Development Index is based on weights derived from the factor loadings of the principal component analysis performed on the time series data of the individual

define our set of LFDCs: we select all Low Income (LI) and Lower Middle Income (LM) countries as well as those Upper Middle Income (UM) countries for which our synthetic FD indicator is, on the scale from 1 to 7, below 3.0. However, we exercise some limited discretion, excluding or including countries (see Appendix 1A). Our set of LDCs includes 112 countries (33 LI, 45 LM, and 34 UM). As with all classifications, our selection is liable to some arbitrariness, but we feel that it represents well the actual diversity of LFDCs.

Figure 1.3 shows the geographical distribution of our LFDC set. It shows that LFDCs are scattered across the world, in South and East Asia, the Pacific, Europe and Central Asia, the Middle East, Latin America, and, with the largest concentration, in North and sub-Saharan Africa.

Table 1.1 lists LFDCs and their FD index scores. The average FD index score of LFDCs is 1.96, with a standard error of 0.54, to be compared with the average of 2.58 (with a standard error of 1.1) for the world set of 187 countries.[35]

The graphs in the different panels of Figure 1.4 illustrate the main characteristics of our set of LFDCs (dark circles) when compared with those of the other countries, developing and advanced (light triangles).

The upper left-hand panel shows the extent to which the level of GDP per capita (expressed in logarithms) and the FD index are positively associated. A simple linear regression on the whole sample between the two variables indicates that a 10% difference in GDP per capita between any two countries is on average associated with a difference of 0.06 points in their FD index score.[36] The lower left-hand panel of Figure 1.4 refers to two individual indicators of financial depth, *domestic credit to the private sector* and *financial system deposits* (both in % of GDP). One can see that LFDC data for both indicators are grouped at the lower range, with an average of 36.19% for the credit ratio and 42.3% for the deposit ratio. For the non-LFDCs the corresponding averages are 87.9% and 87.2%. Also, one can observe quite logically that the two indicators are strongly positively associated, reflecting the crucial role of bank deposits in financing credit to the private sector.[37] The upper right-hand panel of Figure 1.4 shows how the volume of deposits

---

indicators. The IMF FD index is essentially oriented towards measuring the domestic side of financial development, the dimension of international financial integration only reflected by one indicator (international debt securities of government to GDP). As we find this dimension quite important for characterizing the monetary policy environment of LFDCs, we have developed our own index, which, although simpler than the IMF's, assigns a much larger weight to the degree of international financial integration. Note, however, that the linear correlation coefficient between the 2016 values of the two indexes is quite high (0.81). The dataset of the IMF FD index is available at the IMF's website.

[35] This implies a sizable difference between the average values of the FD index in LFDCs (1.96) and non-LFDCs (3.50). This difference is statistically highly significant.

[36] The estimated regression coefficient has a 95% confidence interval of [0.52; 0.65].

[37] A linear regression of the domestic credit ratio on the financial deposit ratio for the whole set of countries, allowing for a difference between LFDCs and non-LFDCs both in the regression constant and in the coefficient of the deposit variable, gives the following result. There is a significant difference between LFDCs and non-LFDCs in the respective regression constants; there is however no significant difference in the respective regression slope coefficients. The co-variation between credit and

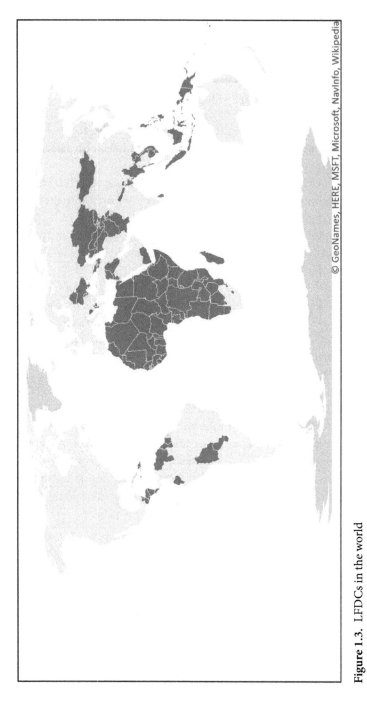

Figure 1.3. LFDCs in the world

in the financial system combines with the extent of the country's banked population (the access variable). The average percentage in the population (aged 15 or more) of *account holders at a formal financial institution* is 37% for LFDCs and 84% for non-LFDCs. The relationship between the two indicators of financial depth is positive but highly non-linear and somewhat heterogeneous: a given ratio of financial deposits to GDP can be associated with different levels of the access indicator, as is apparent in the graph. This can be due to differences in GDP per capita but also to differences in the average size of deposits per account holder.[38]

The last panel of Figure 1.4 reports the scores of the indicator of international financial integration together with our synthetic FD indicator, of which it is a component (scores are in the 1–7 range). The difference between LFDCs and non-LFDCs is also particularly striking for the indicator of international financial integration, with an average score of 1.8 for the former and 3.5 for the latter. A sizeable cross-country heterogeneity can also be noted for this indicator, for LFDCs as well as for non-LFDCs.

1.5 Summary

This chapter had a twofold aim. First, to explain why monetary policy has nowadays become an unavoidable, important dimension of economic policy for all countries around the world, and to discuss its fundamental facets at a general level. Second, to present LFDCs' key structural characteristics—those that matter for addressing the main monetary policy issues their central banks confront. The rest of the book will be devoted to the discussion of these main issues within the specific environment of LFDCs. The principal points highlighted by this chapter are the following.

---

deposits ratios is similar for both sets of countries: an increase of 10% in the financial deposit ratio raises domestic credit to the private sector by 3.8% for LFDCs and by 3.3% for non-LFDCs.

[38] For two countries with the same GDP per capita and the same ratio of financial deposits to GDP, the country with the lower degree of access will have the same ratio of financial deposits to GDP only if the average size of deposits per account holder is larger. This is the case when the distribution of deposits is highly skewed, with large ones concentrated on a small number of accounts. The precise relationship between the two variables is given by:

$D/GDP = (N_1/N_2)(N_2/N)[(D/N_1)/(GDP/N)]$ where D/GDP is the deposit to GDP ratio, N_1 the number of adult account holders, N_2 the number of adults in the population and N the total population. GDP/N is GDP per capita, N_1/N_2 is the ratio of account holders in the adult population, the access indicator, and N_2/N the ratio of adults in the population. Assuming the latter is broadly the same across countries, a lower access indicator necessarily implies a higher average amount per depositor to generate the same deposit to GDP ratio for 2 countries of the same GDP per capita level.

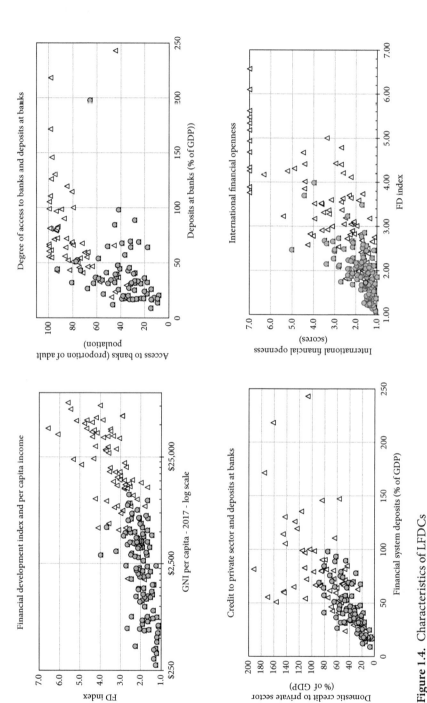

Figure 1.4. Characteristics of LFDCs

Note: The number of countries is 187, of which 112 LFDCs. LFDC's data are represented by the darker dots, those of non-LFDC countries by triangles. Some graphs have been trimmed for extreme outliers. The international financial openness indicator is expressed in scores, over the range 1–7. The score of 7 is attributed to countries for which the sum of external assets and external debt are 1,000% of GDP or more.

Source of data: see text

To understand monetary *policy*, one needs first to realize the crucial role of money in any modern economy. Money is essentially *the* medium of exchange, defined by its general acceptability to make payments and settle debts. The specific form money takes is decided by those who use it. Money's history is that of a succession of innovations that have improved its general acceptability, in particular by making its use more cost-efficient. Money is held for transaction purposes, but also as an asset, a store of value, together with other financial and real assets in agents' portfolios. Changes in the demand or in the supply of money thus trigger a general portfolio reallocation, across all types of asset in the public's portfolios. Disequilibria between money demand and supply spill into the markets for non-monetary assets. This changes prices and yields in these markets, which in turn directly affects aggregate real spending and, ultimately, output and the price level.

Exploiting the relationship between money and the real sector to pursue specific policy goals has become an essential part of the economic policy arsenal. This specific economic policy, monetary policy, has been entrusted to central banks. Central banks are endowed with a special monetary policy capacity because they issue central bank money. The central bank is the bankers' bank, and central bank money is the ultimate means of payment between any two financial intermediaries. Banks are thus dependent on the availability of central bank money to extend credit and thereby issue sight deposits, the other form of money. Central banks are thus in a privileged position to set the conditions on which they issue their own monetary liabilities to banks. This particular leverage on the financial sector is the key channel through which central banks can deeply influence market conditions in the financial sector and thereby pursue their monetary policy goals.

The monetary policy goals are defined by society and entrusted to central banks. Price stability is nowadays the prominent goal—a goal that only monetary policy can be expected to achieve in an efficient way. Central banks have thus been given the mandate to credibly anchor the price level. An associated mandate, also designed to achieve greater macroeconomic stability, is to limit the volatility of output and employment. Central banks use monetary policy not only to keep inflation in check but also to mitigate the effects of temporary external shocks, which cause detrimental output volatility. Central banks thus take advantage of the real effects monetary policy can have in stabilizing real output in the short run.

Concern for financial stability has also fallen historically within central banks' purview. Initially limited to case-by-case interventions as lender of last resort to individual banks experiencing a liquidity squeeze, it has evolved into a fully-fledged role as liquidity insurer and lender of last resort for the financial system as a whole. The mandate therefore often includes the formulation of macro-prudential rules and the reinforcement of supervision to prevent and mitigate the occurrence of threats to financial stability. Central banks face the delicate role of balancing the exercise of their mandate for financial stability with the exercise of their two main mandates, preserving price stability and stabilizing output.

Another mission of central banks is the overseeing of the economy's payments system, to guarantee a safe, efficient, and smooth functioning of the latter. In addition, enhancing financial inclusion has recently become an important mission. Particularly important for LFDCs, where a large part of the population is still unbanked, the mission implies opening up access to financial services to a larger number of individuals and firms. It also includes the need to address the multiple challenges faced by the financial sector, as a consequence of the introduction of new digital technologies. The entrance of fintech firms as providers of financial services to a new range of customers raises special problems.

Conducting monetary policy means setting instruments to reach specific goals. The transmission mechanism from the instruments that the central bank controls to its goal variables is quite complex, and open to great uncertainty in its timing as well as in its final effects. To garner the best chances of keeping their goal variables on track, central banks use a particular monetary policy framework. The latter includes intermediate target variables (e.g. monetary aggregates), which have a close link with goal variables (e.g. inflation) and operating targets (e.g. central bank liquidity) over which the central bank can exert a strong influence with its available instruments. The choice of an appropriate monetary policy framework is in any case a complex one. It is country-specific and depends on many factors, such as the degree of openness of the economy, the nature and reliability of the transmission mechanism of monetary impulses, and the nature, size, and frequency of domestic and external shocks.

Monetary policy in LFDCs operates in a very specific environment, to which the monetary policy strategy needs to adapt. LFDCs are characterized by the following three main features, which can profoundly impinge on the ways in which monetary policy operates in such countries. First, LFDCs have low per capita income—a reflection of various structural factors, widely analysed in the academic literature, which hamper development in mutually reinforcing ways. Second, LFDCs have shallow financial markets, an underperforming banking system, and a reliance on informal finance that is still significant. Third, many LFDCs are also characterized by limited integration in international capital markets. The underdeveloped and segmented nature of the financial system is a huge challenge for the design of monetary policy in LFDCs. Also, the limited integration with international capital markets impairs the proper operation of monetary and exchange rate policies. This is not to deny that such limited integration shields LFDCs from the detrimental consequences of excessively volatile capital flows.

To give an empirical content to the set of countries which may be considered as LFDCs, we use a simple Financial Development Index that synthetizes four individual domestic financial development indicators as well as an indicator of international capital market integration. Using this index as well as some discretion, we constitute our set of 112 LFDCs and illustrate their defining characteristics.

APPENDIX 1A. METHODOLOGY FOR THE SELECTION OF LFDCs

1A(1) Methodology

Our FD indicator is constructed following the methodology of World Economic Forum (2012: appendix A). Normalization is performed on each indicator as a first step. The indicator's value reported for a given country is normalized into a 1–7 *score* according to the following formula: $score = 1 + 6*[(value - min)/(max - min)]$ where max (min) is the indicator's maximum (minimum) value as computed over the whole set of the 187 countries. For example, in 2016 Angola's ratio of domestic credit to the private sector to GDP was 21.12%. The highest ratio reported is 226.13% (Cyprus) and the lowest 3.60% (Afghanistan). Angola's score for this indicator is thus 1.47. To avoid the influence of extreme outliers in the case of the total foreign assets and liabilities indicator, we have set its maximum value at 1,000% of GDP (the actual maximum value being 37,088% for Luxembourg; there are 13 other countries, out of 187, beyond this 1,000% limit). Once normalization is achieved for the five indicators, the country's synthetic financial development indicator is computed as their unweighted average. When, for a country, not all indicators are reported, the average is computed on the available data.

1A(2) Selection of LFDCs

Using the 2017 World Bank's World Development Indicators analytical income classification, we select all Low Income (LI) and Lower Middle Income (LM) countries as well as those Upper Middle Income (UM) countries for which our synthetic FD indicator is, on the scale from 1 to 7, below 3.0.[39] Several countries whose 2016 FD indicator is less than 3 have a generally accepted emerging-market status (Brazil, Colombia, Peru, India, Indonesia, Iran, Mexico, Russia and Turkey). We excluded those from our LFDC set, except Indonesia, which is kept as a representative EME. Similarly, we also exclude Romania and Bulgaria, which are UM countries notwithstanding their 2016 FD indicator of less than 3, given that they benefit, as members of the European Union, from strong support in the process of financial deepening and international integration. On the other hand, we include four countries whose FD index is somewhat above our selection threshold of 3.0. This is the case for Libya, Mongolia, Kiribati, and Venezuela, whose global FD scores are especially upward biased by a single index component. The resulting set of 112 LDCs is presented in Table 1.1.

---

[39] For the income categories, we use the World Bank Analytical Classification (presented in World Development Indicators).

Table 1.1. List of LFDCs and financial development scores (2016)

Country	Score	Country	Score	Country	Score	Country	Score
Afghanistan	1.16	Dominican Republic	2.07	Lao PDR	2.07	Sierra Leone	1.2
Albania	2.15	Ecuador	2.02	Lesotho	1.80	Solomon Islands	1.6
Algeria	1.95	Egypt, Arab Rep.	1.70	Liberia	2.67	Somalia	1.5
Angola	1.56	El Salvador	1.91	Libya	3.70	South Sudan	1.0
Armenia	2.18	Equatorial Guinea	1.74	Macedonia, FYR	2.77	Sri Lanka	2.2
Azerbaijan	2.15	Eritrea	1.26	Madagascar	1.27	St. Lucia	2.6
Bangladesh	1.85	Ethiopia	1.92	Malawi	1.36	St. Vincent and the Grenadines	2.4
Belarus	2.56	Fiji	2.29	Maldives	1.67	Sudan	1.2
Belize	2.21	Gabon	1.65	Mali	1.41	Suriname	1.6
Benin	1.68	Gambia, The	1.91	Mauritania	2.04	Swaziland	1.4
Bhutan	1.87	Georgia	2.66	Micronesia, Fed. Sts.	2.08	Syrian Arab Republic	1.7
Bolivia	2.45	Ghana	1.85	Moldova	2.11	Tajikistan	1.8
Bosnia and Herzegovina	2.50	Grenada	2.61	Mongolia	3.23	Tanzania	1.3
Botswana	2.09	Guatemala	1.95	Morocco	2.12	Timor-Leste	2.4
Burkina Faso	1.82	Guinea	1.22	Mozambique	2.27	Togo	2.0
Burundi	1.27	Guinea-Bissau	1.14	Myanmar	1.52	Tonga	1.6
Cabo Verde	2.48	Guyana	1.85	Namibia	2.85	Tunisia	2.1
Cambodia	2.23	Haiti	1.61	Nepal	2.45	Turkmenistan	2.6
Cameroon	1.46	Honduras	2.22	Nicaragua	1.90	Uganda	1.6
Central African Republic	1.36	Indonesia	2.00	Niger	1.23	Ukraine	2.7
Chad	1.14	Iraq	1.46	Nigeria	1.53	Uzbekistan	2.1
Comoros	1.43	Jamaica	1.89	Pakistan	1.36	Vanuatu	2.2
Congo, Dem. Rep.	1.21	Jordan	2.53	Papua New Guinea	1.68	Venezuela, RB	3.4
Congo, Rep.	2.11	Kazakhstan	2.17	Paraguay	1.91	Vietnam	2.2
Costa Rica	2.59	Kenya	2.11	Philippines	2.06	West Bank and Gaza	1.7
Cote d'Ivoire	1.42	Kiribati	3.99	Rwanda	1.66	Yemen, Rep.	1.0
Djibouti	2.03	Kosovo	2.35	Samoa	2.04	Zambia	1.8
Dominica	2.47	Kyrgyz Republic	1.93	Senegal	1.66	Zimbabwe	1.7

2

The Channels of Transmission of Monetary Policy

2.1 Introduction

We have given in the preceding chapter a short presentation of how central banks take charge of their policy responsibilities within a global monetary policy framework, pursuing principally the crucial goal of price stability, but without neglecting other goals, such as reducing output volatility or preserving financial stability. Within this framework, designed to suit the country-specific environment in which they operate, they handle the set of instruments they have at their disposal in order to influence the macro-financial variables that are the critical determinants of their ultimate goal variables.

In the following chapters, we examine in greater detail the design and use of monetary policy instruments (Chapter 3), the important challenges central banks face when pursuing monetary stability in LFDCs (Chapters 4 and 5), the alternative policy frameworks within which monetary policy can be implemented (Chapter 6), and the use of models in its design (Chapter 7). But before going into these specific policy issues, it is important to fully understand the monetary transmission mechanism (MTM), i.e. to investigate through which channels central banks can affect their ultimate goal variables. For example, how do changes in a central bank's policy interest rates ultimately affect household consumption or firms' investment, or other components of aggregate demand? What is the strength, the time frame, and the reliability of these effects? To what extent do these depend on the country's structural features, economic, financial, and institutional?

It is easy to understand that there is a definite policy advantage, if not a necessity, for a central bank to have as good a knowledge as possible of how changes in its monetary policy instruments work through the economy, and how they affect various types of agents and induce changes in their behaviour, in order to ultimately produce the desired effects on inflation and economic activity.

One important difficulty for central banks is that the MTM is not really well understood. This is the case for all countries. As early as the 1960s Friedman and Schwarz (1963) concluded in their *Monetary History of the United States* that monetary policy shocks affect the real economy with 'long and variable lags'. Despite important available empirical evidence that monetary policy shocks undoubtedly affect inflation and output, precisely how this happens is not very

Monetary Policy in Low Financial Development Countries. Juan Antonio Morales and Paul Reding, Oxford University Press.
© Juan Antonio Morales and Paul Reding 2021. DOI: 10.1093/oso/9780198854715.003.0002

clear, so that the MTM is often referred to as a 'black box' (e.g. by Bernanke and Gertler 1995). This pessimistic view refers to the transmission mechanism in AEs, but a fortiori it also applies to the way monetary policy decisions affect financial and real macroeconomic variables in LFDCs.

Indeed, given the specific financial structure of these countries and the generally less diversified financial behaviour of their firms and households, the transmission channels of monetary impulses are, if not wholly different, at least likely to display varying degrees of discrepancy relative to what is observed in AEs. The main characteristics relating to the rudimentary nature of financial markets in LFDCs were discussed in section 1.4. They all have a direct bearing on the MTM.

The analysis that follows describes in some detail the different channels for transmission of monetary impulses, starting from a more theoretical point of view before taking into account the specificities of LFDCs. Note that these channels, through which actions taken by central banks can ultimately affect output and prices, are not 'monetary policy-specific'. They are also channels through which other shocks, like changes in foreign interest rates or changes in domestic or foreign investors' degree of risk aversion, are transmitted to the real sector. These channels are at the core of the nexus of the multiple interactions between an economy's monetary-financial sector and its real sector. Because of this complexity, disentangling the channels through which monetary impulses are transmitted is empirically challenging.

Figure 2.1 gives a schematic view of the way the different channels of monetary policy connect, more or less directly, the central banks' actions and their main ultimate policy goals. It displays the various and complex interactions between transmission variables. It highlights the many other exogenous factors that also shape the country's monetary and financial conditions and that central banks have to take into account when they design and implement their policy.

Using a classification now commonly used in the literature on the MTM (see e.g. Mishkin 1996), we distinguish six different channels: the interest rate channel; the asset price channel; the credit channel; the exchange rate channel; the expectations channel; and the 'real balances' channel. Note that the importance of each of these transmission channels is very much country-dependent, as illustrated by the results of a survey by the Bank of International settlements (BIS) of African central banks (Christensen 2011).[1] Ultimately the question of the relative strength of the transmission channels is an empirical one. However, what matters more is whether the transmission mechanism is globally effective, and whether monetary policy impulses affect inflation and output in a significant and reliable way,

---

[1] Fifteen central banks responded to the question about the relative importance they attributed to the different transmission channels. They indicated that interest rates, credit, and exchange rate were the key transmission channel for their respective country, although the relative importance given to each varied. Low importance was mostly given to the asset price and expectations channel.

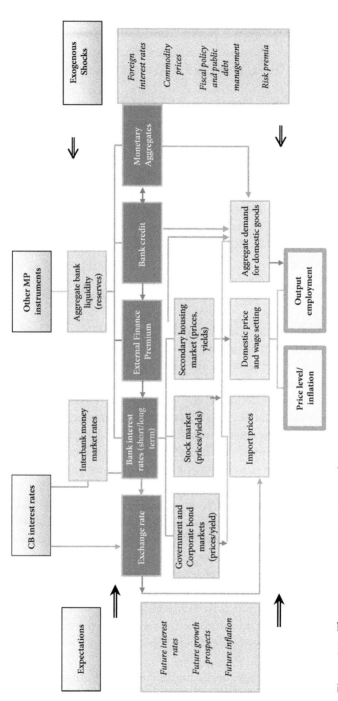

Figure 2.1. The monetary transmission mechanism

although—admittedly only in the short run as far as output is concerned. We shall address both aspects in the following sections.

2.2 The interest rate and asset price channels

The usual presentation of the MTM prominently features the *interest rate channel* as the key channel through which central banks affect aggregate demand. By changing their supply of base money or, more directly, by changing their interest rates, central banks set in motion changes in the whole spectrum of market interest rates, as well as in *asset prices* and in the exchange rate, all of which induce changes in various components of aggregate demand. This 'Money View' of the MTM has been the main work-horse model for describing the interaction between monetary shocks and the real economy (as e.g. in the Mundell–Fleming open economy IS-LM model).

2.2.1 The interest rate channel

According to the Money View, economic agents react to central bank actions by rearranging their portfolio of assets: a decrease in the money supply initiated by the central bank leads agents to draw down their savings with banks and to sell their liquid interest-bearing securities and stocks in order to reconstitute their money balances to the desired level. Financial intermediaries react to the liquidity squeeze initiated by the central bank by curtailing their lending, increasing their borrowing in the interbank market, and selling part of their portfolio of securities, often government securities. Interbank interest rates increase as well as yields on securities, of short maturity but also of longer maturities, if the increase in interest rates is expected to be maintained for a prolonged period. Banks raise their interest rates on savings and time deposits and on non-deposit liabilities to prevent an outflow of funds. Faced with an increase in the cost of their funding, banks raise their rates for all loan categories. The policy-induced general rise in nominal interest rates implies, for given expectations of inflation, a rise in real interest rates. As the *real* cost of borrowing increases for firms and for households, new capital expenditures by firms decrease, as well as residential investment by households. The increase in real interest rates may also decrease current consumption if consumers are induced to save more, postponing their consumption to future periods, for example their spending on consumer durables.[2] Global

---

[2] An increase in the real interest rate has two effects on household consumption: an *intertemporal substitution effect*, which has a negative impact on current consumption, and an *income effect*. If households are net debtors, the increase in interest rates has a negative impact on their disposable income, depressing their current consumption further. If they are net creditors, the income effect

real aggregate demand is in general expected to decrease following a rise in real interest rates, the strength of the decrease depending on the interest rate elasticity of the respective spending category. While most effects of monetary policy are directed towards aggregate demand, changes in interest rates can also affect aggregate supply, through a '*cost channel*' (Barth and Ramey 2001). If firms need to borrow from banks to pay their workers' wages and their intermediate inputs, before receiving the proceeds of the sale of their output, a rise in interest rates increases their costs of production. For given producer prices, aggregate supply thus decreases. Expected effects of a rise in interest rates on both aggregate demand and aggregate supply thus combine to decrease output in the economy. They have, however, opposite effects on prices and thus on inflation dynamics.

2.2.2 The asset price channel

A monetary policy-induced increase in interest rates and in yields of interest-bearing securities has additional effects on asset holders. It increases the opportunity cost of keeping other types of asset, equities and real assets, in their portfolio. Stocks or real assets, like existing residential or non-residential fixed assets, become less attractive relative to interest-bearing securities. Equilibrium on the market for these assets thus implies a downward adjustment in their prices.[3] This is the *asset price channel* of the MTM. Restrictive monetary policy lowers the prices of all existing assets, financial or real. The transmission of these changes in asset prices to the real sector of the economy occurs in two ways. First, through a *wealth effect*. The decrease in asset prices represents a decrease in households' perceived wealth, which may lead them to reduce current consumption, i.e. to save more to reconstitute their wealth and preserve their future consumption opportunities. Second, through a *substitution effect*. Take for instance the housing market. The decrease in market price of existing houses, relative to the cost of building new ones, discourages residential investment. Purchases of existing houses substitute for buying new ones. Similarly, the decrease in quoted stock prices or in the perceived value of non-publicly quoted shares in businesses discourages firms from investing, i.e. from replacing installed physical capital by new one.[4] Both effects have a negative effect on aggregate demand. Figure 2.2

works in an opposite way. In this case the effect of a rise in interest rates on current consumption is indeterminate. Changes in current interest rates will have larger (smaller) income effects if the securities held by households, or in which they are indebted, carry a variable (fixed) interest rate.

[3] Put another way, a hike in interest rates decreases the present value of the asset's future income streams, as the applied discount rate increases with market interest rates.

[4] This effect refers to Tobin's q-theory of investment, where q is the ratio between a firm's current market value and the cost of replacing its stock of physical capital (Tobin 1969). A rise in q decreases the relative cost of new equipment or new buildings. With a higher market value, it is less costly for a firm to issue new shares or to borrow to finance additional investment. Investment thus increases with q and decreases with it.

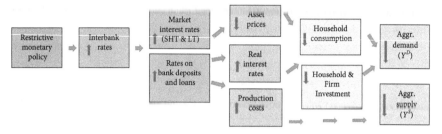

Figure 2.2. The interest and asset price channels

synthesizes how both the interest rate and asset price channels impact aggregate demand (Y^D) and supply (Y^S).

Note, finally, that the asset price channel also concerns the exchange rate, as in an open economy people also hold foreign currency assets in their portfolios. When the central bank initiates changes in the domestic interest rate, domestic agents undertake arbitrage operations between domestic and foreign currency assets. These directly impact the price of the foreign currency, the exchange rate. We discuss these effects in more depth in section 2.4, given that the exchange rate is usually considered as a separate channel of the MTM.

2.2.3 Specificities of LFDCs

While the interest rate channel and the related asset price channel are seen as key channels of monetary transmission in AEs as well as in EMEs, their role can be expected to be somewhat different and possibly more subdued in LFDCs.[5] Indeed, the underdevelopment of financial markets inhibits the arbitrage operations that are a necessary ingredient for the transmission of changes in policy rates to relevant interest rates for households and firms. Interbank markets that operate only intermittently and secondary markets for government or central bank securities that are nonexistent or very shallow loosen the link between central bank rates and banks' loan and deposit rates. This may weaken the role of banks in the transmission of monetary policy in LFDCs where bank-based financial intermediation is dominant.[6] Fortunately, banks' role in the MTM is not confined to setting

---

[5] Note that in many AEs, the role of the interest rate channel strongly decreased after the 2007–8 financial crisis, as central banks have repeatedly cut their policy rates in the aftermath of the crisis. Once interest rates have reached their 'zero lower bound', they have ceased to function as an effective channel on monetary transmission. Central banks have thus resorted to unconventional instruments, like large asset purchase programmes of government securities to inject liquidity into the economy (quantitative easing) or of private securities to improve credit conditions for firms and households (credit easing).

[6] In some LFDCs, notably in Latin America, credit cards have become popular in the upper and middle classes. Interest rates charged for this specific form of consumption finance can, however, be expected to be even less reactive than banks' loan rates to changes in policy rates.

deposit and loan rates, but also includes deciding on the volume of loans to grant to households and firms. We discuss this specific channel and evaluate banks' global role in the MTM in the next section. Even assuming a significant reaction of banks' loan and deposit rates to policy rates, the low degree of access to formal financial intermediation both for small firms and for households reduces the importance of the interest rate in influencing domestic spending (see also section 2.3.3.3.2). Also, a large fraction of the population in LFDCs is too poor to react significantly to changes in policy-induced asset prices. Asset wealth in rural areas can also be expected to be largely immune to monetary policy effects, as it is composed mostly of land and land-related property, the marketability of which is for various reasons often limited. Monetary policy-induced changes in residential property prices in urban areas can, however, have significant impact on current or prospective owners of housing, as real estate represents for them a large part of their wealth, frequently even its most important part. For wealthier households, who own a more diversified portfolio of existing domestic assets, real and financial, including stocks as well as foreign assets, the impact of the interest and asset price channel on their spending follows the mechanism discussed in the two sections above. The same holds for large firms who have access to the banking sector, possibly operate on the domestic stock market, and are in a position to exploit the opportunities offered by international financial intermediation.

2.3 The credit channel and the role of banks

The Money View of a transmission mechanism mainly operating through interest rates has been challenged early on as being too narrow: by focusing exclusively on a 'generic' bond rate as transmission channel, it assumes perfect substitutability between all types of non-monetary financial liabilities, be it government or corporate bonds, treasury bills or bank loans to households or small enterprises.[7] The 'Credit View' of the transmission mechanism therefore departs from the hypothesis of complete financial markets and stresses the role of financial frictions.[8] These originate in informational asymmetries between lenders and borrowers in the credit market. In most cases the borrowers have better information than the

---

[7] An early presentation of a broader MTM based on imperfect substitutability between bonds and bank credit can be found in Brunner and Meltzer (1972).

[8] 'Complete financial markets' is a theoretical notion, dating back to Arrow and Debreu (1954). It implies that for each possible future state of the world there exists a security which only pays if this future state of the world is observed. These contingent securities can be traded without transaction costs, so that agents can reallocate without cost their wealth across time as well as across all possible states of the world. Markets are incomplete if the number of existing state-contingent securities is lower than the number of possible states. Agents cannot in this case hedge themselves optimally against unfavourable future states (e.g. illness, job losses...). Existing financial markets provide a variety of state contingent claims, like insurance contracts, futures, options... but are nevertheless not complete.

lenders on the risks of the project or activity for which they request financing. Banks then play, as intermediaries between lenders and borrowers, a major role in mitigating the adverse consequences of this asymmetric information. They specialize in collecting information about prospective borrowers in order to be able to discriminate amongst good and bad ones and to price their loans according to the quality of their borrowers. They are thereby able to escape, partially at least, the well-known 'adverse selection' problem, and allocate credit in a more efficient way than in the alternative solution, that of 'credit rationing'. They would turn to the latter if they were unable to separate borrowers according to their creditworthiness.[9] Banks also specialize in dealing with moral hazard, the other well-known consequence of asymmetric information. Moral hazard happens when the borrower reallocates the funds received to riskier projects, or takes any other action at the expense of the lender, e.g. by careless management of the collateral that has been committed. Banks can minimize moral hazard by entering into a long-term contractual relationship with their borrowers, by asking them to put up proper collateral, by monitoring broadly their economic performance and accumulating all relevant information about them. The monitoring costs borne by banks in this context are of course charged to their borrowers and are included in the loan rate.[10]

Two variables therefore play a key role in the credit channel of monetary policy transmission: the quantity of *bank credit* and the borrowers' 'external finance premium', the latter being defined as the spread between the firm's cost of borrowed funds and the risk-free rate of corresponding maturity. An alternative definition is 'the difference in cost between the funds raised externally (by issuing equity or debt) and funds generated internally (by retaining earnings)' (Bernanke and Gertler 1995: 28). Focusing on credit volumes or external finance premiums as privileged transmission variables, the literature refers respectively to the *bank credit channel* and the *balance sheet channel*, which we successively discuss in sections 2.3.1 and 2.3.2.

As indicated earlier, it can be expected that these two channels, which bear on both loan volume and loan rate setting by banks, take on a great importance in LFDCs, given their typically bank oriented financial structure and the extent of informational and organizational imperfections in their markets for funds. We discuss in section 2.3.3 the specific role banks play in LFDCs. We survey the

---

[9]   As shown by Stiglitz and Weiss (1981), the credit-rationing solution arises when a bank cannot discriminate amongst borrowers of different quality. The expected profit-maximizing loan interest rate it posts will only attract lower-quality borrowers. The corresponding optimal deposit rate will on the other hand not necessarily attract the amount of funds needed to satisfy all borrowers willing to borrow at the posted loan rate. Optimal credit rationing arises in this case.

[10]   Monitoring costs are a convenient way to introduce 'financial frictions' in macro-models, including DSGE models, following Bernanke, Gertler, and Gilchrist (1999). They include agency costs originating in the costly 'state verification' of the borrower's actual financial situation when the loan is due. On DSGE models, see section 7.3.

results of studies that empirically assess the strength of the MTM through banks' loan rates and credit volume in LFDCs. We also add in this section three specificities of LFDCs which matter for the strength of this broad bank lending and interest rate-setting channel: (i) weak incentives to lend; (ii) a large role of semi-formal and informal financial intermediation; (iii) a significant presence of Islamic banks in several LFDCs.

2.3.1 The bank credit channel

The bank credit channel takes as a starting point that the small and medium-size enterprises that resort to external finance borrow with banks. These enterprises have limited access, if any, to the capital market. Small and medium-sized enterprises are typical in developing countries.

A restrictive monetary policy decreases the reserves of the banks as well as their deposits.[11] With fewer funds to lend, banks will make credit less available to borrowers. This may happen in two ways: either by rationing the quantity of credit supplied or by raising the interest rate bank-dependent borrowers have to pay, and thereby their external finance premium.[12] Either way, one will observe a decrease in investment (I) in capital goods and in new residential housing as well as in consumption of durable goods (C_D). This causes a downturn in aggregate demand (Y^D), as schematically presented in Figure 2.3.

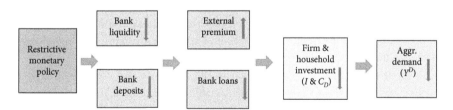

Figure 2.3. Restrictive monetary policy and the bank credit channel

---

[11] Indeed, restrictive monetary policy directly reduces bank deposits when e.g. the central bank performs open-market operations with non-banks, like pension funds or insurance companies, which use their bank deposits to pay the central bank. More often, however, central bank operations are with banks, and the reduction in deposits then occurs following a credit contraction, as banks are unable to renew credit given to clients because of the decrease in their reserves.

[12] See Ramey (1993: 3) who argues that a shift in the supply of bank loans affects real activity either through credit rationing, as in Stiglitz and Weiss (1981), or through a market-clearing change in the risk premium on bank loans, as in Bernanke and Blinder (1988). Note that the increase in the external financial premium comes on top of the general increase in interest rates brought about by the restrictive monetary policy. For this reason, the monetary policy-induced change in the external finance premium is not really considered as a channel parallel to the interest rate channel, but as one which magnifies its effect on the cost for credit and therefore on the real sector (see e.g. Bernanke and Gertler 1995: 29)

Note that the bank credit channel can also be policy-controlled. Indeed, central banks may impose bank credit *ceilings* when 'direct monetary policy instrument' are used. Some LFDCs, albeit in decreasing numbers, continue to rely on such quantitative ceilings on bank credit in order to control aggregate demand and inflation, mainly because alternative instruments, like open market operations, cannot be (or are weakly) undertaken by the central bank when financial markets are underdeveloped (see section 3.2.1). In such a context, central banks also exploit bank credit as the main transmission channel to aggregate demand.

If one abstracts from the very special case where the effectiveness of the bank credit transmission mechanisms depends on whether policy-imposed ceilings are actually binding, the strength of the bank credit channel depends, in general, on a number of factors characterizing the financial environment within which the banks operate. First, for the bank credit channel to be effective, borrowers need to be strongly bank-dependent, without access, or with limited and more costly access, to alternative sources of financing when banks loans are reduced following a restrictive monetary policy shock. This will be frequently the case for small to medium-sized enterprises, which are typical in LFDCs and for which informational asymmetry is most important. Second, banks need to be effectively constrained in their lending activity when outflows of deposits and reserves occur. This will only be the case if they are not in a position to easily compensate their loss of deposits by drawing down their liquid assets or issuing non-deposit liabilities in the market. This lending constraint will typically arise in the smaller, less liquid, less well-capitalized, and less healthy banks. It will also be more common in financial systems where: (i) financial markets are shallow, precluding banks from refinancing themselves by issuing certificates of deposit or borrowing from non-bank financial intermediaries; (ii) access to the international financial markets is limited for domestic banks and the role of domestically incorporated foreign banks in providing liquidity is marginal.

Regulatory constraints on bank capital and liquidity may also affect the strength of the bank credit channel. The so-called 'bank capital channel' (see e.g. Boivin et al., 2010) highlights in this respect the role of the minimum risk-weighted capital requirements recommended by the Basle framework. If restrictive monetary policy induces a worsening of economic conditions, or even the prospects thereof, banks may anticipate an increase in their loan losses, as well as higher risk weights on their existing assets. If they expect their capital adequacy constraint to be soon binding, they will curtail their loan portfolio, this being the most expeditious way to re-establish the adequate ratio of their capital to risk-weighted assets.

2.3.2 The balance sheet channel

Also called the 'broad credit channel', the balance sheet channel focuses on the determinants of the borrower's 'external finance premium', whether the lender is a bank or another (domestic or foreign) lender. A key determinant of this premium is the borrower's net worth, including the value of the collateral committed in the loan contract. Monetary policy shocks, as well as other exogenous financial shocks, affect the borrower's balance sheet. Restrictive monetary policy raises interest rates and decreases asset prices (section 2.2). The borrower's cost on outstanding liabilities increases, the current and expected future profitability of its activities decreases, as well as the value of the collateral. Lenders will require borrowers who have become financially weaker to pay a higher premium, or ration them out by cutting or reducing their credit line upon their renewal. This will decrease investment and households' consumption of loan-financed durables, thereby reducing aggregate demand. This opens the way for second-round effects which magnify the effects of the balance sheet channel. The reduction in aggregate demand and the balance sheet adjustment of liquidity-constrained borrowers, forced to liquidate assets, increases the downward pressure on asset prices and on the values of collaterals. Further increases in the external finance premium produces more credit contraction. It is this amplifying dynamics which has earned the balance sheet channel the name of 'financial accelerator'. It works symmetrically for restrictive and for expansionary monetary policy shocks. It is also well known in the transmission of financial crises, whether homemade or originating in the rest of the world. For these shocks, it also appears to be one of the key mechanisms through which the propagation to the real economy is amplified, sometimes with full force. Banks also fall into the perimeter of the external finance premium channel, as they are themselves borrowers, so that their own net worth and balance sheet strength matters when they set the terms of their lending to firms and households.

In LFDCs, the predominance of banks in financial intermediation therefore implies that restrictive monetary policy can potentially increase the cost of borrowing for firms and households for three cumulative reasons: (i) the policy-induced rise in the risk-free interest rate, which represents the opportunity cost of the bank's funds; (ii) the rise in the borrower's external finance premium requested by banks; (iii) possibly also the rise in the bank's own external finance premium, which adds to its own cost of funds. As a consequence, the aggregate volume of bank credit is reduced.

2.3.3 The role of banks in monetary policy transmission in LFDCs

We focus in this section on the transmission of monetary policy impulses on the two 'bank transmission variables', bank loan rates and bank credit, leaving to section 2.7 the assessment of the full transmission mechanism, from policy variables to output and inflation in LFDCs.

2.3.3.1 Cross-country studies

Mishra et al. (2012) perform a dynamic regression analysis to examine, for a panel of AEs, EMEs and LICs over 1960–2008, the strength of the banks' transmission channels. They report that the links both between the central bank's discount rate and money market rates and between money market and bank rates are weaker in LICs, relative to AEs and EMEs, with substantially smaller short- and long-term pass-through coefficients. Also, the fit of the dynamic specification of the pass-through equation is weaker for the set of LICs, especially for the link between money market rates and bank rates, suggesting that only a small part of the variance of bank rates in LICs can be attributed to changes in money market rates. Mishra et al. (2012) confirm the significantly lower pass-through coefficient for LICs and report that better institutional quality, as proxied by an index of transparency, improves the pass-through of policy rates on bank lending rates across all countries. This factor does not, however, explain by itself the reduced pass-through in LICs. Neither does (at least not in a robust way) the degree of bank concentration, an alternative factor which could help explain the weakness of the bank credit channel in LICs, where competition in the banking sector is generally low. The authors' general conclusion is thus quite pessimistic: results for LICs, for which the bank credit channel could be expected to be the most important channel, indicate this channel to be both weak and unreliable.[13]

Note however that Mishra et al. (2012) concentrate in their panel study on the 'average' LIC's pass-through coefficient. When the same bivariate regression methodology is applied, in an IMF (2010) report, to data at individual country level for a set of 33 sub-Saharan African countries, and with a focus exclusively on the direct pass-through from central bank rates to bank lending rates, results look somewhat different. Heterogeneity stands out: for 27 countries (including 14 in the West and Central African Monetary Unions—WAEMU and CEMAC—and 4 in the South Africa Common Monetary Area), the pass-through is almost full, while for the remaining 6 it is very weak.

Because these studies are only concerned with bivariate relationships between bank lending rates and policy rates, and because they do not seem to lead to robust and uniform results, it seems appropriate to withhold any definitive, sufficiently general conclusion about the strength of the bank interest/credit channel in LFDCs. There is an additional reason for interpreting the results of these two studies with caution. Their regression methodology only considers the direct bilateral relationships between bank (money market) rates and policy rates, without

---

[13] Mishra et al. (2014) reach a similar conclusion regarding a weak bank credit channel in LICs when using an alternative approach and methodology. In this study, they apply a heterogeneous panel SVAR to a sample of 132 countries, including 91 LICs, to analyse the impulse responses of bank lending rates to monetary policy shocks defined, in this case, as innovations in the monetary base. For the group of LICs, one can even observe that the mean response of lending rates to the monetary innovation is wrongly signed. The authors also document that better regulatory quality increases the strength of the response.

controlling for other variables which may have affected both variables. As discussed in IMF (2010: 31–2), exogenous variables may affect bank rates and policy rates in opposite directions, reducing thereby the observed correlation between the two interest rates. This may frequently be the case for supply shocks in LICs. A negative supply shock could induce the central bank to loosen monetary policy, decreasing its policy rate. The shock will nevertheless have a negative effect on business activity and will therefore increase the share of non-preforming loans on banks' balance sheets. Because of this, banks will tend to increase their spread over the policy rate when setting their loan rates. Both rates will in that case possibly diverge, which would imply a *negative* pass-through. Under the assumption that such episodes are more frequent in LICs than in other countries, lower pass-through between bank and policy rates would be the expected result of a typical bivariate regression analysis that only focuses on these two rates and insufficiently controls for the endogeneity of the policy rate.

2.3.3.2 Bank-based studies

Another way to investigate the existence of the bank credit channel is to focus on determinants of the bank credit channel's strength *at the level of individual banks*. As already explained in section 2.3.2, an individual bank's supply of credit will be the more constrained by restrictive monetary policy, the smaller, less liquid, and less well-capitalized it is. Indeed, in this situation the bank will not be able to cushion the monetary policy-induced loss of liquidity and will be forced to restrict its loans. Consequently, and also because its own external premium will be on the rise, it will be forced to raise its lending rates. A small number of studies have applied to LFDCs the methodology used by Kashyap and Stein (1995) to assess the presence of a bank credit channel in advanced countries. This methodology rests on a panel estimation of micro-level bank balance-sheet data. It tests whether the above-mentioned bank characteristics, as reflected in balance-sheet-based indicators, interact with the impact of monetary policy variables on the volume of bank credit. For example, Boughrara and Ghazouni (2009) apply the methodology to four Middle East and North African (MENA) countries, using yearly data over the 1989–2007 period and including all the country's banks in the sample. Their results show that the coefficient of the long-run impact of the monetary policy rate on the growth rate of loans is significantly negative. The evidence on the bank lending channel specifically is, however, rather heterogeneous across countries. Increases in policy rates restrict loan growth more for the relatively smaller banks or the less liquid ones, and/or for those that are less well capitalized. Summing up the evidence, the authors conclude on the existence of a bank lending channel in Morocco, Tunisia, and Jordan, but find the evidence unconvincing for Egypt (Boughrara and Ghazouni 2009: 18).

Similar results based on micro-level quarterly balance sheet data for a set of 20 banks were obtained for Uganda over the 2000–2012 period by Opolot (2013).

His results indicate a significant effect of bank capitalization and liquidity, although not of size, in determining the potency of the effect of monetary policy on the supply of bank loans. Carrera (2010) concludes with a similar panel data approach in Peru, for 22 banks over 2002–12, that the less liquid banks restrict consumer credit more strongly when monetary policy increases interest rates. Bigger banks appear in this study to be able to mitigate the effect of monetary policy on all types of bank credit, while bank capitalization does not appear to matter at all. Abuka et al. (2019) exploit quarterly firm-specific microdata from Uganda's credit registry on accepted and rejected loan applications and on loan originations as reported by banks and other credit institutions. These data, together with banks' balance sheet data, allow the authors to assess the effect of policy rates on loan supply and loan rates across banks, after controlling for macroeconomic factors affecting the demand for loans. The analysis is carried out for 2010–14. The results show that bank loans significantly react to policy-induced increases in the seven-day interbank rate, at both the extensive and the intensive margins: after a monetary tightening, the probability of granting a loan is reduced and the volume of new loans is lower. The pass-through of the interbank rate to the loan rate is strongly significant, and estimated to be close to 0.5. Across banks, the effects of the monetary contraction on credit supply and on loan rates are dampened in the more capitalized banks, as Kashyap and Stein (1995) have found for AEs. However, and contrary to the results of Kashyap and Stein, a similar dampening effect of monetary policy effects is also observed for the *less* liquid banks, both for credit supply and for loan rates. Abuka et al. (2019: 192) explain this result by the tendency of banks in developing countries to allocate a large part of their assets to government or central bank securities, due to the high costs of loan intermediation. The more liquid banks specialize in holding these securities, preferring them to risky and costly loans. Following a rise in policy rates, they worry about a possible increase in the costs of monitoring their loan portfolio and are therefore ready to curtail the volume of their loans more sharply than other, less liquid banks. Moral suasion by the government, according to the authors, may also be responsible for such crowding-out of loans to the private sector by public financing when interest rates increase. The results show that the banks that decrease their supply of corporate loans most are those that have the highest share of government paper on their balance sheet and are thus most exposed to government pressures.

Results from this alternative, individual bank-based approach of testing the bank credit channel therefore seem to broadly confirm its presence. Given the heterogeneity in empirical results, however, it is hard to conclude that the bank credit channel represents a strong and reliable channel for monetary policy.

2.3.3.3 Three additional specificities of bank lending in LFDCs
We explore specific characteristics of LFDCs that may account for a weak role of banks in the transmission mechanism.

2.3.3.3.1 Weak incentives to lend and high excess reserves

An often-suggested explanation for a weak bank credit and interest rate channel is the general weakness of incentives for banks to lend in LFDCs, even though loans to the private sector may be their main source of profit. When the quality of institutions is low, problems of informational asymmetry are worse, loan contracts are costly to enforce, and credit risk is exacerbated. A broad study by IMF (2012) based on bank balance-sheet data of LICs and EMEs over a 50-year period (1960–2010) confirms that LIC banks have an atypically low loan-to-asset ratio and significant excess liquidity. Panel estimates show that the higher a country's institutional quality or the lower its degree of financial repression, the higher is the loan-to-asset ratio of its banks. At the individual bank level, the loan-to-asset ratio is lower for the smaller banks, for the less liquid ones, as well as for those that face the largest credit default risk on their loans.[14]

A closely related issue is the high degree of excess reserves observed in many LICs, but especially in sub-Saharan African (SSA) countries, where excess reserves to deposit ratios up to 20% have not been uncommon, as noted by Saxegaard (2006). Obviously, banks with such a high ratio of excess reserves can compensate for the effects of most restrictive monetary policy impulses and derail the monetary transmission mechanism. Investigating this issue empirically for the Central Economic and Monetary African Community (CEMAC) countries, as well as for Nigeria and Uganda, Saxegaard (2006) concludes that these excess reserves are largely involuntary, in the sense that they are well beyond the level banks would willingly hold for precautionary reasons, as a hedge against unexpected liquidity outflows from private- and public-sector deposits and as a substitute for a nonexistent or unreliable interbank market. He also shows that when a country's banks are in a regime of high involuntary excess reserves, the transmission mechanism of monetary policy shocks is weakened.[15] IMF (2010: 37) and Christensen (2011: 43) also point out the high level of excess reserves in African banks as a significant liability for an effective MTM.[16] They note, however, that a significant decrease in excess reserves has been observed since 2007 in many countries, though not in all. IMF (2019h: 10) indicates, for example, that excess

---

[14] In this study, institutional quality is proxied by various indicators measuring political stability, government effectiveness, the rule of law, and the control of corruption. Financial repression is measured by indicators of government ownership in financial intermediaries, the degree of intervention in the allocation of credit, etc. Credit default risk is proxied by loan loss provisions.

[15] Saxegaard (2006) uses one set of explanatory variables to identify a bank's demand for voluntarily held precautionary excess reserves (e.g. volatility of cash/deposit ratio, of government deposits) and another set to identify involuntary excess reserves (ratio of government deposits to GDP, aid flows/GDP, oil price, etc.). He then uses his estimated series of involuntary excess reserves to detect within a Threshold Vector Auto-regression framework the threshold above (below) which the economy is in a high (low) involuntary excess regime. For each regime he then estimates impulse responses of inflation and output to monetary shocks.

[16] High excess reserves are observed not only in African banks but also in other LFCDs. See e.g. Anderson-Reid (2011) for the Jamaican experience.

reserves remain a policy issue in CEMAC countries. Barajas et al. (2016) document that excess reserves are a characteristic of many emerging and developing countries. They show that this is particularly the case for countries which benefit from large inflows of remittances as a source of low-cost funding.[17] In these countries, mostly LFDCs, the transmission of changes in the policy rate to bank loans is significantly weakened.[18]

There are two intriguing questions about these observed high levels of excess reserves: (i) Banks may wish to keep high reserves because additional lending to the private sector is perceived as too risky; but why would banks hold them when they are not remunerated, as is usually the case, and when at the same time the interest rate on safe government bonds is positive? (ii) Why does the central bank not simply 'mop up' this excess liquidity?

Inexistence or huge imperfections in the functioning of the secondary market for government bonds and of the interbank market, combined with high intermediation costs, imply that banks would willingly hold government bonds only if their yield embodies a high enough liquidity premium. Positive yields of government bonds might therefore carry a zero net return for banks, once the requested liquidity premium and transactions costs are taken into account. It is likely that the development of deeper, efficient secondary markets for government bonds will decrease this liquidity premium, reduce the need to hold large excess reserves, and thus improve the MTM. As to the second question, the answer probably is that the costs of sterilization of this excess liquidity by issuing interest-bearing government bonds or central bank securities are too high—or, in other words, that the government refrains from issuing a too large amount of bonds, as it is quite comfortable with seigniorage revenue generated by existing excess reserves. On their part, weakly capitalized central banks could be reluctant to withstand the costs of issuing securities because this may cause losses obliging them to appeal to the government for recapitalization.[19] Their independence would be compromised and their public reputation would be damaged.

2.3.3.3.2 Formal, semi-formal, and informal financial intermediation

In LFDCs, banks play the major role in organizing financial intermediation between borrowers and lenders. However, often the modern, formal banking

---

[17] Episodes of favourable terms of trade effects in commodity-exporting LFDCs can similarly lead to the build-up of excess reserves in the banking system, as the inflow of reserves associated with the growth of deposits is not matched by a similar growth in the volume of credit.

[18] Barajas et al. (2016) use a panel data approach similar to Mishra et al. (2012) over the 1990–2013 period. While the pass-through coefficient of the policy rate on the loan rate is significantly positive on average for the 92 EMEs and LFDCs in the panel, though low (0.3), it tends towards zero for a country with a ratio of remittances to GDP of about 4–6%.

[19] The adequate level of capital for central banks is a matter of dispute, since they do not face the same risks as commercial banks and regulatory capital does not apply to them. However, most central banks try to show a reasonable net worth. Also, credit rating agencies take into account, among other factors, the financial situation of the central bank in their country risk assessment.

sector lacks reach, providing financial services to only a fraction of the population and following very conservative lending policies, the latter frequently because of regulations to protect savers. Financial intermediation for unbanked households and for micro- and small enterprises that do not have access to the formal banking sector therefore occurs in the informal or in the semi-formal financial sector. As discussed in section 1.4.1.2.3, informal financing still occurs through many community-based savings and credit arrangements or through traditional moneylenders. Informal finance has also been endowed with some structure in many countries, to a varying degree, by the development of microfinance, a donor-supported strategy to foster financial inclusion of the poorest.

The microfinance sector has, over the last three decades, achieved strong growth and outreach across the developing world, has evolved, matured, and diversified (Cull and Morduch 2017). A significant number of microfinance institutions (MFIs) remain active as small community-based NGOs or cooperatives relying on outside grants and retained earnings to finance mostly joint-liability group lending. Others have increased the scale of their operations across the country to make larger, individual loans to their micro-entrepreneur clients. Such a strategy required attracting deposits from the public, which led such organizations to 'upgrade' to a regulated status, turning themselves either into a regulated MFI (also called Non-Bank Financial Intermediaries—NBFI) or into a microfinance bank. While NGO–MFIs are non-profit and microfinance banks are for-profit, semi-formal NBFIs can be non-profit or for-profit (Cull and Morduch 2017: 14). While NGO-MFIs are not—or only weakly—regulated, NBFIs are often regulated by a specific supervisory body, while microfinance banks are regulated by the banking supervisory authority. Microfinance banks cannot, however, in general be assimilated with the formal banking sector, as they retain in principle their original business model, targeting micro- and small entrepreneurs and relying on proximity-based monitoring of their borrowers, as a substitute for adequate collateral.[20] Because of this specific business model, the scope of their asset and liability management is narrower than those of other, universal banks, and their interactions with the central bank remain quite limited.

A key question for monetary transmission is to what extent a monetary contraction, for example, reaches the households and micro- and small firms that rely on microfinance or on another form of informal finance. Although this question has been barely addressed in the literature, several general points can be made. While the central bank has no (or only scant) direct interaction with the MFIs and other operators in the informal sector, the latter are clearly not cut off from the rest of the financial system. Both competition and complementarities

---

[20] A much-discussed issue in microfinance is the conflict MFIs face between their mission to reach out to the poorest and their financial sustainability. The trend towards more for-profit-minded MFIs raises the question of 'mission drift'.

shape the interaction between the formal and informal sectors. Competition is observed to the extent that some borrowers may obtain credit from several lenders, banks, MFIs, or other informal lenders, or to the extent that there are depositors who gauge the opportunity to choose between banks and regulated MFIs. Competition between microfinance and formal finance is strengthened in countries where some MFIs have upgraded to microfinance banks and/or where formal banks have decided to target the upper segment of the MFIs' clients. Complementarity is also an important feature of the interaction between the formal and informal sector, as MFIs use banks to deposit their liquidity or to obtain bridge loans, as do informal lenders, e.g. those who fund the supply of agricultural inputs to farmers.[21]

The transmission channel of (for example) a restrictive monetary policy to the informal financial sector is thus clearly only effective if: (i) banks react to central bank actions by increasing their loan and deposit rates or by restricting the volume of credit supplied to the private sector; (ii) MFIs and informal lenders also increase their loan rates and, possibly, their deposit rates, and constrain their loan volume. The influence of such an indirect effect of monetary policy on the informal sector, and ultimately on the spending decisions of firms and households who resort to this form of financial intermediation, will thus depend on how strong competitive pressures are and how intensively MFIs and informal lenders have to rely on banks for their activities.

Interest rates on microfinance loans are known to be significantly higher than those set by banks, essentially because the smaller loan size and the specific lending technology that involves close monitoring of the borrower imply higher administrative unit costs. Cull and Morduch (2017: 18–9) report that the average median microfinance lender charged a 21% *real* interest rate per year, measured by the average real yields on the portfolios of a large number of MFIs across the world between 2005 and 2009, as recorded by the MIX Market data base.[22,23] They observe that NGO–MFIs charged more than for-profit microfinance banks. Also, interest rates on microfinance loans are thought to be sticky because clients are ready to pay those high rates to get access to credit and to the services of

---

[21] Batini et al. (2010: 20–1) distinguish these two types of interaction between the formal and informal sectors, competition and complementarity, as arising from 'horizontal linkages' (borrowers who first submit their demand for funds to banks and then, if rationed there because of insufficient collateral, to informal lenders) and 'vertical linkages' (informal lenders have access to the formal sector to borrow funds which they then lend to their own clients, taking advantage of their unique position to better select their borrowers and monitor the servicing of their debt).

[22] Rosenberg et al. (2013: 76–8) report similar levels for annual median real rates in the range of 15–24% in 2004–2011. They observe, however, that for this period and for nominal yields, the for-profit lenders had somewhat higher rates than the non-profit MFIs.

[23] The MIX Market database (MIX 2019) contains audited financial account data and many other indicators of the identity and the activity of the MFIs that voluntarily report to MIX (Microfinance Information eXchange). Annual data on interest rates are computed by MIX as the ratio between total income from loans (interest rate and fees) during the year and average annual gross loan portfolio.

MFIs, since they engage in activities expected to generate high returns.[24] MFIs even more than banks tend to rely on customer relationships and are thus even less inclined to adjust the rate they charge to their customers to small changes in monetary policy rates. With respect to the influence that funding costs may have on MFIs' loan rates, an interesting indication is that financing costs represent less than one third of the average yield on loans (Rosenberg et al. 2013: 97). In examining the determinants of MFI loan rates over 1998–2009, Di Bella (2011) however finds that the pass-through of funding costs to loan rates is not significantly different from 1.[25] This suggests that MFIs are not immune to changing financial conditions, at home or even abroad if their financing is of foreign origin. The trend towards for-profit microfinance, and, more generally, the necessity of maintaining sustainability of MFIs as they face a reduction in the share of grants in their financing, can also be expected to increase their responsiveness to changes in domestic financing conditions and therefore, indirectly, to monetary policy. Despite the various points made above about a possible bank–MFI lending channel, there is scant direct evidence connecting monetary policy indicators to microfinance loan rates or loan levels. Taking Bolivia as a case study of a country where microfinance has come to play an important role, we provide in Box 2.1 an illustration of the hierarchy in interest rates applied by MFIs and by banks and of their observed co-movements with the treasury bill rate, an indicator of the stance of monetary policy.

2.3.3.3.3 LFDCs with a dual banking system, conventional and Islamic

Several LFDCs have a financial system in which Islamic banks, i.e. banks which apply the Sharia rules of financial intermediation, coexist with conventional banks in these countries and have seen their market share grow over the past decade. According to the Islamic Financial Services Board (2019: 11, 14), in 2018 there were two LFDCs, Iran and Sudan, where the whole banking system was Islamic, and 11 LFDCs where Islamic banks held a significant share of the domestic banking sector's total assets (larger than 5%).[26] A key characteristic of Islamic banking is that, according to the principles of Sharia, fixed ex ante interest payments are prohibited. Financial instruments need to be based on pre-agreed profit- and loss-sharing (PLS) arrangements of various natures between lenders and borrowers. Bank credits take the form of equity partnerships, leasing-type contracts, or mark-ups on the sale, with deferred payment, of an asset or a

---

[24] This does not, however, necessarily imply that MFIs' clients are insensitive to the level of the interest rate. Cull and Murdoch (2017: 13–14) report evidence of two studies, for Mexico and Bangladesh, that document relativity high interest rate elasticity of the demand for MFI credit.

[25] The panel estimates also show that loan size, productivity, and MFI age reduce lending rates and are the main factors explaining differences among MFIs in the levels of their loan rate.

[26] The latter are (with percentage shares of Islamic banks in total banking assets in brackets): Bangladesh (20), Djibouti (19), Jordan (16), Pakistan (13), Oman (12), Afghanistan (10), Maldives (8), Indonesia (6), Iraq (5), Egypt (5).

Box 2.1. Microfinance in Bolivia

Bolivia has a long experience with microfinance. MFIs started to operate in the country in the mid1980s, in the aftermath of the hyperinflation crisis and the ensuing collapse of the domestic banking system. Supported by international organizations but also by the authorities, who accompanied their development with an evolving regulatory framework, Bolivian MFIs have played an important and pioneering role in the provision of financial services for poor people and for micro-enterprises.[27] They currently operate under the general regime of the 2013 Financial Services Law. This law has strengthened supervisory requirements for the whole financial system but has also imposed interest caps and minimum quotas for credit to specific sectors. It is especially the level at which interest caps are set that has acted as a constraint on MFIs' activity, with possibly detrimental effects on their contribution to financial inclusion (Heng 2015). The average size of loans had to increase, as small loans produce losses, given the interest caps and high administrative costs.

The MIX Market (MIX 2019) database includes for Bolivia 17 financial intermediaries that operate in the microfinance sector—8 microfinance banks and 9 regulated non-bank MFIs. Microfinance banks are NGO–MFIs that have over time upgraded to banking status so as to be able to attract deposits (including sight deposits) in order to finance an enlarged loan portfolio. The latter represented for these 17 institutions an impressive 41% of total credit to the private sector in 2018 (37% if loans to large corporations by MFI banks are excluded).[28] Microfinance banks dominate the sector. The nine non-bank MFIs have only a 7% market share of the MFI sector's total loans but serve up to 38% of the total number of its borrowers.

Figure 2.4 shows the evolution of interest rates for microfinance banks, for non-bank MFIs and for banks in Bolivia from 2003 to 2018. The T-bill rate is taken as a proxy for the policy rate.[29]

While Figure 2.4 is meant to be mostly illustrative, three interesting observations can be made. First, a clear hierarchy of interest rates is apparent. Loan rates of non-bank MFIs are higher than those of microfinance banks, the latter having higher loan rates than banks. Second, there is a general downward trend in interest rates, except for one non-bank MFI. Third, there is some evidence of co-movement between bank rates, MFI loan rates, and the policy rate. This is most clearly apparent in 2007–8, when a restrictive monetary policy pushed the T-bill up.

---

[27] For a thorough discussion of this experience, see Gonzalez-Vega and Villafani-Ibarnegaray (2011).

[28] Loan volume data are from MIX Market and WDI databases.

[29] Interest rates for MFIs are from MIX Market and are nominal yields (ratios between total income from loans during the year and average annual gross loan portfolio). Bank and T-bill rates are from IMF's International Financial Statistics data base.

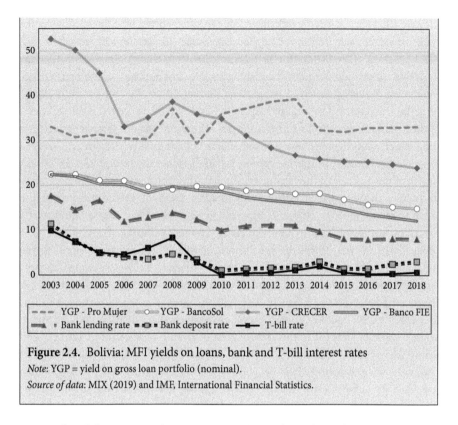

Figure 2.4. Bolivia: MFI yields on loans, bank and T-bill interest rates

Note: YGP = yield on gross loan portfolio (nominal).

Source of data: MIX (2019) and IMF, International Financial Statistics.

commodity (El Hamiani Khatat 2016: 16–7). Bank credit is directed to finance exclusively productive projects. Speculative transactions are forbidden. PLS ratios and cost-plus mark-up rates on leasing-type contracts substitute for conventional banks' loan rates.[30]

The MTM can be expected to be different in a dual banking system, as the impact of central bank policy rates will only affect the funding cost and therefore loan and deposit rates of conventional banks and not those of Islamic banks, at least not directly. A spill-over effect may however occur when competition between Islamic and conventional banks is strong, forcing Islamic banks not to

---

[30] Lewis and Algaoud (2001: ch. 3) offer a detailed description of the basics of Islamic banking. Islamic banks fund themselves by offering current, savings, and investment accounts to the public. Depositors receive no remuneration for current account deposits, which are seen as an interest-free loan contract (*Al-Wadiah* 'safe keeping') and repayable in full on demand. Savings and investment accounts follow the rules of a *Mudaraba* contract. The latter determines the PLS ratio according to which the bank's net profits (and losses) are shared between the bank and its depositors. Financing of households and firms by banks also occurs through *Mudaraba* contracts designed for the borrower's specific projects or through joint ventures (equity partnerships—*Musharaka* contracts). When PLS ratios are difficult to implement, banks offer alternative modes of financing, such as *Murabaha* for foreign trade and working capital (the bank finances the purchase of goods or assets and resells it to the client by instalments on a 'cost plus' basis) or *Ijara* (leasing, mostly for equipment).

deviate too significantly from loan or deposit rates posted by conventional banks when they set their PLS ratios or their mark-ups (El Hamiani Khatat 2016: 17). Such reaction of credit conditions in Islamic banks to changes in policy rates may, however, in general be quite sluggish, especially in countries where market segmentation is important, as in Bangladesh (Sarker 2016: 27). One can thus expect that the transmission mechanism through bank rates is weakened in LFDCs with a dual banking system. In some countries where the Islamic finance segment is important, central banks have devised Sharia-compliant monetary instruments to regulate the liquidity of Islamic banks (Sarker 2016; see also section 3.4.3.2). With instruments to control the Islamic banks' liquidity volume, the central bank may thus have the leverage to activate and monitor the bank credit channel for the Islamic segment of the country's financial system. However, excess liquidity is a frequent feature of Islamic banks in many countries (Islamic Financial Services Board 2019: 59–60). This is the reflection of an insufficient development of Islamic financial interbank markets and of secondary markets for Sharia-compliant government securities, as well as of insufficient sterilization by the central bank (El Hamiani Khatat 2016: 24; Sarker 2016: 28). As already noted in section 2.3.3.3.1, persistent excess liquidity undermines the effectiveness of the bank credit channel. Some empirical content to this observation is given by Zaheer et al. (2013), who study the reaction of 40 banks, of which six are Islamic, to a monetary shock in Pakistan over the period 2002–10. Following the Kashyap and Stein (1995) methodology, the authors show that, faced with a monetary contraction, small conventional banks that are liquid cut their lending less than those that are less liquid, while large conventional banks maintain their loan volume, independently of their liquidity position. Islamic banks, which are small in terms of asset size, are found not to be affected in their loan growth by changes in the policy rate, actually behaving like large conventional banks. While it is difficult to generalize from this single empirical case study, the latter nevertheless seems to indicate that, at the least, Islamic banking does not reinforce the credit channel of monetary policy.[31]

2.4 The exchange rate channel

In an open economy, monetary policy also affects output and prices through its effects on the nominal and real exchange rates. This exchange channel may play a

---

[31] Caporale et al. (2020) also address the bank credit transmission mechanisms for a country with Islamic banking, Malaysia. Although Malaysia is not included in our set of LFDCs, it is interesting to note that their empirical analysis—at a macroeconomic level—using a nonlinear VAR methodology, with monthly data from 1994 to 2015, also indicates that Islamic credit is less responsive than conventional credit to monetary policy shocks. Its response has however increased since 2002—a period which coincides with an increase in the share of Islamic finance—and has become similar to that of conventional bank credit.

significant role in many LFDCs. For it to operate, various conditions need to be satisfied: a flexible exchange rate regime, an open capital account, a sensitivity of aggregate demand to changes in the real exchange rate and of prices to changes in the nominal exchange rate. We discuss each condition in turn in the three following subsections. While we detail the various channels through which exchange rates influence output and prices, we only refer to some selected evidence about their potency. As the exchange rate has opposite effects on output and prices, it is difficult to assess its overall contribution to the transmission mechanism without resorting to a more general empirical model (see section 2.7).

2.4.1 Effectiveness condition I: a flexible exchange rate regime

The central bank has, in such a monetary framework, no exchange rate target, announced or unannounced, and therefore does not intervene in the foreign exchange market. In reality, central banks of LFDCs and EMEs intervene more often than AEs to keep the exchange rate on a desired trajectory, because they are uncomfortable with the anticipated consequences for output and inflation of the actual evolution of the exchange rate. We shall return to this 'fear of floating' symptom in section 6.2, where we discuss exchange rate targeting. We focus here on the transmission mechanism of monetary policy, and assume that the central bank fully accepts the consequences of its monetary policy actions on the exchange rate.

2.4.2 Effectiveness condition II: a sufficiently open capital account

When the country's capital account is sufficiently open to international trade in financial assets, an expansionary monetary policy affects the exchange because it lowers the domestic interest rate. The decrease in the return on domestic currency assets induces investors, domestic and foreign, to rebalance their portfolio, increasing the share in foreign currency assets, at the expense of domestic currency assets. The resulting incipient capital outflows raise the nominal exchange rate (defined as the domestic currency price of foreign currency). The extent of this depreciation, for a given change in the domestic interest rate, will depend on the actual degree of substitution between domestic and foreign currency assets.

2.4.2.1 Uncovered Interest Parity
A well-known benchmark case is the *Uncovered Interest Parity* (UIP) relationship which assumes *perfect substitutability* between domestic and foreign currency assets. As an equilibrium no-arbitrage relationship, UIP implies that expected returns for both assets are equal, when expressed in a common currency. UIP

holds when there are no capital controls or transactions costs for trading between domestic and foreign currency assets and when investors are risk-neutral. Let i_t $\left(i_t^*\right)$ be the current one-period level of the domestic (foreign) currency interest rate on risk-free assets, S_t the current level of the exchange rate (quoted as the domestic currency price of the foreign currency), and $E_t\left(S_{t+1}\right)$ the future level of the exchange rate at $t+1$, the end of the investor's holding period, as expected at period t. UIP is then written as equation (1):

$$i_t = i_t^* + \frac{E_t\left(S_{t+1}\right) - S_t}{S_t} \tag{1}$$

where the RHS of equation (1) represents the expected domestic currency return of a foreign currency asset holding.[32] This expected return has two components: the foreign interest rate i_t^* and the expected change in the exchange rate over the asset's holding period. According to UIP, the current nominal exchange rate is then determined on the one hand by the interest rate differential between domestic and foreign currency assets and, on the other, by the expected future exchange rate. Suppose we start with both domestic and foreign currency interest rates being equal. This implies that the expected change in the exchange rate is nil. A decrease in the domestic interest rate then gives rise to capital outflows, as investors switch to foreign currency assets. The domestic currency thus depreciates. Capital outflows will only cease once investors have restored their portfolio equilibrium. As there is an interest differential in favour of foreign currency assets $\left(i_t < i_t^*\right)$, expected returns on domestic and foreign currency assets can only be equalized if investors are led to expect an appreciation of the domestic currency during the holding period of their investment. This is indeed what happens when capital outflows push the price of the foreign currency $\left(S_t\right)$ up to a level that triggers expectations of a future decline, i.e. of an appreciation of the domestic currency, taking into account the expected future level of the exchange rate $\left\{\left[E_t\left(S_{t+1}\right) - S_t\right]/S_t\right\} < 0$. For portfolio equilibrium to be restored and therefore for capital outflows to cease following the decline in the domestic interest rate, the initial depreciation of the domestic currency must therefore be large enough in

---

[32] Equation (1) is actually a simplified version of the risk-neutral investor's no-arbitrage, portfolio equilibrium relationship. The latter equates the expected end-of-period domestic currency values of two strategies: investing 1 unit of domestic currency in a domestic currency asset with interest rate i_t; investing 1 unit of domestic currency in a foreign currency asset with interest rate i_t^*. The foreign currency asset is bought at price S_t, the current exchange rate, while the proceeds of the foreign currency investment are expected to be converted into domestic currency at the end of the investment period at exchange rate $E_t\left(S_{t+1}\right)$. The no-arbitrage relationship is thus given by $\left(1+i_t\right) = \left(1+i_t^*\right)\left[E_t\left(S_{t+1}\right)/S_t\right] = \left(1+i_t^*\right)\left\{1+\left[E_t\left(S_{t+1}\right)-S_t\right]/S_t\right\}$. Equation (1) in the text is a linear approximation of this no-arbitrage relationship.

such a way that the currency's expected future appreciation fully compensates investors for the lower return on their domestic currency assets. The larger the initial monetary policy induced decrease in the domestic interest rate, the larger will be the initial depreciation, for a given level of the future expected exchange rate. Initial depreciation will also be stronger if investors expect future monetary policy to remain expansive, as they will in this case also revise upwards their expectations about the future level of the exchange rate.[33, 34]

2.4.2.2 Deviations from Uncovered Interest Parity

UIP however, while useful as a benchmark, cannot be expected to hold in LFDCs. There are two reasons for this: (i) Contrary to what UIP assumes, domestic assets are not risk-free, so investors do not in general consider them as close substitutes to safe assets held abroad; (ii) Capital controls, whether they already exist or may be imposed later, hinder cross-border arbitrage between domestic and foreign currency assets.

2.4.2.2.1 Imperfect substitutability between domestic and foreign currency assets
Turning to the first factor disturbing UIP, it can be readily observed that liabilities of LICs and EMEs, whether issued by public or by private agents, carry a so-called 'country risk premium' which reflects the issuer's default risk. Such a 'country risk premium' will indeed be typically observed in the *spreads* between the yield to maturity of domestic currency long-term government bonds issued in USD and the yield on US Treasury bonds of corresponding maturity. It will be larger, the lower the domestic country's rating, i.e. the higher the probability of a default during the bond's life-time. While easily observable for long-term bonds issued in foreign currency, such country risk premiums are also embodied in interest rates of domestic currency debt, whether of long or short maturity or whether issued by the government, by non-financial firms, or by banks.

Thus, not only expected changes in the exchange rate but also expected loss in case of default of the issuer of domestic currency bonds are taken into account by risk-neutral investors. Risk-averse investors will in addition request a risk premium to compensate them for being exposed to both exchange rate and credit risks. The equilibrium relationship between short-term interest rates in domestic currency

---

[33] Note that this analysis of the effects of a decrease in domestic interest rate on the exchange rate relies on a partial equilibrium approach. The changes in the exchange rate will have an impact on output and prices, with feedback effects on domestic interest rates and the expected future exchange rate. A general equilibrium model is needed to describe the full dynamics for long-run equilibrium, e.g. the well-known Dornbusch overshooting model (Dornbusch 1976).

[34] The reasoning is similar for the case when initially $i_t > i_t^*$, i.e. when risk-neutral investors already hold expectations of a future depreciation of the domestic currency. The decrease in i_t will also raise S_t, thereby lowering the expected future depreciation of the domestic currency, so that equality of expected returns is again re-established.

(i_t) and in foreign currency (i_t^*), i.e. between those that are crucial for monetary policy, can then be rewritten in a more general form for risk-averse investors:

$$i_t - dl^e = i_t^* + \frac{E_t\left(S_{t+1}\right) - S_t}{S_t} + \rho\left(B, \theta, \ldots\right) \tag{2}$$

The LHS of the equilibrium relationship reflects the expected return on the domestic currency asset, with dl^e being the annualized percentage domestic currency loss due to default that the investor expects to bear over this asset's holding period. The RHS is the sum of the expected return, in domestic currency, on the foreign currency asset (supposed to be risk-free) and of the requested risk premium, ρ. This risk premium depends positively on the stock of domestic bonds (B) to be held in private investors' portfolios, as well as on a vector θ of other risk-increasing factors, including the volatility of the exchange rate and some measure of dispersion of the probability distribution function of the recovery rate in case of default.[35]

The assessment of the exchange rate channel of the MTM thus needs to take into account that investors do not in general consider LFDCs' domestic currency assets as close substitutes of international, credit risk-free foreign currency assets even when the capital account is fully open.

One can first assume that dl^e is largely determined by the country's fiscal stance and external debt position, and that it is thus independent of current monetary policy actions. The risk premium ρ on the other hand can be affected by monetary policy. Indeed, expansionary monetary policy is in general brought about, as discussed in section 3.4, by purchases of domestic bonds by monetary authorities in exchange for central bank liquidity. The reduction in the stock of domestic bonds to be willingly held in private portfolios will decrease the requested risk premium ρ and thereby, as can be seen from equation (2) above, will weaken the depreciation pressure on the current exchange rate (S_t), for a given change in the domestic interest rate i_t. This 'portfolio balance effect' thus reduces the power of the exchange rate channel of monetary policy transmission. The strength of this mitigating effect is, however, an empirical question.

2.4.2.2.2 A special case: dollarized economies
Partially dollarized economies are a particular case of imperfect substitutability between domestic and foreign currency assets and liabilities. In these economies,

---

[35] Equation (2) reflects, in the portfolio balance approach to exchange rates, the reduced form of the equilibrium between demand and supply of domestic currency bonds in a small open economy. The domestic interest rate incorporates a risk premium which is a function of all the variables that are determinants of the aggregate demand of domestic bonds by the private sector (e.g. perceived risks, real wealth, the degree of risk aversion) and of their supply (government bonds held outside the central bank). When foreign currency bonds are perceived as less risky, as is usually the case for LFDCs, the requested risk premium is positive. See Krugman and Obstfeld (2009: 495–7) for a brief presentation of this approach.

domestic agents have access to domestically issued financial assets denominated either in local or in foreign currency. They do not need to go cross-border to arbitrage between domestic and foreign currency assets. Asset substitutability is thus much greater than in non-dollarized economies. Even more important, the difference in expected returns between rates on, say, 'peso' and dollar deposits with domestic banks will not be affected by 'country risk' factors as is the case with cross-border dollar deposits. A shown by Ize and Levy Yeyati (2003), the only factors which then matter for the portfolio choice between domestic 'peso' and domestic dollar deposits are, besides the difference in expected returns, the volatility of inflation and of the real exchange rate.[36] Given this high cross-currency substitutability of domestic assets, the link between domestic currency interest rates and the exchange rate can be expected to be strong in dollarized economies.

There is however an additional twist to the exchange rate transmission channel of monetary policy in dollarized economies: it may become unreliable or even ineffective if the high substitutability between 'peso' and dollar interest-bearing assets is accompanied by high substitutability in the demand for 'pesos' and dollars as *currencies,* used as cash or sight deposits in day to day economic transactions. Such *currency substitution* implies that foreign currency is used in parallel with domestic money as a medium of exchange for domestic transactions, a temporary store of value, and even a unit of account. If foreign money is able to perform the same functions as domestic money, and if costs of switching from one to the other are low and expected to remain so, the demand for domestic money ceases to be a well-behaved, stable function of the volume of transactions and of its opportunity cost, as given by the domestic interest rate. Expectations of domestic currency depreciation become an additional crucial determinant of domestic money demand. Higher expected depreciation will induce agents to shift out of domestic money and increase their foreign money holdings, putting pressure on the exchange rate and demanding a steep increase in the policy rate to try to contain a large depreciation. Because such changes in expectations may be unrelated to fundamentals, and may indeed be self-fulfilling if currency substitution is high, monetary policy loses its grip on the nominal exchange rate. As a result, monetary policy not only loses a reliable transmission channel, but also faces the challenges of excess exchange rate and interest rate volatility potentially generated by high currency substitution.[37] We return in section 6.5 to the issues raised by dollarization.

[36] Ize and Levy Yeyati (2003) use a mean-variance framework to describe the choice of a depositor who maximizes the expected utility of his real wealth. The optimal portfolio allocation between domestic and foreign currency assets is thus determined by real returns differentials, their variances and covariances.

[37] Models of currency substitution show that if there is complete substitutability between foreign and domestic money, the exchange rate and domestic price level are *indeterminate* (see Vegh 2013: section 5.5). If substitutability is imperfect but nevertheless high, small changes in monetary policy can lead to large changes in the exchange rate. Surveying empirical studies of currency substitution, Vegh (p. 765) notes that the results are still inconclusive, so that 'its impact on the effectiveness of monetary policy remains an open question'.

2.4.2.2.3 Capital controls

Many LFDCs still use exchange controls, as discussed in section 3.2.1.2. These may include various types of restriction on capital movements with the rest of the world, although they vary very much from country to country. Restrictions may be imposed on cross-border trade in various types of assets (e.g. direct investment, debt securities, shares, credit). They may be applied to residents or non-residents, to capital in- or outflows. In order to assess the extent of these restrictions, several authors have relied on the IMF's Annual Report on 'Exchange Arrangements and Exchange Restrictions' (AREAER), which reports in detail for each member country the 'de jure measures' taken to limit capital flows. Among them, Fernández et al. (2016) use a very detailed coding methodology of the AREAER data to measure the degree of a country's financial integration. They compute an 'overall restrictions index' which may vary between 0 (no restrictions) to 1 (restrictions on all type of international transactions). It appears that for 2017, the last year for which their index have been updated, the indicator's value was 0.59 for LI countries, 0.45 for LM as well as for UM countries, and 0.21 for HI countries.[38]

Figure 2.5 combines, for the 43 LFDCs that are included in this database, the 2007 and 2017 values of the 'overall restriction index'. The heterogeneity among LFDCs is clearly apparent according to this 'de jure' measure of capital controls, with a cluster of countries having a relatively open capital account and another group a relatively closed one. It can also be observed that countries have in general maintained, if not slightly increased, the intensity of their capital controls since 2007, the year of the global financial crisis. Only a few LFDCs among the 43 for which data are reported eased their restrictions on capital flows.[39]

Although existing 'de jure' restrictions do not necessarily always represent effective constraints for international trade in assets, it can be concluded from these data that capital controls are still pervasive in LFDCs. This has obvious implications for the exchange rate channel of monetary policy impulses. By limiting arbitrage between domestic and foreign currency assets, capital controls imply that a monetary policy induced decrease in domestic interest rates will only have a weak effect on the exchange rate, or even no effect at all. Capital controls thereby limit or suppress the effectiveness of this transmission channel.

---

[38] The figures represent unweighted averages of the scores of individual countries in each group. The database of Fernández et al. (2016) is publicly available, with updates, and covers 100 countries over the 1995–2017 period. It details regulatory restrictions on international transactions concerning 10 categories of assets. Restrictions indices are computed for capital in- and outflows, the overall restrictions index being the average of both.

[39] Country labels in Fig. 2.5 refer to the World Development Indicators' country codes. Not all data points are labelled, for reasons of clarity.

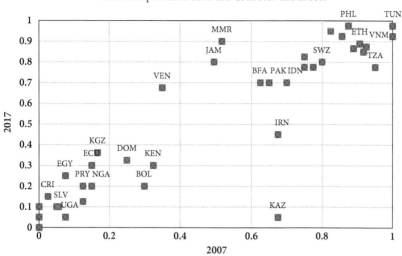

Index of capital controls in LFDCs in 2007 and in 2017

Overall restrictions index of Fernandez et al. (2016) - Data from the June 2019 update

Figure 2.5. Index of capital controls in LFDCs in 2007 and 2017

2.4.3 Effectiveness condition III: real effects on output and pass-through on prices

Exchange rate changes have relative price effects which affect aggregate demand and output. They also impact directly the price level through their 'pass-through' effect. To be an effective transmission channel of monetary policy the exchange rate would need to have strong effects on output and a weak pass-through on prices, thereby reconciling as much as possible its respective effects on the output and inflation targets set by the monetary authorities.

2.4.3.1 Real exchange rates, aggregate demand, and output

Monetary policy induces changes in the *nominal* exchange rate, but what matters for aggregate demand is the change in the *real* exchange rate, i.e. in the price of home goods relative to foreign goods. As most LFDCs are small open economies, the relevant simple macroeconomic model to analyse issues relating to the real exchange rate is the two-sector model, also known as the dependent economy model. Originally developed by Salter (1959) and Swan (1960), it features traded and non-traded goods. The domestic economy produces both types of good, the traded goods at international prices, the home goods at prices which are determined on the domestic market by the interaction of demand and supply. The real exchange rate is then, in this analysis, the relative price of traded goods in terms of non-traded goods (expressed in the same currency units). A monetary policy-induced depreciation of the exchange rate S_t will immediately, for given foreign

currency prices $P_{T,t}^{*}$, raise the domestic currency price of traded goods P_{l}, propor-
tionally to the rate of depreciation, as $P_{T,t} = S_{t}.P_{T,t}^{*}$. This increases on impact the
relative price of traded goods $P_{T,t}/P_{NT,t}$ and raises the demand for non-traded
goods so that aggregate demand for domestic output increases. The strength of
this real spending effect will depend on the relative price elasticity of the demand
for non-traded goods.[40] This change in relative prices—in the real exchange rate—
also decreases the domestic demand for traded goods. But as demand for these
goods is supposed to be perfectly price-elastic, any domestic output of traded goods
not sold at home will be exported. Total demand for domestic output will thus
increase. However, other effects may counterbalance this favourable expenditure-
switching effect on aggregate demand. To the extent that the domestic currency
depreciation decreases agents' real wealth, as further discussed in section 2.4.3.2,
real income may actually decline, leading to expenditure-reducing effects on
domestically produced goods. The ultimate short-run effect of the exchange rate
depreciation on output is thus in general ambiguous (see also Box 6.3).

2.4.3.2 Balance-sheet effects of the exchange rate

Exchange rate changes do not only have effects on output through relative price
effects but may also directly affect aggregate demand through the changes they
bring about in households' and firms' net wealth. While a monetary policy-
induced depreciation of the domestic currency has a positive effect on output
through the expenditure-switching effects discussed in section 2.4.3.1, this
balance-sheet effect works in an opposite way. When a large part of households'
wealth takes the form of cash balances or of nominal domestic currency assets,
the rise in the domestic price level induced by the exchange rate depreciation (the
pass-through effect discussed in section 2.4.3.3) decreases real wealth. This
decreases consumption, as households save more to reconstitute their wealth.
While this channel operates in any country, it takes a special twist in dollarized
economies, where firms and households often have a net liability exposure in foreign currency. A monetary policy-induced depreciation of the domestic currency
will increase the domestic currency value of their net foreign currency debt.
Relative to their income, usually earned in domestic currency, their debt service
will increase. With such a weakened balance sheet, access to credit will become
more difficult, with a higher external premium to be paid in light of the depressed
value of collaterals. We are back to the balance sheet channel discussed in
section 2.3.2. The extent to which the exchange rate may contribute to trigger this

---

[40] This elasticity is generally considered to be low. Corsetti et al. (2011: 408–10, 420) refer to a range
below 1, and use 0.74 for their model simulations. Empirical estimates for developing countries are
hard to come by. One exception is Barja Daza et al. (2005), who estimate for Bolivia a constant elasticity of substitution consumption function using input–output data over 1990–2002. They obtain an
average value of 0.72 for this relative price elasticity of the demand for non-traded goods.

specific balance sheet channel and possibly the accompanying financial accelerator depends on how large the private sector's net foreign currency exposure is. The contractionary effect of devaluations brought about by such a balance sheet effect has been widely studied at a theoretical level in the context of the choice of exchange rate regimes (see e.g. Céspedes et al. 2004 and Box 6.3).[41] It is also a major policy concern in EMEs and LFDCs because of its collateral threats to financial stability, as we discuss in section 6.4.5.2.

2.4.3.3 Exchange rate pass-through on prices

Changes in the exchange rate not only have relative price effects but also directly affect the domestic price level. This is different from most other transmission channels of monetary policy, which only affect aggregate demand and whose final effects on output and prices will be governed by how aggregate supply reacts to the impulse on aggregate demand.[42] A 10% depreciation of the exchange rate mechanically raises the domestic price index by 4% if traded goods enter with a proportion of 40% into consumers' expenditures and if the domestic price of traded goods rises by the extent of the depreciation, as assumed by our simple two-sector model. The latter hypothesis has been questioned by the vast literature on exchange rate pass-through, with the law of one price for traded goods being challenged by 'pricing to market behaviour'.[43] Foreign producers, for instance, might not be able to fully pass-through the domestic currency's depreciation into domestic import prices, if the price elasticity of the domestic demand for their products is high.[44] Such trade-strategic behaviour may decrease the extent of the pass-through on traded goods, in import and export prices. This of course matters for the pass-through of the exchange rate in the general price level, which is the main concern of monetary authorities . An additional important factor needs, however, to be taken into account. Domestic producers and wage earners may set their prices and wages on the basis of their exchange rate expectations, thereby reinforcing the '*global* pass-through'. Indeed, because the exchange rate in many LFDCs is often very closely monitored as a 'headline' indicator of monetary conditions, a depreciation can quickly lead to an expectation's fuelled raise in domestic prices and wages. Whether these effects come into play will crucially

---

[41] It has also been well documented in the context of sizeable devaluations observed in acute crises periods or as part of stabilization policy measures (see e.g. Edwards 1989).

[42] The exceptions are the interest cost channel and the expectations channel, which also affect aggregate supply (see sections 2.2.1 and 2.5).

[43] See e.g. Frankel et al. (2005) for a useful review.

[44] Obviously, the two-sector model with a single traded good is in this case no longer appropriate. Trade barriers, transport and distribution costs, differences in market structures, etc. imply imperfect substitutability between the tradable goods which a country imports or exports. Foreign producers facing e.g. local competitors for similar goods will have to take a high elasticity of demand into account: when setting their price they will not be in a position to pass the depreciation of the domestic currency into higher prices. They will have to dip into their profit margin in order to limit the increase in local currency prices or even to keep them unchanged.

depend, as discussed further in section 4.5, on the credibility of monetary policy and on its performance in anchoring the price level. As this is often a particularly difficult issue in dollarized economies, it is not surprising that their pass-through coefficient is especially high.

A high rate of *global* pass-through has two opposite implications. Monetary authorities can, on one hand, better exploit the exchange rate channel to target inflation.[45] With a high pass-through, an exchange rate *appreciation* has strong inflation reducing effects. On the other hand, the relative price effects of exchange rate changes on output are reduced and balance sheet effects are magnified with a high pass-through, which increases the likelihood that an exchange rate *depreciation* has contractionary effects (see section 2.4.3.2). A high pass-through is however more of a curse than a blessing if changes in the exchange rate are mostly exogenous. Exchange rate shocks are then almost fully transmitted to domestic prices as supply shocks, to which monetary authorities will need to react. They then face a difficult choice: either let inflation raise or tolerate output losses to keep inflation on target (see section 4.2.1). An exchange rate shock with a high pass-through may be a particularly damaging supply shock for economies which import a large part of investment goods and inputs for domestic production, which is the case in many LFDCs. In this case the depreciation will raise domestic producers' prices and decrease investment, leading to lower capital accumulation and a contraction of output, thereby compounding the acuity of the inflation–output policy trade-off faced by authorities.[46]

There exists an abundant empirical literature on the exchange rate pass-through. Frankel et al. (2005) report from a panel study over 1990–2001 that developing countries have in general displayed a much larger 'global pass-through' than advanced economies. They observe, however, a general decline in the developing countries' pass-through coefficient over the 1990s. They also show, at an empirical level, that one crucial factor behind this trend has been the decline in the inflationary environment, together with increased monetary stability. Devereux and Yetman (2014) confirm for a set of Asian EMEs both the evidence of a trend towards a reduced pass-through and its interpretation in terms of improved inflation control. In line with the latter, Ha et al. (2019: 298) report that the pass-through is dampened in countries with greater central bank independence. Aron et al. (2014) provide an extensive survey of pass-through studies for developing countries and EMEs. Drawing attention to many mis-specification pitfalls in the surveyed studies, they finally retain the three following stylized facts: (i) there is little systematic difference between AEs and EMEs, once inflation history is taken into account, the pass-through becoming smaller with a more stable,

---

[45] E.g. Acosta-Ormachea and Coble (2011: 18–19) note that for Peru and Uruguay, two dollarized economies, the exchange rate channel plays a 'substantial role in controlling inflationary pressures'.
[46] See Van Wijnbergen (1986)

anti-inflationary monetary policy; (ii) there is some evidence that the pass-through is higher in developing countries and EMEs with flexible exchange rate and high exchange rate volatility, one possible explanation being that invoicing in local currency is discouraged by too much exchange rate volatility; (iii) in countries in a fixed exchange rate regime the pass-through following a change in the peg is also higher, a possible explanation being that the change in the exchange rate is expected to be permanent (Aron et al. 2014: 137–8).

2.5 The expectations channel

Over recent decades the expectations channel has assumed increasing importance in the design of monetary strategies. Indeed, the dynamics of transmission of monetary policy to aggregate demand, and more generally the efficacy of monetary policy, have been found to significantly depend on expectations about future inflation, interest rates, and exchanges rates held by 'forward-looking' agents.

For a given level of short-term nominal interest rates, agents' expectations of future inflation determine the real interest rate. Expected long-term real interest rates—the ones that matter for the effect of monetary policy on aggregate demand—will depend on both the future short term nominal interest rates and the future inflation rates that agents expect to prevail over the relevant period to maturity. The long-term nominal (real) interest rates reflect the future expected short-term nominal (real) interest rates.[47] The effect on long-term real rates of an increase in short-term rates that is brought about by the central bank will thus, for example, be stronger if people expect the change in policy to be maintained for a number of periods and if they expect it to be effective in reducing future inflation.

Agents' expectation of inflation are also a crucial ingredient of firms' price-setting behaviour and of negotiations between firms and workers about nominal wages. Both shape the aggregate supply relationship that links inflation and output. Inflation expectations thereby directly contribute to determining the terms of the trade-off faced by monetary authorities between their two targets, price and output stability. In particular, the stronger the anchoring of inflation expectations on the authorities' inflation target, the easier it will be for the central bank to achieve price stability while preserving its capacity to attenuate the impact of adverse

---

[47] Recall that the expectation theory of the term structure of interest rates holds that the yield on a bond of n periods to maturity is an average of all the successive one-period interest rates expected over the n periods. When agents are risk-averse, their requested risk premiums for carrying an interest rate risk become additional determinants of the term structure of interest rates. Similarly, a liquidity premium may also be requested by the holder of securities with longer maturities if these securities are, in the absence of a well-functioning secondary market, perceived as less liquid that those with shorter maturities.

short-term exogenous shocks on output. A strong anchoring of inflation expect-ations in turn depends on the credibility of the central bank in pursuing its price stability mandate. Incomplete credibility weakens this expectations channel. We come back to these important issues in section 4.3.

As already discussed in section 2.4, expectations about the future level of the exchange rate matter for today's level of the exchange rate. For example, a restrict-ive monetary policy induces an appreciation of the domestic currency, for a given level of the future exchange rate. If people expect the central bank to maintain its restrictive policy for a prolonged period, they will also expect the domestic cur-rency to be more appreciated in the future. Such a revaluation of the expected future exchange rate has an immediate strengthening effect on the current value of the domestic currency, reinforcing the effects of monetary policy on prices and output through the exchange rate channel. Exchange rate expectations also mat-ter for monetary policy in fixed exchange rate regimes. This is especially evident when agents consider that the exchange rate peg is overvalued and therefore expect a devaluation to occur in the near future. When agents strongly act on these expectations, swapping domestic currency assets for foreign currency assets, the central bank will be forced ultimately to abandon the exchange rate peg, and thus to give up its nominal anchor, once it realizes that it will shortly run out of international reserves to defend it (see section 6.2.3).

Exchange rate expectations and expectations of inflation are linked. When agents expect inflation to be high in the future, they will also expect the domestic currency to depreciate in the short to medium run. A causal relationship between the two expectations also runs the other way. When agents observe large increases in the exchange rate and expect them to be persistent, they will re-evaluate upwards their inflation expectations. This close relationship between inflation and exchange rate expectations is of special importance for monetary policy, and plays a crucial role in choosing a nominal anchor to achieve price stability (see section 6.2.5).

An important issue concerning the role of expectations as a channel for monet-ary policy is how these expectations are formed, and especially how they react to new information about exogenous shocks that will shape future inflation, interest and exchange rates, but also to any news about the central bank's policy reactions to these shocks and to announcements about its future monetary policy. This mat-ters especially for long-term expectations of inflation, for which the anchoring to the central bank's price stability target is the most important policy concern.

Monetary models used for policy purposes, which we discuss in Chapter 7, feature different mechanisms explaining how agents update their expectations.[48]

---

[48] The popular standard New Keynesian model assumes that agents hold rational expectations. Agents are supposed to know how the economy works, as described by the model, and to fully exploit all the information available to them when forming their expectations. Expectations are unbiased and are updated as soon as news about current shocks becomes available or when future events or policy

Whatever the precise mechanism, most share the 'forward-looking', 'updating to new information' aspects of expectations. The earlier 'adaptive' approach has been progressively discarded. Indeed it assumes that agents are 'backward-looking', and form their expectation about a variable's future value exclusively on the basis of its past values, leading to systematic and persistent prediction biases.[49]

Are there reasons to expect that the expectation channel operates very differently in LFDCs? The strength of this channel may partly depend on the strength of the channels it combines with. If, for example, nominal interest rates are a weak channel, this will also be the case for expected real rates. Also, central bank policy announcements about future monetary policy may have less effect on financial markets if the latter are not well developed and thus feature relatively sticky prices and yields. This may not be the case, however, for the exchange rate, which is very sensitive to policy-induced changes in expectations. Price setters and wage setters, in both the formal and informal sectors, can also be expected to react to changes in inflationary expectations, particularly if the observed inflationary shocks are large. The nexus between exchange rate and inflationary expectations is in this respect particularly relevant for LFDCs and EMEs. Whether inflationary expectations can effectively be influenced by the central bank, especially in reaction to inflationary shocks, will crucially depend on the strength of the credibility of the latter's price stability policy.

Central banks in LFDCs need thus to be attentive to the expectation channel, especially if they have previously experienced a history of unbridled inflation. Monitoring it, when inflation surveys are available, and making use of this channel to promote price stability will enhance the effectiveness of their policy.[50]

2.6 The real balance channel

A relevant question for the MTM is whether monetary impulses that take the form of changes in monetary aggregates can be transmitted directly to aggregate

changes are announced. Other models introduce less stringent hypotheses, acknowledging that the information necessary to update expectations is not easily available and is costly to acquire, or relying on some form of bounded rationality (see e.g. Coibion et al. 2017: 8–11). We discuss the New Keynesian model and its hypotheses at more length in section 7.3.

[49] Models where *all* agents are 'backward-looking' are no longer very much used, after the 'rational expectations revolution'. However, there are models used for policy purposes where *some* agents behave in this way, using 'rules of thumb' for forecasting, while others are 'forward-looking'. This is e.g. the case of the New Keynesian Hybrid Phillips Curve, in which inflation expectations combine both adaptive and rational expectations (see 4.2.1.1).

[50] When such inflation expectations surveys of households, firms, or financial markets participants are not available, the central bank task of assessing the state of these expectations and of understanding their determinants is more complicated. While not yet generalized in LFDCs, surveys have become more frequent, especially in countries adopting inflation targeting as monetary framework (see section 6.4).

demand, independently of their effects operating through the other channels described in the preceding sections. Indeed, early monetary theory assumed that real balances directly affected aggregate demand. For given prices, a rise in nominal balances due to expansive monetary policy leads people to eliminate their excess money balances by spending more. This shortcut in the transmission mechanism has been widely used in many theoretical models to describe schematically the role of money in affecting domestic spending. It has also provided the theoretical underpinning to the early IMF's Financial Programming Model and, thereby, the rationale for money stock targeting in many LFDCs, as further discussed in section 6.3.[51]

Beyond being used as a practical shortcut to represent the MTM in general, the real balance effect is also a specific transmission channel, independent of the multiple other channels. As real balances are perceived by consumers as part of their wealth, an increase in nominal (and real) balances resulting from expansive monetary policy encourages them to save less and consume more. This channel may be thought to be of some significance in countries whose financial depth is low and where money is still a major asset in people's financial wealth. There are however some caveats. First, only a relatively small part of the domestic money stock can be counted as private wealth and give rise to consumption effects. Money issued by banks (bank deposits) has private debt as counterparty ('inside money') and therefore cancels out from aggregate private wealth. Only the monetary base issued against international reserves and net claims on the government ('outside money') can be counted as private wealth. Second, real assets and possibly also net foreign currency assets contribute in most LFDCs to a larger part of private wealth than real balances in domestic currency. The real balance effect can thus be expected to be an empirically very weak transmission channel of monetary impulses to private consumption, even in LFDCs.

It is useful to draw attention to a last point. The MTM discussed so far concerns the effects of monetary policy on private-sector decisions that affect aggregate demand or aggregate supply. But spending by the government on goods and services also contributes to aggregate demand. When such spending is financed by the central bank, a direct link between aggregate demand and base money is observed—a link similar to that between real balances and private spending. The recourse to the central bank, increasing the monetary base, allows the government to augment its expenditures, which pushes aggregate demand up. This occurs

---

[51] In this model, designed for an economy with fixed exchange rates and low financial depth, money supply affects directly nominal income through a quantity theory-type relationship. According to this 'monetary approach to the balance of payment' model, the central bank is expected to control nominal income and the level of its international reserves by targeting the domestic credit component of the money stock. See Agénor and Montiel (1999: ch. 13) and Easterly (2004) for a discussion of the IMF's financial programming model.

notwithstanding the other, subsequent effects that the increase in the monetary base may have on aggregate demand through the other channels of monetary transmission.[52] This first-round effect of direct monetary financing of government spending on aggregate demand may be even more important in countries with low financial depth than its indirect, second round effects through interest rates, bank credit, and exchange rates. It therefore warrants special attention from the monetary authorities of LFDCs. We return to the broader question of monetary financing of the government in section 5.2.3.

2.7 How effective is the transmission mechanism in LFDCs?

The analysis in the preceding sections has focused on the different channels of the MTM, taken separately. For each channel, we have described the way it operates and surveyed available empirical studies that assess the strength of its response to monetary policy impulses. Market interest rates as well as asset prices have mostly been found to be weakly responsive to central bank policy rates in LFDCs. There is no unanimity in empirical studies regarding the bank credit channel, expected prima facie to be a dominant channel in LFDCs. The conclusion of the various bank-based studies that we report is that bank credit does indeed react to monetary policy in the selected LFDCs, but that the strength of its response is quite country-specific. Concerning the pass-through from policy rates to bank loan rates, cross-country panel studies of LFDCs mostly indicate that it is small and unreliable. Other country-by-country studies insist again on country heterogeneity, the pass-through being high in some countries, low in others. No clear indications on the factors behind these differences, however, emerge from these studies.

The other channels, the exchange rate and the expectations channel, may also be less potent in non-dollarized LFDCs than in EMEs and AEs. The sensitivity of the exchange rate to monetary impulses is curtailed by the low degree of substitutability between domestic and foreign currency assets and by capital controls. The central bank's capacity to influence agents' expectations in order to more effectively achieve price stability will be low if its credibility is low, which is unfortunately often the case in many LFDCs.

One could expect that the weakness of the response of many transmission variables -to changes in monetary policy carries over to a weak global response of output and inflation. To assess whether such a diagnosis of a weak MTM is to be

[52] Note that the link between a monetary aggregate and the government spending component of aggregate demand is usually not labelled in the literature as a transmission channel of monetary policy. The MTM literature deals with the reactions of the private sector to monetary impulses, and usually discusses the monetary interactions between the central bank and the government separately. An exception is Bofinger (2001: 74–80), who includes central bank-financed government expenditures in a 'quantity theory channel'.

retained for LFDCs, it is however indispensable to look into the global effects of monetary policy on its two ultimate target variables, inflation and output, irrespective of the channels through which these effects operate—or, more precisely, taking their combined effects into account.

Empirical analysis of the transmission of monetary policy impulses on output and prices in LFDCs has been mainly carried out through three different methodologies. We briefly discuss their main findings.

2.7.1 The SVAR approach

A first, frequently used approach is the *Structural Vector Autoregression (SVAR)* methodology, originally developed to study the MTM in AEs (see Box 2.2) and also largely applied in EMEs and LFDCs, either for individual countries or for group of countries.

Mishra and Montiel (2012) offer a comprehensive survey by geographic region of these studies, of their methodology and their results. Their conclusion is that there is 'absence of evidence for strong monetary transmission' (Mishra and Montiel 2012: 25). They also note that the lack of positive evidence may either reflect the actual situation of the MTM in LICs or be due to methodological shortcomings of these standard studies. The arguments that support the first hypothesis involve the structural specificities of LFDCs and have already been discussed at length in this chapter. The methodological problems that make it more difficult to empirically detect an effective MTM in LFDCs than in AEs are multiple. They include the unavailability of data for sufficiently long periods and at sufficiently high frequency, as well as their often low quality, the result of multiple sources for measurement errors. It also includes, importantly, the difficulty in identifying for many LFDCs a single monetary variable (e.g. discount rate, bank reserves, monetary base) that consistently reflects, over the whole estimation period, the central bank's policy impulses. The fundamental methodological difficulties are well illustrated by Li et al. (2018). They carried out simulation experiments to explore the power of SVAR to detect the MTM in LICs. Examining different obstacles to uncovering the MTM in LFDCs with an SVAR empirical approach, they conclude that 'the power of the VARs to reject the null that the "MTM is missing" is very low' (Li et al. 2018: 130).[53]

---

[53] Li et al. (2018) use a calibrated standard open-economy DGSE model composed of 4 equations: an aggregate demand equation, a New Keynesian Phillips Curve, the uncovered interest rate parity, and a monetary policy interest rate reaction function. Each equation is supplemented with a specific shock. Two models that imply different identifying restrictions for the SVAR are proposed: the standard one, usually assumed by studies of the MTM in AEs, and a LIC version. One of the key differences is that the central bank's policy rate reacts contemporaneously to shocks in the AE model, but with a lag in the LIC model. 1,000 data samples of 40 periods are generated for each model. Each sample is

Box 2.2.   SVAR models of the MTM: a quick overview

A Structural Vector Autoregression (SVAR) model of the MTM is, in a nut-shell, a system of simultaneous equations—the reduced form of a structural model—representing the dynamic interactions of all the variables which matter for monetary transmission. It would e.g. include, in a simplified version, a policy interest rate, output, and prices. Each variable is a function of current and past values of all the variables in the system. Identifying restrictions that relate to the underlying structural model are used to extract for each variable a series of pure innovations (shocks) that are uncorrelated among themselves. This ensures e.g. that the monetary policy shock is indeed an exogenous shock, i.e. a reflection of a discretionary policy change. It is thereby identified as separate from the contemporaneous reaction of the monetary policy variable to contemporaneous output or price shocks. The identification restrictions thus impose a causality-type structure on the contemporaneous interactions between the variables. One may assume, for example, that output and prices do not react contemporaneously to a policy rate shock, but only with a lag, while the policy rate itself reflects both the discretionary monetary policy shock and the reaction of the monetary policy variable to contemporaneous shocks on output and prices. This particular identifying hypothesis assumes that authorities react immediately to shocks emanating from the private sector, while the latter reacts with a lag to a monetary shock. Provided that sufficient identifying restricting are imposed, an estimated SVAR system can be used to trace, for each variable, the path of its reactions over time to a contemporaneous shock to any of the included variables, its 'impulse response function' (IRF). In particular, it provides, for a given economy and time period, the estimated dynamic responses of output and prices to an initial, exogenous monetary shock. This is why the SVAR approach has become popular in studying the MTM.

A crucial point of SVAR models is their identification structure, which greatly matters for correctly estimating and interpreting the impulse responses to monetary shocks. In the three-variable model taken as example, three restrictions are necessary for identification. Various types of identification restrictions can be imposed. A frequent approach is the Choleski or recursive identification model (Christiano et al. 2005). Variables are ordered according to the number of contemporaneous shocks which affect them. Zero restrictions on contemporaneous effects are then imposed. For example, output would only react to its own contemporaneous shock, prices to their own shock and to output shocks, and the monetary policy variable to each of the three shocks. Such recursive identification can become more difficult with larger

Continued

Box 2.2. *Continued*

---

models of the MTM, as these would also include e.g. one or several market interest rates, the exchange rate, a monetary aggregate, and bank credit. Robustness of the IRFs to a particular identification can be assessed by considering alternative sets of recursive identification constraints. Other, non-recursive identification methods are also used. Theory-motivated identification restrictions are imposed on the contemporaneous effects of a given shock on the other variables, such as: zero restrictions (no effects), sign constraints, or restrictions on the long-term effects of the shock on the variables (e.g. no long-term effect of the monetary shock on real variables). Linear constraints can also be imposed across contemporaneous effects of shocks. Extensions to the SVAR methodology have been developed in order to better measure the MTM by improving identification of the shocks. The Factor Augmented VAR (FAVAR) supplements the VAR model variables with a limited number of factors. The latter are unobserved variables that synthesize useful information, e.g. about credit conditions, that is extracted from a larger set of variables, external to the model (Bernanke et al. 2004). Threshold VARs are used when there is a presumption that there have been changes in monetary policy regimes during the estimation period (see e.g. Caporale et al. 2020).

2.7.2 Using microdata

A second approach used by some studies assessing the MTM in LFDCs focuses on microdata. This includes the studies that analyse the bank lending channel at the level of individual banks, several of which have been discussed in section 2.3.3.2. Among them, the study by Abuka et al. (2019) goes one step further, as it also uses micro-data for real economic activity and for inflation to explore the global effects of monetary policy in Uganda. They find that real activity, as measured by the number of applications for commercial constructions at the district level or by the volume of exports, by district and destination country, is significantly affected by monetary policy, the effect being mediated through

---

the result of an independent draw of the 4 shocks. An SVAR estimation is then applied to each sample, and the impulse response functions (IRFs) of the four endogenous variables to the monetary shock are recovered with their confidence intervals. The authors show that if a researcher applies a SVAR only to one of the dataset generated by the LIC version of the model and uses the appropriate identification restrictions, she will nevertheless fail in half the cases to reject the hypothesis of no transmission. Moreover, the power of detecting the MTM decreases when the MTM is calibrated to be weaker. It also decreases when the researcher mistakenly uses the AE identification restrictions for the monetary policy variable on a sample generated by the LIC model. The power to detect the MTM, even a powerful one, becomes very weak in this case.

the bank lending channel. The same holds for non-food inflation, measured at the district level.

2.7.3 A narrative approach

Berg et al. (2018b)) adopt a third approach, the *narrative approach*, to evaluate the strength of the MTM in the East African Community (EAC).[54] Following a large and persistent commodity price shock in 2010–11, a concerted decision to react vigorously to control inflationary pressures was taken by the monetary authorities of the four EAC countries. Three central banks (Kenya, Tanzania, and Uganda) reacted with sharp rises in their policy rates or with other restrictive monetary policy measures, in line with their particular monetary policy framework.[55] Such strong reaction was quite unexpected in the respective economic and financial communities, as gradualism was until then the usual response of their central banks to shocks. This tightening of monetary policy, both strong and largely unanticipated, can thus be considered as an 'exogenous event', a restrictive monetary shock aimed at reducing inflation, and announced as such. Studying how this monetary policy shock affected the economy in these countries allowed the authors to gain interesting insights into the operation of the MTM. They 'find clear evidence of most elements of the standard transmission mechanism in most of the countries' (Berg et al. 2018b: 106).[56] The authors also note that the strength of the MTM was greater for those two countries, Uganda and Kenya, whose monetary policy framework allowed for a clear and transparent signalling of the policy measures taken by the central bank. The authors also note that there is only mixed evidence that financial depth is a prerequisite for an effective MTM. Also, a general high level of banks' excess reserves did not seem to impair the MTM in the countries studied.

Such a narrative approach is less general than cross-country SVAR studies. It also specifically focuses on the effects of large, negative monetary shocks, leaving aside the issue of the effects of more moderate or of expansionary monetary policy measures. It provides a useful alternative to the SVAR methodology, however, when the reliability of the latter for assessing the MTM in LFDCs is questionable.

---

[54] The narrative approach to assessing the effect of monetary policy has been pioneered by Romer and Romer (1989). Its aim is to observe what happens to output and prices when there has been a major shift in monetary policy, i.e. a change in monetary policy that is not itself a reaction to developments in real output. Shifts are identified by an examination of the data and historical records of policy-making.

[55] As the reaction of Rwanda's central bank was somewhat more subdued, the country was used as control in the narrative approach.

[56] Effects varied however across countries: in all three countries inflation fell sharply, the pass-through to short-term interest rates was quick and significant, and the exchange rate appreciated. Growth of bank credit also decelerated. In Kenya and Uganda, but not in Tanzania, lending rates responded significantly, though partially, to the shock. Output contracted quickly in Uganda, more moderately so in Tanzania, and not at all in Kenya.

The Berg et al. (2018b) study is therefore reassuring in the sense that it points to actual global effectiveness of the MTM in LFDCs. It thereby reinforces the available evidence provided by some studies—though not by all—of effectiveness of specific transmission channels as discussed in the preceding sections.

2.8 Summary

This chapter has looked at how, and how strongly, monetary policy decisions affect through different channels the financial and the real spheres of the economy. While the list of channels is very much the same for LFDCs, EMEs, and AEs, their absolute and relative strength is often quite different, as they are shaped by LFDCs' key specificities. The analysis developed in this chapter has shown that the MTM in LFDCs is handicapped in each of its channels, for structural reasons. Many of the empirical studies we report tend to confirm this. The interest rate and asset price channels are curtailed by the weak development of crucial interbank and secondary security markets. The bank credit channel, expected to be strongest in economies with a mostly bank-based financial structure, does not seem to live up to this challenge. This is because a large part of financial intermediation occurs outside the formal sector, and also because asymmetric information on the credit market is high and incentives to make loans are therefore low. The exchange rate channel, when operational, is found to have ambiguous effects on output, as a result of the interaction of opposite effects—expenditure-switching vs expenditure-reducing effects—of a monetary policy-induced depreciation. The extent of the latter's pass-through to prices will depend on the degree of openness, but appears to be dampened in countries experiencing a stable, price stability-oriented monetary policy. While there may be reasons to downplay the expectations channel because the interest and asset price channels are not fully operational in LFDCs, it is nevertheless not to be neglected. Expected inflation matters for price setting in the whole economy, formal or informal. It also matters for exchange rate expectations, with which it interacts. It is a crucial channel for a successful monetary strategy oriented towards price stability, in LFDCs as much as in AEs or EMEs.

Our analysis of the MTM in LFDCs does not dispel the impression that it really is a 'black box', to borrow again the term used by Bernanke and Gertler (1995). On the other hand, empirical studies that have assessed the effects of monetary policy shocks on real activity and inflation in LFDCs are mostly consistent with a MTM that is effective although not very strong, and possibly also more uncertain than in AEs and EMEs. This is obviously a general conclusion, characterizing an average LFDC. It needs to be qualified country by country, in terms of the actual development of the country's financial system and of its monetary policy framework. Notwithstanding that general observation, all LFDCs gain from improving their MTM. They can achieve this by expanding the range of the central bank's monetary policy instruments and its interactions with the banking sector. A complementary approach to improve the MTM and gain monetary policy effectiveness can clearly be pursued by enhancing the credibility of the central bank and the transparency of its monetary policy, as well as by adopting a coherent monetary framework with a clear nominal anchor. We discuss each of these important issues in the following chapters.

3

Monetary Policy Instruments

3.1 Introduction

Monetary policy is pursued in every country within a specific framework that links monetary policy's ultimate goals to a set of intermediate and operating variables over which the central bank can expect to have a significant and reliable effect, using the range of instruments it has at its disposal. Central banks set their instruments so as to affect in the desired way, either directly or indirectly, the key intermediate or operating variables, i.e those variables which, like interest rates, exchange rates, and monetary and credit aggregates, act as monetary policy transmission variables (see section 1.3.3).

In Chapter 2, we discussed the various channels through which monetary policy impulses are transmitted to the economy's real and financial sector, influencing in their combined effect the central bank's final goal variables, inflation, output, and financial stability. The strengths of each of these channels and their reliability as transmission variables of the central bank's action are shaped by the country's structural features, both economic and institutional. This is particularly true for LFDCs, for which the monetary policy transmission mechanism appears to be much less diversified and reliable than is usually observed in AEs. It is in this context that LFDCs' central banks have to deploy their monetary policy framework, choosing their intermediate and operating variables and using their available set of instruments to implement their monetary policy.

We focus in this chapter on a detailed analysis of the instruments of monetary policy, postponing the discussion about monetary frameworks to Chapter 6.

The spectrum and choice of instruments vary greatly across countries, as they are influenced by several factors, like the legacy of past practices and the lessons derived therefrom, financial depth, degree of independence of the central bank from the government, and exchange rate regime. One also needs to acknowledge the influence of the former colonial powers and of the international financial institutions in the institutional design of the central banks of most LFDCs. Many LFDCs try to emulate in their monetary policy the practices of AEs, but nevertheless differ among themselves in many aspects. Finally, within a given country, the selection of instruments will depend importantly on the choice of intermediate and operating target variables (see Chapter 6).

When contrasting the use of monetary policy instruments in LFDCs and in AEs, two major differences can be noted from the start. First, while the prevailing

Monetary Policy in Low Financial Development Countries. Juan Antonio Morales and Paul Reding, Oxford University Press.
© Juan Antonio Morales and Paul Reding 2021. DOI: 10.1093/oso/9780198854715.003.0003

situation in the AEs is of structural liquidity deficits that make banks dependent on the central bank, the situation in LFDCs is often quite the opposite. Banks tend to hold large surpluses of liquidity, either for precautionary reasons or because their lending does not proceed at the same pace as the growth of their deposits. Interbank markets are consequently small in most LFDCs. It must be reiterated that the situation differs from country to country and is likely to evolve over time. Second, lack of infrastructure and distortions created by policies often appear to be obstacles to the deployment of monetary policy instruments. Domestic bond and equity markets, when they exist, are very small in LFDCs, as noted in section 1.4.1.2. Stock exchanges, brokerage houses, and dealers' institutions are painfully inadequate. As a result, concerns about the cost to central banks of using securities and other market instruments may limit their active use, as noted by Gray and Pongsaparn (2015). These structural factors lead in LFDCs, relative to AEs, to an over-reliance on instruments of an administrative type, like reserve requirements, or on instruments where the initiative lies with banks and not with the central bank, like windows that allow unconditional refinancing or depositing with the central bank for authorized banks.

In what follows we discuss the different types of instruments, their nature and purpose in the implementation of expansionary or restrictive monetary policy, and how they are used by the central bank to manage bank liquidity and short-term interest rates.[1] We discuss each instrument first at a conceptual level, before illustrating its use for selected LFDCs. Before turning to each instrument, it is useful to clarify the distinction between direct and indirect monetary policy instruments.

3.2 Direct and indirect instruments: a typology

The term *direct* refers to the one to one correspondence between the instrument (such as a credit ceiling) and the intermediate policy objective (such as a credit aggregate). Direct instruments are mostly non-market instruments and were applied widely in the past, in AEs as well as in developing countries. While the industrial countries shun them nowadays, after the financial liberalization reforms of the 1980s and 1990s, several are still in use in a significant number of EMEs and LFDCs, notwithstanding the general trend to more market-oriented instruments.

In a nutshell, direct instruments are regulations and controls that directly affect the asset composition of the balance sheet of financial intermediaries. They tend to make monetary policy a subset of development policy. As mentioned in section 1.3.2.3, monetary policy in LFDCs was, before the market-oriented

---

[1] For related literature, see Alexander et al.(1995), Van't dack (1999), Schäechter (2001), and Buzeneca and Maino (2007).

reforms of the 1980s and 1990s, indistinguishable from credit policy. As such, it was geared to the general objectives of governments regarding economic development. Direct instruments used in this context impose on the banking sector, through explicit regulations by the government and the central bank, ceilings or floors on interest rates or credit volumes to be granted to targeted sectors. Sectors of the economy that benefit from such preferential credit policy usually include selected public enterprises or the export-oriented private sector, and quite frequently the government itself. Often, monetary policy has, in this view, also a redistributive assignment for the benefit of specific categories of the population. For instance, banks are required to make loans to first-time buyers of houses, for their own occupancy and up to a certain value, at interest rates below market rates.

Indirect instruments are intended to influence the underlying supply and demand conditions in the market for central bank money, the monetary base, which plays a crucial role in the making of monetary policy. More precisely, indirect instruments, either rule-based or market-based, are instruments that affect the central bank's supply of, or demand for, its own liabilities, which the banks need as reserves. The main rule-based indirect instruments are reserve requirements and credit and deposit standing facilities. Market-based indirect instruments involve asset transactions between the central bank and the banks, undertaken on a voluntary basis and at market prices. At the initiative of the central bank, they take the form of open-market operations with different types of domestic securities and of interventions in the foreign exchange (FX) market.

Indirect instruments alter the size and composition of the balance sheet of the central bank. With indirect monetary policy instruments, the central bank sets the conditions to which it agrees to supply additional liquidity to the market, or alternatively to retrieve it. Also, imposing required reserves for monetary policy purposes creates a floor for the demand for base money. The central bank is thereby in the position to determine the volume of base money in circulation and to influence domestic short-term interest rates. These indirect instruments are more connected to monetary policy than direct instruments insofar as they clearly aim at monetary variables rather than at the volume and allocation of bank credit.

IMF (2012: fig. I.3: 8) reports for 140 countries the relative frequencies observed in 2010 of the use of the various types of monetary policy instruments in each of the three income categories (AEs, EMEs, and LICs). Four features stand out: first, the still high percentage of LICs resorting to direct instruments (33% vs 23% and 22% for AEs and EMEs respectively); second, reserve requirements are used in practically all (98%) of LICs and EMEs, while 20% of AEs do not use this instrument; third, standing facilities are very popular in all three categories (above or close to 90%); fourth, more than half of LICs conduct open-market type operations in the primary government bond market, while this is only the case for 10% of AEs and 22% of EMEs.

3.2.1 Direct instruments

There are several types of direct monetary policy instruments: interest rate controls, credit ceilings, and mandatory allocation of credit or specific lending requirements. Also, high reserve requirements, often coupled with high statutory liquidity ratios, can be considered as direct instruments. In addition, some countries use exchange rate controls, which strictly speaking are not monetary instruments but are nevertheless used to complement monetary policy instruments or even to substitute for them. We therefore briefly discuss them in this context.

3.2.1.1 The use of direct instruments in LFDCs
As already indicated, a significant proportion of LICs still resorted in 2010 to direct instruments. Since then, however, more LFDCs have liberalized their banking systems, making them more market-oriented, often but not always under pressure from the international financial institutions. Liberalization has meant the gradual substitution of direct instruments by indirect instruments. However, the process has not always followed a monotonic trajectory, and policy reversals also have happened. Direct instruments have not been discarded in all LFDCs, as evidenced by the examples of Bolivia, Kenya, Vietnam, and Zambia given in the next section. Tellingly also, the central bank of Fiji lets its monetary policy rely mainly on indirect instruments, but keeps direct instruments at hand for the case 'when indirect measures are ineffective in addressing underlying economic issues where macroeconomic stability is threatened' (Reserve Bank of Fiji 2013: 4).

3.2.1.1.1 Types of direct instruments
Interest rate controls are a preferred direct instrument. Ceilings on bank lending interest rates or preferential discount rates for selected bank borrowers have similar direct effects on borrowing costs, while caps and floors on bank deposit interest rates aim at determining the conditions of funding the bank's assets. For instance, Kenya introduced in 2016 interest rate controls with the avowed aims of reducing the cost of borrowing, increasing access to credit, and increasing return on savings. Similarly, Bolivia introduced caps on interest rates in 2013, along with regulations on sectoral allocations of credit.

Other direct instruments are also still used in some LFDCs. In Vietnam, where the banking sector is still partly state-owned, bank-by-bank credit growth ceilings are imposed. Government directives provide for a sectoral allocation of credit to priority sectors, and there are caps on the share of consumer loans in the total loan portfolio.[2] The Bank of Zambia fixes commercial banks credit ceilings

---

[2] The State Bank of Vietnam intends to abandon over the medium term the current administrative allocation of credit and replace it with market-based instruments, as reported by IMF (2019g: 11).

for different economic sectors and activities, and also determines interest rate caps.[3]

Such sectoral allocations of credit take the form of floor levels or minimum growth rates of credit to priority sectors, like agriculture or the more generic 'productive sectors', or even directly to the government. Although this is less frequently the case, directed credit may also be used to set a ceiling on global credit growth. It is to be noted that the 'preferential credit view' of monetary policy is often observed in a situation of 'fiscal dominance' (see section 5.2.3), when the central bank is forced to accommodate the government's financial needs, or those of public enterprises, at favourable terms, below current market conditions. This is the case, for instance, in Vietnam, where the central bank has, in addition to loans to state-owned enterprises, been making up for capital shortfalls in state-owned commercial banks (IMF 2019g: 62). Also, the Bolivian Central Bank has a sizeable fraction of its assets in loans to state-owned enterprises.

3.2.1.1.2 Advantages and disadvantages of direct instruments

Direct instruments have several *advantages*, of which the main one is having bank credit aligned to the government's priorities and development plans. Credit can be channelled to strategic sectors of the economy, as defined by the authorities in their development plans, and to the financing of the government. Also, interest rate ceilings on loans may grant consumers protection. In turn, a ceiling on deposits rates may impede excessive risk-taking by banks at the expense of their depositors, especially by those banks that are in financial distress.[4] Also, interest rate floors for deposits are seen as a protective measure to small depositors under the assumption that they are ill-informed and hence can suffer abuses from the banks. In the view of the authorities of some LFDCs, imposing minimum deposit rates contributes to promote saving by the public at large.

With the renewed emphasis on financial stability after the international financial crisis of 2007–9, some of the direct instruments, particularly those related to interest rates, may be assessed in the light of prudential regulations. Indeed, excessive price competition on loans or deposits among banks may cause undesirable risk-taking in view of the asymmetric information problems that plague the financial system. In these circumstances, market interest rates do not necessarily allocate credit in an efficient way.

Whatever the caveats, the *disadvantages* of direct instruments cannot be underestimated. They may distort resource allocation and potentially impinge on the efficiency of financial intermediation. Binding interest rate ceilings, whether on deposits or credits, lead to credit rationing. Such ceilings may also undermine the

---

[3] Source: website of Bank of Zambia (https://www.boz.zm/monetary-policy-instruments.htm).
[4] Ceilings on deposit interest rates prevent the practice of 'gambling for survival', a strategy a bank in distress may otherwise be tempted to adopt.

banking sector's profit margin, possibly intentionally, with the unintended consequence of inhibiting the sector's development. Also, they may end up in negative
real interest rates, if nominal rate ceilings are not adjusted quickly enough to a
rising inflation rate. Negative real interest rates, if lasting, cause inefficient allocations of capital. More broadly, there is the likelihood of financial disintermediation (a shift from bank finance to direct financial intermediation), of accentuation
of informality in financial transactions, and of the appearance of (primitive)
forms of shadow banking.[5] It has been argued by the IMF that the Bolivian
regulations on sectoral allocations increase stability risks for commercial banks.[6]
Concerning the 2016 imposition of interest rate controls in Kenya, Alper et al.
(2019) conclude their empirical analysis by noting that these controls 'led to a
collapse of credit to micro, small and medium enterprises; shrinking the loan
book of small banks; and reduced financial intermediation' (p.2).

Direct instruments may freeze market shares and hence suppress healthy
competition. The priority lending of banks to the government greatly reduces
budgetary discipline, and crowds out credit to the private sector when the latter
relies mainly on the domestic financial sector, as is the case of most domestic
enterprises in LFDCs. Also, whether the regulations embodied in the direct
instruments meet their objectives is difficult to verify. For instance, the assignment of credit to preferred sectors is often circumvented, as loans in favourable
terms are redirected to sectors for which they were not intended.[7] Lastly but
importantly, with globalization and increasing integration with international
financial markets, direct instruments are more difficult to apply and their efficacy
is under question.[8]

3.2.1.2 Exchange controls

Exchange rate controls are typically used on a temporary basis to stem undesired
inflows or outflows of foreign currency and to protect the exchange rate peg.
Exchange rate controls refer to different types of administrative restriction on
current or capital account transactions in foreign exchange by both residents and
non-residents. They include repatriation measures and surrender requirements of
export receipts to the central bank, prior authorization of payment for imports,
multiple exchange rate practices, prohibitions, quotas, taxes, or reserve requirements

---

[5] Shadow banks are non-bank financial intermediaries that perform banking functions similar to
those of the traditional commercial banks but get around the rules and the supervision that apply to
the latter. Sometimes shadow banks are sister institutions of the commercial, regulated banks.

[6] See e.g. Heng (2015) and IMF (2018b: 65).

[7] E.g. loans to the manufacturing sector at preferential rates or with preferential conditions are
deviated to commercial firms. In Bolivia, in the 1970s, it was well known that commercial conglomer-
ates used their repair shops as a façade of industrial activity to benefit from favourable interest rates.

[8] See Fry (1995: ch. 18) for an early and in-depth discussion of interest rates and selective credit
policies in developing countries.

on capital account flows.[9] Such exchange controls are designed to make access to foreign currency administratively difficult and time-consuming. Exchange rate controls are used to bypass the radical shifts in monetary policy that would be needed to address an exchange rate crisis if the central bank were to rely solely on indirect monetary policy instruments. For instance, in the case of a severe balance-of-payments deficit, keeping the exchange rate fixed entails a persistent drain on international reserves. To stem foreign currency outflows, monetary policy would need to become sufficiently restrictive, for a long enough period, to correct the current or capital account disequilibrium at the root of the loss of international reserves. This may produce severe consequences for domestic output and employment. To avoid this dilemma—of choosing between either abandoning the exchange rate peg or coping with the domestic costs of a monetary policy aimed at protecting it—countries often resort to exchange rate controls, particularly in LFDCs. These are used on a temporary basis when the exchange rate peg is viewed by the authorities as fundamentally in equilibrium and when the current pressures on the FX market are expected to be reversed later. This is typically the case for countries with a sufficiently open capital account when they face huge short-term capital in- and outflows. Similarly, if the country is not on a peg but has a flexible exchange rate regime, unbridled capital outflows may force an over-rapid depreciation of the currency. This pushes the country to resort to or reinforce controls on capital operations, as the recent cases of Nigeria and of Argentina, an EME, illustrate.[10]

While many countries resort explicitly to controls on the exchange rate or capital movements, others use interventions of their central banks in the FX market, coupled with soft regulations, to avoid excessive speculation on the exchange rate. A good example is given by Indonesia, which since 2005 has adopted a fully-fledged inflation targeting and moved to a flexible exchange rate regime. Bank Indonesia has intervened occasionally in the FX market, mainly to contain appreciation pressures on the exchange rate. While moving to a flexible exchange rate regime, Bank Indonesia employed regulations limiting or even prohibiting rupiah transactions by non-residents, and enacted rules for banks on their net FX positions.[11]

In LFDCs, exchange controls are however mainly used to sustain artificially an overvalued exchange rate for prolonged periods. This is for instance the case when the political authorities of a given country highly value the implicit subsidy to imports that an overvalued exchange rate entails, and are unwilling to face the inflationary consequences of a devaluation of the domestic currency and its

---

[9] The IMF issues yearly a detailed report on the exchange restriction practices of its members (see e.g. IMF 2019a: 20–27).

[10] Bank of Nigeria (2018: 37), and *The Economist* (2019).

[11] For a thorough account of the Indonesian experience, see Bank Indonesia (2005), OECD (2008), and Ramayandi and Rosario (2010).

attendant political costs. When international reserves are scarce and when there is strong reluctance to adjust the external disequilibria with domestic monetary or fiscal measures or to devalue, exchange controls appear an easy way out to resolve this conundrum. We discuss in depth in section 6.2 these difficult issues confronting policy-makers when a fixed exchange is the cornerstone of the country's monetary framework.

To briefly assess the extent of the use of exchange controls, one can mention, based on 2018 data reported by IMF (2019a; 55–65), that in our set of 112 LFDCs, 18 do not have a unified exchange rate, 10 operate dual exchange rates and 8 multiple exchange rates; 15 also are still under the IMF's article XIV status which authorizes restrictions on payments for current account transactions as transitional arrangements.[12] Also many EMEs and some LFDCs use capital controls, sporadically and at different intensities for macroeconomic stability, including exchange rate stability.

Fernández et al. (2016) have constructed synthetic indicators for a large array of 'de jure' capital controls for a set of 100 countries over the 1995–2013 period. We have already discussed their study in section 2.4.2.2. We only mention here a telling result. Of the 39 LFDCs of our set included in their list of countries, 14 are categorized as having, over the sample period, capital controls on more than 70% on average (and no year less than 60%) of the international transactions subcategories included in the analysis. Only 9 of the 39 LFDCs are considered 'open', i.e. having on average less than 10% and in no year more the 20% of capital account transactions subject to controls. The 16 other ones fall in between these two extreme categories. More generally, either de jure capital controls or, more often, a de facto weak integration with the international capital market isolate LFDCs from the often speculative capital flow gyrations that plague the EMEs.

While potentially useful to manage temporary stresses on a country's foreign currency market, exchange controls have, like all direct instruments, important drawbacks, especially if they are used over a prolonged period. By constraining access to foreign currency through administrative measures, they not only impose direct procedural costs but, worse, decrease efficiency in the allocation of resources, rationing foreign exchange to some sectors or individuals while subsidizing access to it for others. Liberalization of the capital account is known to be fraught with the danger of excessive volatility of capital flows and ensuing macroeconomic instability. Hence resorting to exchange controls can be considered as a useful, albeit temporary, shielding strategy. They need however to be designed so as not to excessively curtail access to favourable opportunities for long-term

---

[12] The general regime for IMF members follows article VIII of the Articles of Agreement. This article prohibits restrictions or discriminatory practices applied to current account payments without the IMF's prior consent. It does not, however, exclude the use of restrictions on capital account transactions.

external private and public sector financing and for international portfolio diversification. Also, long-lasting exchange controls generate informal parallel exchange markets, which bypass the formal financial sector and completely escape the purview of the central bank. Parallel exchange rates can diverge substantially from the official exchange rate. This puts additional pressure on it and entail major efficiency costs, as discussed in Box 6.1.

3.2.2 Indirect instruments

Central banks have an array of indirect instruments that they use to target interest rates, exchange rates, or base money. Indirect monetary policy instruments allow the central bank to influence the variables of interest through its direct interaction with the commercial banks. Some of the indirect monetary policy instruments are rule-based, but the trend is to use market-based money market operations, at the discretion of the central bank. Few LFDCs employ the whole gamut of indirect instruments. A noteworthy exception is that of the Central Bank of Armenia, which uses the whole range of indirect instruments of monetary policy (Central Bank of Armenia 2019).

3.2.2.1 Central bank liquidity and the interbank market
As already discussed in section 1.2.3.3, a key aspect of the leverage the central bank has on banks is the provision of central bank liquidity, the ultimate means of payment among financial intermediaries. Banks need central bank liquidity to meet their reserve requirements and for the timely settlement of their interbank compensation balances. Also, they may have recourse to central bank liquidity to meet unexpected cash withdrawals by depositors. Less often, banks may need liquidity support for operations with the treasury or for market transactions with the central bank. The central bank is thus in a position, as bankers' bank, to profoundly influence banks' behaviour in the money and credit supply process, by affecting the availability of banks´ liquidity directly or by determining the conditions on which banks have access to it.

Central banks manage the liquidity of the system by using their indirect instruments to intervene in the interbank market. It is in this market that the commercial banks borrow or lend reserves among themselves, usually for short periods and at the so-called interbank rate of interest. The type of instrument used by the central bank to intervene on this market may depend on the type of operating target it pursues, either targeting the interest rate or the level of reserves held by the commercial banks at the central bank or, more generally, base money. Often, central bank interventions use a combination of several instruments to achieve the desired target for interest rates or bank reserves.

Information on the size of the interbank markets in LFDCs is scant, unfortunately. However, it is possible to deduce from several case studies, without being completely off the mark, that interbank markets are significantly underdeveloped in most LFDCs. Banks tend to maintain exceptionally large excess reserves, as further discussed in section 3.3.1.1, and secondary market trading of securities is largely absent, given the tendency to hold them until maturity. Persistently large surpluses of liquidity hold back the development of an interbank market of a significant size. In addition, there is a shortage of supporting trading institutions like brokers, dealers, and so on. Also, the standardization of terms and conditions for securities trading is incipient, settlement systems are insufficiently developed and, more generally, the interbank payment system is neither liquid nor strong. These conditions impair the reach of indirect instruments and channels of transmission of monetary policy, as discussed in Chapter 2. Yet, over time, indirect instruments themselves can contribute to the development of an interbank market, as stressed by Buzeneca and Maino (2007). Vigorous liquidity-absorbing open market-type operations by the central bank can give strength to the interbank market.

Many LFDCs do not have an active interbank market that operates on a permanent basis. Interbank transactions are sporadic, on/off operations. Borrowing or lending in these markets is a very small fraction of the banking sector's total loan portfolio. Often, transactions are limited to very few counterparties, in very fragmented banking systems. Buzeneca and Maino (2007) report that the percentage of banks in developing countries—a category that to a significant extent overlaps with our set of LFDCs—making use of the interbank market is lower than what is observed in AEs and EMEs. The same holds for the percentage of collateralized transactions. However, these data may be outdated, as many LFDCs have been pursuing efforts to strengthen their interbank markets.

Several illustrations may give some additional indications about the state of interbank markets in LFDCs. In Myanmar, the interbank market is currently almost nonexistent, yet some efforts are being made by its central bank to form an interbank market for foreign exchange transactions (see IMF 2019d). A similar comment can be made in relation to the interbank market in Indonesia. Most operations are unsecured and overnight, in a segmented market. Many transactions involve foreign exchange swaps, either between foreign banks and large domestic banks or inside a group of small domestic banks (IMF 2018a: 34). In the countries of the West African Economic and Monetary Union (WAEMU), the interbank market is also shallow, as is the secondary market for bonds. Chronic excess liquidity and over-reliance on the common central bank explains this state of affairs. Transactions, when they happen, usually are within the same group of affiliated banks (Kireyev 2015: 12; IMF 2019e: 10). Segmentation of the interbank market thus appears as a prominent feature of LFDCs, and can be attributed to the extensive asymmetric information about counterparty risk which still prevails in many of these countries' banking systems.[13]

3.2.2.2 The management of bank liquidity

At any moment of time, the liquidity of the banking system is the result, on the one hand, of various factors exogenous to the central bank and, on the other, of deliberate actions by the central bank to manage liquidity and keep it in line with its operating goals. Both are directly reflected in the central bank's balance sheet.

3.2.2.2.1 The balance sheet of the central bank and the monetary base
In its simplest and synthetic form, a central bank balance sheet captures, on the liability side, the issuance of monetary base, i.e. those central bank liabilities which circulate as ultimate means of payments. The asset side then reflects the counterparts of the monetary base, its supply side. Each one is a channel through which the monetary base is issued. While the central bank directly controls some of them, it has only an indirect influence, or none at all, on others. Table 3.1 illustrates a central bank's stylized balance sheet for the case of Paraguay.

The largest item of the monetary base is the demand for currency by the public, and to a minor extent by banks for their operations with the public. In many LFDCs, currency in circulation still plays a major role in the size of the monetary base because of the extent of their informal production and labour markets. Central banks can exchange bank reserves with currency both ways. Banks can use banknotes to constitute reserves at the central bank. In turn, central banks can give back reserves by returning banknotes freely, should banks need them to satisfy the requests of depositors converting their deposits to currency. Central banks usually accommodate fully the public's demand for currency. Bank reserves are the second— smaller though crucial—component of the monetary base. They are the sum of required reserves, as imposed by the central bank, and of reserves held beyond the required ones. Banks hold the latter for settlement of operations with other banks, with their clients, with the treasury, or with the central bank itself, as well as for general precautionary purposes. Bank reserves may be the operating target in themselves or they may be a means to attain the targeted short-term interest rate or the targeted money base. In any event, demand and supply of reserves are central to monetary policy.

It is standard practice to regroup the operations that affect the supply of base money into two main categories: those that change the central bank's Net Foreign Assets (NFA) and those that change its Net Domestic Assets (NDA).

---

[13] A commentator in Bolivia once stated that there are blue-blooded banks and plebeian banks. Blue-blooded banks transact only among themselves, while plebeian banks rely on the central bank for their liquidity needs.

Table 3.1. Central Bank of Paraguay: stylized balance sheet, 31 December 2018

Assets 2018 (in billions of guaranies and % change with 2017)			Liabilities 2018 (in billions of guaranies and % change with 2017)		
Net foreign assets (NFA)	48,354	4.6%	Currency in circulation	13,757	6.2%
Net domestic assets (NDA)	−28,653	2.7%	Bank reserves	5,944	10.4%
Net position on the public sector	−8,854	5.6%			
Net claims on deposit money banks	1,200	−1.1%			
Other domestic items (net)	−20,999	1.3%			
of which Monetary control instruments	−12,228	−6.8%			
Bank deposits in foreign currency	−8,938	−0.2%			
Monetary base	**19,701**	**7.4%**	**Monetary base**	**19,701**	**7.4%**

Source: Data from Central Bank of Paraguay and IMF (2019f, p.38); the guarani is Paraguay's currency (5,926 guaranies = 1USD at end 2018); year-to-year percentage changes in absolute values of items

In contrast with AEs, where international reserves are a small item in the balance sheet of their central banks, international reserves are frequently the most important item on the asset side of the balance sheet of central banks in LFDCs.[14] Changes in NFA reflect the central bank's interventions in the FX market. In many LFDCs, central banks maintain a target, or target range, for the exchange rate (see section 6.2.1). They thus need to match the excess demand (the excess supply) of foreign currency that materializes in the FX market at the target rate by buying back (issuing) base money in exchange of foreign currency. Changes in NFA over a given period are therefore the net result of current and capital account transactions of the economy observed at the prevailing exchange rate. Their impact on bank liquidity has to be taken as given by the central bank if the exchange rate target is to be maintained at its desired level, barring the use of direct exchange controls.

Changes in NDA arise through different channels. In LFDCs, operations of the central bank with the government are a main source of changes in the supply of base money. Central bank credit to the government raises the monetary base as soon as the government makes payments out of its freshly credited central bank deposit. Both outstanding currency and bank reserves increase as a result. Alternatively, base money decreases when the government accumulates funds in its central bank deposit account. It is therefore the net position of the central bank with respect to the government that matters, as counterpart of the monetary base. This position can at times be a net liability position, as is the case for the central bank of Paraguay by end 2018 (see Table 3.1).[15] The actual net position of the government at the central bank cannot usually be directly controlled by the latter for the short-term management of bank liquidity, although some coordination with the government on the timing of expected payments and receipts helps.[16]

The other main factor in changes in NDA is the central bank's net claim on banks. This position is directly shaped and monitored by the central bank through its monetary policy instruments. When it grants credit to banks it raises banks' reserves; when it accepts remunerated fixed-term deposits it decreases them (see section 3.3.2). When it engages with them in a money market

---

[14] They are also closely monitored, and often their changes are targeted in the financial programme that countries are expected to follow when they are borrowing from international financial institutions (see Box 6.6).

[15] Such a net liability position can also reflect a sterilization operation initiated by the central bank but carried out by the government. The proceeds of a treasury bill issue are deposited with the central bank and are not spent. This operation decreases the monetary base, and appears as a decrease of the net position of the government at the central bank (see section 3.4.1).

[16] The institutional framework regulating the access of the government to central-bank financing is a crucial aspect of the capacity of the central bank to implement its monetary policy in an independent way (see section 5.2). In many LFDCs, monetary financing of the government is still pervasive. However, it is sometimes curtailed, e.g. when limits on net credit to the government are imposed in the monetary programme defined at the beginning of the fiscal year.

operation, it also directly affects the bank reserve component of the monetary base (see section 3.4.2).

The last component of NDA is a residual, encompassing many different items of the central bank's balance sheet, some of which do not vary much over time and play no role in the supply of bank liquidity, like the central bank's own equity position or its property assets. Other items, however, do matter: this is the case when the residual NDA includes the central bank's liabilities (bills or fixed-term deposits) issued to absorb banks' liquidity for monetary policy purposes, or when it includes the foreign currency liabilities of the central bank with the domestic banks, which can be sizeable and quite variable in heavily dollarized economies. Both cases clearly apply to Paraguay, as shown in Table 3.1.

Figure 3.1 illustrates, for the case of Bangladesh, the contributions of the various components in the central bank's balance sheet which account for the growth rate of its monetary base over 2008–2018.[17] Analysis of the factors influencing bank liquidity is a crucial part of the assessment of monetary policy, particularly for countries where, as in Bangladesh, the central bank uses the monetary base as operating target.[18] The monetary base is referred to as 'Reserve Money' in the terminology used by the Central Bank of Bangladesh.

Figure 3.1 clearly shows the dominant role played over the period by changes in NFA and in net claims on the public sector in explaining the growth rate of the monetary base in the country, both components often acting in a compensating

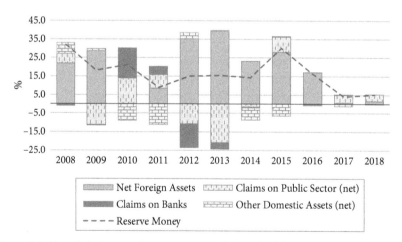

Figure 3.1. Bangladesh: contributions to annual growth of the monetary base
Source: Central Bank of Bangladesh: Reserve money and its sources; authors' computations

---

[17] The growth rate of the monetary base is shown as the sum of the contributions of all its counterparts. The contribution of a counterpart is its growth rate over the period, weighted by its initial share in the monetary base.
[18] See Central Bank of Bangladesh (2019: ch. 4).

way.[19] Monetary policy actions of the central bank of Bangladesh thus needed to gear, as much as possible, the two remaining sources of bank liquidity—net claims on banks and other net domestic items—towards a path compatible with the programmed growth rate of the base money.

3.2.2.2.2 Managing bank liquidity

To manage bank liquidity, i.e. the 'bank reserves' component of the monetary base, in a sufficiently precise way, the central bank needs to estimate the amount of liquidity which would be spontaneously in circulation if it did not intervene. This amount is often called the Autonomous Liquidity Position (ALP). Changes in ALP reflect the combined effect of each autonomous factor, notably changes in NFA and in the net position of the public sector, but also in the demand for currency by the public. Once the ALP has been estimated, the central bank decides on the monetary operations it needs to perform to reach the desired level of bank liquidity, or alternatively the target interbank interest rate. Monetary operations of the central bank will inject, or absorb, liquidity to attain the specific operating target given the ALP. Box 3.1 gives a brief overview of the main liquidity forecasting issues.[20]

Figure 3.2 shows how the central bank intervenes when its operating target is, say, the overnight interbank interest rate (ONIR). The equilibrium level of the ONIR results from the interaction between the demand and supply of bank reserves. The demand of reserves is given by the DR schedule. It is a downward-sloping function of the ONIR, which represents the opportunity cost of holding excess reserves. The position of the DR schedule is mostly determined by the required reserves imposed by the central bank, an increase in the latter shifting the DR schedule to the right. Figure 3.2 represents a situation where the initial level of reserves, R_0, given the autonomous liquidity factors, is reflected in the vertical schedule TSR_0. Given the position and shape of the demand for reserves, the available R_0 level of reserves would push the ONIR rate below the targeted rate, to $ONIR_0 < ONIR^*$. The central bank therefore intervenes to retrieve liquidity from the market, shifting the total level of supplied reserves (as pictured by the vertical TSR schedule) to the left, to its R_1 level, so as to let the ONIR rate reach its targeted level, $ONIR^*$.

There are four broad categories of instruments for liquidity management by the central bank, to be discussed in greater detail in the following sections: minimum reserve requirements (section 3.3.1), standing credit and deposit facilities

---

[19] This reflects in part automatic liquidity sterilization by the government through its deposit at the central bank. When e.g. liquidity is abundant as a result of large increases in NFA, financing of the government becomes easier. The recourse to the central bank credit becomes less important. Also, some proceeds of the government's auctions of bills or bonds can then be temporally deposited at the central bank and act as a sterilization factor.

[20] For a thorough account, see e.g. Gray (2008).

Box 3.1. Liquidity forecasting

To prevent excess bank liquidity or liquidity shortfalls to arise and threaten to derail its monetary policy, a central bank needs to forecast as precisely as possible the banks' net liquidity needs, over both short- and long-term horizons. Net liquidity needs equal the difference between the banks' demand for reserves and the net supply of liquidity that arises from the various autonomous factors that are regrouped in the autonomous liquidity position (ALP). If the projected need, over a given horizon, is positive (negative), the central bank has to be ready to inject (retrieve) liquidity in (from) the market within this time frame.

(i) Forecasting the banks' demand for reserves is not an easy task. Banks hold reserves, as desired reserves and as excess reserves. The main components of desired reserves are the required reserves that are set by the regulations of the central bank. Required reserves are easy to forecast, under the assumption that banks comply with them. Desired reserves also include the precautionary reserves held for instance because the payment system is slow and unreliable, the interbank market is shallow, or access to central bank liquidity is difficult or expensive. Banks' truly excess reserves are the reserves held involuntarily, beyond the desired reserves. Excess reserves are often estimated, as a short cut, by the reserves held above required reserves, but such estimates neglect precautionary reserves, which may at times be important. Actual excess reserves reflect involuntarily accumulation of reserves, when banks find it difficult to invest according to their usual asset allocation strategy. To correctly assess the global liquidity needs that will be compatible with monetary policy's targets, the central bank needs to forecast, as accurately as possible, the level of reserves that banks would *voluntarily* want to hold. This may be especially difficult in LFDCs, where excess reserves are a frequent structural problem because of the underdevelopment of their financial sector.

(ii) Forecasting the ALP is the other challenge. As discussed in this section's text, these concern the three following items of the central bank's balance sheet: the currency held by the non-bank public and by banks in their vaults; the net credit position to the government; and net foreign assets. An increase in the demand for currency tightens the liquidity available to banks, while an increase in any of the two other factors expands it.

(iii) There is normally a definite pattern of the demand for cash by the public. As a share of the total demand for money, it will be a function of the factors that determine the latter, mostly nominal income and expected inflation. As a demand for a specific form of money, cash, its long-term trend will depend on institutional factors, like the degree of informality or the development of new payments devices, like mobile money. In the short run, it will mostly be impacted by seasonal fluctuations. Daily and weekly fluctuations as well as spikes in the days preceding major holidays are common. These cash movements are relatively well predictable. Dollarized economies face an additional uncertainty, that of likely demand shifts between the domestic and the foreign currency.

(iv) The net credit of the central bank to the government is more difficult to predict in the short term. The government's budget is normally formulated on a yearly basis, and movements within the year are rather unpredictable, more so on the income side than on the expenditure side. Central bank financing of the government is forbidden by law in many countries, though ways to bypass it are not uncommon. Most changes in the net credit to the government, then, occur through changes in the government's current account deposits at the central bank. It has been observed, particularly in countries experiencing an export boom with concomitant windfall tax revenues, that one major factor of expansion of the monetary base was the use by the government of its deposits at the central bank, especially when the government has adopted a policy of 'spend all that you can'. Forecasting of liquidity becomes then substantially more difficult. A few governments resort to rules like $t+2$ disbursements. These disbursements are made two days after the treasury has informed the central bank that it will use its deposits. Even fewer governments have timely and detailed schedules for the use of their accounts.

(v) Changes in NFA occur when the central bank acts as counterparty in the FX market. Forecasts of the ALP originating in NFA use projections for the most important items of the balance of payments. Many LFDCs are commodity exporters, and a main input for the projection of export revenues is the forecast of commodity export prices. Forecasts of imports are easier than those of exports, as imports usually have a close relationship with GDP. Disbursements related to foreign aid and foreign lending usually follow a definite pattern that makes them predictable. Service of the foreign debt, interest plus amortization, can also be easily predicted on the basis of the loan contracts.

To be a useful support for monetary policy-making, forecasts of the banking system's net liquidity needs have to be established frequently and for specific horizons. Daily forecasts, if possible, should track liquidity needs in the time spans between the scheduled open-market operations of the central bank. They should at least cover the banks' maintenance period of required reserves. Regular forecasts on longer horizons are needed if the central bank intervenes with instruments of longer maturities (see section 3.4.3.1). Such a regular forecasting process requires the timely availability of high-frequency data of good quality, as well as an adequate research capacity within the central bank.

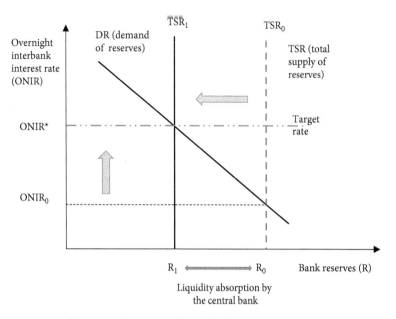

Figure 3.2. Equilibrium in the overnight interbank market

(section 3.3.2), open market-type and open market operations (OMOs) with domestic securities (section 3.4), and FX interventions (section 3.5). While OMOs and FX interventions are market-based instruments, standing credit and deposit facilities as well as reserve and statutory liquidity requirements are rule-based instruments.[21]

In terms of Figure 3.2, increasing reserve requirements will shift DR, the demand for reserve schedule, to the right, pushing up the equilibrium ONIR. Alternatively, an open market purchase by the central bank of securities or of foreign exchange from banks, which increases the banks' reserves, will push the ONIR down, as TSR, the total reserve supply schedule, moves to the right. As discussed in section 3.3.2, standing credit and deposit facilities can help the central bank set a ceiling, or a floor, to the level of the interbank rate.

Managing bank liquidity and short-term interbank rates is a key stage for the implementation of monetary policy by the central bank. Suppose, for instance a sale of securities by the central bank. This tightening of monetary policy results in fewer bank reserves. With fewer reserves, the commercial banks, taken globally, will have either to reduce their lending or will have to attract more deposits from the public, or attract deposits that are not subject to reserve requirements, like long-term deposits and certificates of deposit, or issue non-deposit liabilities. The tightening puts pressure on interest rates and credit conditions faced by

---

[21] This classification is used by Buzeneca and Maino (2007).

borrowers, thereby activating the transmission of the central bank's monetary action to aggregate demand, as discussed in Chapter 2.

3.3 Regulation-based instruments

3.3.1 Reserve requirements

Bank reserves are deposits made by the commercial banks at the central bank plus the currency kept in their vaults. In many countries, but not in all, the monetary authority requires the banking institutions to hold a minimum amount of reserves at the central bank. The fraction of deposits that banks (and quasi-banks) are required to hold as reserves is called the 'required reserve ratio'. As discussed in section 3.2.2.2, management of bank reserves by the central bank plays an important role in the conduct of monetary policy.

3.3.1.1 Required and excess reserves

Central banks determine, through their regulations concerning required reserves, the most important portion of reserves. Banking institutions, of course, can and do maintain reserves in excess of those required, for settlement of balances, and as a precaution to cover both expected and unexpected liquidity needs.

Not all LFDCs require banks to hold minimum reserves. Since reserves that are not compulsory are often unremunerated or are remunerated at below market rates, they are expected to be small. Nevertheless, banks in LFDCs usually hold larger voluntary excess reserves than in AEs and EMEs. It could be expected a priori that, for the great majority of LFDCs, reserve requirements would constitute the binding variable determining the marginal demand for central bank reserves because the required reserve ratio is often high, significantly higher than in the AEs. Yet it is observed that LFDCs customarily hold unusually large excess reserves. As already mentioned, there is a precautionary motive to maintain reserves, but banks' reserve holdings in LFDCs often go well beyond this motive.[22] Also, banks in LFDCs hold high excess reserves because of the poor working of their interbank markets and the still rudimentary state of development of their secondary markets for short-term central bank or government paper. When banks decide on their optimal holding of reserves, they take into account the trade-offs between the opportunity costs of excess reserves and the risk of shortfall of reserves. The latter risk refers to their potential inability to respond to large cash

---

[22] Saxegaard (2006) analyses the behaviour of banks with regard to excess reserves for several sub-Saharan African countries. He concludes that there is also, beyond the precautionary motive, an involuntary holding of reserves. Excess reserves are in this case the result of very low lending opportunities, possibly coupled with significant inflows of deposits, especially government deposits (Saxegaard 2006: 42). See section 2.3.3.3.1.

withdrawals or deposit outflows by their clients, while being at the same time unable to borrow at affordable interest rates and reasonable conditions. If such an event occurred, banks could expect to incur stiff penalties from the central bank, or even, in extreme cases, risk default or intervention by the banking supervisory authorities.

If banks hold large excess reserves, it is obvious that required reserves do not really constrain their behaviour—at least not as much as the monetary authorities could wish for. This slack therefore weakens the transmission mechanisms of monetary policy, as discussed in section 2.3.3.3.1.

3.3.1.2 Characteristics of reserve requirements

A great majority of LFDCs have reserve requirements. Characteristics of reserve requirements vary across countries. Required reserves are applied to different types of bank deposit, from demand to time and savings deposits. A bank's required reserves are thus computed as the product of the amount observed, at a specified date or period, for each category of its deposits and the respective minimum reserve ratios.

The reserve ratios can be either uniform, according to maturity or currency, or differentiated according to one or both criteria. Federico et al. (2014) report on the reserve requirement systems applied in 52 countries, including 37 developing countries. Within this subset, about one third had uniform reserve requirement ratios in 2011. The others applied, in roughly equal proportions, reserve ratios that varied according to maturity, to currency, or to both (Federico et al. 2014: table 1). Using the database updated to 2015 by the authors, we report in Figure 3.3 the average reserve ratio as well as the applied reserve requirement system for the 20 LFDCs for which 2015 data were available. Two points are

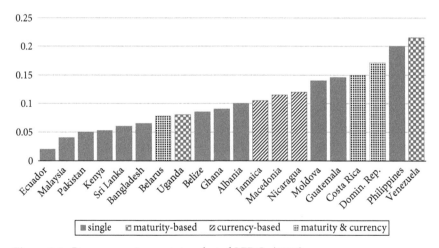

Figure 3.3. Reserve requirements in selected LFDCs (2015)

Source: Authors' elaboration based on Federico et al. (2014), updated database

worth mentioning. First, the majority (60%) of these LFDCs use a uniform, single ratio system. Second, one observes a relatively large cross-country range for the average required reserve ratio, from 2% for Ecuador to 21.5% for Venezuela.

The broad trend in the past 30 years in LFDCs has been one of general reduction in the reserve ratios and unification of the required rates for different types of deposits. The decline has been far from smooth, with frequent changes over the business cycle, and has even sometimes been reversed. Reserve ratios remain significantly higher in developing countries than in AEs. Also they change more frequently. This is confirmed for the 20 LFDCs selected in Figure 3.3 from the 2015 database of Federico et al. (2014): from 2005Q1 to 2015Q3, one observes 82 changes in the reserve ratio in this set, roughly once every 10 quarters for the average LFDC country, while almost no changes were observed for AEs over the same period.

The 'reserve base'—the deposits which are subject to required reserves—includes demand deposits as well as quasi-money deposits, with the exception of fixed-term deposits with long maturities (e.g. two years or more).[23] In many LFDCs, foreign currency deposits are also subjected to reserve requirements. However, reserves on foreign currency deposits can often be constituted in domestic currency.

Reserve requirements also depend on two other regulatory principles: the date at, or period over which, the deposits subject to reserve requirements are taken into account for the computation of the amount of required reserves the banks need to constitute; and the time period over which banks are expected to comply with the reserve requirement, the so-called maintenance period. Indeed, since meeting reserve requirements at all times and on a contemporaneous basis may cause liquidity problems for banks, regulations generally allow banks to use required reserves as liquidity buffers. To this end, the amount of required reserves to hold is based on the average of the daily values of deposits observed over a given period starting before the actual maintenance period, as defined by the central bank. For example, the Central Bank of Kenya stipulates that the reserve ratio to be maintained is based on a required reserve ratio of 5.25% and on the daily deposit average over a period extending from the middle day of the previous month to the middle day of the current month, with the additional proviso that the reserve ratio cannot at any day fall below 3%.[24]

---

[23] When such deposits are exempted from reserve requirements, the depository banks tend to impose high penalties if clients withdraw before term, with the aim of minimizing the need to nevertheless build reserves against these deposits. Note that some countries allow the long-term time deposits that are exempted from reserve requirements, either in domestic or in foreign currencies, to be negotiable in the capital market. This feature makes deposits resemble bonds, but with the important difference that the former have more seniority than the latter in case of forced closing.

[24] Source: https://www.centralbank.go.ke/monetary-policy/(as of August 2020). In Bolivia, required reserves are based on the deposit average over a 14 day period determined by the Superintendence of Banks, and the maintenance period for compliance with the reserve requirements is also 14 days,

Some countries remunerate the required reserves at close to market rates while others do not. Remunerating required reserves, and sometimes even excess reserves, aims at decreasing their opportunity cost for banks. Developing countries tend to be less inclined than AEs to provide such remuneration.[25]

3.3.1.3 Effects of reserve requirements

Required reserves have several monetary functions. First, they are an instrument of monetary control, often the main one, to the extent that they are an important determinant of the total demand for reserves held by the banking system and insofar as they make the commercial banks dependent on the central bank.[26] Second, changes in minimum reserve ratios can be used by central banks to offset major expected changes in autonomous liquidity. In particular, increases in the required reserve ratios may be used as a substitute for FX interventions. They have indeed been frequently used in EMEs, sometimes also in LFDCs, to sterilize short-term capital inflows or, in commodity-exporting countries, to sterilize the effects of large current account surpluses in the balance of payments, as noted by Céspedes et al. (2012).[27] In a way, reserve management substitutes for interest rate policy in several LFDCs.[28] An extreme example is that of Venezuela, which changed regulations on required reserves 13 times between 2005 and 2015.

Third, increases in the required reserve ratios can signal to the public that the monetary stance is tightening. Also, high required reserves are included in the set of prudential measures designed to avoid banking crises (see section 3.6.1).

Required reserves have advantages as well as drawbacks. Their main advantage is to strengthen the role of central banks as suppliers of ultimate liquidity. They thereby facilitate the achievement of the central bank's operating targets. They also provide for increased day-to-day stability of the interbank market rates if the maintenance period for averaging is sufficiently long. Finally, there is also a fiscal side to the reserve requirements. Reserves that are not remunerated or are remunerated at below market rates contribute to the central bank's profit. The government can then collect the corresponding seigniorage through its participation in the central bank's profits.

---

starting 8 days later than the period of required reserves. Over the maintenance period, constituted reserves have to meet on average the required ratios. Ratios differ by maturity and currency.

[25] Buzeneca and Maino (2007) noted that according to the 2004 IMF survey only 40% of reporting developing countries provided such a remuneration.

[26] Note that the declining use of currency in favour of deposits with banks or even with non-banks, encouraged by new information and communication technologies (see section 1.2.2), erodes the reliance of banks on central bank liquidity and forces the central bank to adapt the ways it uses its instruments to keep control of market liquidity and interest rates.

[27] Federico et al. (2014) similarly conclude that EMEs have, since 2004, frequently resorted to reserve requirements as a macroeconomic stabilization tool, and have done so as a substitute or complement to traditional, interest rate-based, counter-cyclical monetary policy.

[28] The active management of compulsory reserves, with frequent changes in its regulation, was declining until the international financial crisis of 2007–9. It has resurfaced in several LFDCs since then.

There are also drawbacks to required reserves. First, reserve requirements, if unremunerated or remunerated below credit market rates, are like a tax on financial intermediation. This tax is passed through to the banks' customers, either to their borrowers or to their depositors, depending on the market power of the banks in each market. Borrowers may pay a higher interest rate and/or depositors receive a lower interest than otherwise, i.e. without this 'tax'. This could lead to 'disintermediation', a shift from bank finance to direct financial intermediation, for which funds are collected by issuing marketable securities not subject to reserve requirements. However, in many LFDCs, the disadvantage of direct inter-mediation relative to bank finance is structurally so large that ultimately high reserve requirements only contribute to globally hampering financial deepening.

Second, liquidity buffers allowed by high reserve requirements discourage the formation of an active interbank market, reducing the scope for a market-based monetary policy.

Finally, a complex system of reserve requirements may paradoxically compli-cate the central bank's liquidity management. Tracing the effects on bank liquidity of reserve requirements that are differentiated along currency and maturity is more difficult than when they are uniform. As noted by Buzeneca and Maino (2007: 12), the forecasting of the demand for reserves is indeed facilitated when requirements are uniform, since the forecast errors are likely to be smaller if there are no shifts among different types of deposit that result from differences in reserve requirements. Buzeneca and Maino (2007) also point out the complica-tions that differentiated reserve requirements imply for controlling monetary aggregates. Possibly for these reasons, a trend towards unification of the required rates for different types of deposit is observed.

3.3.2 Credit and deposit standing facilities

In its interaction with banks to manage market liquidity and interest rates, the central bank may offer standing facilities. Through its credit facility it gives banks access to additional liquidity at their own initiative. Through its deposit facility it allows banks to deposit excess liquidity. The central bank sets the interest rates and determines the rules at which banks have access to these two facilities. Most LFDCs central banks have a standing credit facility, fewer a deposit facility.

3.3.2.1 Credit facilities
Credit facilities date back to the origin of central banking, when the central bank became the bankers' bank and provided short-term credit through its 'rediscount window'. Central banks either rediscounted bills of exchange that issuing firms had discounted with their bank or discounted bankers' acceptances (see Box 3.2). Although some LFDCs still operate a rediscount window, through which they

Box 3.2. Discounts and rediscounts

Discounting consists in loaning less than the face value of the loan. The annual-ized percentage difference between the amount actually received with the loan and the latter's face value is the implicit interest rate. Discount was a common operation of private banks before the advent of central banks. They discounted 'real bills', bills that were backed by transactions on real goods, originating in commercial operations of a self-liquidating nature and safe from default risk. Banks would issue currency notes in exchange for these bills. These notes were fully convertible to metallic money, and therefore generally accepted as means of payments, while the bills were not.

The monopoly for the issuance of money given to central banks, towards the end of the nineteenthth century, changed the nature of the discount oper-ations. Banks continued to discount merchants' bills but could no longer issue currency notes, but only deposits. To satisfy their clients' demand for central bank currency, banks needed access to central-bank refinancing. The central bank would rediscount the letters of change which the banks presented at its discount window. Discounting by the central bank was unrestricted, provided these bills met the standards of quality or bore personal guarantees. During the 1970s, however, central banks started to pay closer attention to the control of bank liquidity and monetary aggregates. From a more theoretical view-point, it was pointed out that free central-bank rediscounting had the disad-vantage of causing wide fluctuations in the money supply and hence in the price level. To mitigate this risk, central banks at times set ceilings to the quan-tity of rediscounts that they granted. This marked a striking difference from the earlier regime, as it put an end to central banks' automatic and unlimited refinancing of 'real bills'. Discounting in this sense was progressively aban-doned, and replaced by the set of indirect monetary policy instruments cur-rently used to attain the central bank's operating target. The demise of the traditional form of discounting bills of exchange was also fostered by the high transactions costs implied by this form of credit to the private sector, relative to more modern forms of business finance, like straight loans. Nowadays, (re) discounts may still be among the operations allowed in the statutes of central banks of some LFDCs, but they are not very frequent and the loans that go through them are small. The term 'discount window' has, however, frequently been kept to denominate a standing facility through which the central bank supplies banks with short-term credit. Eligible collateral for the latter now-adays encompasses a broad set of safe assets, especially treasury or central bank bills. The associated central bank policy rate is still called the discount rate. Some countries also use the terms 'Lombard window' and 'Lombard rate', which is believed to date back to the credit practices of the great merchant bankers of Lombardy in medieval Italy.

provide short-term refinancing to banks, new forms of standing credit facilities have become much more common. Nowadays banks borrow at a permanent central bank facility for very short maturities, against collateral of predefined eligible assets, mostly government or central bank securities. Overnight is the usual maturity, but some central banks in LFDCs allow maturities of one week, or even longer. Standing credit facilities are restricted to commercial banks, although exceptionally some quasi-bank institutions have access to them. The interest rate banks have to pay is set by the central bank at a pre-announced level that is higher than the rate at which it makes it liquidity available through its other money market operations (see section 3.4). Banks therefore access this window only if they are not able to obtain the necessary liquidity in the interbank market or by participating in the other liquidity-providing operations of the central bank. Given that the lending is very short-term and more costly, the facility is intended to satisfy liquidity needs that are temporary and residual. Indeed, it is the case in many countries that, at the end of each business day, the counterparts' debit position on their settlement account with the central bank is automatically considered to be a request for recourse to the marginal lending facility.[29] On the other hand, the supply of central bank liquidity through this facility is, in principle and under normal circumstances, infinitely elastic at the announced interest rate. The interest rate of such a 'marginal' lending facility therefore acts as the *ceiling* for the overnight interest rate in the interbank market. The overnight rate will only breach this ceiling if the central bank curtails aggregate lending under this facility. This may happen in exceptional circumstances but also be part and parcel of the facility's design.[30] The latter is, for example, the case in WAEMU, where individual bank limits are imposed for accessing the one- or seven-day marginal lending facilities (BCEAO 2018: 48). In Kenya too, access to the overnight standing facility is not automatic, and the guidelines governing it change from time to time.[31]

The central bank provides liquidity to a bank under the marginal lending facility in the form either of collateralized loans or of repurchase agreements ('repos'). The latter have become more and more frequent, in line with the more general practice of central banks of resorting to repos for fixed-term liquidity-providing operations (see section 3.4). In the case of an overnight repo for example, the central bank purchases from the bank, in a bilateral transaction, a predetermined security and the bank agrees to buy it back the next day, at a predetermined price.

---

[29] In Bolivia, in a slight variant of this, requests of central bank liquidity are automatically granted for transactions within the Real Time Gross Settlements system of payments.

[30] Collateral constraint affecting a large number of liquidity-stressed banks may also lead to a rise of the interbank rate above the standing lending facility's rate.

[31] An interesting prudential feature of this standing facility is that banks that access this resource twice in a week are subjected to increased supervision (https://www.centralbank.go.ke/monetary-policy/).

The central banks of Armenia, the Dominican Republic, Nigeria, and Paraguay, as well as of those of WAEMU, operate such a repo-based standing liquidity-providing facility, while the central banks of Costa Rica, Kenya, Nicaragua, Tajikistan, and Zambia operate through overnight secured loans.[32] Some central banks, like those of Bolivia, Nigeria, and the WAEMU, also provide intra-day credit to prevent gridlocks in the Real Time Gross Settlements System (RGTS) of interbank payments, thus ensuring the smooth functioning of the latter. Intraday credit needs to be collateralized but is interest-free. Overdue intra-day credits are usually sanctioned with a penalty interest rate. Finally, note that notwithstanding the open access to a permanent credit facility, a central bank can also respond to a given bank's specific liquidity needs in a more discretionary way, in its role of banker's bank and lender of last resort (see also section 3.6).

3.3.2.2 Deposit facilities

Many central banks that have a standing credit facility also offer a standing deposit facility. This is currently the case for, among others, the central banks of Armenia, Costa Rica, Nigeria, and Paraguay. On the other hand, neither Nicaragua nor the WAEMU have deposit facilities, although they have standing credit facilities.[33] Most of these deposit facilities are overnight. Deposits are remunerated at a pre-announced interest rate. There are usually no limits to the amounts banks may, individually or collectively, deposit though this facility. The interest rate on the deposit facility then acts as a *floor* for the overnight interbank interest rate.

3.3.2.3 Policy roles of standing facilities

The two standing facilities play a double monetary policy role. First, the lending and deposit facilities both act as safety valves, in the face of unexpected liquidity developments in the interbank market. Without them, the interbank interest rate would display much larger volatility, especially towards the end of the reserve requirement maintenance period, when some banks scramble for liquidity to fulfil the requirements. As discussed in sections 3.3.2.1 and 3.3.2.2 the overnight lending facility caps the overnight interbank rate and the overnight deposit facility puts a floor on it. If both are operational, the interbank rate will be within a 'corridor', whose average level and width are determined by the two standing facilities' policy rates.

Second, the policy rates of lending and deposit facilities have an important signalling role when the central bank uses the short-term interbank interest rate as operating target. As such rates signal the upper and lower limits of a corridor for the short-term interbank interest rates, they provide a clear indication of the

---

[32] Source: websites of respective central banks (2020) and CEMLA (2018).
[33] Source: websites of respective central banks (2020) and CEMLA (2018).

monetary policy stance. Setting the corridor's limits is usually done with reference to the central bank's *monetary policy rate* (MPR), the key rate on which the
central bank relies to announce the orientation of its monetary policy and enact it
(see section 3.4). When setting this rate, which signals its current target for the
short term interbank rate, the central bank also simultaneously sets its overnight
credit rate, at *MPR+x %*, and its overnight deposit rate at *MPR–y %*. The corridor
around the *MPR* thus has a width of *(x + y)*. If *x=y*, the corridor is symmetrically
set around the MPR, but this is not necessarily so. The central bank of Nigeria, for
example, operates a wide and asymmetric corridor. The narrower the corridor,
the tighter the control maintained by the central bank on the average level of the
interbank rate. Figure 3.4 illustrates this for the Central Bank of Egypt, which
uses the standing facility policy rates to closely anchor the overnight (O/N)
interbank rate, its operating target, to its main refinancing rate (the 7-day repo
rate). The latter has been set by the Bank, during the reported period, at the very
centre of the 100 basis point-wide corridor. Market operations initiated by the
Bank can then be used to guide the interbank rate within the corridor. The width
of the corridor is, however, often larger than what is illustrated for Egypt in
Figure 3.4, as is currently the case in Armenia (300 basis points) or in Nigeria
(700 basis points).[34]

For central banks that do not operate a deposit facility, the signalling role for
the stance of monetary policy is usually assigned to the standing credit facility's
interest rate, together with the main policy rate. Monetary policy announcements
then set the applicable levels for both rates. The spread between the standing
credit rate and the main policy rate signals the degree of control authorities wish

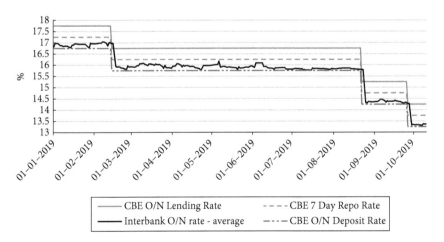

Figure 3.4. Central bank policy rates and the interbank rate in Egypt
Source of data: Central Bank of Egypt and *Macrobond* database

---

[34] Data on websites of Central Bank of Armenia and of Bank of Nigeria, as of Aug. 2020.

to exert on the interbank market. The larger the spread, the larger the potential variability of the short-term interbank rate. A large spread, maintained over a prolonged period, may however also have positive aspects. By making access to central bank liquidity more costly, it favours the development of a more active interbank market and opens greater opportunities for use by the central bank of more market oriented monetary policy instruments.

3.4 Money market operations

The purpose of the central bank's money market operations is manifold. Their aim is to manage the liquidity of the market, to steer interest rates, and to signal the stance of monetary policy. Money market operations consist in the sale, or purchase, of eligible assets by the central bank. In most developing countries, the eligible assets are restricted to government securities, central bank paper, and foreign exchange. The operations take place either in the primary market (open market-type operations) or in the secondary market (open market operations— OMOs). The primary market is the market where central bank and government securities are offered for sale for the first time. Such sales are used by the central bank to withdraw liquidity. The secondary market is the market in which the securities are remarketed, being offered for resale. Operations in the secondary and FX markets enable the central bank to inject or absorb liquidity from the system.

Open market-type and OMOs available to central banks fall into three broad categories: (i) issuance on primary markets of central bank or government paper; (ii) outright or reverse operations in the secondary markets; (iii) interventions in the FX market.

Note that central banks in LFDCs often operate actively only on a subset of these markets. Indeed it is only in the AEs and the most advanced EMEs that monetary authorities have a choice of markets in which to operate, and can expect that the effects of actions in one market will rapidly and predictably spread to other markets.

3.4.1 Operations in the primary market

Operations in the primary market are operations in which the central bank issues its own paper or customized treasury bills from its portfolio for liquidity-absorption purposes.[35] Placement of central bank securities is less frequent in LICs than in

---

[35] E.g. the Central Bank of Bolivia had a long-term government bond in its assets portfolio but issued short-term securities backed by the long-term bond. The latter were akin to covered bonds.

middle- and high-income countries. Gray and Pongsaparn (2015: 7–8) report from a 2013 IMF survey on monetary policy instruments that only 17% of LICs issued central bank securities, vs 38% for the upper middle-income countries, the category with the highest share. Liquidity management associated with the primary issuance of short-term securities has been particularly relevant when the economy is experiencing large net inflows of foreign exchange. Typically, these derive from commodity exports earnings or from short-term capital inflows. The securities offered for sale are generally of short maturity, and the transaction is conducted under any of several types of available tender procedures. The sales procedures are discussed in section 3.4.4. The transaction implies a full transfer of ownership to the buyer, without any repurchase clause. At maturity, the buyer can redeem the security at face value at the central bank. When the security is redeemed, market liquidity increases again.

In a number of LFDCs, the central bank also sells, for monetary policy purposes, government securities on the primary market. The proceeds of the sale are in this case frozen in a government account at the central bank, implying a temporarily sterilization of market liquidity. These operations are of the open-market type and are organized similarly to the issuance of central bank paper. The maturity of the government securities issued is generally longer than those of the central bank.

Such interaction with the government for monetary policy purposes can occur in a more direct way through the management of government deposits at the central bank. A transfer of funds that the government holds in its deposits with financial intermediaries to its deposit accounts at the central bank reduces market liquidity; a transfer in the opposite direction increases it—assuming that the deposits of the government with financial institutions are not subjected to 100% reserve requirements. This type of sterilization operation implies for the central bank a strong coordination with the government relative to the issuance of its own certificates, and possibly therefore a loss of its autonomy.[36] Gray et al. (2013: 109) indicate that among the 121 central banks reporting to the 2010 IMF survey on monetary policy instruments, 32% undertook sales of government paper and 44% managed government deposits at the central bank for monetary purposes. Also, among the survey's 25 central banks from African countries—almost all LFDCs—a significant number engaged in such operations: 30.8% of them in sales

The central bank could split the long-term bonds into short-term securities. This 'customization' made possible the short-term operations.

[36] An additional issue is the cost-sharing of a sterilization policy based on the issue of government securities. If the central bank issues its own certificates for sterilization purposes, it bears the full cost of the interest to be paid to the investors. If sterilization occurs by freezing the proceeds of the issuing of treasury bills or bonds in the government's deposit at the central bank, the cost is shifted to the government's budget if the deposit is not properly remunerated, which is frequently the case.

of government securities and 34% in transfers of government deposits to or from the central bank.[37]

When issuing marketable certificates is difficult to organize because of lack of proper market infrastructure, central banks of LFDCs wishing to sterilize liquidity for a given period may rely on fixed-term deposits as an alternative . In doing so, however, they forgo a key benefit of central bank securities, namely its contribution to the development of an active money market (Gray and Pongsaparn 2015: 8). When central banks issue securities, the term structure of the securities they sell in the primary market and the regularity of such operations, with fixed schedules, are particularly important—especially when secondary markets are underdeveloped, as is the case in most LFDCs.

Commercial banks can economize on the transaction costs and reduce uncertainty regarding future short-term rates by acquiring securities with long maturities. However, this preference may not coincide with the preferences of the central bank, given that the longer the maturity, the less frequently the banks will return to the central bank for requesting or depositing liquidity. Therefore the central bank will not have the opportunity to influence effectively, through its other regular operations, the liquidity of the banking system. It may hence partially lose control of the liquidity of the financial system (see 3.4.3). As noted by Gray and Pongsaparn (2015: 14), the maturity of central bank securities is usually short-term, less than one year. Longer maturities are typically designed to address lasting structural liquidity surpluses. Here are a few examples of the variety of practices: Securities of the Central Bank of Armenia have maturities of 91–182 days (Central Bank of Armenia 2019: 11). The Central Bank of Costa Rica issues monetary stabilization bonds with maturities from 1 to 10 years, at fixed or variable rates.[38] Bank Indonesia issues two types of certificate, in the context of a domestic banking system that includes both conventional and sharia-compliant banks. Conventional certificates were issued in 2018 with a maturity of 9 and 12 months. The sharia-compliant Bank Indonesia sukuks are issued in several tenors, from one day to 12 months, to counterparties involved in sharia finance. The aim of organizing regular auctions of Bank Indonesia sukuks is to support the development of sharia money market instruments and improve the liquidity of this market (Bank Indonesia 2018: 72, 82).[39] The Central Bank of Bangladesh organizes, for liquidity

---

[37] Gray and Pongsaparn (2015: 13) indicate, however, that only a few cases of central banks issuing government securities for liquidity sterilization purposes have been reported in the IMF's internal 2013 survey on monetary policy instruments. They cite only the example of the Reserve Bank of India, an EME.

[38] Bonos de Estabilización Monetaria (see the Central Bank of Costa Rica website: https://www.bccr.fi.cr/seccion-inversiones-bccr).

[39] The prohibition of interest payments which are fixed ex ante and the general principle of profit-and-loss sharing are key characteristics of sharia-compliant financial transactions (see section 2.3.3.3.3). The Bank Indonesia *sukuks*, instead of paying a fixed interest rate, share with the holder of the certificate a joint ownership over a portfolio of sharia-compliant assets that back the certificate,

management purposes, weekly auctions of its own short-maturity bills as well as of government treasury bills and bonds of longer maturities (Central Bank of Bangladesh 2019: 25).

3.4.2 Outright and reverse operations in secondary markets

3.4.2.1 Outright operations

An outright transaction implies a full transfer of ownership from the seller to the buyer. The central bank may buy or sell eligible assets, securities, without any type of commitment to reverse the operation. Gray et al. (2013: 110–1) indicate that about two thirds of all central banks reporting in the IMF 2010 survey on monetary policy instruments conducted outright sales and purchases of securities and foreign exchange. When undertaken, the outright sales of securities are highly concentrated on government securities and central bank paper. Among the reporting central banks of the African region, 64% declared pursuing such outright operations. However, as the survey question does not distinguish between sales and purchases of securities, sales of government paper in the primary market may have been included as outright operations, as in many countries the fine distinction between open market-type operations and true OMOs is not necessarily made when reporting to surveys. There are some reasons to believe that the sales are mostly in the primary market. Outright sales on the secondary market of securities in the central bank's portfolio have a significant disadvantage relative to sales on the primary market or even to reverse operations. With outright sales it is difficult to precisely target the maturity of the liquidity absorption operation, as the latter will depend on the residual maturity of the security sold.

3.4.2.2 Repurchase and reverse repurchase operations

OMOs are mostly conducted through reverse operations, either to inject liquidity into the market or to absorb it for a period predefined by the central bank.

To inject liquidity, the most common instruments used are *repurchase agreements* (repos), through which the central bank buys eligible assets with a repurchase clause.[40] Central bank repos are short-term operations, with a pre-specified maturity, say 7 days to 3 months, and they are executed through

---

as in a covered bond. At maturity, Bank Indonesia repurchases the investor's share in the portfolio, which parallels the reimbursement of a conventional security. It also pays out his share in the income earned (Bank Indonesia 2018: 83).

[40] Repos are financial instruments that are also commonly used in interbank operations, in lieu of collateralized loans. With respect to the latter, they benefit from the additional protection provided by the actual transfer of ownership of the underlying asset to the repo asset-purchasing party. Repo operations also enjoy greater flexibility and security within standardized global master agreements, and are handled within a market infrastructure designed to facilitate asset transfers and settlements of transactions.

standard tenders. When the central bank executes repos, ownership of the asset is transferred to the central bank. The engaged parties agree, however, to reverse the transaction through a forward transaction that re-transfers the asset to the initial seller at a future point in time, i.e. the seller bank repurchases the asset from the central bank at a price that is agreed on when the transaction is initiated. The percentage difference between the repurchase price and the purchase price in a repo corresponds to the interest due on the amount of central bank liabilities made available to the counterparty. In other words, the repurchase price includes the interest to be paid to the central bank. Repos are similar to a collateralized loan but can be more flexibly operated by the central bank and are more secure from a legal viewpoint. For repo operations, central banks may prefer securities with short maturities, as these would have a lower market (or pricing) risk should the counterparty bank not meet its commitment to repurchase them. If the paper has a long maturity, central banks may impose a 'haircut' i.e. a percentage reduction of its market value.[41]

Reverse repos are structured as repos and are used by the central bank to absorb liquidity from the interbank market. In a reverse repo, the seller of the security is the central bank and the counterparty bank the purchaser. The central bank commits to buy the security back at a specified date.

Foreign-exchange swaps also involve reverse transactions with the sale, alternatively the purchase, of foreign exchange by the central bank. Swaps have the same logical structure as repos, but foreign exchange or securities denominated in foreign currency are used instead of securities in domestic money (see section 3.5.3). Swaps do not involve any exchange rate risk, as counterparties agree, when the swap is negotiated, on the foreign currency price at which the transaction will be reversed.

A large and increasing number of LFDCs take on reverse transactions with securities. This trend reflects the growing number of LFDCs that have adopted a monetary policy framework centred on short-term interest rates as an operating target. The use of foreign-exchange swaps is in general about half as frequent than the use of reverse transactions with securities among all central banks, according to 2010 and 2013 IMF surveys on monetary policy instruments (Gray et al. 2013: 111; Gray and Pongsaparn 2015: 11). There are no reasons to believe that this is different for LFDC central banks. Indeed, in the 2010 survey, 62% of central banks from LICs reported using repos and only 24% foreign exchange swaps

---

[41] The asset transferred to the central bank through the repo is valued at market value less a 'haircut' percentage, which is a function of the combined credit and liquidity risks. Credit risk materializes when the counterparty bank is not able to honour the repurchase of the asset. Liquidity risk is about the possible loss that arises when the asset has to be sold in the market by the central bank because of the bank's delinquency. With underdeveloped secondary markets, the repo's market value is often determined by the estimated shadow price of the security, given an estimated interest rate and the remaining time to maturity at the moment the repo is concluded.

(IMF 2012: 8). Finally, repo or reverse repo transactions conducted by central banks in LFDCs may not necessarily be done on a regular basis. Intermittent OMOs may occur, for instance when the interbank market is characterized by low activity or when secondary markets are shallow.

3.4.3 Allocating market instruments to policy needs

In order to achieve their operating target in an efficient way, central banks need to optimally combine the whole set of instruments at their disposal. Reserve requirements and the policy rates on credit and deposit facilities are set intermittently, with a long-term view of the market liquidity situation and its expected developments. Many central banks in LFDCs now signal, as EMEs and AEs do, the stance of their monetary policy by announcing a 'Monetary Policy Rate' (MPR). This key rate is their announced target rate for the short-term interbank rate. Central banks also frequently set the rates of their standing facilities simultaneously with their MPR, and in close reference to it (see section 3.3.2.3). Money market operations are then the instruments used to steer the interbank rate towards the announced target. To achieve this, central banks need to operate market instruments over a sufficiently large range of maturities. Only thus will they be equipped to address successfully the expected short- and long-term changes in market liquidity, which also requires adequate liquidity forecasts (Gray and Pongsaparn 2015: 19).

3.4.3.1 Long-term liquidity management
Structural excess liquidity, a very frequent situation in many LFDCs, is addressed by the regular issue of central bank long-term securities. This is for example the case of the Central Bank of Paraguay, which issues monthly its own certificates, the *letras de regulación monetaria*, which have up to 18 months' maturity (Central Bank of Paraguay 2016). The same objective can be achieved by regular open-market sales of securities of long tenor, as for example those operated on a frequent and regular basis by the Bank of Nigeria for government securities, with tenors ranging from 90 to around 360 days.[42] The mopping up of structural excess liquidity can also be attained with reverse repos or by the issue of fixed-term deposits, as Bank Indonesia does. The two types of operation are possible for maturities of up to one year.[43] Similar longer-maturity market operations can be deployed to cope with structural excess demand of liquidity. Such structural interventions may follow a regular time schedule, but some central banks also

---

[42] Data from website of Central Bank of Nigeria: https://www.cbn.gov.ng/rates/govtsecurities.asp
[43] See website of Bank Indonesia: https://www.bi.go.id/en/moneter/operasi/operasi-pasar-terbuka/Contents/Default.aspx0

undertake longer-term money market operations when the need arises and at their discretion. For instance, they may create temporary facilities through which the banks can borrow, with maturities going, say, from one week up to three months and renewable for additional periods.[44]

3.4.3.2 Control of short-term liquidity fluctuations

Short-term and very short-term fluctuations in market liquidity can, however, only be addressed if the central bank has close contact with the market, i.e. if banks are frequently,—say at least on a weekly basis—encouraged to participate in the auctions organized by the central bank. Indeed, it is through these auctions in the primary or secondary market that the central bank has the opportunity to minutely steer the interest rate or the volume of liquidity of the interbank market towards its target level (see section 3.2.2.2.2). This requires setting up a regular schedule for the auctioning of repos/reverse repos, possibly also for foreign-exchange swaps, and for the issuing of short-term securities. The maturity structure of these instruments, as well as the volume of the central bank's interventions, need to be adapted to the specificities of the country's interbank market for liquidity management to be effective. Central bank interventions and the impact of their policy rates weaken if these occur at too low a frequency or if their volume is small relative to the size of the banks' aggregate balance sheet (Gray et al. 2013: 81).

Offering a sufficiently rich range of maturities for instruments actively used by the central bank may also bring about additional benefits. For instance, it may contribute to develop the interbank market itself, especially its repo segment, and to increase competition within it. It will also help establish a benchmark yield curve (Gray and Pongsaparn 2015: 19). Both expected benefits would facilitate liquidity and asset management within the banking system and thereby strengthen the interest rate channel of monetary policy transmission.

Consider the following examples of how the short-term management of bank liquidity is organized by selected LFDCs' central banks. BCEAO, the central bank of WAEMU, organizes, for banks subject to reserve requirements, two main repo refinancing operations, on a weekly basis for 7 days repos and on a monthly basis for 28 days repos. There is a close connection between these open-market operations and the announced monetary policy rate (MPR), as the latter is the floor bid rate for both variable interest tenders.[45] The *Central Bank of Armenia*'s main policy interventions are the weekly scheduled liquidity providing seven-day repo

---

[44] In Bolivia, banks can borrow from the central bank against their liquid assets as collateral for periods that start with one week, but the liquidity supply of the central bank is not perfectly elastic. It is in tranches and takes a stepwise form. Interest rates may be increasingly higher for the subsequent tranches than for the first tranche.

[45] See website of WAEMU's Central Bank: https://www.bceao.int/fr/content/instruments-de-mise-en-oeuvre-de-la-politique-monetaire

variable-rate auctions in which its MPR also applies as minimum bid rate (see also section 3.4.4 below). It also intermittently organizes tenders for three-month repos.[46] *Bank Indonesia* signals its MPR through its seven-day reverse repo rate. Repos and reverse repos of one week's to three months' maturity for conventional securities are offered in daily auctions. Daily reverse repo tenders, based on sharia compliant securities for the same range of maturities, also take place.[47] Besides the monthly issues of its *letras de regulación monetarias* for structural liquidity-absorbing purposes, the *Central Bank of Paraguay* conducts daily fine-tuning operations . These consist of variable-rate auctions which are arranged as repos or as reverse repos, depending on the liquidity situation. The MPR of the Central Bank of Paraguay determines the maximum bidding rate (MPR+5bp) for fixed-term deposits and the minimum bidding rate (MPR–5bp) for repo tenders (Central Bank of Paraguay 2016: 12).

Many central banks in LFDCs also operate outside the frequency and maturity of their standard operations to cope with unexpected liquidity developments, following the example of central banks of some AEs, like the European Central Bank (ECB). For instance, overnight to longer-maturity reverse repos are conducted for liquidity absorption whenever the central bank feels that there is an excess of liquidity. This can be done at any time of the working day. Collecting fixed-term deposits or offering collateralized loans are also frequently part of such so-called *fine-tuning operations*. They can occur through a quick tender initiated by the central bank or on a bilateral basis, through direct negotiations with selected bank counterparties. Often, they are conducted during the last days of the reserve maintenance period (see section 3.3.1.2), e.g. to absorb existing excess liquidity balances before the start of the next maintenance period. The frequency of such fine-tuning operations will depend on the frequency of the central bank's regular interventions but also on the accuracy of its liquidity projections.

3.4.4 Allotment procedures

Auctions are by far the preferred method of sale of securities, either involving central bank and government securities sold by the central bank for monetary purposes in the primary market or outright sales or reverse transactions in the secondary market. Over-the-counter operations constitute only a small fraction of central banks' operations in the money market.

---

[46] See website of Central Bank of Armenia: https://www.cba.am/en/SitePages/fmoopenmarketop-erations.aspx
[47] See website of Bank of Indonesia: https://www.bi.go.id/en/moneter/operasi/jadwal/Contents/Default.aspx

A first type of auction procedure is the *fixed-rate auction,* also called *volume tender.*[48] The central bank announces, before the auction, the yield it is willing to offer on its securities or the interest rate at which it agrees to provide, or retrieve, liquidity for a given time period. Each participant informs the central bank of its bid amount. After collecting the bids, the central bank sets the volume it wishes to allocate and defines the allotment ratio––the ratio between the volume available for allocation and the total volume of bids. Each participant receives the amount that corresponds to his initial bid times the allotment ratio. In the case of a *full-allotment fixed interest rate,* the central bank announces that all bids will be accepted. Under this system, the central banks lets the market decide on the volume of liquidity to be retrieved or to be issued. This type of fixed-rate system avoids the pitfall of overbidding which frequently occur when the central bank decides on both the interest rate and the volume (see Box 3.3).

The second type of auctions is variable-rate auctions. Central banks of LFCDs that use auctions for allotment overwhelmingly employ this type of auction. In standard tenders for repos and reverse repos, the bids of participants are submitted in terms of proposed interest rates. In AEs and EMEs, when the central bank auctions off its own securities or government securities for monetary purposes, auctions are usually conducted as variable-price—or multiple-price—auctions. Indeed, the securities that are auctioned off usually carry a fixed interest rate or are zero coupon securities, the latter often being the case for central bank paper. Price auctions of fixed interest rate securities can, however, also be considered as interest rate auctions, as the security's yield is inversely related to its price. The difference between price auctions and interest rate auctions is formal, and thus does not bear on the essence of the procedure. LFDCs resort to price auctions more rarely. In variable interest rate tenders, each bid specifies both the interest rate and the amount proposed at that rate.

The procedure followed by central banks in managing a variable interest rate auction can be illustrated conveniently by the two examples given in Table 3.2. The first example concerns a liquidity-providing repo organized by the Central Bank of Armenia, the second a liquidity-absorbing issue of central bank paper organized by the Central Bank of Paraguay.

Seven bids have been entered at the Central Bank of Armenia for the seven-day repo tender reported in Table 3.2. The bids complied with the floor rate set by the central bank—its Monetary Policy Rate (MPR). In its allocation procedure, the central bank decided to allot only 93% of the total amount requested. Having ranked all the bids in ascending order of proposed interest rates, the central bank first satisfied the bid with the *highest* interest rate, subsequently bids with

---

[48] For a formal presentation of fixed and variable price (or interest rate auctions), see European Central Bank (2011: box 5: 38). The ECB's modalities for tenders has served as template for many countries, with relatively minor deviations depending on the depth of the LFDC's financial markets.

Table 3.2. Standard variable interest rate tenders at the central banks of Armenia and Paraguay, October 2019

	Central Bank of Armenia	Central Bank of Paraguay
Type of operation	Repo[a]	Issue of CB securities[b]
Maturity (days)	7	553
Trade date	23 Oct. 2019	23 Oct. 2019
Submission threshold bid rate (%)	5.50[d]	– [e]
Number of bidders	7	12
Total bid amount[c]	64,500	755,000
Lowest presented rate (%)	5.51	5.25
Highest presented rate	5.61	5.75
Total allotted amount[c]	60,000	520,000
Marginal (cut off) rate (%)	5.56	5.60
Average rate (%)	5.61	5.50

Notes: [a] Main refinancing operation; [b] *letras de regulación monetaria*; [c] In millions of domestic currency (drams and guaraníes); [d] Imposed minimum rate; [e] The imposed maximum bid rate was not reported.

Source: Websites of the respective central banks.

successive lower interest rates, until the total liquidity available was exhausted. The tender's cut-off rate, its marginal rate, is the lowest rate taken into consideration for allotment of funds. All the bids *above* the cut-off rate were satisfied in full. Bids *at* the cut-off rate received the residual amount to be allotted. Each participant, if selected, was then expected to pay the interest that he offered in his bid. If there were many bids at the marginal rate, each bidder was satisfied in proportion to the amount to be allotted at this marginal rate. Obviously, the average interest rate at which the bidders obtained their liquidity through this repo tender exceeded the cut-off rate.

The procedure for tenders concerning liquidity-absorbing operations follows symmetrical rules. The tender reported in Table 3.2 for the issue of the Central Bank of Paraguay's 18-month securities recorded 12 participants. The Central Bank decided to issue 69% of the total amount requested by the bidders. In this tender, the first bids to be satisfied were those with the *lowest* interest rate, successively all those up to the cut-off rate. Those below the cut-off rate received the full amount of securities requested in their bid, those at the cut-off rate shared the residual amount to be allocated. Obviously, the average interest rate at which the bidders obtained their securities through this tender was below the cut-off rate.

Variable interest rate auctions are competitive, and in principle benefit the central bank. The average interest rate it receives on its lending operations is

---

Box 3.3. Advantages and disadvantages of auction modalities

The volume tender with fixed interest rates has the disadvantage of inducing banks to overbid in order to make sure to get at least what they actually need. The consequence of this is that some participants receive less than they desire if other participants overbid by a larger extent. This grossly blurs the tender procedure as it cumulatively increases overbidding behavior.

The variable rate auction in its American modality has the advantage that it enforces competition and precludes collusion among market participants. Moreover, the central bank benefits, in the case of repos, from the difference between the marginal interest, the lowest accepted bid rate, and the higher rates paid by the other successful bidders. Similarly, it profits, in the case of reverse repo or of issuing of securities, from the difference between the marginal rate, the highest accepted rate, and the lower interest to be paid to the other successful participants. The central bank benefits from the so-called 'consumer surplus'.

The drawback comes from the 'winner's curse' which can characterize multiple price auctions. It occurs when a bidder, not knowing the prices of other bidders, and putting, according to her subjective beliefs, a high intrinsic value on the security being purchased, offers a price that is substantially higher than the prices of other, more cautious bidders. She will obtain her desired amount but at a price way too high, implying too low a yield. With a price closer to the cut-off price, she would have been allotted the same quantity. The winner's curse may dissuade participation of some financial institutions in the auctions or lead participants to bid a lower price than otherwise in subsequent auctions (Gray and Pongsaparn 2015: 18). The auctions will have a smaller market than otherwise. There is a large body of literature on the 'winner's curse'; a standard reference is Milgrom (1989).

At the beginning, variable-rate auctions were of the sealed envelope type in most LFDCs. With the advent of electronic platforms, the auctions are now open, and at all times a bidder knows where her bid stands in relation to other bids. This open process mitigates the winner's curse but it has the drawback that bidders tend to wait until the end of the bidding time to place their bids. From this follows a bunching of bids with the same interest rate.

---

higher, and the average interest rate it pays on the securities it issues or in other liquidity-absorbing operations is lower. There is however a drawback, as some participants may be discouraged by the 'winner's curse'. Box 3.3 gives an account on the advantages and disadvantages of the different types of auction.

The auctions described above are sealed-envelope American auctions. Sometimes a so-called Dutch option, or single-price option (Gray and Pongsaparn

2015: 17), is chosen. Bids are entered and ranked as in an American auction, and in the same way the central bank selects the marginal rate so as to exhaust the total amount of liquidity it has decided to supply or to retrieve. However, in the Dutch auction, all successful participants pay, or receive, the same interest rate, the marginal rate. The amount of liquidity or of securities each bidder receives corresponds to a given proportion of the amount he has bid for. This proportion equals the ratio between the amount set by the central bank and the total amount of successful bids.

The eligible participants in the auctions will vary across countries, but in general the counterparties are financial institutions subjected to the regulation and supervision of the banking authorities. They have to be in full compliance with the prudential regulations. In addition, some technical requirements may be asked of them, like proof of significant activity in the money market, or in the FX market when foreign exchange swaps are concerned. In general, repos are only available to banks, while the primary market is open to all financial institutions.

Some central banks supplement their money market operations conducted on a weekly basis (or a longer periodicity) with daily operations on their money desk. On the money desk, the securities unsold in the auction of liquidity-absorbing operations are sold at the average price of the last auction plus a penalty. The demand for securities on the money desk is met on a first-come first-served basis until the residual stock of the week's auction is exhausted. Some countries opt instead for a volume auction of the residual stock, with settlement at a pre-specified hour of the day. While use of the money desk is more common for liquidity absorption operations, it is also possible for liquidity provision operations like repos. Similar rules apply, but recourse to repos on the money desk is more expensive than in auctions.

3.5 Interventions in the foreign exchange market

Within the policy toolkit the central bank has at its disposal, interventions in the FX market play an important and specific role. FX interventions consist of sales or purchases of foreign exchange against domestic currency, and are predominantly aimed at influencing the exchange rate, its level, its target path, or its volatility. Indeed, the exchange rate is a key variable in most economies and particularly in LFDCs, where it is often chosen as an operating target (see section 1.3.3.3). Central banks in LFDCs, regardless of their exchange rate regimes, intervene in varying degrees in the FX market. Countries that peg their exchange rate to the currency of a major economy intervene when necessary in the FX market, buying and selling foreign exchange at the rate fixed by the monetary authorities. Countries that do not peg their exchange rates usually have a system of managed float. In a few cases, and then generally only for short periods, they adopt a clean float. With a managed float, central banks intervene in the market buying and selling foreign exchange, building up their foreign assets or running them down in order to align the exchange rate with the target.

3.5.1 Objectives of FX interventions

FX interventions designed to influence the exchange rate may be carried out for different purposes (see e.g. Adler and Tovar 2014: 9; Basu and Varoudakis 2013: 5–6). First, the central bank may intervene to keep the exchange rate on its target path, a path chosen as consistent with the exchange rate's fundamentals and therefore aligned with monetary policy's domestic targets, inflation, and output. Interventions are carried out to prevent a persistent appreciation of the domestic currency that would lead to significant overvaluation, with detrimental consequences for external competitiveness and for growth, or alternatively to prevent a persistent depreciation that would compromise the inflation target. The latter is particularly crucial for countries for which the pass-through from the exchange rate to domestic prices is high.

Second, central banks use interventions to contain exchange rate volatility. Temporary shocks to the current or capital accounts of the balance of payment may generate major fluctuations in the exchange rate. LFDCs are especially vulnerable to external price shocks and FX interventions are used, along with other monetary policy measures, to dampen their effect on inflation and output (see section 5.3). Global financial shocks to the exchange rate, taking the form of large and quickly reversible capital inflows, mostly affect EMEs. In these countries, central banks have resorted to FX interventions to moderate appreciation of the domestic currency, building up a cushion of foreign exchange to be used when capital flows are reversed and when, as a result, the domestic currency suffers strong depreciation pressures. Such FX interventions avoid large short-term swings in the exchange rate. Central banks thereby actually provide domestic agents who have run up foreign currency debt with an insurance against the depreciation of the domestic currency. This contributes to the country's financial stability (Domanski et al. 2016: 70). Because of their low integration with international capital markets, only a limited number of LFDCs are currently exposed to this type of shock and, if that is the case only moderately so. However, LFDCs whose financial sector is heavily dollarized may nevertheless find the financial stability aim of such FX interventions to be quite relevant (see section 6.5.2.1).

Third, FX interventions are crucial when FX markets are shallow, even in normal times. When agents who wish to sell or buy sizeable amounts of foreign currency cannot find in the FX market the necessary counterparties to complete their transaction at reasonable exchange rates, the central bank can step in. By intervening as 'market maker' on the FX market, it provides liquidity and decreases exchange rate uncertainty.

Finally, central banks intervene in the FX market to optimize the level of their stock of international reserves, which is a strategic variable for many countries and particularly for LFDCs, as discussed in section 3.5.4. FX interventions to build up or decrease the stock of international reserves have to be managed in a timely manner so as to interfere as little as possible with the desired path for the exchange rate.

3.5.2 Types, effects, and limits of FX interventions

Most central banks intervene on the spot FX market, usually by outright sales or purchases of foreign exchange. Such interventions are similar in many ways to open-market operations with domestic securities, and have the same monetary policy implications. For example, interventions in the FX market to impede nominal appreciation of the exchange rate result in an accumulation of foreign reserves. Its counterpart is an increase in base money that implies a more expansionary monetary policy. Domestic interest rates are pushed down, which mitigates the appreciation pressures. Central banks may however wish to limit the ensuing inflationary pressures and real overvaluation of the exchange rate of the more expansionary monetary policy, and try to offset the intervention's liquidity creation with restrictive open market-type operations, for example by issuing central bank securities. In the process, they sterilize the liquidity effects of their spot market intervention. A *sterilized intervention* is thus an exchange of foreign exchange against domestic currency securities instead of against domestic liquidity. When interventions in the FX spot market are fully sterilized, the domestic interest rate remains unchanged.[49] This contrasts with unsterilized interventions, whose effect on the exchange rate is strongly enhanced by their consequences on domestic interest rates.

With a sterilized intervention the central bank can thus, in principle, target the exchange rate and the domestic interest rate separately, using two instruments, FX interventions to target the former, and open-market operations to target the latter. Recent studies focused on EMEs find that sterilized interventions are indeed useful as a supplementary instrument for keeping the exchange rate in

---

[49] Partial sterilization often occurs automatically when there are standing facilities. Liquidity creation resulting from FX purchases by the central bank will push the interbank rate to its floor, to the rate of the deposit standing facility. Any excess liquidity at this rate will then be automatically absorbed, as banks will increase their deposits at the central bank. To achieve full sterilization—i.e. to bring the interbank rate back to its initial level—restrictive open-market interventions that fully offset the liquidity created by the foreign exchange purchases are, however, necessary.

line with its fundamentals, prevent lasting misalignments and limit exchange rate volatility (Ostry et al. 2012; Basu and Varoudakis 2013; Blanchard et al. 2015; Patel and Cavallino 2019).[50] Sterilized interventions are effective for management of the exchange rate through two channels: a portfolio balance effect and a signalling effect (Ostry et al. 2012: 11). The first channel operates through the risk premium, the wedge between domestic interest rates and the expected return on foreign currency assets (see section 2.4.2.2.1). Investors who consider that both assets are imperfect substitutes take into account such a risk premium in holding the outstanding stocks of both assets in their portfolios. Sterilized interventions change the relative supply of domestic vs foreign currency assets, affecting the risk premium and thereby the exchange rate.[51] The lower the substitutability between the domestic and foreign currency assets, the stronger the expected portfolio balance effect. Such imperfect substitutability between domestic and foreign assets is clearly a reasonable assumption for EMEs and, a fortiori, for LFDCs.[52] The second channel through which interventions affect the exchange rate is the signalling channel. By intervening to keep the exchange rate on target, the central bank signals its intention to adhere to it. When the central bank has sufficient credibility, this conveys information about the future stance of its monetary policy and anchors agents' expectations about the future level of the exchange rate. This in turn stabilizes the exchange rate on the spot market and limits the necessity of further interventions.

There are, however, limits to FX interventions. In the case of interventions to counter depreciation pressures on the domestic currency, the limit is the stock of available international reserves (see section 3.5.4). To avoid coming close to this limit and possibly triggering an exchange rate crisis, the central bank will need to abandon full sterilization and complement its sales of foreign currency on the FX market with a tightening of monetary policy, usually by raising its policy rates or alternatively by increasing banks' required reserves. In an extreme case, when there is 'fear of floating' prompted by the inflationary consequences of exchange rate depreciation, intervention of central banks in the FX market as well as tightening of monetary policy can be very vigorous. In the symmetric case of revaluation pressures, the limit to the use of sterilized interventions is less clear. There is

---

[50] While the overall empirical evidence about the effects of FX interventions on the level and volatility of the exchange is still somewhat mixed, many studies points to its effectiveness, particularly in the case of EMEs. For brief surveys, see Ostry et al. (2012: 11–12) and Patel and Cavallino (2019: 32).

[51] E.g. a sterilized intervention by the central bank to counter depreciation of the domestic currency implies a decrease in the supply of domestic currency assets available for investment purposes to private residents and non-residents. This results in a decrease in the risk premium on domestic assets requested by investors to hold the new asset mix in their portfolio. With unchanged foreign and domestic interest rates, this in turn leads to the appreciation of the domestic currency, relative to its level before the intervention.

[52] Domestic bond markets are small in LFDCs. The sterilization of FX purchases or sales by the central bank can therefore imply large disequilibria between supply and demand on these markets, and thereby have a large effect on the equilibrium risk premium and hence on the exchange rate.

no limit in principle to the amount of reserves a central bank can accumulate. However, reserves have an opportunity cost (see 3.5.4) and the sterilization part of the intervention is itself also costly, as the central bank has to pay interest on the securities it issues or the reverse repos it carries out. Also, the absorption capacity of such securities by the domestic market may be limited. To minimize costs and avoid crowding out the domestic security and credit markets, the central bank may need to adapt its monetary policy, lowering its policy rates or reducing required reserves.

Thus, when sterilized FX interventions have reached their limit, domestic monetary policy has eventually to be adjusted to preserve the exchange rate target. This will occur if the shocks to the exchange rate are particularly large. It will also be inevitable if interventions are needed, not to counteract shocks that may lead to temporary deviations of the exchange rate from its fundamental equilibrium value, but to support an exchange rate that is fundamentally over- or undervalued. We discuss this issue of consistency between an exchange rate target and domestic inflation and output targets in section 6.4.5.2.

Central banks can also carry out their exchange rate interventions outside the spot FX market by operating on the FX forward or other FX derivatives markets, when such markets are sufficiently developed and liquid. A central bank may, for example, sell foreign currency forward against the domestic currency at its target exchange rate. The impact of such an intervention on the forward exchange rate would then be quickly reflected in the spot rate through interest rate arbitrage operations.[53] Central banks can also issue FX options or intervene as counterparty in cross-currency swaps.[54] Through FX interventions of this type, beyond

---

[53] The current period forward exchange rate $F_{t,t+1}$ is linked to the spot rate S_t through the covered interest parity (CIP): $(1+i_t) = (1+i_t^*)(F_{t,t+1}/S_t)$. Like the UIP, it is a no-arbitrage condition which equalizes the end of period values, in domestic currency, of holding domestic and foreign currency risk-free securities, carrying respectively interest rates i_t and i_t^* and initiated with an exchange rate of S_t domestic currency per foreign currency units (see section 2.4.2.1). The difference between CIP and UIP is that in the former, the investor covers his exchange rate risk on the forward market, while for the latter the position is unhedged. Contrary to UIP, CIP thus strictly holds even if investors are risk-averse—barring some possible deviations if there are transactions costs. As a result, covered interest arbitrage operations guarantee that any changes to $F_{t,t+1}$ brought about by the central bank's forward interventions, are directly transmitted to the spot rate S_t, the latter varying in the same proportion as the forward rate.

[54] By e.g. selling FX call options, the central bank can offer a hedge to agents having a foreign currency liability, as the option grants them the right, but not the obligation, to buy foreign exchange at a predetermined price from the central bank. The option will be exercised and the central bank will lose reserves if currency depreciation pushes the exchange rate above the option's exercise price. With a cross-currency swap, a type of interest rate swap used e.g. by Brazil, the central bank can also offer a hedge to agents exposed to the risk of a depreciation of the domestic currency (Domanski et al. 2016: 71). As in the case of sales in the forward market or sales of call options, the central bank bears the exchange risk, as these transactions are settled at the spot exchange rate prevailing at the contract's maturity. Note that cross-currency swaps are not to be confused with regular FX swaps, which are a repo operation based on foreign exchange. Such FX swaps are without exchange rate risk, contrary to the cross-currency swaps, in which the central bank takes an open position in the forward leg of the contract (see Adler and Tovar 2014: 42).

those on the FX spot market, central banks can have an effect on the current exchange rate, without an immediate impact on their international reserves. Central banks of AEs as well as of some EMEs rely on the use of such instruments of FX intervention to manage their exchange rate (Domanski et al. 2016). Most LFDCs, however, have to stick to regular spot market interventions until their financial market structure has reached sufficient maturity.

3.5.3 Modalities of FX interventions

Concerning the procedures used to intervene on the FX market, most central banks in LFDCs undertake outright sales or purchases of foreign exchange. Most operations with foreign exchange are over-the-counter operations, do not have well-established frequencies, and take place as soon as the demand (or the supply) emerges. If the exchange rate is not pegged, the sales procedures can be the same as the ones described in section 3.4.4. In Armenia, for example, foreign exchange transactions are executed through auctions, of a quick-tender type (Central Bank of Armenia 2019: 18). Occasionally, central banks use FX swaps for short-term interventions in the FX market. They consist of simultaneous spot and forward transactions in domestic currency against a foreign currency. The central bank buys (or sells) foreign currency in the spot market and at the same time sells (or buys) it back in a forward transaction at a specific date and a pre-agreed price. Banks that temporarily need central bank liquidity can buy their foreign currency at the central bank and then reverse the operation at the specified forward date. More often it is the central bank which needs the foreign currency in the context of foreign reserve management, and which will enter into a swap arrangement with the commercial banks. FX swaps are similar to repos (or reverse repos) on domestic securities and are mainly used as instrument for the management of central bank liquidity (see section 3.4.2.2). Their temporary effect on the exchange rate may, however, be a useful complement to outright interventions on the FX spot market, for example, to address short-lived illiquidity situations in this market.[55]

3.5.4 Concept and roles of international reserves

International reserves are the main determinant of the capacity of a central bank to conduct FX interventions. Their role is, however, broader. According to the

---

[55] FX swaps may also take place sporadically between a domestic central bank and a foreign central bank. These swaps are used more by EMEs than by LFDCs, within a multilateral framework, e.g. within the Chang Mai Initiative (see Appendix 6A(1)). These swaps are not monetary policy instruments proper, but rather instruments used by central banks to manage their foreign currency liabilities in order to fortify their international reserves.

conventions of the IMF followed by most countries, international reserves are 'those external assets that are readily available to and controlled by monetary authorities for meeting balance of payments financing needs, for intervention in exchange markets to affect the currency exchange rate, and for other related purposes (such as maintaining confidence in the currency and the economy, and serving as a basis for foreign borrowing)' (IMF 2009: 111).

Conventionally, official reserve assets comprise monetary gold (i.e. gold owned by the monetary authorities as a financial asset and sometimes as a commodity), foreign-exchange and other claims on non-residents, holdings of IMF's Special Drawing Rights (SDR), the reserve position at the IMF, and other assets that are liquid and readily available for international transactions. However, the above categorization of international reserves is not without ambiguities. It is a gross concept, and does thus not take into account the future drains on reserves which can result from short-term FX liabilities or from off-balance sheet positions in the markets of FX derivatives. The IMF's concept of Net International Reserves follows when these items are deducted from official reserves (IMF 2016a: 4). More comprehensive still is the concept of the central bank's Net Foreign Asset (NFA) position, which takes into account foreign-currency assets that are not included in the concept of official reserves but also nets out the total amount of the central bank's external foreign-currency liabilities, for example those vis-à-vis multilateral official lenders.

LFDCs hold international reserves to facilitate their international payments, but also for precautionary reasons, regardless of their exchange rate regime. During the two last decades global foreign exchange reserves have increased more than sixfold at world level, more rapidly than the volume of international trade. This feature has been especially observed in China and in other EMEs and developing countries (World Bank 2019: 1). Globalization, recurrent shifts in commodity prices, and the repercussions of the financial crisis in the AEs have contributed to this trend.

The level of international reserves is of key importance for LFDCs. Their economies are in general weakly diversified. This renders them very vulnerable to external shocks, while they also have limited access to the international capital market to smooth domestic consumption and investment. The shock-mitigation role of international reserves is particularly important for commodity exporters, for heavily indebted countries, and for countries with fixed exchange rate regimes (see also Appendix 6A(1)).

In a 2018 World Bank survey on reserve management practices, the motive of holding reserves to 'provide self-insurance against potential external shocks' was unanimously selected as highly relevant by all the reporting central banks from LICs and lower-middle income (LM) countries, respectively 9 and 28 central banks. The motive of holding reserves to 'service external debt or obligations' was seen as highly relevant by all reporting central banks from LICs, and by 82% of central banks from LM countries. A third motive, 'conduct foreign exchange policy', was indicated as highly relevant by respectively 78% and 61% of central banks from low-income and lower-middle income countries (World Bank 2019: 3, 12). In a similar survey undertaken by the Bank of International Settlements (BIS) and focused on central banks of African countries, the top priority for holding reserves is 'to fund essential imports', according to the 26 reporting central banks. The second and third priorities are to 'alleviate FX shortages of the government' and 'to stabilize exchange rate movements when these affect domestic inflation'. The latter is, according to this survey, seen as particularly important for countries where the pass-through of the exchange rate is high, which is especially the case for countries whose financial sector is highly dollarized (Schanz 2019: 2–5).

The upkeep of reserves is costly. The net cost is given by the difference between the cost of maintaining them and their return. The gross cost can be the return on alternative assets in which the central bank could have invested, either in other less liquid FX assets or in domestic-currency assets. It can also be the cost of borrowing in FX if the country has been borrowing to replenish its reserves, for instance, to meet the foreign exchange asset target agreed with the IMF. It can also be the domestic interest rate if reserves are acquired through sterilized interventions, as reserves are in this case financed by interest-bearing central bank liabilities. Whatever the precise metrics, the net cost of reserves is in general positive, as the return of reserve assets is generally low, given that these assets need to be liquid and without significant credit risk. If one takes the sovereign bond spread as a first approximation, one can observe that the upkeep cost of reserves can be significant for low-income countries (Schanz 2019: 6).

While the benefits of holding reserves are very clear, it is difficult to assign them a numerical target value. It is thus quite difficult to determine an 'optimal stock of reserves' which would be derived from precisely balancing their benefits with their costs. International institutions like the IMF offer guidance in this respect (see e.g. IMF 2016a). In practice, there are rules of thumb which can quickly be referred to in order to assess reserve adequacy, like whether the stock of reserves covers at least three months of imports or whether reserves are enough to cover the official short-term external debt. Both metrics should be set at higher thresholds if the country is heavily dollarized.

3.6 Instruments of financial stability

Beyond their main mandate to carry out monetary policy in order to achieve price stability, as well as contributing to output stability, central banks have also been entrusted with a responsibility for financial stability. They may share this responsibility with specific bodies that regulate the financial sector, but are nevertheless always closely involved in preserving financial stability because of their function of lender of last resort (see section 1.3.2.6). We briefly discuss in this context the financial-stability instruments that have been deployed by central banks in LFDCs. We focus on those instruments that overlap monetary policy instruments or are organized in close parallel to them.

3.6.1 High required reserves

Along with their monetary-policy functions of control of liquidity, as discussed in section 3.2.2.2.2, required reserves have also traditionally been justified, when set at a relatively high level, as a means of protecting customers' deposits. Banks can indeed, regulations permitting, dip into their required reserves to cushion large unexpected deposit outflows. High reserve requirements then constitute a first line of defence against a bank run, but cannot obviously substitute for other necessary measures of prudential control. In the same vein, changes in reserve ratios have been used recently in LFDCs, as well as in EMEs, as a macro-prudential tool, frequently as a substitute for monetary policy, the latter being understood in a narrow sense as interest rate policy.[56] Reserve requirements are then managed to dampen—more effectively than changes in interest rates—boom and bust cycles in bank lending. Also, increases in required reserve ratios applied to foreign-currency bank deposits have been used to de-dollarize the banking sector in heavily dollarized countries. Since de-dollarization reduces financial fragility, such a reserve requirement policy can be interpreted as directly contributing to guaranteeing financial stability (see section 3.6.4).

3.6.2 Statutory liquidity requirements

In some countries, reserve requirements are superseded by, or combined with, liquid asset requirements. Statutory liquidity requirements are often lumped together with required reserves, but they are different in terms both of yield and of destination. They are required more for prudential reasons than as instruments of monetary policy.[57] The liquidity ratios can be quite high. A sizeable number of countries in our LFDC set have statutory liquidity requirements in the 20–30% range.

---

[56] On this point see Federico et al.(2014).

[57] Statutory liquid assets requirements were used as monetary policy instruments in several AEs before the 1980s. In countries where banks held large portfolios of liquid government securities, central banks imposed high liquid asset requirements to prevent banks emasculating restrictive monetary policy measures by selling government securities. These direct monetary policy instruments were discarded in the 1980s as distorting the banks' portfolio allocation, and as leading to 'financial repression' in favour of the government (Monet and Vari 2019).

Box 3.4. Reserve plus liquid asset requirements: the Bolivian system of 1997

A major reform to enhance financial stability occurred in Bolivia in 1997 with the introduction of liquid asset requirements. In addition to cash reserve requirements, the financial institutions have to hold a percentage of their deposits in liquid assets deposited into two funds. The first fund of liquid assets is in domestic currency (FLA-DC) and the second is in foreign currency (FLA-FC). All deposit-taking institutions, banks, and quasi-banks are subject to the regulation. All deposits, either checkable accounts, savings passbooks, or term deposits, are included. Only term deposits in domestic currency with maturities over one year and in foreign currency with maturities of two years or more are exempt. The regulations apply to deposits in domestic currency and in foreign currency.

Banks receive shares in each fund. The two funds of pooled liquid assets are collectively managed under the auspices of the central bank. Treasury bills and notes of different maturities compose the FLA-DC, which is directly operated by the central bank. Liquid assets are thus remunerated at the market rate of the lowest-risk securities. Regulations of the central bank fix the assets allowed in the FLA-FC portfolio, the management of which is delegated to a foreign-asset manager.

The key point of the reform was to allow financial institutions to borrow short-term in domestic or foreign currency from the central bank, with their assets held in the FLA-FC and in FLA-DC respectively as collateral. This specific central-bank lending is allowed within the first two successive tranches of 40% and 30% of the fund, with higher borrowing costs and more stringent conditions for the second. Lending against the last tranche would only be considered in very exceptional circumstances and with even more stringent conditionality.

The system described above has served well the central bank of Bolivia and the private financial institutions. As circumstances changed, however, the regulations were modified. First, the ratio of liquidity requirements became differentiated with regard to the currency of the deposit. Second, an additional marginal ratio was established for deposits in dollars.

Assets dedicated to compliance with liquidity requirements may or may not be deposited with the central banks. If deposited with the central bank, acting as a trustee, they will be invested in government paper. If the liquid assets are not with the central bank, they are invested in assets authorized by the central bank and sometimes through the central bank which then acts as an intermediary. The latter closely monitors whether each individual bank complies with the set minimum ratio. Averaging liquidity requirements over a maintenance period is often allowed, so that both cash reserve and liquid asset requirements are operated in a similar way. Box 3.4 shows how the Bolivian central bank organized such liquidity requirements. The central banks of Pakistan, Algeria, and Armenia, to name but a few, also impose liquidity requirements, in parallel with cash reserves.[58]

Mandatory liquidity ratios have been imposed for many years in EMEs and in LFDCs as an important and easily employed instrument to strengthen the stability of the banking system, especially for heavy dollarized countries or for countries facing regular short-term capital in- and outflows. In response to the 2007–9 global financial crisis, comprehensive liquidity requirements were also introduced in the 28 AEs and EMEs that are members of the Basel Committee on Banking Supervision. Many non-member countries, including developing countries, have decided to progressively implement at least part of these regulatory standards. There are many facets to the Basel III regulatory framework, principally rules for capital adequacy but also rules that target banks' liquidity. The prudential framework includes two compulsory liquidity ratios, the Liquidity Coverage Ratio (LCR) and the Net Stable Funding Ratio (NSFR).[59] It is to be expected that in an increasing number of LFDCs that currently use country-specific statutory liquidity requirements, these Basel III international liquidity standards will progressively substitute for the current rules. According to the Financial Stability Institute (2015) survey on the implementation of Basel rules, the new standards have already been adopted, or were expected to be adopted within four years of the survey, by many central banks or supervisory authorities of LFDCs.[60]

3.6.3 Exceptional operations as lender of last resort

The lender of last resort (LOLR) function is one of the more complex and delicate functions of central banks, fully linked to their mission of preserving financial stability. The LOLR function applies more frequently in the case of idiosyncratic liquidity crises, but its relevance appears even more sharply in the case of systemic crises. The special facilities set up by central banks to operate in the exceptional

---

[58] In 2018, conventional and Islamic banks needed to hold respectively 19% and 18% of their deposit base and other borrowing in liquid approved securities, on top of the applicable 5% cash reserve ratio. See website of the Central Bank of Pakistan: http://www.sbp.org.pk/m_policy/mpf-03.asp

[59] The LCR requires banks to fully cover with high-quality liquid assets the cash outflows that can be expected to occur within 30 days in a stress scenario. The NSFR takes a longer-term perspective, requesting banks to match less liquid and longer-term assets with stable funding (capital, customer deposits or other liabilities maturing in more than one year). While the two concepts are conceptually clear, their implementation has to deal with many complex issues in order to tailor the set of rules to the specificity of the country's banking system.

[60] The supervisory authorities of as many as 35 countries belonging to our set of LFDCs declared in this 2015 survey their intention to implement the Basel III Liquidity Coverage Ratio. Note however that several of these countries have yet to fully implement this framework, and continue, like e.g. Pakistan, to rely on their own specific liquidity requirements imposed by the central bank.

context of their LOLR function (see Box 3.5) should not be confused with the monetary policy instruments they deploy in normal times. Short- or long-term emergency liquidity loans are employed to assist solvent banks whose access to private financial markets is temporarily impaired and are thus afflicted with severe liquidity problems. Short- and long-term lending is in normal times used by the central bank to influence market liquidity through standard procedures aimed at all banks without discrimination. Emergency lending to a solvent but illiquid bank will however be channelled through specific facilities, like second-tier discount windows, and will be priced at substantially higher rates than those that apply to usual lending by the central bank. LOLR credits are extended with suitable collaterals that usually go beyond government securities. Central banks determine what assets other than government securities are acceptable collateral. In particular, collateral provided by well-rated loans extended by the private banks to firms and households may be acceptable.

Box 3.5. The central bank as lender of last resort to banks in liquidity distress

---

LOLR interventions by central banks have been guided by Bagehot's rule. Formulated in 1873 by the British economist Walter Bagehot, it states that central bank credit to banks should flow freely, against good collateral, and be granted at penalty rates. Solvent banks have no problem in putting up good collateral. The penalty interest rate has a double purpose. First, banks have recourse to the central bank truly of last resort. To avoid going for a central bank credit, banks will keep sufficient liquid assets. Also, they will do their best to go to the interbank market before appealing to the central bank. Second, it pushes the debtor banks to repay the loan from the central bank as soon as they can.

Central banks face two major difficulties in managing LOLR support, however. First, it is often difficult to distinguish a solvency problem from a liquidity problem. Liquidity shortages in a given bank may reflect underlying solvency problems. Second, recourse to the LOLR facility may carry a stigma that reinforces the isolation from the interbank market of the assisted bank, and sometimes hastens the withdrawal of funds by depositors instead of stopping them as expected; also, because of this stigma, banks that effectively have major liquidity needs shy away and delay their borrowing until it is too late.

The provision of LOLR support by central banks also carries moral hazard risk, i.e. the risk of inviting imprudent behaviour within the financial system. A fully-fledged set of prudential rules is needed to minimize this risk and to provide for a resilient financial system in which recourse to the LOLR remains truly exceptional.

The potential need for rapid action should unexpected market developments occur makes it desirable to retain a high degree of flexibility in the choice of instruments. This is why there are, in the toolbox of central banks, exceptional operations for liquidity provision, with frequency and maturity that are not standardized. Their use will depend on circumstances. There may be some advantage for the central bank to cultivate 'constructive ambiguity' about its LOLR interventions, so as to foster prudent behaviour among banks (Freixas 1999). Note, however, that norms and regulations applying to LOLR interventions are very useful, even when they are broad, to avoid charges of discretionary behaviour on the part of the central bank. There is a delicate balance to strike between flexibility and predictability.

In the case of a financial crisis, liquidity problems are not limited to an individual bank but are systemic. Extensive LOLR liquidity support by the central bank is in this case the first large-scale step to preserve the stability of the financial system. This tool of crisis containment has been used on a large scale in every countries that has faced banking crises since the 1970s. Also, lower- and middle-income countries tend to rely on this tool for longer periods after the start of a crisis than high-income countries (Laeven and Valencia 2018: 13). At some point, however, it becomes clear that the crisis is no longer about a global liquidity squeeze but has evolved into a bank solvency problem. Tools of crisis resolution other than LOLR liquidity provision then become necessary, like bank recapitalization measures or the setting up of asset management companies to purchase and administer non-performing bank assets. Those fall outside the direct responsibility of the central bank, although the latter may continue to play some coordination role in the resolution of the crisis.

3.6.4 Lender of last resort in dollarized economies

The central bank faces multiple challenges when the country's financial system is heavily dollarized.[61] The foreign currency then supersedes the domestic currency in its main functions, and a large part of financial intermediation is performed in foreign currency. Nicaragua, Cambodia, Kazakhstan, and Albania (among others) are LFDCs where dollarization (euro-ization for the latter) is still high. In section 6.5, we discuss in depth how dollarization complicates the choice of an effective nominal anchor, as it very much constrains the selection of an appropriate intermediate monetary policy target. An additional challenge for the central bank in dollarized economies is, however, that of maintaining financial stability in a dollarized environment. This implies a broadening of their LOLR responsibility,

---

[61] We use 'dollarization' as a generic term. Although the dollar is the leading currency in this respect, the foreign currency which competes with the domestic currency may also be the euro (euroization in the case of Central and Easter European economies) or the yen (yenization) or, possibly in the future, the renminbi once it becomes fully convertible.

with the latter extended to cover the provision of liquidity in foreign currencies to domestic banks.

Systemic liquidity stress on the market for domestic dollars in partially dollarized economies can occur when there is a perceived increase in country risk or in the solvency of its banking system.[62] This may trigger a bank run out of domestic dollar deposits into US dollar cash or into cross-border dollar deposits. Such a run on domestic dollar bank liabilities cannot be handled by the central bank by providing domestic currency liquidity. If there is a cash drain in dollar bills when small depositors panic, banks can respond to the withdrawals by converting their foreign currency reserves held at the central bank into cash in US dollar bills. The withdrawals of large depositors are covered first with the deposits that banks hold abroad, but once these have been run down, banks will ask support from their central bank. The central bank of a dollarized economy thus has to use its international reserves to finance the supply of US dollar bills to the public or to settle payments with the foreign banks that are the recipients of the cross-border transfers of dollar deposits.[63]

If the central bank withheld its support, the liquidity tensions on the dollar interbank market would immediately spill over onto the FX market, possibly precipitating a large depreciation of the domestic currency. The latter would undermine the stability of the banking sector, given the extensive unhedged foreign-currency exposure of bank borrowers.[64] Central banks in heavily dollarized countries therefore need to build a sufficiently large cushion of international reserves, much larger than in non-dollarized economies, taking into account the extent of the domestic public's foreign currency bank deposits.[65]

Given the crucial importance for financial stability of liquidity in the domestic dollar money market, many central banks of dollarized economics have implemented two sets of measures: (i) precautionary measures to prevent foreign currency liquidity crises, and (ii) monetary policy-type interventions mechanisms to assist banks in managing their foreign-exchange liquidity.

High required reserves on foreign-currency deposits and high statutory liquidity requirements in foreign-currency assets are typical prudential measures (see sections 3.6.1 and 3.6.2). Both represent, when fully backed by the central bank's international reserves, readily available foreign currency resources which can be mobilized in case of a bank run. Both also give banks some flexibility in the

---

[62] See Gulde et al. (2004) for a discussion of the events that triggered runs on domestic dollar liquidity in several Latin American countries (Argentina, Bolivia, Mexico, Paraguay, and Uruguay) during the 1990s and early 2000s

[63] To supply dollar bills at short notice is also a logistical challenge for central banks, as they usually only hold a tiny fraction of their international reserves as vault cash.

[64] See section 2.4.3.2, where the 'balance sheet' effect of the exchange rate is discussed.

[65] Note that in the 1990s some central banks in heavily dollarized EMEs had negotiated contingent foreign currency credit lines with some international banks. The most notable case was Argentina. These contingent credit lines are of no avail in the case of a fully-fledged banking panic.

day-to-day management of their foreign-currency liquidity if some averaging over the maintenance period is allowed, making it less necessary for the central bank to intervene in the dollar money market (Baliño et al. 1999: 17). Direct interventions by central banks to facilitate foreign-currency liquidity management by domestic banks include the following measures: clearing and settlement of domestic transactions in foreign currency in their books; issuing of central bank securities denominated in foreign currency or indexed to the exchange rate; repos or collateralized central bank credit in foreign currency; and FX swaps (Baliño et al. 1999: 18–9; Gulde et al. 2004: 16–7). These instruments were used by central banks in the 1990s in heavily dollarized Latin American countries like Bolivia, Argentina, Peru, and Uruguay to 'enhance flexibility in the use of international reserves, limit exchange rate volatility, and, in some cases, to facilitate the domestic recycling of dollar liquidity' (Gulde et al. 2004: 18).

Such instruments are still currently in use in several heavily dollarized LFDCs. The central bank of Cambodia, for instance, issues certificates of deposits in foreign as well as in domestic currency, in tenors ranging from seven days to one year. Cambodian banks are also allowed to borrow through overdrafts intra-day dollar liquidity from the central bank. Having overhauled in 2018 its set of monetary policy instruments, the Central Bank of Nicaragua offers a whole array of instruments in foreign currency. It regularly issues through auctions its own certificates of deposits denominated in dollars, with maturities of up to 1 year.[66] It organizes liquidity-providing repos, which are in domestic currency but indexed on the US dollar exchange rate. It also operates an overnight deposit standing facility in dollars, with a pre-announced interest rate. The Central Bank of Kazakhstan has helped banks facing high dollarization of their liabilities to reduce their foreign-exchange exposure by providing them with short-term and even long-term FX swaps at an advantageous interest rate. Note that when central banks set the interest rate on their monetary policy instrument denominated in domestic dollars, they do not have much room relative to the benchmark US dollar rates of similar maturity. The domestic dollar rate diverges from the latter by the country risk premium, over which the central bank has only scant control. In any case, it is the degree of substitutability between domestic dollar assets and dollar assets in the anchor country which determine the admittedly limited degree of discretion the central bank may enjoy in setting its own interest rates for operations in dollars.

Finally, it appears that central banks of partially dollarized economies have a strong incentive to enlarge the space of their domestic currency in their country's financial system, in order to strengthen the effectiveness of their monetary policy and to limit the specific vulnerabilities dollarization implies for financial stability.

---

[66] They were issued in significant amounts, as the outstanding amount represented 4.6% of gross international reserves in 2018 (Central Bank of Nicaragua 2019: 96).

To foster such a de-dollarization process, they need first to firmly establish the credibility of their commitment to achieve and maintain price stability. Additional measures can then be introduced to progressively reverse dollarization. Reserve and statutory liquidity requirements that are higher for foreign currency than for domestic currency deposits will increase the cost of financial intermediation in dollars. This will be reflected in higher rates for dollar bank loans and lower rates on dollar deposits, decreasing their appeal to residents. Also helpful are measures to enhance the attractiveness of the local currency, for instance through the development of domestic currency interbank and security markets, as well as prudential rules, like limits on foreign exchange net open positions, designed to induce banks to better internalize the various risks their operations in foreign currency impose not only on themselves but on the whole financial system.

3.7 Summary

This chapter has been devoted to the presentation of the whole array of monetary instruments that LFDCs' central banks may use to achieve the operating and intermediate targets of their monetary policy framework. For each instrument, we have discussed its specific purpose, the context, mechanism, and modalities of its use, and its advantages but also possible drawbacks, with special reference to central banks in LFDCs, in general or on the basis of the experience of selected countries. Several points are worth recalling:

- Direct monetary policy instruments, through which the central bank inter-venes in a regulatory way to direct banks' asset allocation or interest rate-setting, are still more common in LFDCs than in AEs and EMEs. Exchange controls, relating to current or capital account transactions, also fall into this category and are still in use in a number of LFDCs.
- With a market-oriented monetary policy, central banks rely on indirect monetary policy instruments, through which they can influence bank liquidity and short-term interest rates, in line with the target they have set for the monetary base or for the interbank rate. Rules-based indirect instru-ments, like reserve requirements or standing credit or deposit facilities, relate to the demand for central bank liquidity and to the ceiling and floor rates for the short-term interest rate. Market-based interventions in the money market allow the central bank to inject liquidity into the market or to withdraw it for varying time periods. Most central banks in LFDCs have decided to evolve towards a market-based monetary policy and have thus set up at least part of the available array of indirect monetary policy instruments. However, the shallowness of the interbank market and of the secondary markets in debt securities still impairs the central bank's

open-market operations in many LFDCs. They are organized irregularly or have a low rate of participation. This hinders the central bank's capacity to closely manage market liquidity. The task is especially difficult in a situation of persistent excess reserves in the banking system, another characteristic of many LFDCs. For this reason, many central banks, especially those which have opted for a monetary policy based on an announced policy rate, also operate overnight credit and deposit standing facilities. Setting the rates on these facilities allows them to gain closer control on short-term market interest rates.

- Many central banks in LFDCs carry out interventions on the FX market to regulate the path of the exchange rate. This is often of crucial importance given the vulnerability of LFDCs to external shocks. As the FX market is often shallow, the central bank intervenes as 'market maker', using its international reserves as buffer stock. Interventions on the FX market have direct consequences for liquidity and interest rates in the domestic money market. Central banks sometimes wish to neutralize these effects through sterilization operations, aiming at dissociating their exchange rate policy from their domestic monetary policy. Such sterilization operations can be effective if the degree of substitutability between domestic and foreign currency assets is low, which may still be the case in many LFDCs.

- Central banks in LFDCs often complete their monetary policy arsenal with statutory liquidity requirements. The latter, together with high reserve requirements, are intended to prevent liquidity crises in the domestic banking crisis and to minimize the need for the central bank to intervene as lender of last resort. Exceptional interventions by the central bank to provide liquidity as lender of last resort are also crucial to head off a systemic banking crisis, as has been experienced in many countries, including several LFDCs. When the country's financial system is heavily dollarized, the central bank's role of lender of last resort is broadened, so as to include also the monitoring of liquidity in the domestic foreign-currency money market. To address severe liquidity tensions in this market, the central bank may need to intervene through monetary policy-type interventions in foreign currency, with the backing of its international reserves.

4

Monetary Policy Trade-Offs and Monetary Policy Credibility

4.1 Introduction

Chapters 2 and 3 documented two crucial aspects of the monetary policy framework: the monetary transmission mechanism and the arsenal of monetary policy instruments. For monetary authorities to be able achieve the goals given by their mandate, they need to be able to rely both on a sufficiently large set of monetary policy instruments and, more importantly, on the efficient transmission of monetary impulses initiated through the use of these instruments to the economy's real sector and the goal variables they endeavour to influence.

This chapter adds two further aspects of the making of monetary policy: first, the trade-offs between monetary policy goals and secondly, central bank credibility.

We first discuss the different goals monetary policy is expected to pursue. As already briefly discussed in section 1.3, there is a global consensus that central bank's priority should be to achieve and maintain price stability. Such a priority is based on standard monetary theory and motivated by a large empirical body, justifying and giving evidence, respectively, of the monetary roots of the inflation process. Preserving price stability is, however, not the unique facet of the central bank's mandate. Central banks are also entrusted with the mission to use their capacity to affect the real economy in the short run, in order to mitigate the effects of domestic or external shocks on output and employment. In addition, as lender of last resort, they cannot escape their responsibility to intervene when a financial crisis hits and threatens to disrupt the domestic financial sector. Such an ultimate responsibility in turn calls for a central bank to adopt a preventive approach to guarantee the stability of the domestic financial sector, minimize the probability of crises, and mitigate their effects. Entrusted with these three mandates—price stability, output stabilization, and financial stability—but endowed with only one generic instrument—monetary policy—central banks are confronted with trade-offs. Favouring price stability entails output costs and may also be detrimental to financial stability. Alternatively, addressing as a priority the need to stabilize output may kindle inflationary developments. Section 4.2 explores the analytical foundations of these trade-offs and their empirical characteristics, with a focus on those which take into account the structural features of LFDCs. They are directly relevant for assessing how the trade-offs in these countries can be managed by central banks.

Monetary Policy in Low Financial Development Countries. Juan Antonio Morales and Paul Reding, Oxford University Press.
© Juan Antonio Morales and Paul Reding 2021. DOI: 10.1093/oso/9780198854715.003.0004

Section 4.3 addresses another crucial issue for the effectiveness of monetary policy: the credibility of central banks. A central bank is credible when private agents have high confidence in the specific monetary policy goals it announces and in the strategy it follows in order to achieve them. Credibility is crucial because agents are forward-looking and make economic decisions on the basis of their expectations about inflation and the business cycle. According to the theoretical literature, central banks with low credibility are confronted with unfavourable trade-offs between price stability and output stabilization. Solidly anchoring inflationary expectations helps central banks achieve low inflation with only minimal deflationary effects on output. Central banks have low credibility when agents believe that they are susceptible to deviating from their promise to keep inflation low in order to achieve short-term gains in output, or to reduce the real value of public debt or to finance budget deficits. This is the case, in particular, when there is a close political relationship between the central bank and the government, when the government is able to corner the central bank into a situation of 'fiscal dominance'. To avoid such a situation and endow the central bank with the necessary credibility, monetary policy institutions need to be designed so as to guarantee the central bank political and economic independence. Central bank independence is thus a strong signal for agents to be confident in the central bank's capacity to fulfil its mandate. In addition, credibility will be substantially enhanced if the independent central bank pursues its monetary policy in a transparent way, providing agents with information about the context in which it has taken its decisions, and explaining and justifying the latter. We provide in section 4.3 an analysis of the conceptual aspects of credibility, before focusing on its main ingredients—central bank independence and accountability. Surveying relevant empirical studies, we report on recent trends in central bank independence and transparency, with a spotlight on LFDCs. We also discuss the available cross-country evidence on the association between central bank independence and inflation performance.

4.2 Price stability and other goals of monetary policy

Monetary policy, broadly understood, has the capacity to determine the general price level and the rate of growth of prices, i.e. the inflation rate.[1] Central banks are therefore mandated to achieve price stability or, at least, to aim for a moderate rate of inflation.

However, most if not all central banks have a broader mandate, explicit or implicit. They are also expected to help mitigate the volatility of domestic output, i.e. to decrease the amplitude and length of economic cycles by pursuing an output

---

[1] This strong assertion can be subject to some qualifications, especially from the side of the fiscal theory of the price level. This theory holds that in circumstances of 'fiscal dominance', it is fiscal and not monetary policy which needs to provide the nominal anchor. See Appendix 5A.

stabilization policy. Finally, they have to take responsibility for the stability of the financial system.

Strong priority is given to price stability in the central banks' mandate, especially in developing countries which have often experienced serious bouts of high inflation. Box 4.1 briefly reviews the cost of inflation, and recalls the arguments behind this crucial priority given to price stability as the main target for monetary policy.

If price stability is not the unique goal of monetary policy—if the central bank also needs to worry about output volatility and financial stability—it may face important trade-offs. It may be a daunting challenge to reconcile the effects of its monetary policy, a single instrument, on three different goals. Giving precedence to one may hinder the other(s). Globally, optimal monetary policy may involve some arbitraging between these three goals. The actual ordering of the goals will depend on the circumstances and the preferences of the government and central bankers. Sections 4.2.1 and 4.2.2 discuss in depth each of these trade-offs, especially for central banks of LFDCs.

The trade-offs between price and output volatility have been studied for many years, starting with the pioneering work of Phillips (1958). The additional goal of financial stability has a long history, but it acquired more urgency with the international financial crisis of 2008. This additional goal has given rise to acute controversies on the use of monetary policy to this end.

4.2.1 The trade-off between inflation and output volatility: theoretical aspects

Central banks have the capacity to use monetary policy to influence not only the general level of prices but also real output. This may be the case because changes in monetary variables do not have an effect only on nominal prices and wages, but also on real variables. There is a consensus that monetary policy can affect output and employment directly in the short run, within a time span of about six quarters. However, the reaction of prices and wages, which is seldom instantaneous, wipes out the effect of monetary policies over the longer run. The more flexible prices and wages are, the shorter-lived the output and employment effects of monetary policy. Indeed, it is the inflexibility of nominal wages and prices in the short run that causes a monetary impulse to have real effects. If all prices and wages were fully and instantly flexible, the monetary impulse would immediately increase them in a proportional way, leaving real balances, real interest rates, real exchange rates—and consequently real output—unchanged.[2] However, this is not

---

[2] Thus, changes in the level of the nominal supply of money do not have real effects. Its effects are only on nominal variables like price level and nominal wages. This property is known as the 'neutrality of money', also as the 'classical dichotomy'.

Box 4.1. The costs of inflation

In evaluating the costs of inflation, the distinction between anticipated and non-anticipated inflation is crucial. With anticipated inflation there are only small costs, like the more frequent repricing of goods in outlet stores or incomes that are pushed to higher unindexed tax brackets when there is progressive income taxation.

On the other hand, with unanticipated inflation the costs can be very high. First, unanticipated high inflation blurs and distorts relative prices. It makes agents believe that changes in relative prices are taking place when in fact they are not. At the same time, some sectors may be late in adjusting their prices so that changes in relative prices actually do occur. The ensuing distortions in relative prices induce a misallocation of resources and hence severe efficiency costs.

Second, high inflation tends to be highly variable, increasing uncertainty, discouraging private investment, distorting allocation between fixed and variable income assets, between real and financial, or between domestic and foreign currency assets. Persistent, high, and variable inflation may well deter the development of an efficient financial market in domestic currency.

Third, distortions in relative prices are conducive to unwarranted wealth and income transfers. Wealth is transferred from creditors to debtors. This may entail intergenerational transfers, as the older are generally creditors while the young are debtors. The transfers of income are also important, from fixed income earners (wage earners and pensioners) to variable income earners (entrepreneurs, traders, all agents that are price-setters). Changes in wealth and income may lead to social conflict that aggravates inflation. High inflation penalizes the poor. While the rich can find ways to protect themselves from it (e.g. with dollarization), the poor have neither the information nor the means to do so.

An ongoing inflation process may, if unchecked, accelerate over time, and may even degenerate into hyperinflation. The costs in terms of foregone output can be very high in a highly inflationary environment. Speculation yields a higher reward than productive activities, and entrepreneurial talent is diverted from production.

High inflation spurs 'defensive' strategies in the public, like indexation of wages, pensions, rents, and so on. Indexation has the undesirable feature that it perpetuates inflation and accelerates it after adverse exogenous shocks. Indexation introduces rigidity exactly when flexibility is most needed to cope with exogenous shocks. The other 'defensive' strategy is dollarization, i.e. the use of a foreign currency in functions of domestic money, with lasting effects. High inflation pushes dollarization, but even when inflation subsides dollarization may continue. Such strong persistence in the long term consequences of short term inflationary shocks is referred to as hysteresis.

the real world. Prices are rigid in the short run, and it takes time to adjust to disequilibria brought about by monetary or real shocks. Firms react to these disequilibria by adjusting their output and employment.

Because monetary policy affects real output in the short run, central banks that pursue a policy of inflation control while simultaneously worrying about output volatility realistically face a well-known trade-off: a restrictive monetary policy designed to reduce the rate of inflation has negative effects on output in the short run; expansionary monetary policy designed to mitigate the effect of a deflationary shock on output will push inflation up. This is a well-known trade-off.

In order to illustrate the challenge that monetary authorities face when they have to address both inflation and output volatility, we use a graphic presentation of the economy's short-term equilibrium, in line with the existing macroeconomic theory developed for AEs. In the simple model, presented in the next three subsections, the equilibrium of output and inflation in the short run results from the interaction between the economy's aggregate supply and aggregate demand. The short-run aggregate supply relationship between output and inflation is captured by the well-known neo-Keynesian Phillips curve (NKPC) (see section 4.2.1.1). The second relationship combines two aspects: the dependence of aggregate demand on inflation; and the systematic behaviour of monetary authorities who influence aggregate demand in order to reach a combination of output and inflation which is consistent with their policy goals. This is the aggregate demand– monetary policy reaction curve (AD_MPR) (see section 4.2.1.2). Both relationships are shown in Figure 4.1 as respectively the NKPC and AD_MPR curves. Short-run equilibrium is given by their intersection.[3] The equilibrium of inflation and output following a negative supply shock is characterized in section 4.2.1.3. We then discuss in section 4.2.1.4 whether and how this type of model, which has strongly influenced the thinking and policy-making in AEs, can be relevant to LFDCs.

4.2.1.1 The Phillips curve

Originally developed by Phillips (1958) as a relationship between nominal wage inflation and unemployment, it has repeatedly been reformulated and is nowadays usually recast as a relationship between the rate of inflation and the 'output gap', i.e. the percentage deviation of actual output from its 'natural' long-run level.[4] Its current formulation has been developed within the New Keynesian macroeconomic approach. This general-equilibrium modelling approach, developed in the

---

[3] This presentation follows Clarida et al. (1999: sections 2 and 3) and Walsh (2000). It is the simplest, 'rock-bottom' model of optimal monetary policy. Its extensions have been numerous and have inspired the development of larger models, for which often only numerical solutions are available. These models are called 'Dynamic Stochastic General Equilibrium' (DSGE) models, whose main features are discussed in Ch. 7. Of various degrees of complexity, they are used to simulate the dynamic path of the economy towards a steady state, once it is hit by a shock, nominal or real. The parameters used for the simulations are either estimated or directly set to calibrated values.

[4] More precisely, the equilibrium level of output one would obtain under fully flexible prices.

1990s and 2000s and inspired by earlier 'real business cycle' models, is based on microeconomic foundations with forward-looking agents, households, and firms, who optimize intertemporally and hold rational expectations. Its Keynesian feature lies in the addition of nominal frictions into the 'real business cycle' framework, imposing rigidities of nominal prices and wages, i.e. abandoning the hypothesis of full flexibility of nominal prices and wages. These features make the New Keynesian approach particularly well suited to study the effects of monetary policy on inflation and on real output.

The following specification of aggregate supply, called the 'New Keynesian Phillips curve' (NKPC), has gained wide acceptance in current New Keynesian macroeconomic models. It features the economy's *supply side*, describing the result of the interaction of firms that set prices and output in the output market and agents who offer labour inputs in the labour market.

$$\pi_t = \beta E_t \pi_{t+1} + \kappa x_t + u_t \tag{1}$$

The current rate of inflation π_t in equation (1) depends on three factors:

- the rational expectation inflation rate, expected for next period $E_t \pi_{t+1}$ and based on information available at the current period t;
- the current output gap x_t;
- a current stochastic supply shock u_t.

All variables are defined in percentage deviations from their long-run (steady-state) equilibrium values. The first factor reflects the role of expectations held by agents about future inflation in determining current inflation. When firms revise their price, expected future inflation is taken into account in setting the new price. The coefficient of expected inflation in equation (1) is β, the discount factor $(\beta < 1)$. The way such expectations of future inflation are formed is, however, difficult to assess in practice. The original NKPC postulates that agents hold rational expectations, i.e. that they behave as knowing how the inflation rate is determined, and as being able to use optimally any information available to make the best forecast, $E_t \pi_{t+1}$. A more realistic approach is the so-called *hybrid* NKPC. It postulates that a subset of agents form their expectation of future inflation in a quite unsophisticated way, picking last period's inflation rate as a good forecast of next period's inflation rate. In this case, the model's expected inflation rate is a combination of $E_t \pi_{t+1}$ and π_{t-1}. We stick, however, to the original version to keep the model's graphic presentation as simple as possible.

The coefficient κ is the key coefficient of the NKPC, as it shapes the trade-off between inflation and output. The degree of nominal price rigidity is the main determinant of κ. This coefficient depends on the proportion of firms which at any given period keep their prices unchanged. The underlying price rigidity in this model was developed by Calvo (1983). It assumes that firms are monopolistic price-setters, and set prices using a mark-up over marginal costs. However, in any given period a fixed proportion of firms do not change their prices. If a firm's prices are rigid, it is optimal for it to adjust its output to the demand it faces. When a firm is offered, randomly, the opportunity to change its prices, it sets them according to current and future expected real marginal costs, the latter being an increasing function of the volume of output, as given by the firm's production function. This is the reason why, in the aggregate, the inflation rate is a positive function of both expected inflation and actual output (or output gap).[5] The larger the degree of price rigidity, the smaller the value of κ. The NKPC in Figure 4.1 exhibits the relationship between inflation π_t and the output gap x_t. The larger the degree of price rigidity, the flatter the curve.

4.2.1.2 The aggregate demand/monetary policy reaction function

Aggregate demand is negatively related to the expected real interest rate, as household consumption as well as household and firm investments decrease when the latter rises.[6] For given expected inflation, aggregate demand is therefore negatively related to the *nominal* interest rate.

In this simple presentation, we shall suppose that the nominal interest rate is the instrument that authorities use to reach their monetary policy goals.[7] By choosing the nominal interest rate, and thereby a level of aggregate demand, they can achieve, more or less closely, a target output gap. Any chosen output gap will be, in equilibrium, associated with a corresponding rate of inflation. Because monetary authorities cannot affect inflation and output gap independently of each other, they cannot obtain their most preferred option, which would be inflation on target and zero output gap.[8] They must choose how to use their instrument, the nominal interest rate, to reach the best balance between two imperfect achievements: too high (low) inflation, relative to target ($\pi_t > 0$; $\pi_t < 0$); too low (high) output, relative to its natural level ($x_t < 0$; $x_t > 0$).[9] This trade-off determines at any time how monetary authorities set their interest rate, given information about the state of the economy that is available to them, in particular taking into account the relationship between π_t and x_t as given by the Phillips curve. By

---

[5] Note that the NKPC is derived from the linearization around steady-state of a complex, non-linear solution to the firms' price-setting equilibrium relationship. Inflation and output–gap variables are thus defined as percentage deviations from their steady-state values.

[6] Durable goods are investment-type goods. Their consumption by households is guided by similar considerations to those that are conducive to investments by firms.

[7] Other monetary instruments, e.g. open-market operations used for targeting monetary aggregates, can be used to target the desired specific nominal interest rate.

[8] This parallels the Tinbergen principle, according to which one needs two instruments to reach two targets simultaneously.

[9] Recall that x_t and π_t are defined as percentage deviations from their steady-state values, and that in steady state, inflation is on target and output is at its natural level $\left(\pi_t = 0 = x_t \right)$.

carrying out such a 'systematic monetary policy' focused on aggregate demand (i.e. x_t), monetary authorities can address deviations of inflation and the output gap from their respective targets in an optimal way, according to the relative weight they assign to their two goals, stabilizing inflation around target and stabilizing output.[10] The result of such an optimal monetary reaction for the two target variables can be described by the AD_MPR relationship shown in equation (2).[11]

$$x_t = -\frac{\kappa}{\xi}\pi_t + v_t \qquad (2)$$

where:

κ is the key structural Phillips curve parameter linking π_t and x_t as discussed above;
ξ is the relative weight monetary authorities attach to stabilizing output $(x_t \rightarrow 0)$ relative to reaching their inflation target $(\pi_t \rightarrow 0)$;
v_t is a stochastic shock which combines two types of shocks: (i) pure demand shocks, unobserved by the monetary authorities when they set the interest rate to target x_t; (ii) the deviation of aggregate demand from target due to imprecise monetary control.

This optimal systematic monetary policy relationship can be interpreted in the following way: when inflation increases, following e.g. a supply shock, the central bank moderates the rise in inflation by reducing the demand for output through restrictive monetary policy. It does so according to its relative preferences: the more conservative it is with respect to inflation (the smaller ξ), the larger the decrease in output it will accept for any tolerated increase in inflation. The AD_MPR curve in Figure 4.1 reflects this optimal accepted trade-off between short-term outcomes for inflation and output. The stronger the central bank is in fighting inflation, the flatter is the slope of the AD_MPR curve in the $\pi_t - x_t$ space. The inverse of the slope of the AD_MPR curve in Figure 4.1 (i.e the ratio κ/ξ in equation (2)) therefore indicates what is often called the 'sacrifice ratio', the percentage decline of output which the central bank accepts in order to decrease the inflation rate by 1%.

---

[10] In this simple approach, we suppose that optimal monetary policy is of the 'discretionary' sort, i.e. set for given expectations of inflation. We postpone to section 4.3.1 the discussion of optimal monetary policy under discretion and under commitment.

[11] As shown by Clarida et al. (1999), this relationship can be derived from the minimization of the expected value of discounted future quadratic losses resulting from the deviations from target for inflation and output, under the constraint given by the Phillips curve:

$$Min E_t \sum_{i=0}^{\infty} \beta^i \left[\xi x_{t+i}^2 + \left(\pi_{t+i} - \bar{\pi} \right)^2 \right] \text{ wrt to } x_{t+i}$$

s.t. $\pi_{t+i} = \beta E_t \pi_{t+i+1} + \kappa x_{t+i} + u_{t+i}$ for all periods.

Solving for the first-order conditions leads to the AD_MPR relationship given in the text, assuming that $\bar{\pi}$, the inflation target, is zero.

4.2.1.3 Equilibrium after a negative supply shock

In the NKPC model, supply shocks are at the root of the trade-off between output and price stability. This challenges monetary policy. If only shocks to aggregate demand were observed, no such trade-off would exist. Monetary policy would intervene, neutralizing the changes in aggregate demand, thereby stabilizing output and automatically bringing prices back to their target level. Supply shocks, on the other hand, move output and prices in opposite directions giving rise to a trade-off between stabilizing inflation and stabilizing the output gap.[12]

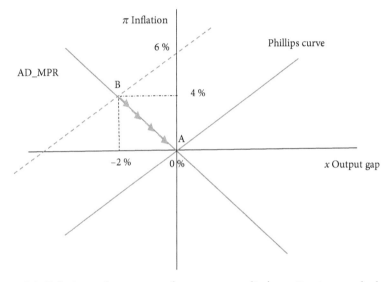

Figure 4.1. Inflation and output gap after monetary policy's reaction to a supply shock

---

[12] Strictly speaking, this is only the case for supply shocks that have different effects on the natural, flexible price level of output and on its efficient, welfare-maximizing level targeted by the central bank. This assumes realistically that there are not only nominal but also real rigidities. It is in this case not possible to simultaneously achieve price stability and the efficient level of output. Price stability would stabilize output at its natural level, but leave a positive gap between output and its efficient, welfare-relevant level. If there are only nominal rigidities, as assumed in the original New Keynesian framework, real effects only arise because firms change their nominal prices in a non-synchronized way. With zero inflation, all firms are satisfied with the existing prices, relative prices are no longer distorted, and output is stabilized at its natural level, which coincides with the efficient, welfare-relevant output level targeted by authorities. In such a context, monetary policy would only need to focus on price stability. This has been termed a 'divine coincidence' by Blanchard and Galí (2007). Mark-up shocks (Clarida et al. 1999: 1667 n. 15) or real wage shocks (Blanchard and Galí, 2007) are however supply shocks that introduce distortions between the welfare-relevant efficient output and the flexible-price, natural output. The 'divine coincidence' thus no longer holds, and monetary authorities are faced with a trade-off between inflation and the welfare-relevant output gap. In open economies, real exchange misalignments will have similar effects. This will also be the case for supply shocks of foreign origin.

To illustrate how monetary policy works in this model, we discuss the case of a *negative supply shock*, which is typically the most difficult challenge for monetary authorities.

We start in Figure 4.1 from a long-run equilibrium (point A), with inflation at the authorities' target level and output at its natural level $\left(\pi_t = 0 = x_t \right)$. Inflationary expectations are fully aligned on the inflation target. A negative supply shock ($u_t < 0$ in equation (1)), which we suppose has some persistence, shifts the Phillips curve upwards, for two reasons. First, the current effect of the shock pushes up prices. Second, expectations for next period's inflation also increase as the shock is expected to persist. Both effects would combine to raise inflation from its initial level of 0% deviation from target to a deviation of 6%, if the output gap were to remain at its initial level. However, authorities will react to this combined shock according to their optimal reaction function, which shapes the AD_MPR curve (see section 4.2.1.2). A restrictive monetary policy is implemented, causing the output gap to become negative in order to mitigate the increase in inflation. This optimal trade-off is illustrated by point B. This represents the economy's short-term equilibrium after the shock and after optimal monetary policy measures have been taken: the increase of inflation is limited to 4%, but at the cost of a temporary output gap of −2%. The more conservative the central bank (the more horizontal the AD_MPR curve), the more output it is willing to sacrifice to check the rise in inflation. Note that, barring other shocks, the economy will return to its long-run equilibrium once the shock has died down and people's expectation of inflation have adjusted to the actual dynamics of the inflation rate. The latter will gradually move back to the inflation target, along the AD_MPR curve, as the adjustment of expected inflation shifts the Phillips curve back to its original position. At point A, output is also back at its natural level.

4.2.1.4 The Phillips curve in LFDCs

The important issue of the optimal trade-off between inflation stabilization and output volatility has mostly been discussed in the context of AEs. A number of influential contributions have shaped the academic discussion on this issue (see e.g. Clarida et al. 1999). This discussion has most often rested on the results of simulations of simple or more complex DSGE models, whose set-up could be expected to provide a rigorous analysis of alternative monetary policy rules and lead to relevant policy recommendations (see Chapter 7). The same approach has also been used in a number of papers devoted to optimal monetary policy in EMEs and LICs (see e.g. Berg et al. 2010).

It is therefore tempting to use the discussions about optimal monetary policy in AEs to inspire policy recommendations for LFDCs. Before taking this step, it is however necessary to (at a minimum) assess whether the key aspects of the theoretical and empirical framework around which the discussion is organized remain relevant for LFDCs.

4.2.1.4.1 The relevance of the Phillips curve in LFDCs

To what extent is the neo-Keynesian Phillips curve, as given by equation (1), a relevant depiction of the link between inflation and output and in LFDCs, even if one considers its hybrid version? The latter is more realistic, as it does not postulate that all agents hold rational expectations of future inflation, but allows some of them to form these expectations in a backward-looking way. Given the low degree of financial awareness which characterizes many LDCs, the hybrid version would clearly be the preferred specification of the Phillips curve for these countries.

Second, beyond the question of how inflationary expectations are formed, a deeper question is to what extent the specific structure and workings of the LFDCs' labour and output markets are reasonably captured with the neo-Keynesian Phillips curve representation of the inflation–output relationship.

To be sure, the Phillips curve has long been seen as inappropriate for countries with large employment in the agricultural and public sectors (Nugent and Glezakos 1982; Wicker 1986). More generally, informality is a key characteristic of LFDCs' labour and output markets. In the informal sector there are no formal contracts. Often, employment is highly dependent on family labour which is remunerated in kind rather than with money wages. Box 4.2 discusses in more detail the implications of informality for the underpinnings of the Phillips curve in LFDCs.

Despite the huge differences in the structure of labour and output markets in LFDCs relative to AEs, there seems to be some consensus in the literature that the Phillips curve remains relevant for LFDCs as a representation of the supply side of the economy. Any theoretical or empirical analysis developed for monetary-policy purposes needs to assess the interaction between price- and wage-setting as well as output supply decisions. More generally, the Phillips curve describes the link between inflation and the business cycle, i.e. real economic activity, a link which also seems to be present in LFDCs, notwithstanding the significant informal sector. A careful characterization of this relationship is therefore clearly relevant for monetary analysis in LFDCs. Some caveats are, however, in order, as it is not necessarily straightforward to adopt in LFDCs the way the Phillips curve is specified and empirically estimated in industrialized countries.

An important point in this respect concerns which business cycle measure should be used in LFDCs to capture the link between real activity and inflation. Which business cycle variable will provide, together with inflation's other determinants, the best inflation forecast, making it possible for authorities to assess with sufficient confidence a possible trade-off between price stability and output stability? According to the theoretical framework that we have discussed, it is the output gap, the percentage difference between the actual and natural levels of output (see equation (1)). However, the concept of natural output, i.e. the equilibrium level of output under fully flexible prices and wages, cannot be easily assessed empirically. Mistakes can lead to the wrong policy prescriptions. This is true in AEs, but much more so in LFDCs, where a large portion of global output

Box 4.2. Informal markets and the New Keynesian Phillips curve

A high degree of informality in labour, goods, and service markets is observed in many developing countries. Loayza (2016: 3) reports that 'the typical developing country produces about 35 percent of its GDP and employs over 70 percent of its labour force informally', with corresponding median figures of 40% and 88% for sub-Saharan African countries. The informal sector has many facets, and it is very difficult to pin down its characteristics, as there is great heterogeneity across countries. The traditional view is that the informal sector grows with workers who cannot find a job in the (preferred) formal market. However, informality may also arise when the costs of formality are too high. These costs arise from taxation and regulatory measures that deal with work conditions, wage policies, severance payments, licences to operate, and so on. There may be a voluntary decision to enter into informal self-employment or into small-scale enterprises operated by mostly, but not only, family labour. The costs of entry to the informal labour market are lower than those of entering into the formal sector, but they are far from being negligible. In particular, the self-employed and the small-scale firms (often very small) face significant difficulties in their access to credit markets. Either they are excluded and have to depend on their own or their family savings, or they have to pay higher risk premiums than enterprises in the formal sector. Often the main source of external finance is from informal lenders who charge steep interest rates.

This high degree of informality is an important factor in the interaction between inflation and real economic activity and the implications thereof for monetary policy. In the informal sector there is great flexibility in wage-setting and high mobility across occupations. In the formal labour market, institutions are frequently rigid, probably more so than in the AEs. While average wage rigidity may not be as significant as in the AEs, there may be other rigidities in the formal sector like administrative price controls on some staples, monopolistic price-setting for services of state-owned enterprises and in some goods markets, or high government subsidies on fuels (from gasoline to cooking liquid), as well as important menu costs of changing prices.

Even in the formal sector, explicit labour contracts and collective bargaining are rare. Moreover, an important fraction of the labour force is in the public sector, where salaries are largely determined by fiscal constraints. The proportion of unionized workers is smaller than in the AEs and in the EMEs. In most cases there is no unemployment insurance, and the informal labour market serves as a buffer in case of job loss.

A key issue, regarding the Phillips curve in the New Keynesian setting, is about the interaction between informal and formal markets confronted with demand or supply shocks, and its effects in terms of output, employment, and price- and wage-setting. This has been addressed by DSGE models that introduce dual labour markets with various types of friction (see Batini et al. 2010 for an early review). Castillo and Montoro (2012) consider an *integrated* labour market, in which firms, because of regulations, face higher hiring costs when they offer a formal job to the more productive workers. These hiring costs into formal employment increase with labour market tightness. When this happens as a result of an aggregate demand shock, firms turn to workers in the informal sector. This softens the increase in the firms' marginal cost. Output prices therefore increase by less and output by more when informal employment can act as a buffer. As the model assumes that the same degree of price rigidity characterizes the two sectors, the Phillips curve is *flatter* when the informal labour market is large.

Other models consider, however, a *dual* labour market: workers who cannot find a job in the formal sector, characterized by real wage rigidities, turn to the flexible-wage informal sector (e.g. Batini et al. 2011; Fiess et al. 2010). The informal sector acts as a shock-absorber with respect to the formal sector. An expansion in aggregate demand increases output in both sectors and puts an upward pressure on wages, especially in the informal sector. Real marginal costs and prices thus rise in both sectors. Countries with a significant informal sector have a low overall wage rigidity as well as a high overall price flexibility—due to more flexible prices in the informal sector (see e.g. Batini et al. 2011). Both these characteristics point to a steeper Phillips curve. O'Connell (2011: ii57) notes: if 'the formal sector is a sideshow relative to a dominant informal economy [...], actual output tracks natural output, and monetary policy has no stabilisation role at all' This implies, at the limit, a *vertical* Phillips curve.

originates in the informal sector, about which data is scarce or imprecise. Some studies of the Phillips curve in LFDCs bypass this issue completely and stick to the approach commonly used in AEs, i.e. measuring the output gap as deviations of actual output from a computed trend output, presumed to give a good approximation or potential natural output (e.g. Barnichon and Peiris 2008, for a panel of sub-Saharan African countries; Rodriguez 2010, for Peru; Arbatli and Moriyama 2011, for Egypt; Ball et al. 2016, for India).[13] All conclude that the output gap has a significant effect on inflation. Other studies go back to the original approach under which the New Keynesian Phillips curve was derived: the original key explanatory variable of

---

[13] Statistical methods used to compute trend output include simple methods (e.g. quadratic trends) or more sophisticated ones (e.g. Hodrick–Prescott filters). Another approach is to estimate long-run equilibrium output through a typical production function (see e.g. Barnichon and Peiris 2008).

inflation is the real marginal cost of output, according to the underlying Calvo (1983) model of staggered pricing. Although deviations of the latter from its steady state can be assumed to be proportional to the output gap under suitable hypotheses, other variables have been used as proxies for marginal costs.[14] Galí et al. (2005) show that the labour income share (or the ratio between real wage and labour productivity) performs, for US data, empirically better than the output gap.[15] Batini et al. (2005) develop for the UK a more general, open-economy approach, adding the relative price of imported inputs as determinant of marginal output costs, and also taking employment adjustment costs into account.

Saz (2011) adheres to the latter approach for his estimation of the hybrid New Keynesian Phillips curve for Turkey, an EME. He argues that the labour share is a particularly weak indicator of marginal costs, given the extent of the informal economy, and therefore uses a composite index of labour and non-labour costs in his Phillips curve specification. Valdivia (2008) follows a similar open-economy approach of marginal costs for Bolivia. Andrle et al. (2015) specify, in their semi-structural New Keynesian open-economy model for Kenya, two hybrid Phillips curves, one for the food sector and one for the non-food sector. Both food and non-food inflation are related to real marginal costs in the respective sector. In each case, the real marginal costs respond to the domestic output gap and to the real exchange rate, the latter defined respectively in terms of food and non-food prices.

All in all, it seems that the Phillips curve approach remains, in its hybrid version, a relevant representation of the supply side of LFDCs' economies. Care must be taken, when the Philips curve is applied to the data, to choose an appropriate and sufficiently broad measure of marginal output costs, taking due account of the country's labour market characteristics and production structure.

4.2.1.4.2 Characteristics of the Phillips curve in LFDCs

Once the relevance of the Phillips curve concept for LFDCs has been accepted, it is its specific empirical characteristics which crucially matter for assessing the trade-off between inflation and output volatility. The following two aspects particularly deserve attention in a Hybrid New Keynesian Phillips curve for LFDCs: the relative degree of backward- versus forward looking behaviour in forming expectations of inflation; and the size of the coefficient of the marginal cost–output gap variable, i.e. the importance of the business cycle in the Phillips curve equation. The slope of the Phillips and the implied dynamics curve of inflation determine the trade-off between inflation and output volatility faced by the monetary authorities.

---

[14] E.g. with a Cobb–Douglas production function.

[15] Specifications with the output-gap variable often lead to insignificant estimates for its coefficient in the estimated Phillips curve equation, even for industrialized countries. On the contrary, Bleaney and Francisco (2017) point, in their panel study of both developed and developing countries, to a strong and statistically significant positive correlation between inflation and the output gap, but a weak and not significant one for low-income countries.

Assuming they have the capacity to influence aggregate demand in a reliable way through monetary policy measures, they can handle this trade-off according to their preferred arbitrage between price stability and low output volatility.

(i) If the Philips curve appears to be *steep*, i.e. if a small change in real economic activity has a strong effect on inflation, placing a strong control on inflation has limited output costs. The Phillips curve is steep when prices are sufficiently flexible, i.e. when firms quickly adapt their prices to changes in their marginal costs, and when marginal costs react sufficiently strongly to changes in real output. Authorities can then implement a restrictive monetary policy when inflation rises above target, following some exogenous shock, without worrying too much about the negative consequences on output of such policy. Indeed, as soon as monetary policy measures start reducing aggregate demand, firms will quickly moderate their price increases, in reaction to reduced sales and reduced marginal costs. This dampens inflation but simultaneously, mitigates the decrease in aggregate demand initiated by monetary policy. Faced with such a quick reaction of inflation to monetary policy, inflation targeting can be achieved with limited resort to monetary policy measures, so that policy-induced changes in output will also be of modest size. A steep Phillips curve therefore facilitates inflation targeting. Its implied downside, however, is that authorities will have to significantly sacrifice price stability if they wish to use monetary policy to stabilize output in face of exogenous shocks.

With a *flat* Philips curve, the opposite reasoning holds. Output costs to maintain price stability will be high, as only a strongly restrictive monetary policy will succeed in subduing inflationary pressures when price rigidity prevails. On the other hand, monetary policy could then be used to help stabilize output in the face of shocks, with only a modest effect on inflation.

(ii) The way expectations of future inflation are formed by agents is another crucial issue that shapes the trade-off between price and output stability. The original New Keynesian Phillips curve postulates that people hold 'rational expectations', i.e. that they know the way monetary authorities act. They react quickly to changes in monetary policy, provided they feel that monetary authorities have strong credibility (see section 4.3). Authorities committed to stabilizing a high-inflation economy will be able to achieve this with a minimum of cumulative sacrifice of output. Indeed, forward-looking and rational firms will immediately adapt their price-setting behaviour to an expected lower-inflation environment, thereby mitigating the degree of restrictiveness of monetary policy to be applied by authorities. Also, theory shows that, when all agents hold rational expectations, authorities experience a more favourable trade-off between price and output stability when they use monetary policy to address shocks to inflation or to output.[16]

In general, however, a significant proportion of agents form their expectations of inflation in a backward-looking way, which is the assumption of the hybrid New Keynesian Phillips curve. If this were the case for all agents, monetary policy action would be totally deprived of any beneficiary announcement effects on current inflation. Also, backward-looking expectations of inflation increase the persistence of changes in current inflation and output. After an exogenous shock to current inflation, it takes time for inflation, as well as for output, to return to their respective target, even if the shock itself does not persist. The same holds for current monetary policy interventions whose effects also become persistent. This 'endogenous' inertia of inflation and output greatly complicates monetary policy decisions with respect to the inflation-output stability trade-off.[17]

What do empirical estimates of the Phillips curve for developing countries tell us? They are, unfortunately, contradictory. Rodriguez (2010) suggests that the Phillips curve for Peru was very flat during 1980–2005. The point estimate of the output gap coefficient on current inflation is 0.03—while the implied proportion of backward (forward-looking) agents is estimated at 60% (40%). This result of a flat Phillips curve is in line with the results of the calibrated New Keynesian model featuring informal labour markets proposed by Castillo and Montoro (2012) (see Box 4.2). Other studies point, however, to a steeper Phillips curve in developing countries. Ball et al. (2016) find a significant and substantial reaction of inflation (more precisely of core inflation) to the output gap in India over 1996–2014—with a point estimate of the output gap coefficient on current inflation of around 1.0.[18] They also report a slow adjustment of expected inflation. Saz (2011) reports for Turkey (2005–9) robust and reasonably high correlations (of around 0.5) between inflation and the constructed marginal cost index, as well as between the latter and the output gap. His estimates of the hybrid New Keynesian Phillips curve imply that a large majority of firms take a forward-looking perspective in forming their expectations of inflation. They also imply, given the Calvo model of price-setting used in this study, that in any given month 65% of firms change their prices, indicating a mean duration of prices changes of 1.5 months (Saz 2011: 32). This points to quite a high degree of price flexibility and,

---

[16] See e.g. Clarida et al. (1999, section 4.2).
[17] See Walsh (2010: Section 8.4.5.)
[18] This means that a 1% increase in the output gap increases on impact the core inflation rate by 1% (see equation (1)). Core inflation is defined in this study as the weighted median inflation rate based on wholesale prices. Core inflation thus excludes all large changes in individual prices of goods and services included on the consumption price index. Those concern, most often, changes in the prices of food and energy.

together with the other results, to a steep Phillips curve. Arbatli and Moriyama (2011) provide estimates for Egypt (2005–10) which are consistent with a relatively steep Phillips curve: the point estimate of the output gap coefficient in the Phillips curve is 0.49. They also report that the proportion of agents forming their inflation expectation in a forward-looking way can be estimated to be about two thirds.

Studies of price-setting behaviour at a micro-level, based on price changes observed for individual items included in a given price index, at a much disaggregated level, can also provide useful information about the degree of steepness of the Phillips curve in developing countries. Indeed, for any given sensitivity of real marginal costs to the business cycle, the Phillips curve will be steeper, the lower the degree of price rigidity. Studies for AEs indicate that, at the product level, the duration between price changes is between one and two quarters.[19] The limited number of available studies for developing countries tend to show a lower degree of price rigidity. Alidou (2014) reports for Ghana, for 1990–2013—a period during which inflation was at times quite high, with a peak of 60% in 1995—an average frequency of price changes of 94% in a given month, i.e. an almost-monthly adjustment of prices in items included in the CPI. Kovanen (2006) reports for CPI prices in Sierra Leone over 1999–2003—a period of relatively moderate but volatile inflation—a median monthly frequency of price changes of about one-third, indicating an average duration of prices of about 2.6 months.[20] Food prices in particular, appear to be adjusted quickly, virtually every month. Assessing in this study the determinants of changes over time in the frequency of price changes, the author points to past monthly inflation rates as well as to inflation uncertainty as key explaining factors. Nchake et al. (2015) document price-setting behaviour by retail outlets in Lesotho and South Africa over 2002–9, when inflation in both countries was relatively moderate. They find that the monthly frequency of price changes is 41% for Lesotho and 17% for South Africa (an average duration of respectively 2.4 and 5.9 months) These results for South Africa confirm that of a previous study by Creamer et al. (2012), who estimated, over the 2001–7 period, the average price duration for CPI components at 5.0 months and at 6.1 months for items in the producer prices index. Julio et al. (2009) evaluate consumer prices in Colombia to be relatively sticky over the 1999–2008 period of relatively moderate inflation, with a mean monthly frequency of price changes of about 21% (a median of 12%). This is significantly

---

[19] See Vegh (2013 box 8.1, pp. 366–7), which reports the results of studies which analyse the degree of stickiness of individual prices in 20 industrialized countries and 4 emerging market/developing countries. Most reported durations of price changes are between 4 and 6 months. With the exception of one study for the US, the average durations are all above 3 months for industrialized countries. Reported studies for Brazil, Chile, and Sierra Leone feature shorter durations.

[20] For a product i, the duration of price changes expressed in months d_i is inversely linked to their monthly frequency f_i by the following relationship: $d_i = -[1/\ln(1 - f_i)]$ (see e.g. Gagnon 2007: 12), of which $d_i = 1/f_i$ is an approximation.

lower than the 46% mean frequency found by Medina et al. (2007) for approximately the same period (1999–2005) for Chile, a country with a lower inflation rate (2.7%) than Colombia's, but with a memory of a hyperinflation in the not too distant past and accompanying indexation practices—a possible explanation of the paradox, as suggested by Julio et al. (2009). Gagnon's (2007) study of Mexico (1994–2004) also calls attention to the link between inflation and the frequency of price changes: he finds a mean monthly frequency for non-administered prices of 33% for the 1995–7 high-inflation sub-period (average annual inflation of 27%) and of 23% for the 2003–4 low-inflation (average annual inflation of 4%) sub-period, with corresponding average durations of 3 and 7 months).[21]

It is somewhat difficult to generalize from the limited set of micro-level studies of price-setting behaviour, given the heterogeneity in the macroeconomic context of the case study countries, as well as the differences in periods of analysis and in measurement methodologies. One can, however, conclude that most of the reported studies point in the direction of a higher degree of individual price flexibility in developing countries than in AEs. This suggests, in turn, that the result of a steeper Phillips curve found by the several macro-studies reported in this section may find its origin in the larger degree of flexibility of prices observed at the level of individual products.

4.2.1.4.3 *The trade-off between price and output stability in LFDCs: some policy implications*

With a close-to-vertical Phillips curve, monetary authorities face a relatively favourable trade-off between price and output stability. Given the modest output cost of achieving a given reduction in inflation, authorities will be induced to pursue price stability more vigorously. Note that this may particularly be the case in countries where the informal sector is large and where, accordingly, prices are quite flexible and the Phillips curve is particularly steep. Nevertheless, the LFDCs are known to be frequently subject to huge supply shocks, like food and energy price shocks. As illustrated in Figure 4.1, these cost-push shocks, represented as upward shifts in the Phillips curve, simultaneously deteriorate the welfare relevant output gap and increase inflation. It is those types of shock which justify the policy relevance of the price–output trade-off, even for LFDCs. When such shocks are large, price stability cannot be the only target pursued by authorities. Even with a reduced direct output cost, monetary policy actions designed to keep strict price stability will amplify the economic downturn caused by the shock. These output costs cannot be ignored and need to be taken into account when

---

[21] Gagnon (2007) notes that the increase in the *average* frequency of price changes with inflation is only observed for an annual rate of inflation higher than 10–15%. Below this threshold, price changes are also often price decreases, which weaken the link between the *average* frequency and the inflation rate.

monetary policy decisions are taken, so as to strike a proper balance between the authorities' two conflicting targets. We discuss external price shocks more in depth in section 5.3.

The importance of the size of the informal sector poses an additional challenge for monetary policy in LFDCs. When choosing their optimal trade-off between price and output stability, monetary authorities need to be able to properly assess movements in both target variables. Monetary policy acts through changes brought about in aggregate demand, affecting output and prices in both the formal and informal sector. Prices in the informal sector can be expected to be reasonably well included in the global price index used for defining the inflation target. However, it is questionable whether output originating in the informal sector is reliably measured and fully included in GDP or in other usual business cycle indicators. If only formal output is reasonably well observed, changes in it could still be sufficiently informative of changes in global output, if there exists a significant positive correlation between outputs of both sectors, formal and informal. The few existing empirical studies of the cyclical interaction between informal and formal markets provide, however, rather ambiguous results. For example, Fiess et al. (2010) study this interaction for four Latin American countries and conclude that the informal sector reacts pro-cyclically in the case of a positive demand shock to the non-traded sector—it expands—but reacts counter-cyclically in the case of a negative shock to the traded sector—it also expands—reacting in this case as a buffer.

Taking monetary policy decisions on information only based on movements in formal output can thus clearly be challenging when uncertainty about the co-movements of output in both sector is high. It certainly points to the necessity for monetary authorities to address this uncertainty, preferably by developing appropriate statistical tools to acquire good perception of the structural interactions between the two sectors and ultimately to achieve a comprehensive measure of their economy's global real activity.

4.2.2 Financial stability as an additional goal of monetary policy

The financial crisis of 2008 in AEs raised concerns that central banks had in the pre-crisis period put an excessive focus on price stability, neglecting the warning signs of the build-up of important financial imbalances and failing to act upon those. The question of whether financial stability should fall within the purview of central banks is not really arguable. Whether their mandate to preserve financial stability is explicit or implicit, they are entrusted as the financial system's lender of last resort. Also they are responsible for organizing an efficient payment system and for guaranteeing its integrity. As such, they are called to intervene when a financial crisis breaks out. All central banks have done so over the last decades; indeed, they have done their best to avoid full disruption of the financial system and to mitigate effects of the crisis on real economy activity. To this end, they have resorted to a variety of measures, not only expansionary monetary policy but also more 'non-conventional' measures.[22]

In this context, monetary policy has been given the responsibility of 'cleaning up' after the crisis (Mishkin 2011). Limiting the contribution of monetary policy to financial stability to this sole role of cleaning up after the crisis was the dominant view among central banks in AEs, up to the 2008 financial crisis. The alternative view—of 'leaning against the wind' and of raising interest rates, to penalize over-rapid credit growth or to prick nascent financial asset price bubbles, so as to quell early enough any emerging financial imbalance—was deemed complicated, inefficient, or even counterproductive. It was argued that financial imbalances that have the potential to lead to a financial crisis are often difficult to identify as such. Rapid bank credit growth may just be accompanying and facilitating a strong, productivity-led growth of the economy or financial deepening in LFDCs. Raising interest rates too quickly or too strongly in such a situation could be counterproductive.

Also, the interest rate is seen as too blunt an instrument to be useful for checking ongoing booms in financial asset prices (Agénor and Pereira da Silva 2013: 12). If the boom is fuelled by exuberant expectations of ever higher prices in the near future, the interest rate would need to rise to quite high levels to be effective in checking the boom. Such a policy move would obviously have detrimental effects to the real economy, especially to interest rate-sensitive sectors, such as housing and construction, or to small and medium-sized enterprises, whose working capital is highly dependent on credit.

Both scepticism over the capacity of monetary policy to help prevent the outburst of financial crisis and huge confidence in its ability to clean up after the crisis -contributed to an attitude of 'benign neglect' with respect to the build-up of financial imbalances. Faced however with the huge and protracted costs generated by the 2008 financial crisis, central banks had to reconsider their position and reinterpret their financial stability mandate. Many central banks in the AES and EMEs shifted their focus and adopted a preventive approach to financial crises, targeting systemic risk in the financial system within a broad 'macro-prudential'

---

[22] Non-conventional monetary policy instruments have been used by the central banks of the main AEs to avoid the implosion of the financial system. They include: (i) enhancing access to low-cost central bank liquidity for banks and extending it to other financial intermediaries; (ii) expanding global liquidity through large-asset purchase programmes ('quantitative easing'); (iii) pushing down yield spreads by sterilized purchases of mortgage-backed securities, corporate bonds, and covered bank bonds or by swapping short- for long-term securities in the central bank balance sheet ('credit easing'). In addition, (iv) negative policy rates on central bank deposits were introduced to induce banks to increase their lending; finally (v) a new policy of 'forward guidance' aimed at keeping also long-term rates at a low level by giving financial markets the assurances that monetary policy rates would remain at their bottom level for a prolonged period of time.

framework. Such a framework goes beyond pure monetary policy measures and involves specific instruments of prudential supervision. A central bank that takes into account financial-stability aspects when it sets its policy interest rate or adjusts its reserve requirements clearly faces a trade-off with the two other goals which are part of its mandate, price and output stability. The extent of the trade-off between financial stability on one side and price and output stability on the other is difficult to evaluate. This trade-off has an intertemporal dimension, as monetary policy is to be used to influence the probability and the depth of a crisis happening in the medium term (IMF 2015a).[23] This means augmenting interest rates above what would be strictly necessary to keep the best output–inflation trade-off in the short run. To reinforce financial stability and thereby expect less—or at least less severe—future crises, one needs to accept lower output and lower inflation, possibly for several periods, i.e. until the threats to financial stability have subsided.

Such a difficult trade-off can be mitigated, if not avoided, by resorting to macro-prudential instruments.[24] Such measures, such as countercyclical capital buffers, loan-to-value limits, and dynamic loss provisioning, directly aim at dampening financial cycles (IMF 2015a).[25] Implementing these regulatory instruments within the domestic financial sector in an efficient way, and managing them so as to quickly quell developing threats to financial stability, helps central banks to use monetary policy, prioritizing price and output stability. To do so, central banks will need to maintain a close collaboration with the other regulatory authorities in charge of prudential control, so as to minimize possible conflicts between financial stability and the two other goals. This is particularly important for central banks whose mandate does not authorize them to directly set the instruments of macro-prudential control. Since the global financial crisis, many central banks have however seen their financial stability mandate enlarged, and do now have the opportunity to exercise effective macro-prudential control.

---

[23] One can use calibrated DSGE models to assess these trade-offs by simulating optimal policy responses to shocks in economies with financial frictions, and by adding financial stability as argument of the intertemporal welfare function to the usual ones, price and output stability. Reviewing these studies, IMF (2015a: 21) suggests that welfare improvements of pure 'leaning against the wind' policies are generally 'small and state (or shock) dependent'. However, these models are still too stylized to be able to capture the dynamics of fully-fledged financial crises, so that no definite conclusion can yet be drawn.

[24] See e.g. Woodford (2012: 22). He justifies introducing financial stability into the welfare function in an inflation targeting-cum-output gap strategy within a model with financial frictions and endogenous crisis states. However, he also notes that the 'leaning against the wind' role of monetary policy may be less crucial if effective countercyclical macro-prudential instruments exist—instruments that 'could ensure that significant variations in marginal crisis risk never occur, even when conventional interest rate policy is used purely to minimize the variability of inflation and the output gap'.

[25] The list of systemic risk prudential control instruments also includes household debt-to-income ratios, reserve requirement ratios, bank leverage ratios, limits on interbank exposures, limits on domestic- and foreign-currency loans, concentration limits on bank portfolios, capital surcharges on systemically important financial intermediaries, and levies/taxes on banks (see Cerutti et al. 2017).

Financial stability is clearly an important goal shared by all countries, advanced, emerging, and low-income. However, the extent to which this goal will be addressed by a 'leaning against the wind' monetary policy, as discussed, will vary from country to country, depending on the country's financial structure, its monetary policy transmission mechanism, and the scope and efficiency of its instruments of prudential control. In many LFDCs, interest rates set by the central bank have a limited effect on bank credit and on banks' interest rates, given the rudimentary money markets and the structural excess liquidity in the banking system (see section 2.3.3). Any 'leaning against the wind' monetary policy may thus fall short in achieving the expected quick and strong curtailing effect on bank credit, while nevertheless ultimately generating (if maintained over several periods) an unwarranted restrictive effect on spending and output.

In many LFDCs, the limited role to be assigned to a 'leaning against the wind' monetary policy is also justified by the following observation: banking crises in these countries in the past have typically *not* been caused by a credit and asset price boom–bust scenario, followed by a sudden increase in banks' non-performing loan portfolio and in losses on their marketable net assets, as has been the case in many crises in AEs and EMEs.[26] Instead, banking crises have often been triggered by external shocks hitting an already fragile banking sector. The vulnerability of the banking sector in many LFDCs could have been the confluence of various interacting factors: inefficient or imprudent lending practices (e.g. inadequate risk assessment and control procedures, connected lending); heavy government intervention in lending decisions; strong concentration of loans in a handful of commodity exporting firms; heavy exposure to exchange rate risk; weak prudential supervision and unsustainable macroeconomic policies. When the financial system is initially already in a fragile position, any sudden external shock can precipitate the banking crisis. Acute negative shocks to the terms of trade impact the export sector and have a strong recessionary effect on global output that raises the banks' ratio of non-performing loans to total assets. For LFDCs which are on some kind of fixed exchange rate regime, a sizeable overvaluation, generated by inappropriate macroeconomic policies, distorts relative prices in the economy, and weakens its tradable goods sector and therefore indirectly the banks' balance sheets. A sharp devaluation, at some point necessary to correct the exchange rate misalignment, can threaten financial stability. Devaluation may have contractive effects on real income and output, as discussed in Box 6.3. As a consequence, banks will be confronted with borrowers who face severe difficulties in servicing their credit obligations. This risk is enhanced in dollarized economies, as borrowers in foreign currency see the domestic-currency value

---

[26] Marchettini and Maino (2015) e.g. explain that cyclical credit indicators are not good predictors of financial crisis for countries with low financial depth. Indicators relating to the structural safeness of a financial system perform better for these countries.

of their debt increased by the devaluation (see section 6.5.2.1). Banks may fall into insolvency as a consequence.

Because sizeable exchange misalignment affects the soundness of the banking sector and because subsequent realignments, often sudden and sharp, are a direct threat to financial stability, LFDCs aim at maintaining a stable level for the real exchange rate. The desideratum of a stable real exchange rate acquires even more significance in the case of heavily dollarized countries. To the extent that monetary policy helps to achieve this rate, it directly contributes to its third goal—financial stability. But this is attained, not through intervening in the financial cycle with a 'leaning against the wind' policy in a strict sense, but by pursuing traditional goals of global long-term macroeconomic stability (see also section 6.4.5.2).

The majority of LFDCs are now engaged, at various speeds, in a process of financial deepening and closer international financial integration. The history of financial crises teaches us that financial liberalization and deregulation need to be carefully framed and supervised in order to avoid pitfalls which can lead to sudden short-term capital inflows, excess credit, unsustainable leverage of financial intermediaries, and asset bubbles, as well as their reversals. The limited role assigned in LFDCs to a 'leaning against the wind' monetary policy to guarantee financial stability implies the adoption, as in AEs and EMEs, of a set of macro-prudential instruments. Macro-prudential regulations will be tailored to the country's financial and institutional development, taking into account its capacity to monitor and enforce observance by relevant domestic and foreign financial intermediaries. Whether or not the central bank is directly in charge of macro-prudential policy, it is still its full responsibility to ensure that its monetary policy is adequately backed by an efficient framework of prudential rules, guidance, and surveillance.

4.3 The importance of institutional credibility for monetary policy effectiveness

When discussing the contribution of monetary policy to macroeconomic stability, both theory and practice stress the crucial importance of credibility. A central bank is credible when private agents and markets are confident that it is fully committed to pursue clearly announced goals, and is giving a strong priority to price stability in the medium to long run. A credible central bank manages monetary policy in a way that always remains consistent with these announced targets. Credibility is deemed essential for a central bank to actually achieve its main goal, price stability, at the lowest costs in terms of foregone output.

In what follows, we first discuss some conceptual issues regarding monetary policy credibility before discussing how it can be achieved. We focus particularly on central bank independence and on transparency of the monetary policy process, both of which are recognized as essential to generate high credibility for policy-makers.

4.3.1 Monetary policy credibility: conceptual aspects

4.3.1.1 The inflation bias of discretionary monetary policy

Recognition of the crucial role of credibility for public policies in general, and for monetary policy in particular, goes back to Kydland and Prescott (1977) and Barro and Gordon (1983), who pin down the outcomes of policies when agents rationally anticipate actions by policy-makers and act upon them in their best interests.[27]

Schematically, the reasoning in the Barro–Gordon (1983) model goes as follows. The monetary authority pursues a twin goal of minimizing inflation as well as output variability around their respective target levels (see section 4.2.1). The output target level is set, possibly under political pressures, at a level which is higher that the natural level output, the level the economy achieves once all prices and wages have adjusted.[28] The authorities act in a discretionary way, i.e. they do not feel bound by any initial commitment, nor by any rule nor by their own reputation. Because there is no effective commitment to its inflation target, the central bank is tempted to engineer a 'surprise inflation'. When the inflation rate is higher than the expected rate, i.e. the rate agents have actually embedded into their wage negotiations and their price setting, output increases in the short run, along the Phillips curve (see section 4.2.1.1). A surprise inflation thus pushes output above its natural level and provides authorities with short-run benefits. This is tempting, even for well-meaning and competent policy-makers. However, agents anticipate this incentive and take into account the likelihood of authorities succumbing to this temptation, and adjust their inflationary expectations accordingly. Prices and wages are reset and, as a result, output does not rise above its natural level and inflation is higher than the authorities' target rate. This outcome of strategic interaction is known as the 'inflation bias' generated by 'discretionary' monetary policy: inflation is above the target level set by the central bank without this in any way improving the output side of the central bank's loss function, as output

---

[27] The concept of a policy's credibility is closely linked to the concept of 'time (in) consistency'. A policy is time-consistent if, being optimal at period t, it remains optimal as time passes—at period t+1, t+2, . . . Only time-consistent policies are fully credible, as by definition there is no incentive for the policy-maker to change them. Taking the strategic interaction between policy-makers and rational agents into account, it appears that many policies are not time-consistent and therefore a priori not credible, unless complemented by specific commitment mechanisms.

[28] Authorities would set a target level of output which is beyond the natural rate of output if they deem the latter to be inefficient, as a result of real frictions in the economy, provoked e.g. by wage rigidities. Political reasons may also play a role if the central bank is not independent of the government (see section 4.3.2).

remains at its natural level. Appendix 4A gives a detailed presentation of the Barro–Gordon (1983) model, explaining how the inflation bias is the outcome of the interaction between agents who hold rational expectations and a monetary authority which has incentives to renege on its promises.

The 'excess inflation' outcome of a discretionary monetary policy is therefore clearly a dead-weight loss for society. Eliminating this inflation bias is thus a desirable objective. This can be achieved when monetary authorities are credible, i.e. if they are able to convince agents that price stability is their ultimate goal and that they will not deviate from this commitment and engineer a surprise inflation, whatever the short-term gains they could extract thereby in terms of additional output.[29]

The theoretical literature (e.g. Clarida et al. 1999; Galí 2018) also points to an additional advantage of credible monetary policies. When agents believe that the central bank is really committed to its medium-term inflation target, the central bank is in a better position to react to supply shocks. Because a credible central bank is able to dampen agents' expectations of future inflation, a persistent negative supply shock will have less inflationary impact during the whole period of adjustment to the shock. The credible central bank thus globally faces a better output–inflation trade-off over the adjustment period to the shock than if it had low credibility or no credibility at all.[30] Low credibility thus gives rise not only to an inflation bias but also to a 'stabilization bias'—the weakening of output stabilization policies.

The credibility of monetary policy can therefore be considered as some kind of public good which society should strive to provide. A way to do this is to design monetary policy institutions within which responsible authorities have the

[29] Short-term gains in output may not be the unique motive tempting monetary authorities to 'cheat' agents by engineering a surprise inflation. A reduction in the real value of public debt denominated in domestic currency or the collection of additional seigniorage (both examples of inflation tax) are also strong motives for authorities to succumb to the temptation of surprise inflation.

[30] This important aspect of credibility is discussed in detail in Clarida et al. (1999: 1681–1682), Galí (2008: 102–6), and Galí (2018: 93), the main argument being the following: A fully credible central bank which reacts to a persistent cost-push shock with a restrictive monetary policy has the capacity to redistribute and smooth over time the deviations of inflation and output from their efficient allocation. Compared to the results a discretionary policy could achieve, inflation will increase by less and output will decrease by less at the time of the shock. During the period of adjustment to the persistent effects of the cost-push shock, inflation will remain lower, but so will output. This redistribution and smoothing of welfare costs across time is globally welfare-improving. This can be achieved by the fully credible central bank because it can influence the expectations of future inflation and future output gaps of rational agents. The latter understand that the central bank's monetary policy reaction to the shock is not limited to the current period but will be followed through until the shock has died out. They adjust their expectations accordingly. A central bank with no credibility cannot make commitments about future monetary policy and has no influence on agents' expectations of future inflation and output gaps. Acting in a discretionary way, it can only affect the current output gap to dampen the shock's current inflationary effects. As a result, its policy actions lead to a larger decrease in output and a lower dampening of inflation than in the full-credibility case. More generally, optimal stabilization policy leads to excessive fluctuations both in output and in inflation when the central bank has no credibility, relative to what is achievable when it benefits from full credibility on behalf of agents.

capacity to generate credible policies. How to ensure credibility for monetary authorities' future actions, through reputation, rules, commitment, or binding promises, is one of the key issues in designing monetary policy institutions capable of delivering price stability.

4.3.1.2 Solutions to enhance credibility

Several solutions to the credibility problem have been advocated by the theoretical literature and to a large extent implemented and experimented with over the last 20 years in many AEs as well as in developing economies.

Rogoff (1985) recommended leaving monetary policy in the hands of a 'conservative' central banker, a policy-maker with a substantially stronger aversion for inflation than the median voter. The central banker's reputation of being a hardliner on inflation, with a consistent track record in this respect, would help minimize the inflation bias of a discretionary policy while simultaneously preserving his capacity to stabilize output shocks.

An alternative approach is to impose rules which constrain policy-makers to adhere to a low inflation target, and which 'tie their hands', keeping them from engineering inflation surprises. Fixed exchange rates, of the hard peg variety, are a popular example of such a rules-based policy. Authorities constrain themselves to align their inflation target to that of the country to whose currency they have chosen to peg their domestic currency. By promising to keep the peg, they 'tie their hands' and renounce to any autonomous discretionary monetary policy. In the late 1970s and early 1980s, a monetary targeting rule was introduced in several AEs, without much success, as the relationship between money growth and inflation became unstable and unreliable after some time.[31] The other rule-oriented credibility mechanism is strict inflation targeting: the central bank announces a target rate of inflation and gives it full priority, with maximum transparency about its current policy actions and those intended in the future.

Too tightly specified rules have advantages but also drawbacks, the main drawback being the inability of monetary authorities to stabilize the effects of short-term shocks, e.g. of commodity price hikes in LFDCs. Output stability could be enhanced at the expense of temporary deviations from the price stability goal. A particularly strong commitment to the two types of rule mentioned above is therefore not necessarily desirable. It is also probably unnecessary to achieve robust credibility for monetary policy.

History teaches that fixed exchange rates can work as efficient nominal anchors, even if they allow for the possibility of readjustments when fundamental

---

[31] Friedman (1968) promoted a strict rule implying that a central bank should let the money stock grow at a constant rate. In practice no central bank has followed such a strict rule, preferring to announce a target range for money growth, adapting the range to current economic situation and, quite often, tolerating persistent deviations from it.

imbalances in the country's balance of payments occur. Monetary aggregate rules have never been strictly enforced, to say the least. Similarly, inflation targeting has never been implemented in its strictest form. Flexible inflation targeting, which allows for transparent and well-justified deviations from the inflation target in the case of temporary output shocks, has become the norm among central banks which have opted for this type of rule-based mechanism of creating credibility. Chapter 6 discusses in detail the specific aspects, particularities, advantages, and disadvantages of these three types of nominal anchors.

Whether authorities are of the inflation hardliner, conservative central banker type, or whether they adhere to a specific policy rule with sufficient commitment and consistency, the key point is that the private sector must be convinced that authorities are determined to stick to their target of keeping inflation low over the medium term. Expectations of inflation then converge to the level targeted by the authorities. Deviations of actual inflation from target are also easily corrected when authorities have sufficient credibility. If a temporary supply shock pushes inflation above target, the convergence towards it will be quicker and it will entail smaller output losses if expectations remain anchored to the medium term target. If this were not the case, because of the authorities' low credibility, restrictive monetary measures taken by authorities to dampen inflationary pressures would be seen by agents as recurrent negative inflation surprises. If the authorities wished to converge rapidly on their inflation target, protracted output losses would be the price they would have to pay.

4.3.2 Central bank independence

The dismal performance of monetary policy authorities in keeping inflation in check, not to mention achieving price stability, as observed in many countries, has been attributed to the domination of a country's central bank by the government. An over-deep implication of the central bank in the country's political process can only result in nurturing fiscal dominance. Short-term-minded politicians, underestimating the social costs of inflation, would pressure the central bank to accommodate monetarily bulging fiscal deficits and to manage monetary policy in line with the political business cycle. This is particularly true in LFDCs, where the risk of fiscal dominance is particularly high.[32] Such a view has been largely backed by empirical research and theoretical analysis, and has led to the recommendation that central banks should become independent from politicians, in order to be able to pursue credibly their principal goal of price stability.

---

[32] See section 5.2.

4.3.2.1 Characteristics of central bank independence

The three salient features of central bank independence (CBI) are as follows: (i) political independence, which implies guarantees that the appointment and removal of central bank governors and of other members of the board do not suffer from political interferences and that their mandates are sufficient long and do not overlap with those of government officials; (ii) a clear legal mandate concerning monetary policy goals, with price stability as the main objective; (iii) economic independence in the sense that the central bank has the capacity to use its monetary policy instruments and manage its balance sheet independently of government interventions. Importantly, the latter includes the prohibition of direct financing of the government and, more broadly, the public sector—barring exceptional circumstances, declared by a qualified majority of the central bank's board. This latter feature of CBI is especially relevant for LFDCs.

A useful distinction between *goal independence* and *instrument independence* was made by Debelle and Fischer (1994). With *goal independence* the central bank sets its targets, like a specific number for the inflation rate. However, in many countries such targets are determined outside the central bank, for instance by the ministry of finance, although this is frequently done in consultation with the central bank. Goal independence would be a facet of what we have called above political independence. With *instrument independence* the central bank enjoys complete freedom in managing its instruments, like its policy interest rate.

Allowing the central bank to gain its independence has in many countries necessitated major changes in the institutional framework within which day-to-day monetary policy is pursued and has implied major adjustments in the statutes of central banks. Legal independence is however to be distinguished from de facto independence. Several central banks are not legally fully independent from the government, which is often their only or majority shareholder, but have full economic independence in the sense that they have the capacity to pursue their policies without political interference. The essence of CBI seems to lie in instrument independence. Many independent central banks may not be goal-independent but they are always instrument-independent. This is for example the case of the Bank of England, where the government sets the numerical inflation target, and of the Central Bank of Brazil, where the inflation target is set in coordination with government ministers. Hammond (2012: 8) observes that such joint determination of the numerical target by the central bank and the government was practised in most of the 27 inflation-targeting countries surveyed, but that all the central banks benefited from instrument independence.

4.3.2.2 Trends in central bank independence

Many studies have tried to measure the degree of 'de jure' (i.e. legal) CBI by using a synthetic indicator. This indicator aggregates the coded values given to the different legal or regulatory characteristics of the monetary policy framework that are likely to contribute to CBI.[33] The synthetic indicator of CBI probably most often used in empirical studies for various sets of countries and periods is the Cukierman, Webb, and Neyapti (1992) indicator.[34] Arnone et al. (2007) performed a large comparative analysis for 68 central banks in the late 1980s and 162 central banks in 2003. They conclude that political autonomy of central banks in developing countries has been much lower than in EMEs and AEs. On the other hand, it appears that central banks in developing countries have significantly increased their economic (operational) autonomy between the two reported time periods.

Garriga (2016) offers the most complete coverage of CBI to date, covering 182 countries for 1970–2012, using the Cukierman et al. (1992) indicator. Figure 4.2 presents Garriga's latest data (2012) for CBI together with 2011 data for the synthetic Financial Development Index that we have constructed to identify our set of LFDCs (see Appendix 1A). Data are reported for two sets of countries: the 95 LFDCs and the 80 medium to high financial development countries. Note that only countries for which data for both variables were available are included. The CBI index ranges from 0 to 1, the FD index from 1 to 7.

The average CBI score is 0.58 for LFDCs and 0.65 for the countries with a higher level of financial development. LFDCs are thus characterized by a somewhat lower CBI, on average. However, although statistically significant at 1% level, this difference in the average value of CBI indexes is not very sizeable. Figure 4.2 also shows, more generally, that CBI levels exhibit a large variance across countries, for any given level of financial development. Only a weakly positive association between CBI and the level of financial development can be detected statistically across the 175 countries. CBI levels in 2012 therefore do not seem to be very much constrained by the level of financial development experienced at that moment, contrary to what one could have expected.

The differences in CBI across countries observed in the snapshot reported in Figure 4.2 need, however, to be interpreted as the result of the combined effects of different factors that may have influenced a country's monetary institutions over the previous 20 years. They need to be assessed in a historical perspective, but identifying them is a challenging task. Dincer and Eichengreen (2014), for example, report results from a 100-country study which show that CBI has increased over the 1998–2010 period in the more open economies and in countries that

---

[33] Coding assigns values, e.g. in a range from 0 (lowest level of independence) to 1 (highest level of independence), to legal characteristics of the monetary framework within different categories (like political and economic autonomy). E.g. the shorter the term of office of the governor, the lower the assigned score. Also, in regard to the way a central bank's objectives are defined, 0 will be assigned if those objectives do not include price stability, 1 if the latter is the only objective and if the central bank has the final word if this conflicts with the government's objectives. The scores of each category are then weighted before being added up to obtain the overall CBI score.

[34] Grilli et al. (1991) propose an alternative indicator which uses a methodology similar to that used later by Cukierman et al. (1992).

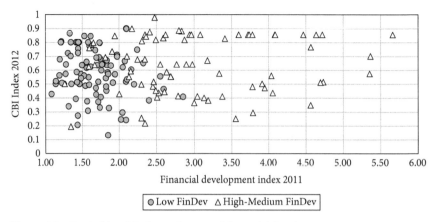

Figure 4.2. Central bank independence and financial development
Sources: CBI index 2012: Garriga (2016); FDI index.

have experienced IMF conditionality; on the other hand, they do not find evidence that higher institutional quality reinforces CBI. Polillo and Guillén (2005) insist on the sociological and political aspects of central bank independence. They hypothesize that countries embark on reforms towards increased CBI mostly under external pressures, driven by international economic, cultural, and political competition in the context of increased globalization. They provide empirical evidence for such a 'normative effect', indicating that CBI increases when a country's exposure to foreign trade and foreign investment becomes larger and when it becomes involved with IMF lending. They also document an 'imitation effect': countries opt more easily for stronger CBI when their trading partners or competitors have independent central banks.

Garriga (2016) reports that CBI has evolved at differential paces across regions. While 'de jure' CBI has improved worldwide, the largest and more rapid increase in CBI has been observed in the group of Eastern Europe and 'post-Soviet' countries, where the most recent (2012) average level of CBI is even above the one observed for Western Europe and North America. Latin America also achieved a strong, though gradual, increase in CBI, reaching a level close to, but still somewhat below, the Western Europe and North America average. Asian countries have also been on an upward trend, though not as successfully, remaining in 2012 below the Latin American average. In Africa and the Pacific, the evolution towards increased CBI has been timid, the average of the index improving only modestly from the level observed in the 1970s—a level close to those observed at that time in Western Europe, North America, and Latin America. Garriga (2016) also notes that not all institutional reforms of central banks have increased CBI. Indeed, of the 382 reforms she has identified for the whole set of countries over 1970–2012, 14.7% have in fact decreased CBI.[35] This indicates that the observed worldwide trend of increasing CBI is not necessarily irreversible.

Relative to this issue, there have been concerns that the 2007–8 financial crisis weakened CBI. The reason for this is that many central banks had to intervene strongly to ensure the stability of the financial system, and had to do so in close cooperation with the political authorities. Also, central banks, in the aftermath of the crisis, have seen their mandate extended to include financial stability, which not only adds an additional trade-off to the pursuit of price stability (see section 4.2.2) but also requires closer coordination with government bodies. The pursuit of a truly independent monetary policy thus becomes more difficult (see e.g. Fischer 2015). Finally, many central banks have taken increased risks on their balance-sheet positions by resorting to non-conventional monetary instruments, possibly thereby weakening their financial independence from the government.[36] To assess this threat to CBI, De Haan and Eijffinger (2016) investigated whether significant changes in CBI, as measured by the Cukierman et al. (1992) index, have occurred since the great financial crisis. Comparing for 78 countries CBI levels in 1995–2007 with CBI levels in 2007–8, they conclude that their data do 'not suggest that CBI has decreased after 2007' (p. 14).

The observation that de jure CBI is not necessarily associated with de facto CBI has prompted researchers to look for an alternative indicator of CBI, based on actual behaviour rather than on legal features. This may potentially be important in countries where institutions are often weak, as in LFDCs, and where there can be a wide gap between formal rules and current practice. Cukierman et al. (1992) propose in this case to use the turnover rate of central bank governors (TOR) as a better indicator to measure effective CBI. The underlying argument is that a more rapid turnover indicates a lower CBI, as it suggests the possibility of the

---

[35] Bolivia is a case in point for LFDCs: the central bank's economic independence was weakened during the past decade when central-bank lending to public enterprises was made possible again. For EMEs, other examples are Hungary and Turkey where their respective governments have recently taken steps to exert a closer political control over their country's central bank.

[36] Many central banks have on their balance sheet accumulated bonds with long maturities and/or with non-negligible risk of default through large asset purchases, and have financed them by issuing short-term liabilities held by commercial banks as reserves. A possible general increase in interest rates could weigh heavily on central banks' profit and loss account and debilitate their current budget. Central banks in LFDCs that are called upon to act as LOLR and bail out banks can also end up with large credit risks on their balance sheet. In general, central banks cannot become insolvent, as they have the ability to issue non-interest-bearing liabilities, in principle without limit. However, resorting to seigniorage cannot be unlimited, but above all endangers price stability (see section 5.2.1). Also, central banks that have accumulated a large amount of foreign-currency liabilities cannot really rely on seigniorage to spend their way out of their financial woes. Recapitalization of the central bank by the treasury may therefore sometimes be the only way to allow the central bank to pursue its price stability goal while at the same time fully assuming its financial stability responsibilities (Buiter 2008: 11). This assumes that these two goals are fully shared by public authorities and the central banks, in which case concerns about central bank independence are moot.

government changing the governor frequently and picking the monetary authorities most favourable to their own policies, or the government firing those who offer strong resistance. However, such an interpretation of the turnover rate indicator is not straightforward and possibly doubtful or even misleading. Indeed, according to De Haan and Eijffinger (2016), who review the political-economy aspects of choosing turnover rates as indicator of CBI, the most important objection is that 'a high tenure of the central bank governor could also reflect that the governor behaves in accordance with the wishes of the government' (p. 14).

4.3.2.3 Central bank independence and transparency

Changes in a country's institutions designed to enhance the central bank's independence and endow the latter with sufficient legal guarantees have in general been associated with two additional major changes in the monetary policy framework. The first was to require greater accountability from central bank officials. This was seen as necessary to preserve the legitimacy of central bank policy decisions. Central bank officials, now entrusted with greater political and economic autonomy, had not been elected, and their performance could at best be assessed in hearings with the legislative bodies. The second change was to require greater transparency about the monetary policy decision process. This was also intended to alleviate concerns about insufficient democratic legitimacy of an independent central bank. This meant in practice requesting the central bank to announce its goals and publicly justify its policy decisions, explaining their motivation, the context in which they were taken, and how they could be expected to serve the announced goals. Beyond the aim of enhancing democratic legitimacy, a crucial feature of transparency is that it decreases uncertainty surrounding the monetary policy process, thereby contributing to a better anchoring of inflationary expectations. This helps the central bank not to lose credibility when it deviates from its announced inflation target in a discretionary way, in reaction to an external price or output shock. Because the central bank explains the reasons for the actions it takes, agents recognize that the deviation from the inflation target is only temporary and does not threaten the medium-term price stability goal. A transparent way to implement monetary policy thus enhances central bank credibility and improves monetary policy effectiveness.

The methodology used by researchers to measure the transparency of the monetary process is similar to that used to measure central bank credibility. For a given central bank, a synthetic transparency index is computed as the weighted sum of coded scores assigned to different characteristics reflecting the transparency of the different aspects of the monetary policy process. These aspects include the degree of openness with respect to the policy objectives pursued, the analytical methods (e.g. models, forecast techniques), and the economic data used to support monetary policy decisions within the chosen monetary framework (e.g. inflation targeting). The transparency features included in the indexes also focus on the way monetary policy decisions are reached, e.g. whether detailed reports are made available—notably a regular 'Inflation Report'—on how extensively the policy measures taken are motivated and justified, on how quickly and comprehensively they are communicated, e.g. whether the minutes of the Monetary Committee are published within a short time, and so on.[37]

Dincer and Eichengreen (2014; 2015) report transparency scores for 120 central banks for 1998–2014. Similarly to what has been observed for CBI, they note a general upward trend of the transparency index. This shows that CBI and transparency go hand in hand—which is to be expected, as both reflect the same concern, namely that of improving the effectiveness of monetary policy. The extent of transparency reached differs widely, however, across income groups. Over the whole period, central banks in high-income countries display the highest transparency index, the low-income countries the lowest. All groups show increased transparency over the period, most of the improvement being observed from 1998 to 2006. Some fallback is also noted for the upper-middle income group after 2007. Dincer and Eichengreen (2014) note, unsurprisingly, that the transparency index is higher when countries have stronger political institutions, deeper financial markets, more open economies, and a flexible exchange rate.[38]

Figure 4.3 focuses more precisely on the differences between LFDCs and the AEs and EMEs, combining the data on CBI and transparency for those countries for which both the Dincer and Eichengreen transparency index and the Garriga CBI index were available. Panel A shows for individual countries of each of the two groups (51 LFDCs and 69 other countries) how central bank transparency has evolved from 1998 to 2014. The scatter graph of panel B displays for the most recent available year (2012) the degree of association between individual countries' transparency and independence indexes.

Two main observations can be made. First, the earlier observation that transparency has increased is confirmed for almost every individual country. The average level of transparency of LFDCs has increased from 2.0 to 4.6, that of the other countries from 5.0 to 7.9, within the 0–15 range of the index. Although the typical LFDC country had lower central bank transparency, both in 1998 and 2014, relative to the other countries, and quite significantly so, there is nevertheless a large heterogeneity among the two groups. Second, one observes, for the most recent period for which the respective indices are available, that CBI displays, across countries, a positive, highly significant association with central bank transparency. This is to be expected, as a country's achievements in terms of both central bank independence and transparency reflect the degree of the country's willingness to implement the necessary institutional reforms. However, as can also be

---

[37] The 'Inflation Report' has been for many countries an important and significant instrument in developing an explicit inflation targeting strategy (see section 6.4).

[38] The latter seems to imply that the need for transparency is higher with flexible exchange rates. According to Dincer and Eichengreen (2014: 213), this is so because, with flexible exchange rates, 'success of maintaining a peg no longer suffices for verifying the ability of the central bank to attain its monetary policy goals'.

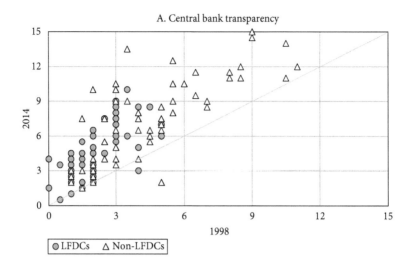

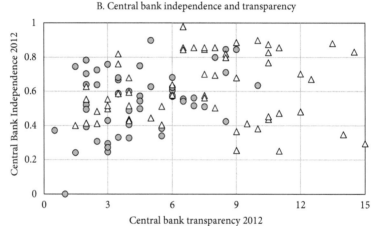

Figure 4.3. Central bank independence and transparency

Sources: Data for central-bank independence are from Garriga (2016) and for central-bank transparency from Dincer and Eichengreen (2015: table 1a).

observed, there is a huge heterogeneity between countries in this respect: some central banks score low on the transparency scale but are very independent; very transparent central banks may have low independence.

4.3.2.4 Effectiveness of central bank independence and transparency

4.3.2.4.1 *Central bank independence and inflation*

Since the early 1990s, numerous empirical studies have tried to assess the extent to which CBI mattered for keeping inflation low. Early studies concluded that there existed a significant negative link between de jure CBI and inflation for AEs.

This is, for example, reported by Alesina and Summers (1993) for OECD countries in 1955–88. Evidence for developing countries was found to be much weaker: Cukierman, Webb, and Neyapti (1992) conclude that de jure CBI was indeed, in 1950–1989, inversely related to inflation for industrial countries, but that this was not so in developing countries, in which the relationship was not statistically significant. However, a significant link between CBI and inflation was found for developing countries when the alternative measure of 'de facto' CBI, the turnover rate of central bank governors, was used.

These early studies gave rise to many others, which differed in many dimensions.[39] Klomp and de Haan (2010) identified 59 cross-country or panel studies, published or not, carried out from 1991 to 2006, and performed a meta-regression on the results of these studies. A meta-regression synthesizes the results of a set of studies with respect to a crucial parameter—in this case the parameter of the CBI index in the inflation equation—while taking into account the specific characteristics which differentiate one study from another.[40] The authors conclude from their results that there indeed exists a negative and significant relationship between inflation and legal indicators of CBI in OECD countries. However, the results are sensitive to the CBI indicator and the estimation period used. They also indicate that for developing countries a negative association between inflation and CBI can be established when the central bank turnover rate is used as CBI indicator.[41] Later studies broadly confirm that CBI matters for inflation, but also that results are not unambiguous and are quite sensitive to the sample used.[42] Garriga (2016) notes in this respect that, for a simple specification of the inflation process, the coefficient of her legal CBI index is negative and statistically highly significant in a large sample (182 countries, yearly data 1970–2012), both for developed and for developing countries. However, this is not the case when the same methodology is applied to more restricted samples used in other studies. Agoba et al. (2017) study the relationship between legal CBI and inflation for a set of 48 African countries over the period 1970–2012. Their results fail to show a clear negative effect of CBI on inflation, except when this explanatory variable interacts with financial depth indicators, suggesting that a sufficiently high level of financial development is a condition for CBI to reduce inflation.

[39] The number of countries included, the dependent variable (average inflation, a dummy for low/high inflation performance, even logs of inflation for countries with extremely high inflation rates), the CBI indicator used (legal or turnover rate), the control variables (degree of openness, the exchange rate regime, financial depth), the cross-section or panel data approach . . .

[40] The meta-regression of Klomp and de Haan (2010) focuses on the estimated t-statistics of the coefficient of the CBI indicator and takes into account the meta-independent variables. The latter reflect the characteristics of the study (all coded as dummy variables) such as CBI indicator type, method of estimation, control variables included in the specific study, estimation period, and type of publication. The estimated constant of the meta-regression is taken as the 'true' value of the t-statistic of the CBI coefficient on inflation, as estimated by the 59 studies.

[41] Klomp and De Haan (2010), however, note that the TOR indicator of CBI may be endogenous to the inflation performance, in which case the results of studies using this indicator may be biased.

[42] See e.g. Acemoglu et al. (2008), Crowe and Meade (2008), and Arnone and Romelli (2013).

Many factors can account for the disparity of results obtained in testing the link between CBI and inflation performance. The major, although inevitable, weakness of the CBI indicators, whether de jure or de facto, lies in their capacity to measure CBI in a sufficiently precise way, along with the difficulty of isolating CBI from other contemporaneous changes in the country's monetary policy framework or, even more broadly, in its institutional organization. Also, there may possibly be methodological problems in the empirical approach.[43] However, despite these caveats, we may on the whole conclude that there exists a body of empirical evidence that seems to confirm the expected, theoretically founded, link between CBI and low inflation performance, even if the evidence is not always systematic and unambiguous. These studies contributed to sustain empirically the case for CBI, forcefully advocated by the monetary theory developed in academic circles. In addition, the case for CBI was empirically reinforced by the success stories of early adopters of an inflation-fighting strategy which prominently included CBI.[44]

4.3.2.4.2 Central bank transparency and inflation

In one of the very few studies of the effects of *central bank transparency* on inflation, Dincer and Eichengreen (2014: 236) note that central bank independence and transparency 'go together' as they find their origin in the same search for greater monetary policy effectiveness.[45] Using their synthetic transparency index, they report, for a sample of 100 central banks for the 1998–2010 period, that greater transparency is associated with lower volatility of inflation and also, though less consistently so, with a lower average inflation level. Combining both central bank independence and transparency indices as explanatory variables, they conclude (p. 233) that 'the two variables are jointly significant in most specifications' used to explain the average level and the variability of inflation.

---

[43] Among the issues are the possible endogeneity of the CBI index in the inflation regression and the existence of latent factors which influence both inflation (the dependent variable) and the CBI index (the independent variable). Changes in political regimes may both influence inflation rates and initiate central bank reforms which will be reflected as changes in the CBI indicator. Also, differences in society's attitude towards inflation aversion can determine their differences both in inflation performance and in the degree of CBI they choose. If the CBI index is endogenous, it is difficult (if not impossible) to assess the effect it might have on inflation performance as least squares estimates will be biased. Proper estimation with instrumental variables may take care of the endogeneity bias in the inflation–CBI equation, but are not readily at hand.

[44] These includes mostly AEs, like New Zealand, the UK, and the countries now members of the Eurozone. Remember that for developing countries, the leverage exerted by international institutions also played a major role in the advancement of CBI. IMF-sponsored adjustment programmes pushed countries into severing the link between the central bank and the government so as to weaken the risk of fiscal dominance, which is a major explanatory factor of many countries' dismal inflation rates.

[45] Crowe and Meade (2008) also address this issue but in an indirect way. Using the variance of the private sector's forecasts of inflation as a measure of the quality of public information about monetary policy, they find that increased transparency is associated with more accurate private-sector forecasts, suggesting that transparency may operate in decreasing forecast errors of market participants and better anchoring their expectations.

4.3.2.4.3 Real effects of central bank independence and transparency

Systematic empirical studies on the effects of central bank independence and transparency on real variables are virtually nonexistent. The very early and unsophisticated, correlation-based study by Alesina and Summers (1993) on CBI and its macroeconomic performance concludes, for their sample of 16 AEs, that although CBI reduces the level and variability of inflation, it does not have a discernible effect on real variables (real interest rates, unemployment, growth). The panel data study by Garriga (2016) reports a globally positive association between CBI and growth in developing countries (but not in AEs) and a negative association between CBI and unemployment in AEs (but not for developing countries). Such studies do not pretend that their results are evidence of a strict causal link between CBI and real variables. Their results may therefore not hold in a fully-fledged econometric specification, similar to those used in assessing the effects of CBI on inflation. To our knowledge, no such study exists. The existing preliminary evidence seems, however, to indicate absence of any harmful effect of CBI on real variables. As pointed out by Fischer (2015: 4), it does not appear that there is a cost to the documented benefit that CBI helps restrain inflation.

4.4 Summary

This chapter has focused on two key aspects of the monetary policy process: (i) the trade-off between the three goals which fall within the purview of central banks—price stability, output stabilization, and financial stability; and (ii) the role of central bank credibility in enhancing the efficacy of monetary policy as well as the contribution of central bank independence and transparency in reinforcing this credibility. We now briefly summarize the main points of this discussion, with a particular focus on aspects which specifically concern LFDCs.

The trade-off between price stability and output stabilization is epitomized in the neo-Keynesian Phillips curve. The flatter the Phillips curve in the inflation–output gap space, the more costly it is, in terms of lost output, for monetary authorities to bring down inflation, e.g. after a cost-push shock. The degree of price rigidity is the key determinant of the shape of the Phillips curve: the less flexible the prices, the flatter the Phillips curve. Our survey of empirical estimates of the Phillips curve in developing countries, and of studies of price-setting behaviour at a micro-level, leads to the conclusion that the Phillips curve in LFDCs is relatively steeper than in the AEs, as a consequence of a substantially higher degree of price flexibility. This characteristic can reasonably be traced back to the existence in LFDCs of large informal product and labour markets, characterized by high price and wage flexibility respectively. LFDCs therefore enjoy a relatively favourable trade-off between price stability and output stabilization. As a result, monetary authorities in LFDCs have often, not unsurprisingly, chosen to give higher priority to the former. This standpoint is reinforced, in countries with a large informal sector and a weak statistical infrastructure, by the difficulty of measuring changes in the global output gap. However, two specific features of LFDCs suggest that output-gap stabilization should not altogether be excluded from policy priorities: their particularly high vulnerability to cost-push shocks, with strong effects on output; and the relatively high persistence of inflation expectations, which implies a slower response of actual inflation to restrictive monetary policy and therefore a higher persistence of the associated negative output gaps.

LFDCs also manage monetary policy to preserve financial stability. LFDCs are particularly concerned about avoiding the overvaluation of their real exchange rate and its likely follow-up, an abrupt exchange rate crisis with sharp negative balance-sheet effects on businesses and banks. In tranquil times monetary policies aim to avoid significant exchange rate overvaluation while simultaneously pursuing the goal of price stability. In turbulent times, when the exchange rate rapidly depreciates, monetary policy is used to rein in the exchange rate fall, closely synchronizing interventions in the foreign exchange market and changes in the policy interest rate. Monetary policy thus can avoid or, at a minimum, attenuate the costly output costs that financial crises often entail.

Central bank credibility is particularly important for LFDCs. Theory suggests that central banks with low credibility face an unnecessarily high rate of inflation, as well as a less favourable trade-off between price stability and output stabilization. Empirical studies linking inflation to measures of the degree of CBI have broadly corroborated the negative relationship between both variables implied by theory, although not unequivocally so. A central bank benefits from credibility if it is able to instil confidence in the monetary policy it plans to implement and in its unwavering commitment to fulfil its mandate, which prominently includes price stability as a medium-term goal. Such confidence is destroyed when the central bank is at the behest of the country's government, for whom short-term output gains or easy monetary financing of public-sector deficits often prevail over the price stability goal. The latter situation is not uncommon in LFDCs where 'fiscal dominance' is frequent, directly resulting from a functional relationship between the central bank and the government. It is in this context that independence of central banks from the political process has been advocated as an institutional means to enhance credibility. Empirical measures of CBI indicate that it is at present still significantly weaker in LFDCs than in other countries, but also that much progress has been observed over the last 20 years. Recommendations of the IMF have played a significant role in this evolution, as well as (more diffusely) peer pressure induced by globalization.

Finally, another important ingredient of central bank credibility is transparency of the monetary policy process. Greater transparency contributes to central banks' legitimacy. As importantly, it increases the confidence of economic agents in the central bank's goals and in the seriousness with which it will pursue them.

This boosts credibility. Greater central bank credibility in turn increases monetary policy effectiveness. Again, LFDCs appear to have at present lower central bank transparency scores than other countries. Improvements over the last 20 years have been observed, but have remained modest.

One can thus conclude that wide scope for improvement remains, in terms of both central bank independence and transparency, for those LFDCs wishing to enhance their central bank's credibility and policy effectiveness.

APPENDIX 4.1

The Barro-Gordon model and the inflation bias of discretionary monetary policy

The Barro-Gordon (1983) model has three key hypotheses as ingredients:

(i) Monetary authorities try to achieve the optimal balance between their twin targets: deviations of the rate of inflation π_t from its target (say 0%) and deviations of output from a given target level. Authorities choose a target output level which is higher than the natural level, which they consider too low because of various real inefficiencies, e.g. real wage rigidities. Authorities choose their optimal inflation rate taking the agents' expected inflation rate as given, thus implementing a discretionary monetary policy.

(ii) The economy is described by a New Keynesian Phillips curve (of the type of equation (1) in section 4.2.1.1) according to which the output gap—the difference between output and its natural level—increases in the difference between actual inflation π_t and expected inflation.

(iii) Agents have rational expectations: they understand how the economy works and are able to make the best forecast of the actions taken by the authorities. Their rational forecast of equilibrium inflation is noted $E[\pi_t]$. Rational expectations are equivalent to perfect foresight when there are no stochastic shocks.

In its simplest version the Barro–Gordon model can be explained in a one-period framework and under the hypothesis that interaction between agents takes place only within one period and that there are no shocks. The interaction between the two 'players', the authorities and private agents, is illustrated in Figure 4.4, which is adapted from Figure 22.4 in Barro and Grilli (1994: 441).

The line labelled $\pi_t = \Theta\left(E[\pi_t];...\right)$ reflects the authorities' decision to implement, through monetary policy, the inflation rate π_t that is consistent with their optimal inflation–output mix. This inflation rate is an increasing function of agents' expected inflation rate $E[\pi_t]$. Indeed, suppose that agents initially expect zero inflation—the target authorities have announced. Authorities then set a positive inflation rate, so as to benefit from the increase in output this surprise inflation will generate. However, they also have to bear the cost of positive inflation. The resolution of this trade-off determines π^0, the optimal inflation rate that corresponds to zero expected inflation. When agents expect $E[\pi^s]$, the

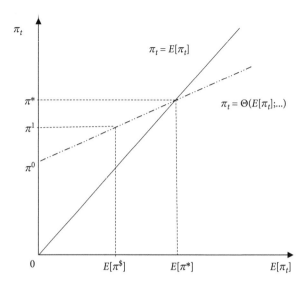

Figure 4.4. The inflation bias of discretionary monetary policy

authorities similarly set a higher inflation rate, again in order to engineer surprise inflation. However, for the same inflation surprise and therefore the same output effect, the cost of higher inflation now weighs in the authorities' welfare function relatively more than the benefit of higher output. This dampens the optimal increase in inflation, which increases from π^0 to π^1, i.e. by less than the rise in expected inflation from 0 to $E\left[\pi^\$\right]$. The slope of authorities' optimal response to changes in expected inflation is thus less than 1.

The 45° line labelled $\pi_t = E\left[\pi_t\right]$ describes how private agents' inflation expectations react to changes in the inflation rate chosen by authorities. Under perfect foresight, agents understand the optimal strategy pursued by the monetary authorities and set their expectations accordingly.

Equilibrium occurs at the intersection of the two lines, at π^*. This inflation rate simultaneously satisfies the authorities' optimal discretionary strategy and corresponds to the agents' rational forecast. The disturbing aspect of this equilibrium is that it entails a positive rate of inflation without any output gains, as there is eventually no inflation 'surprise'. If no inflation surprise is possible, given the rationality of agents' expectations, a preferred equilibrium for both the private sector and monetary authorities would be an actual, perfectly anticipated, zero inflation rate—the point of origin in Figure 4.4. However, this cannot be an equilibrium under discretionary monetary policy. As indicated above, monetary authorities would have, for $E\left[\pi_t = 0\right]$, an incentive to choose a positive rate of inflation. Since agents recognize this incentive, $E\left[\pi_t = 0\right]$ is inconsistent with rational expectations, and the non-cooperative equilibrium ('Nash equilibrium' $\pi^* = \Theta\left(E\left[\pi^*\right];...\right)$ is the unique possible equilibrium. The positive inflation which characterizes this equilibrium is often referred to as the outcome of the *inflationary bias* of discretionary policy. Only this equilibrium is time-consistent, in the sense that neither the central bank nor the agents have any incentive to change their policy or their expectation of inflation. More desirable outcomes— equilibria with $\pi < \pi^*$ —are not time-consistent and therefore not credible. They can only be achieved if authorities find a way to persuade agents that the announced inflation rate will actually be implemented—that they will not renege on it and resort to surprise inflation.

5

Monetary Policy

Dealing with Fiscal Constraints and External Price Shocks

5.1 Introduction

In Chapter 4 we discussed the main issue of monetary policy faced by central banks, the necessary arbitrage between two main conflicting goals that fall within their mandate: achieving price stability and attenuating output volatility. The stability of the financial sector is a third goal that comes under their responsibility, in coordination with the supervisory authorities. This complicates their main task. Achieving these three goals systematically and with maximum efficacy requires a high degree of credibility from monetary authorities. The credibility enjoyed by the central bank is itself crucially determined by its independence from the government.

In this chapter we examine two significant challenges the monetary authorities face in the exercise of their broad mandate, particularly in LFDCs: managing the constraints imposed by the fiscal features of their economy, and reacting to major external price shocks.

In all countries, but particularly in LFDCs, fiscal issues are extremely important in defining the reach of monetary policies. Often, central banks are called to finance the gap between the budget deficit and available market finance. Deficits are frequent because of weak taxation powers and rigid expenditures. Expenditures expand in good times, particularly for commodity-producing countries, but do not contract sufficiently in the cyclical downturn. Financing the deficit with borrowing in the market is often difficult: domestic debt markets are usually still in their infancy, access to the international private capital market is limited, and borrowing from international financial institutions often carries high conditionality while disbursements are slow. The government's frequent reliance on central bank monetary financing often has undesirable consequences for price stability, making the central bank unable to fulfil its mandate and undermining its credibility. The major threat is 'fiscal dominance', i.e. the subordination of monetary policy to fiscal needs. In the first section of this chapter, we analyse, at a conceptual and empirical level, the different aspects of the interactions between fiscal and monetary policy.

A second major challenge for monetary authorities in many LFDCs is how to address the consequences, for the domestic price level and for economic activity,

Monetary Policy in Low Financial Development Countries. Juan Antonio Morales and Paul Reding, Oxford University Press.
© Juan Antonio Morales and Paul Reding 2021. DOI: 10.1093/oso/9780198854715.003.0005

of changes in international commodity prices. In this chapter we consider shocks to the external price of the two commodities that weigh heavily in the economies on many LFDCs: oil and food.

We provide a theoretical analysis of the monetary authorities' options with regard to the domestic effects of these shocks on prices and activity. For each commodity we distinguish between net exporters and net importers. We mostly focus on the case of oil shocks, then extend the analysis to food shocks, given sufficient similarities between the two. Monetary policy's reaction to the shock will vary according to whether the country is a net exporter or net importer of the commodity. For oil exporters, many problems arise from the incomplete coordination between the central bank and the government that benefits on impact from the windfall income brought about by the price hike. In any case, for net exporters and importer alike, monetary policy will need to address the trade-off between mitigating the direct and indirect inflationary effects of the price increase and the negative output effects of a restrictive monetary policy. In addition, the policy responses will differ according to the type of exchange rate regime.

5.2 Fiscal constraints on monetary policy

Coordination between monetary and fiscal policy is clearly one of the main challenges faced by LFDCs. In this section we give an in-depth analysis of how fiscal policy can constrain monetary policy. We first discuss how seigniorage results from the inability of the government to meet its intertemporal budget constraint by raising taxes, reducing primary expenditures (i.e. expenditures excluding interest payments on government debt), and borrowing in the market. Seigniorage reflects the government's command of real resources obtained by issuing money. In general, high inflation risks are linked to high seigniorage. We provide some illustrations of the importance of seigniorage in selected LFDCs. We present the various modalities of fiscal dominance discussed in the theoretical literature and examine how they may be applied to the context of LFDCs.

5.2.1 Central banks, government financing, and seigniorage in LFDCs

As discussed in section 1.3.2.1, central banks in LFDCs, like many central banks in the AEs, started as purveyors of fiduciary money (bills and coins) to the economy. The issuing of currency was largely, although not uniquely, determined by fiscal needs. The financing of governments by central banks went further ahead after the latter were granted a monopoly on the issuance of money and when they progressively abandoned the gold standard.[1] On too many occasions, governments could borrow from their central banks whatever amount they needed to finance the deficits that could not be financed by borrowing from the market. Often governments in LFDCs called the central bank to finance programmes and projects of the public sector at large, including those of state-owned enterprises. In addition, central bank credits at subsidized rates to favoured sectors, as well as sales of foreign exchange at preferential, non-market rates, are to be viewed as operations guided by fiscal concerns, as stressed in IMF (2004). Similarly, fiscal motivations were at play when the central bank used administrative measures, like high reserve and statutory liquidity requirements (that often are met with government bonds), to mop up the liquidity it originated in the first place. These forms of financial repression were driven by fiscal needs.[2]

Many LFDCs still find it difficult to wean their central banks from the historical tradition of being the financiers of their governments. Because of the weak taxation powers of governments, many (though not all) LFDCs have resorted to seigniorage, often extensively and frequently. Seigniorage is the amount of real resources that the central bank can command from the issuance of money. It plays the complementary role of financing the budget shortfall. Fiscal deficits can be financed, partially or totally, with seigniorage, which is added to debt financing or substitutes for it (see Box 5.1). Notice that this link leads to a close relationship between debt management and monetary policy.

'Printing money' and other forms of seigniorage alleviate fiscal distress and allow governments to avoid the (generally) costly repudiation of public debt. With recourse to seigniorage, governments can still remain solvent. In other words, they can still stay within the limits of their intertemporal budget constraint. Equally important from a political viewpoint, seigniorage avoids the accumulation of arrears to non-financial 'preferred' claimants, like government's employees or pensioners.

---

[1] Before the establishment of central banks, private banks could issue currency notes, generally backed by gold. They were often lenders to the government, but their loans were constrained by the gold standard. The central bank monopoly, coupled with the abandonment of the gold standard, gave more space to the borrowing of governments.

[2] An extreme case of this form of financial repression surged in the eve of the Bolivian hyperinflation of the 1980s. The required reserves in foreign currency of the banking system deposited with the central bank were lent by the central bank to the government to meet the latter's obligations to foreign creditors. Then, when the central bank could not return the deposits in foreign currency to the banks, because of the failure of the government to repay its debt in dollars, the latter enacted in 1982 a de-dollarization measure. This measure stipulated a forced conversion of debt contracts in foreign currency into domestic currency. This administrative form of de-dollarization caused capital flight and accelerated inflation. The natural financial alternative for the government to satisfy its needs would have been to issue bonds in foreign currency in the domestic market. The success of this action would have depended on the willingness of the public to buy the government's securities, and the demanded yield would probably have been higher than the interest paid on the central bank reserves. That this path was not followed suggests a strong form of financial repression. It must however be noted that the domestic market for government bonds did not exist at that time, although it could have been created from scratch.

Box 5.1. Seigniorage and government financing

Seigniorage is defined as the real resources captured by the sovereign as a result of its monopolistic privilege of issuing base money through the central bank. The demand for base money is the sum of the demand for currency by the public and for reserve deposits at the central bank by financial intermediaries, amongst whom it is the ultimate means of settlement (see section 1.2.3.3). Any new issue of base money for which there is a corresponding demand gives rise to seigniorage (S), as defined by $S \equiv \dot{B}/P$ where $\dot{B}$ is the period change (indicated by a dot above the character) in the nominal monetary base and P the price level. When expressing this in continuous time, we get:

$$S \equiv \frac{\dot{B}}{P} = \frac{\dot{B}}{B}.\frac{B}{P} = \mu.b \tag{1}$$

where μ is the continuous growth rate on the nominal monetary base B and b is the real monetary base (B/P). Defining π as the inflation rate, we can express the relative change in the nominal monetary base μ as the sum of the growth rate of real balances b and the inflation rate (the relative change in P):

$$\mu = \frac{\dot{b}}{b} + \pi \tag{2}$$

S can thus be shown to be the sum of two components:

$$S = \left(\frac{\dot{b}}{b} + \pi\right).b = \pi.b + \dot{b} = T_{\text{infl}} + \dot{b} \tag{3}$$

The first component is the inflation tax $(T_{\text{infl}} = \pi.b)$. The inflation tax reflects the decrease in the real value of outstanding base money. When inflation is positive, people need to increase their holdings of currency, just to keep unchanged their real balances. The resulting increase in nominal base money reflects a transfer of real resources to the issuer.

The second component originates in the desired changes in real balances. It can be positive even when inflation is nil. For example, an increased demand for real balances can result from higher transactions in a growing economy or from a decreasing opportunity cost when inflation abates.

The relationship between seigniorage and inflation is a non-linear one: when inflation increases, the inflation tax component of S rises (the 'tax rate' increases), but the demand for real balances will decrease (the 'tax base' decreases), thereby mitigating the inflation tax receipts. Beyond a sufficiently high rate of inflation, S will start declining with further increases in π. This non-linear relationship between S and π is known as the 'seigniorage Laffer curve'. Note also that, for a given inflation rate, S increases with the demand for real base money. High reserve requirements, still very often encountered in LFDCs, are therefore a way to capture seigniorage. When reserves are remunerated, however, part of the seigniorage is transferred back to banks.

Ceteris paribus, the substitution of debt by seigniorage increases inflation risks. The risk is increased when the debt in domestic currency is large and inflation is not fully anticipated by the markets, as governments may then be tempted to inflate with money printing in order to dilute the real value of their liabilities. If a heavily indebted government wishes to limit the recourse to seigniorage, it will have no choice but to take fiscal measures that reduce the primary fiscal deficits, current and future. However, this is not always feasible, as governments rarely have full control of their primary balance, and also because imposing the burden of adjustment on the citizens may be politically difficult to carry through. Nevertheless, in LFDCs with a modicum of institutional development, central banks make an effort (albeit not always successful) to keep a lid on lending to the government, with the objective of limiting inflationary risks. Limiting credit to the government is thus frequently a major challenge for central banks.

Central bank loans to the government often give rise to excess liquidity, which cannot always be absorbed through money market operations. On the contrary, in many LFDCs, high fiscal deficits financed with monetary issuance have put a brake on the development of government securities markets and of an active interbank market. This is turn inhibits the efficient use of open market operations and, more generally, the development of more sophisticated financial markets.

Furthermore, many LFDCs have a fixed exchange rate regime. This regime, combined with limited access to the international capital market, as is the case for most LFDCs, puts the burden of controlling the money supply to avoid balance of payments problems in the long run on limiting credit to the government, the main source of money supply. Excess money supply in such a regime may lead to an exhaustion of international reserves and may end up in catastrophic devaluations of the currency. To prevent this, the straightforward recommendation is to put a ceiling on central banks' net credit to the government.[3]

---

[3] This is also a main lesson drawn from the financial programming exercise of many central banks, based on the monetary approach to the balance of payments, whose main advocate was the IMF (see section 6.3.2).

The relationship between fiscal deficits, money growth, and inflation has long been a central element in the analysis of high inflation and the process that leads to it. The studies of hyperinflation point to repeated high fiscal deficits financed with monetary issuance as its ultimate cause, at least for those LFDCS with small or nonexistent markets for public debt. Notice, however, that even seigniorage has limits, and attempts to surpass these limits lead to hyperinflation, which fortunately remains a rare phenomenon.[4] Episodes of hyperinflation are characterized by extremely high and unstable inflation rates with no equilibrium levels.

5.2.2 Seigniorage in selected LFDCs

We illustrate the importance of seigniorage for the financing of government deficits in selected LFDCs (Bolivia, Ghana, Kenya, and Sri Lanka) over the two last decades in Figure 5.1. We also separate total seigniorage into its two components, as discussed in Box 5.1. The figure reports government net lending, total seigniorage, and inflation tax, as defined in Box 5.1, all expressed in percentage of GDP. Bolivia, a heavily dollarized economy until around 2008, is a special case for which a foreign currency component of seigniorage can be identified.

The following observations can be made. For the four selected countries, seigniorage represents on average between 1% and 2% of GDP over 1990–2014.[5] This percentage remains modest, though significant, relative to their average budget deficit, which ranges from 2.5% to 7.6% of GDP (see right-hand panels of Figure 5.1). However, in specific periods the contribution of seigniorage to government financing can be significantly larger than average: witness 6% in Bolivia in 2007, 3.2% in Kenya in 1993, and 3% in Ghana in 2010.

The inflation tax component of seigniorage in general plays a major, often dominant role, except for Bolivia (see left-hand panels of Figure 5.1). In terms of period averages, the inflation tax represents 89% of total seigniorage for Kenya, 80% for Sri-Lanka, 61% for Ghana but only 30% for Bolivia. Recall that the difference between total seigniorage receipts and its inflation tax component originates in increases in the demand for real base money (see Box 5.1). This component usually plays a larger role when the inflation tax (and inflation) abates (e.g. in Ghana in the second half of the period), reflecting increased demand for real balances due to lower opportunity costs and possibly to a more stable and growing economy.

---

[4] Hyperinflation appeared historically in the wake of armed conflicts or of severe external shocks, like that caused by the debt crisis in Latin America in the 1980s.

[5] This is also the range observed, with some exceptions, for the 1980–2005 annual averages of seigniorage in the 47 sub-Saharan African countries investigated by Baldini and Poplawski-Ribeiro (2011). Significant outliers are Nigeria (9.9%), the Democratic Republic of Congo (9.2%), and Angola (4.8%).

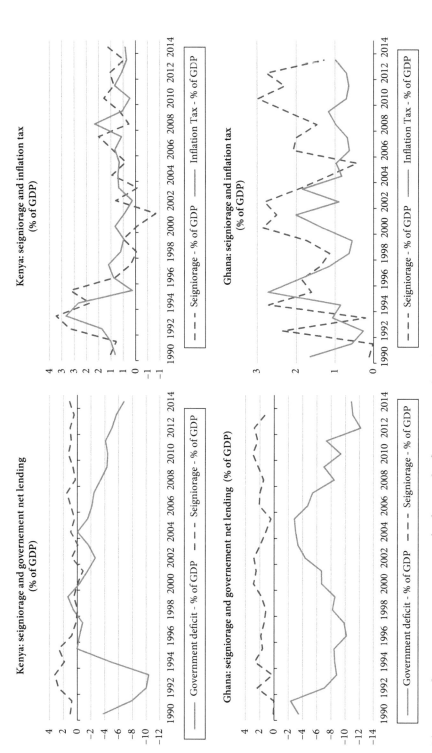

Figure 5.1. Seigniorage, government net lending, and inflation tax in selected countries

Source: IMF, International Financial Statistics and World Economic Outlook.

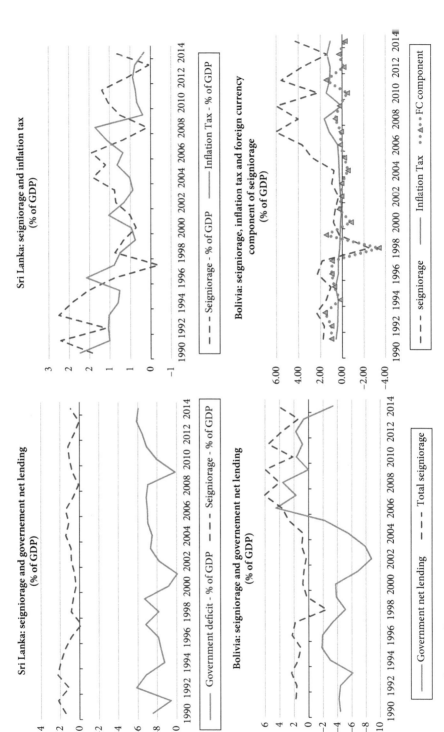

Figure 5.1. Continued

Bolivia is a special case. Because of an earlier high inflation episode, the country had already in the 1990s a highly dollarized financial system. More recently, a de-dollarization process was set in motion. Both dollarization and de-dollarization have shaped the evolution of seigniorage over the period. As a result of dollarization, including currency substitution, the demand for domestic currency base money had shrunk considerably, which explains why the inflation tax has been so low over the period. As can be seen in Figure 5.1, it is only since 2008 that the inflation tax has become once more comparable with levels observed in other countries, reaching 1.5% of GDP—a consequence of the de-dollarization process. Dollarization also meant that the central bank issued base money expressed in foreign currency: banks had to hold foreign currency deposits with the central bank to comply with reserve requirements which were imposed on banks' foreign currency liabilities with the public. As a result, increases in the foreign currency part of the monetary base also gave rise to seigniorage: in a dollarized economy, the change in the real monetary base ($\dot{b}$ in equation 3 of Box 5.1) has therefore to be split into its domestic and foreign currency component. A foreign currency component is therefore added in the graph for Bolivia. As can be seen, it modestly contributes to seigniorage over the period (by 0.2% of GDP on average), while it plays a more important role in seigniorage's short-term changes during the first half of the period.[6] Finally, a major change in the sources of seigniorage in Bolivia can be observed since 2005 as a consequence of the de-dollarization process. As can be seen from Figure 5.1, the significant increase in seigniorage since 2005 is not explained by inflation tax or by the foreign currency component of the monetary base. It is therefore due to the remaining component, the increase in the demand for real balances in domestic currency base money, which is a direct manifestation of the ongoing de-dollarization process.

5.2.3 Fiscal dominance of monetary policy

Fiscal dominance arises whenever monetary policy eventually has to adjust itself to the financing needs of the government. It is a phenomenon encountered in advanced economies (AEs) as well as in developing countries. It is very pervasive in emerging market economies (EMEs) and in LFDCs.[7] There are, however,

---

[6] Reserve requirements on banks' foreign currency deposits were imposed early on, before the start of our observation period. Seigniorage receipts from issuing monetary base in foreign currency have presumably been high during the build-up of these reserves. They have been more limited since, mostly reflecting changes in required reserve ratios. It can however be expected that continuation of the de-dollarization process will progressively decrease the demand for the foreign currency component of the monetary base, implying systematically negative contributions of the foreign currency component to seigniorage.

[7] Zoli (2005) offers a comprehensive survey for EMEs. See also Moreno (2003).

important structural differences relating to fiscal dominance between industrial countries and developing countries:

- In LFDCs, markets for government bonds in domestic currency are generally rudimentary or in their infancy.[8] They are growing particularly in countries where inflation has been subdued for some years. LFDCs with a fixed exchange rate backed by large international reserves are more likely to have significant markets for bonds in domestic currency, albeit still small relative to AEs.[9] Note also that the low depth and small degree of diversification which characterize the LFDCs' financial sector are not conducive to the development of sizeable markets for public securities.
- A substantial portion of public-sector debt liabilities in LFDCs is in foreign exchange or linked to foreign exchange. Hence claims on the government are real claims. They cannot be repaid with domestic money—i.e. by issuing non-interest-earning liabilities—as is the case when the debt is nominal and in domestic currency. To repay the foreign currency debt, seigniorage does not meet the purpose, and taxes have to be collected, the receipts of which need to be converted into foreign currency.[10]
- The institutional arrangements that prevail between the central bank and the ministry of finance are often characterized in LFDCs by much closer interdependence—at a functional and organizational level as well as at the level of economic policy design—than what is observable in industrialized countries;
- The tolerance to public indebtedness is usually much lower in developing countries than in the AEs. This structural feature relates to the credibility problems linked to the countries' track record of debt defaults and renegotiations on foreign currency debt.[11] It is also, more generally, related to their institutional weaknesses. Note that this low debt threshold makes more difficult the placement of government securities, often leaving money issuance as the only available option.

---

[8] Debt markets in domestic currency in most Latin American LFDCs disappeared in the 1930s because of dynamic consistency problems, as creditors feared that governments could not offer a credible commitment not to dilute their obligations through inflation. The few LFDCs, and several EMEs, that maintained domestic currency debt markets, did so with bonds indexed to inflation. Only at the very end of the 20th century did nominal debt markets in domestic currency resurface in these countries.

[9] Actually many LFDC governments would prefer to borrow in their domestic markets, even if these loans carry higher interest rates and shorter maturities than loans extended by the international financial institutions, in order to escape conditionality imposed by these lenders.

[10] Obviously, governments can issue money to buy the foreign exchange needed to honour external debts, but at the cost of depleting international reserves and putting depreciation pressures on the exchange rate. Notice that the depletion of international reserves to reimburse external debt coming due leaves unchanged the *net* external debt of the country's public sector (central bank included). Repayment of the net external debt necessarily involves the use of new real resources.

[11] It is to be noted that no LFDC government has defaulted on its public debt in domestic currency in recent times. Governments realize that in doing so they would lose access to a hard-won source of financing.

There are many facets to fiscal dominance. Sargent and Wallace (1981) provide the theoretical framework describing how monetary policy loses its capacity to control the inflation process when the government is not inclined to satisfy its intertemporal budget constraint—its solvency constraint—by levying taxes or curtailing spending. Seigniorage then becomes, sooner or later, the adjustment variable: the central bank is forced to step up the monetary growth rate, with the inflation rate following suit. Box 5.2 discusses the dynamics of such a fiscal dominance process.

Box 5.2. Fiscal dominance and its dynamics

In the classic analysis of Sargent and Wallace (1981) on fiscal dominance, the government sets current and future budgets and determines the amount of financing through bond sales and seigniorage to finance fiscal deficits. Seigniorage finances the gap between financing needs and the amount of bonds that the government can sell to the public. The gap is covered by the printing press (and banks' reserve deposits at the central bank). Sargent and Wallace (1981) assume in their analysis that the bonds issued are real bonds, so that the real value of debt is immune to inflation. They also assume that people expect the government to honour fully its liabilities. In this setting, they show that the government loses its ability to control inflation whenever the real rate of interest exceeds the growth rate of real GDP. Without recourse to seigniorage, the debt would in this case be put on an explosive path.

More generally, consider a small open economy, as are most LFDCs. The government can finance a given budget deficit either by borrowing abroad or drawing down its foreign reserves held with the central bank (i.e. by increasing its net external debt), or by issuing domestic bonds in the domestic market, or, finally, by borrowing from the central bank in domestic currency. The size of the real government budget that must be financed determines the borrowing needs. The budget financing gap, i.e. the part of the budget that cannot be financed with debt, will be assigned to the central bank. The money base increases by whatever amount is required to close this financing gap in domestic currency. The central bank thus generates seigniorage revenue by lending in domestic currency to the government. If deficits are continuously large and determined with little or no consideration of the outstanding stock of public liabilities, debt could increase boundlessly. Once the public debt reaches a plateau, it becomes increasingly difficult to place more debt, since solvency becomes an issue for the market. When the government's solvency is in doubt—a case not considered by Sargent and Wallace (1981), but obviously

Continued

Box 5.2. *Continued*

---

encountered in some countries—new debt can only be issued at increasingly higher interest rates, further eroding debt sustainability. The demand for bonds that can be issued in domestic or in foreign currency thus sets an upper limit on the stock of bonds relative to GDP. Beyond this limit, access to the debt market closes and the risk of default becomes more manifest, especially if international reserves are low. Such a risk materializes if debt renegotiations are not in the offing. This pushes the government to resort all the more to monetary financing. Hence, inflation is the likely result of recurrent high fiscal deficits, even if for a while they are financed by bonds. Countries in this situation can then find themselves on a path of high inflation or even hyperinflation.

The danger of runaway inflation is enhanced whenever the public can substitute away from domestic currency and avoid the inflation tax by holding foreign currency, buying foreign currency assets or non-perishable goods. This erodes the inflation tax base, forcing the government to raise inflation to generate the necessary seigniorage receipts. Large increases in the government's debt will thus eventually require over time significant increases in seigniorage. Notice, however, that it is the high expansion of money prompted by fiscal needs that will lead to inflation. Hence inflation is still a monetary phenomenon, with fiscal roots in this case. When budget deficits involve, currently or in the future, a monetary expansion and inflation, the literature on fiscal dominance (e.g. Carlstrom and Fuerst 2000) speaks of a 'weak form of the fiscal theory of the price level'. Alternatively, we can label it a 'weak form of fiscal dominance', as opposed to the 'strong form of fiscal dominance' featured by the fiscal theory of the price level, as discussed in Appendix 5A.

While the Sargent–Wallace channel of fiscal dominance singles out money financing to generate seigniorage revenues, there are other channels through which fiscal policy curtails monetary authorities' capacity to aim at price stability. To improve its intertemporal fiscal balance, the government may, as indicated in section 5.2.1, take policy measures of a 'financial repression' type. The aim is to decrease the real value of its interest-bearing debt in domestic currency through unanticipated inflation or through balance sheet ratios, imposed on financial intermediaries and requesting them to increase their holdings of public sector bonds. Governments in LFDCs worried about the costs of servicing their debts fix or try to influence the interest rates of monetary policy, aiming at nominal interest rates well below the level necessary for fighting inflation. Also, when markets for domestic currency securities are thin, the real interest rate tends to increase with the level of public debt, in order to induce holders to accept devoting a higher share of their portfolio to public sector bonds. This may also encourage the government to exert pressure on the central bank to use monetary policy to counteract the rise in interest rates.

The expectation that the government may not necessarily be committed to fully honouring its debt obligations provides another channel of fiscal dominance. Indeed, history shows that governments in many LFDCs have not always respected their intertemporal budget constraint, which has often led to financial crisis whose resolution called for debt rescheduling or even forgiveness. The economic literature offers two quite different approaches to such expectation-based mechanisms of fiscal dominance:

- First, according to the well-known and empirically well-documented 'classic' approach, high public debt levels may destabilize expectations on the exchange rate insofar as they originate in concerns about the solvency of the government and give rise to fears of default. Once such expectations develop, they have a significant impact on interest rate risk premiums and on the exchange rate (see section 2.4.2.2.1). Once expectations of devaluation have set in, the central bank may act by increasing domestic interest rates to avoid actual devaluation. While this may prevent the burden that an actual devaluation would immediately impose on the real value of the foreign currency part of the debt, it nevertheless raises the current and future costs of servicing the debt. Such 'unfavourable expectations' therefore increase the subordination of the central bank to fiscal considerations, even when there is no monetary financing of the deficit and the government is financing itself by placing debt with the public, abroad or domestically.

- A second approach to an expectation-based mechanism of fiscal dominance has more recently been developed by the 'fiscal theory of the price level' (FTPL), particularly in the context of AEs where it has attracted much attention. The Appendix to this chapter presents a detailed and critical analysis of fiscal dominance according to the fiscal theory of the price level. It also examines its relevance for LFDCs and reports on its few empirical studies. According to the FTPL, fiscal policy shocks, such as an unexpected increase in government transfers to households, that at any moment of time worsen people's expectations about the government's solvency prospects, may have *direct* inflationary effects. Because people think that the government will not increase taxes in the future, as would be necessary to guarantee its solvency, they feel in some way richer and therefore consume more. This raises the price level and decreases the real value of the domestic currency part of the public debt, up to the point where the government's solvency is again fully restored and any 'wealth effect' has disappeared. Monetary policy is unable to do anything about this. It is forced into a 'passive' role. If the central bank resists and if it tries to gain control of the inflationary dynamics unleashed by the fiscal shock by raising interest rates, it quickly runs into the risk of actually reinforcing inflation, as higher interest rates further reduce the government's solvency and induce debt instability. This generates, along the same lines as described above, a further inflationary shock. This counterintuitive effect of a restrictive monetary policy has been labelled the 'paradox of tight monetary policy' by Loyo (1999), the first to have applied the FTPL to an EME (Brazil).

- Is such a 'strong form of fiscal dominance', according to which the price level and inflation are determined by fiscal policy independently of changes in the money stock or in monetary policy, relevant for LFDCs? The discussion of the FTPL in the Appendix shows that the strong form of fiscal dominance is probably less relevant to LFDCs than the more conventional 'weak form of fiscal dominance' discussed in Box 5.2. Also, the empirical evidence in support of FTPL (a theory mostly based on expectation mechanisms) is methodologically difficult to obtain. The rare existing empirical studies specifically devoted to the FTPL nevertheless seem to suggest that for some LFDCs, the relevance of a FTPL-type fiscal dominance cannot be discarded.

Whatever the mechanisms through which fiscal dominance operates, its consequences are serious: monetary policy becomes unable to guarantee a nominal anchor for the country. As a consequence, the road is opened to high inflation episodes and possibly to a debt crisis, as fiscal dominance usually has its roots in the government having put public debt on an unsustainable path. Both types of crises will leave the post-crisis task of monetary policy much more difficult than if fiscal policy had been disciplined and had not interfered with monetary policy. Entrenched high inflationary expectations can make it very difficult for monetary policy, and very painful for the economy, to restore price stability after the crisis (see section 4.2). Actual debt renegotiations with creditors, resulting in debt or debt service reductions, will eliminate the country's debt overhang and give its government a breathing space. It will, however, also leave a legacy of suspicion of moral hazard with respect to the public finance management. Investors' feeling about the credibility of the government's future debt commitments will be more reserved. At the least, this will translate into higher risk spreads on public-sector bonds and make debt financing more costly. It may also increase the probability that people, when faced with a shock that entails significant negative effects on the fiscal balance, will react as predicted by the fiscal theory of the price level, with renewed inflation as a consequence (see the Appendix to this chapter). Both could, if unchecked, rekindle the danger of renewed fiscal dominance on monetary policy.

Given the destructive effects of fiscal dominance, a standard policy recommendation for most countries, and especially, for developing countries, is to insulate monetary policy from fiscal policy. This recommendation is, however, difficult to apply in practice if fiscal deficits are sizeable.

To avoid repetition of the financing of fiscal deficits with money printing, many countries have promulgated legislation to tie the hands of the government, barring by law its access to financing by the central bank. The quest for legal independence of central banks in Latin America was motivated more by the need to contain inflation by separating monetary policy from fiscal policy than by the fear, which prevailed in the AEs, that monetary authorities would 'cheat' the public with respect to their commitment to price stability in order to ensure short-term output gains (see section 4.3.1).

Legal independence was seen as the cornerstone of the central bank's key mandate to control inflation (see section 4.3.2.1). Yet, without a solid fiscal position, central bank independence, either legal or de facto, cannot by itself ensure low inflation. Some LFDCs have, over the last two decades, introduced fiscal rules (Schaechter et al. 2012) that contribute to keeping fiscal deficits low as well as constraining expectations on the fiscal front. The enforcement of such rules depends very much on the institutional strength of the country, which is often weak in LFDCs. Short of explicit fiscal rules, many LFDCs have however made efforts for many years in terms of institution-building, under the auspices of international financial institutions and development agencies, to improve the quality of public management, to keep public debt on a sustainable path, and to minimize the interference of fiscal policy with monetary policy.

5.3 External price shocks and monetary policy

The vast majority of LFDCs have small open economies, and as such they are subjected to strong exogenous shocks that can affect both prices and output. Monetary policy can, if properly focused, respond to these exogenous shocks, stabilize prices, and mitigate their undesired effects on output, despite the institutional weaknesses of the LFDCs that set limits to its efficacy. Managing the trade-off between price and output stability when nominal prices are rigid and when other real rigidities are present in the economy is a difficult challenge, as discussed in section 4.2.1. We should recall, in this respect, that LFDCs give, in most cases, more weight to price stabilization than to output stabilization, which is often for them a less explicit target.

Shocks can be diverse: they can be demand or supply shocks, real or financial, caused by international or domestic factors. For LFDCs, the most important shocks originate in the international economy and are trade-related. In this section we exclusively focus on the two main external shocks monetary policy has to deal with in LFDCs: increases in oil and food prices. Both are at the root of acute trade-offs between price and output stability. We briefly document the important role played by these two shocks, before examining at a more theoretical level how monetary policy can contribute to cushioning their detrimental effects.

5.3.1 Oil and food price shocks in LFDCs

Shocks to commodity prices, especially oil prices, and shocks to the international prices of food are of particular relevance to LFDCs. These shocks have large effects on the consumer basket and on domestic output and prices; they are frequent and persistent; they are very visible; and they are likely to influence actual and expected inflation as well as output trajectories. They are in addition not only pure price shocks. They usually also combine with significant shocks to the country's aggregate demand and to its fiscal and external balance. Monetary policy needs to confront the economy-wide repercussions of these external shocks.

Primary commodities and most food staples are tradable goods, whose prices are fixed internationally. LFDCs are price-takers for these goods. The policy responses to shocks will vary across countries, depending on their condition of being a net exporter of oil (or food) or a net importer. LFDCs have structurally a high dependency of their exports on a narrow set of primary commodities and strongly rely on imported intermediate inputs and capital goods. External price shocks therefore usually have more severe consequences than in AEs. Also, as discussed in Chapter 2, the channels of transmission of monetary policy are substantially narrower and less predictable in LFDCs than in AEs, which impairs the efficacy of monetary policy in softening the shocks. The economies of the LFDCs are fragile and volatile, and exogenous shocks, if not well managed, can leave a deep and lasting imprint that hinders their growth prospects and may contribute to political instability. This emphasizes the need to carefully tailor the policies to cope with them.

The foreign price shocks act as a combination of supply and demand shocks to the domestic economy. This combination has a bearing on the trade-offs between price stability and output stability, as monetary policy can deal better with shocks to demand than with shocks to supply. Supply shocks indeed imply a trade-off between price and output stability, which demand shocks usually do not (see section 4.2.1.3).

As a telling illustration of the relevance of such shocks, a significant part of the inflation pressures observed in many LFDCs in 2008 and 2011 can be attributed to global movements in international food and oil prices, which peaked during these years, as shown in Figure 5.2. As noted by IMF (2011: 107) the food price peak in 2008 'contributed about 5 percentage points to headline inflation in emerging and developing economies on average but only about 1 percentage point to advanced economy inflation'. More generally, as documented in IMF (2011), the pass-through of international food prices into domestic food prices,

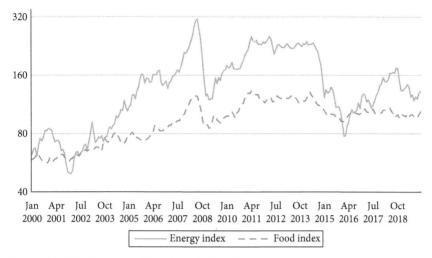

Figure 5.2. World commodity prices: fuel and food
Source of data: IMF, Primary Commodity Price System, index 2016 = 100, log scale

as well as of crude oil prices into domestic transport prices, is significantly higher for developing countries than for AEs.[12]

There is little controversy around the classical tenet that in the long run, when prices fully adjust, inflation is directly dependent on monetary growth within national boundaries. In the short run, however, inflation of consumer prices can be caused by changes in international prices. Higher international oil or food prices can affect domestic output prices, either directly or via the pass-through to other domestic markets and especially through the wage–price spiral.

For LFDCs, trade shocks are more important than capital account shocks. According to some estimates, they can explain close to 50% of the changes in output.[13] Yet some LFDCs in the middle income range have some exposure to the international capital markets and are vulnerable to its swings. Risk premiums may increase either idiosyncratically in a given country or because there is a generalized increase for all LFDCs or for regional subsets. Sudden stops in financing and capital flight are more common to EMEs, but they also happen, albeit significantly less frequently, in LFDCs, even though the latter are poorly integrated with the international capital market.[14] Also, foreign interest rate shocks may put

---

[12] E.g. Charry et al. (2018: 376) note for the case of Rwanda: 'food and oil price shocks have accounted for the bulk of inflation dynamics, particularly in 2008 and 2011.'

[13] As estimated e.g. by Kose and Riezman (2001: 70) for a set of African countries. Note also that during the international financial crisis of 2007–9, LFDCs barely felt its direct restrictive financial effects, mainly because of their isolation from active capital markets. However, the current account of their balance of payment was affected as a result of the recession in AEs.

[14] As an example, consider what happened, after 2009, when investors of the AEs, in their search for yield, placed funds in 'exotic' bonds issued by LFDCs in Africa and Latin America. These flows

pressure on LFDCs' exchange rate and domestic interest rates, especially on those already more integrated with the global financial market.[15]

We specifically select increases in oil and food prices as monetary policy's most serious external shock challenge in LFDCs. We concentrate our analysis on price rises, for which the inflation–output trade-off is the most difficult to manage. Commodity price declines can be analysed in a symmetric manner, *mutatis mutandis*. The trade-off can in this case be expected to be less difficult to deal with. The favourable mechanical effects of commodity price decreases on the price level ease the task of monetary policy of reaching its inflation target. Monetary authorities can then more easily turn their attention to managing the arbitrage between the price shocks' effects on aggregate demand and output on the one hand and on the domestic price component of inflation on the other.

Note that oil and food price shocks to the domestic economy can also result from sharp upwards adjustments to the administratively set, or subsidized, prices for these two types of goods.[16] Indeed, when international prices for oil of food rise, their officially capped domestic prices will rise, with a lag, and only after black market transactions have undermined the former price ceiling. They are adjusted upwards infrequently but sharply, catching up with past increases in international prices and taking into account expected future developments in them. Huge rises in domestic prices for oil and food can also be the direct conse-quence of the dismantling of subsidies. These sharp adjustments of domestic prices to international prices can be broadly treated and analysed in the same way as exogenous increases in oil and food prices when their domestic price is not subject to administrative controls.

We distinguish in our analysis between countries that are net exporters and those that are net importers of those commodities. We use the open-economy traded/non-traded goods model as theoretical reference in our discussion.[17] Our

came in many instances to a halt or were reversed when the terms of trade of the issuing LFDCs significantly deteriorated, leading markets to reevaluate their repayment possibilities.

[15] Although LFDCs' external debts usually carry fixed interest rates and are often concessional, some have been issued at variable interest rates. In this case, debt service is vulnerable to changes in the world interest rate. More generally, regardless of the contractual conditions on interest rates, a tightening of credit in the main financial centres might derail the expected refinancing of maturing debt or limit opportunities to issue new debt.

[16] Both oil and fuel are in general carefully monitored by authorities in LFDCs. Fuel prices are usually subjected to administrative controls, and although most food products have flexible prices, the prices of some basic staples are often subjected to caps fixed administratively. When prices are capped by the government at overly low levels, as is often the case in LFDCs, shortages and black markets develop. In black markets prices are more flexible, yet competition on these markets is weak and price signals are unreliable. Inside information on the sources of supply carries a huge premium.

[17] Simple open-economy models are of two types: the Mundell–Fleming model, with a domestic good in which the domestic economy is fully specialized and an imported foreign good; the Swan–Salter–Corden model, where the domestic economy produces a traded good and a non-traded good. This second model corresponds to a small open economy which has no influence on the price of the good which is internationally traded (be it an exportable or an importable good). This model fits best the case of LFDCs.

analysis is set in a simple, partial equilibrium framework, as we essentially wish to draw attention to the issues that shocks raise for monetary policy, identifying their direct effect on prices and incomes, as well as their indirect effects on the exchange rate and on external and fiscal balances. A full assessment of the coordination issues that external shocks raise between monetary, exchange rate, and fiscal policies, however, requires a more ambitious, general-equilibrium approach. Full-fledged macroeconomic general equilibrium models can be helpful in this respect, as we discuss in section 7.3.3. Box 7.3 also briefly presents the characteristics of the DSGE model used by Dagher et al. (2012) to analyse windfall shocks in LICs.

5.3.1.1 Oil price shocks

A frequent foreign price shock for an LFDC is given by the unexpected increase of the price of a main commodity export and the windfall income that comes with booming exports sales.[18] The income effects of an export price boom are the most noticeable, but effects on the marginal costs of production are far from negligible when the leading export good is also an input used in domestic production. This is the case, for instance, for oil, natural gas, and some agricultural products.[19] The same increases in international commodity prices will, however, have opposite income effects on countries which import these commodities.

Consider the case of oil. An immediate impact of a higher price of oil will be to put pressure on the consumer price index (CPI) in both net oil exporters and net importers. Further, the marginal costs of domestic producers will be affected, as oil is an important input for the traded goods sectors and, to some extent, for the non-traded sector. Increases in the CPI may later induce second-round effects if there is, formally or informally, wage indexation. In addition, since increases in oil prices may be mitigated by additional subsidies on oil, designed to compensate consumers for the international oil price hike, there will be a direct bearing on the government's non-oil fiscal deficit. While these price effects of an oil price shock are common to both oil-exporting and importing countries, the induced income effects of the price shock are fundamentally asymmetric and need to be discussed separately.

5.3.1.1.1 Oil price shocks in oil-exporting countries

In most oil-exporting LFDCs, the largest portion of the windfall is captured by the government, either because of the high taxation of the multinational

---

[18] Windfall export incomes can also be observed without changes in international prices, e.g. when a country's export capacity increases following the discovery of oil or of other mineral deposits. We do not discuss this here, as our focus is on the specific trade-off between price and output stabilization that price shocks imply for monetary policy.

[19] On the other hand, the leading export sectors may be metal ores that have no or little use as inputs for domestic enterprises.

companies that exploit the oil deposits or because the exploitation is in the hands of state-owned enterprises.[20] The effects on the economy of such a price-induced windfall gain will crucially depend on two key factors: the way the government will spend the extra revenues on consumption and investment or postpone spending and accumulate financial assets; and the way the central bank will manage the effects on domestic monetary condition of the influx of foreign exchange associated with windfall export receipts. The latter will crucially depend on the country's exchange rate regime. We organize the discussion around an exchange rate regime's two extreme forms: a fully fixed and a fully flexible exchange rate.[21] Though actual experiences of LFDCs often diverge from those two extreme exchange rate regimes (see section 6.2.1), contrasting the results of the analysis for both regimes provides useful benchmarks for a country which allows limited flexibility of the exchange rate when dealing with windfall gains (see also section 5.3.2.3).

5.3.1.1.1.1 The case of a fixed exchange rate regime. Figure 5.3 illustrates schematically how the government's and the central bank's policy choices may combine, as well as the respective outcomes of these different policy mixes in the context of an fixed exchange rate regime.[22] We discuss each combination in turn.

Case A. The government spends the windfall. This case is depicted in branch A of Figure 5.3. The government increases its non-oil fiscal deficit. Typically, a large part of these additional expenditures financed by the oil windfall is on non-traded goods. Figure 5.4 shows how this affects equilibrium in the country's non-traded sector. The demand schedule for non-tradables shifts outwards. The output effect of this increase in demand will be partially checked by the upward shift in the supply schedule, caused by the increase in marginal costs. The latter is observed to the extent that oil is a significant input and that its domestic prices track closely the international price, which might not always be the case. Both demand and

---

[20] Among the many LFDC net oil- or other fuel-exporting countries are Algeria, Angola, Bolivia, Cameroon, Ecuador, Equatorial Guinea, Nigeria, and Kazakhstan.

[21] As already mentioned, we focus our analysis only on the effects of oil price increases. The analysis developed for the case of an oil price hike can be developed in a symmetric way for the case of a sharp decline of the oil price. Instead of a windfall gain, the government will experience a huge income loss. The way this loss is managed by the government—whether there is an immediate curtailing of government spending or a temporary smoothing over time of reductions in spending— will be of crucial importance for the macroeconomic effects of the shock, symmetric to the case of a price increase. The same applies to the type of coordination between the government and the central bank with respect to the policy of international reserves and the exchange rate policy followed by the latter. A crucial difference will, however, exist in terms of acuteness of effects. In the case of an oil price bust, the inevitable decrease in aggregate demand and output as well as the inflationary effects of exchange rate depreciation, a consequence of the depletion of international reserves, will be felt more severely than the consequences of a symmetric oil price hike. In this setting, both monetary and fiscal policy will have an important role to play. See Torvik (2018) for a discussion of monetary policy reactions to a negative oil price shocks in oil-exporting countries.

[22] Fig. 5.3 is adapted for the case of an oil-exporting country from fig. 12.1 of Berg et al. (2018a), focusing on the effects of aid inflows.

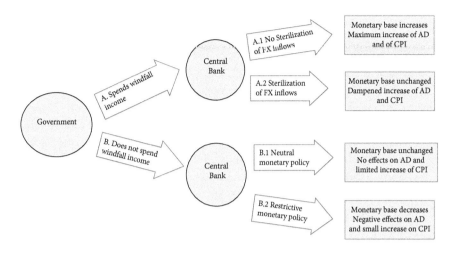

Figure 5.3. Monetary and fiscal policies with oil windfalls in a fixed exchange rate regime

Note: AD is aggregate demand, CPI the consumer price index.

Source: adapted by authors from fig. 12.1 of Berg et al. (2018a)

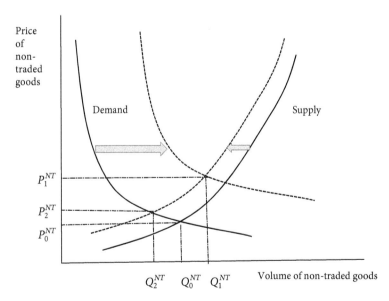

Figure 5.4. Effects of an oil price increase on the non-traded sector of an oil-exporting economy with a fixed exchange rate

supply effects combine to increase the price of non-tradables (from P_0^{NI} to P_1^{NI}), as well as its output (from Q_0^{NT} to Q_1^{NT}). Given an exogenous foreign currency price of all tradables and a fixed exchange rate, the country's real exchange rate, as measured by the relative price of non-traded vs traded goods, appreciates. This reflects the loss in competitiveness of the non-oil tradable sector, which has also witnessed an increase in its marginal costs. Demand for tradables thus increases, both because of the content of tradables in the additional government expenditure and because of the adverse shift in competitiveness. Because of the latter, domestic supply of tradables also contracts. The non-oil trade balance deteriorates.[23]

The country's additional oil revenues will lead to an accumulation of international reserves as well as to an expansion of the domestic monetary base as counterpart. Observe that this increase in the monetary base occurs at the initiative of the government when there is little coordination between the government and the central bank. Indeed, the gain in international reserves would not have a monetary bearing, nor would it cause real appreciation, as long as the government revenues stayed on deposit at the central bank. However, as the government withdraws the funds to finance its expenses, the money base will increase. Movements in the deposits of the government at the central bank then become a main source of money creation. This monetary accommodation of the windfall income-induced government spending implies that the latter has its full effect on aggregate demand (tradables and non-tradables).[24] This scenario assumes that the central bank remains totally passive with respect to its purchase of foreign exchange from the government. It does not sterilize the foreign exchange inflow (Branch A1 in Figure 5.3).

In the alternative scenario (Branch A2 in Figure 5.3), the central bank uses open-market operations to mitigate the monetary effects of the oil windfall-induced government spending. This will be the case if monetary authorities have a strong preference for price stability. These sterilization operations, which involve sales of securities in domestic currency, siphon liquidity from the market and raise the domestic interest rate.[25] The outward shift in the demand schedule in Figure 5.4 will thus be dampened. This will cushion the increase in the price of non-tradables and thereby in the CPI. The restrictive monetary policy will also dampen second-round

---

[23] These real exchange rate effects of oil price increases in oil-exporting countries on non-oil sectors are often referred to as 'Dutch disease', in reference to what has been observed in the 1960s in the Netherlands after the discovery of natural gas. The deterioration of the non-oil trade balance is a typical effect often observed in oil-exporting LFDCs. It implies, within the sector of non-oil tradables, a decline in exports and an increase in imports, including those that compete with domestic production.

[24] As long as the government has an overall budgetary surplus, there will be no need for monetary financing of its overall budget, which is boosted by windfall oil revenues. There is always, however, in the case discussed above, a monetary accommodation of its non-oil budgetary deficit.

[25] The central bank could also neutralize the monetary effects of the windfall by directly reselling the foreign exchange in the market. However, this is seldom the case, as central banks prefer to hold on to this foreign exchange.

effects on wages and reduce expectations of future inflation, both of which mitigate the inflationary effects of the oil price increase. Note, however, as mentioned in section 3.5.2, that monetary policy, especially for liquidity-absorbing open-market type operations, has only a limited and temporary reach in a regime of fixed exchange rates, unless the capital account remains sufficiently closed.

With high capital mobility, the withdrawal of central bank money through open market operations induces a capital inflow from abroad of similar magnitude, which forces the central bank to increase the monetary base by an equal amount. As in this case the exchange rate regime limits the effectiveness of monetary policy, avoidance of second-round effects may have to rely on other means.[26] However, many LFDCs still have a de facto closed capital account. One can thus conclude that the sterilization policy discussed above is a useful strategy for LFDCs' central bank to pursue price stability in the face of an oil price shock and concomitant spending of the windfall income by the government.

In principle, the government could smooth the effects of the windfall by spreading its expenditures over a sufficiently long time. However, this custodial role is not always fulfilled as expected.[27] In most cases, the rents that accrue to the government will stay in its coffers only for a short period of time before being spent. Governments typically will increase employment in the public sector and public investment. The government wage bill and that of its contractors, in the case of public investment, grows and becomes a main channel of transfer of government revenues to the domestic private sector.

Case B. The government does not spend the windfall. This is depicted in Branch B of Figure 5.3. There is no change in the non-oil fiscal deficit. There will be only relative price and marginal costs effects of the increase of the price of oil. There will be no significant direct effects on aggregate demand. The demand schedule for non-tradables in Figure 5.4 thus does not shift. The government can either invest its savings in foreign assets, say in sovereign wealth funds, or use them to reduce the public external debt. Also the savings can be directly held as deposits at the central bank, allowing the bank to shore up its foreign reserves. With the central bank adopting a neutral position, keeping the monetary base unchanged (Branch B1 in Figure 5.3), CPI still increases because of the mechanical effect on the consumer basket and the marginal cost-induced price increase of non-tradables (from P_0^{NT} to P_2^{NT} in Figure 5.4), but this increase is much smaller than

---

[26] E.g. through incomes policies that limit wage increases in the formal sector, particularly wages in the public sector.

[27] See Collier and Gunning (1999) for the reasons that justify the custodial role of the government in managing the windfall export receipts, taking into account existing differences in private vs public savings rates and in private vs public rates of return on investment.

when the government spends the windfall income (P_2^{NT} instead of P_1^{NT}). Output of non-tradables decreases (from Q_0^{NT} to Q_2^{NT}), as does output of non-oil tradables.

However, even if the government does not spend its oil windfall income, which limits the inflationary effect of the oil price shock, an inflation-conscious central bank may still wish to dampen further the increase in domestic prices which follows the oil price increase. It can do this by selling foreign exchange in the market or by using other open-market operations to absorb liquidity (Branch B2 in Figure 5.3). This causes a leftwards shift (not shown) of the demand schedule for non-traded goods in Figure 5.4 and further decreases total output.

Consumers may anticipate that resources that are not spent currently will be spent at some point in the future. If consumers were fully Ricardian and not credit-constrained, they would increase their consumption from the outset in anticipation of higher transfers from the accumulated rents in wealth funds or from future lower taxes.[28] The increase in consumption resulting from a higher expected permanent income would, however, be distributed over time, so that current consumption would only increase modestly. Ricardian consumers may also have incentives to borrow against their higher expected permanent income, for investing in housing or other constructions, especially if few other opportunities for wealth diversification exist, which would be the case if the capital account of the balance of payments is de facto closed. Under these hypotheses, more consumption and more construction investment would also shift aggregate demand and put pressure on prices, particularly of non-traded goods and the CPI. So, even if the government were to fully neutralize the oil boom windfall gains, one could still observe real appreciation and inflationary pressures if the country's consumers are far-sighted (Ricardian) and if they are not credit-constrained. Neither hypothesis, however, is very likely in the context of LFDCs.

Often governments in oil-exporting LFDCs fix the price administratively or heavily subsidize the production and commercialization of fuels for the domestic market. It is only in some rare cases that they let the domestic price of fuels adjust fully to the international price movements of oil. With administrative fixing of prices, the domestic supply of oil is lower than otherwise. Moreover, if oil is produced by state-owned enterprises, the lower receipts from domestic sales impact the fiscal budget. Also, subsidies to consumers or to domestic non-oil producers impair the fiscal budget and are a way to redistribute (albeit quite inefficiently and regressively) part of the government's windfall gain. They account in Figure 5.4 for part of the shift in aggregate demand which pushes up the price of non-tradables.[29]

---

[28] On the issue of Ricardian versus non-Ricardian agents in the broader fiscal policy context, see also Appendix 5A(1)

[29] As is well known, these policies also imply that incentives to develop alternative sources of energy, which could substitute for oil, are weak. This keeps producer countries in a vulnerable position if the price of oil were to abruptly decline.

5.3.1.1.1.2 The case of a flexible exchange rate regime. Case A. The government spends the windfall. With fully flexible exchange rates, there will be no automatic monetary accommodation, as is the case with a fixed exchange rate regime. Instead, a nominal exchange rate appreciation will occur as the government sells its foreign currency oil receipts in the market for foreign exchange. The implicit assumption in this appreciation mechanism is that there is an imperfect substitution between domestic currency and foreign currency assets.[30]

As shown in Figure 5.5, the demand for non-tradables increases as a result of additional government spending. Part of this increase is however dampened by the decrease in the domestic currency price of non-oil tradables which follows the nominal appreciation of the domestic currency, whose effects are depicted by the darker arrows in Figure 5.5. This currency appreciation also shifts the supply schedule of non-traded goods to the right, partially counteracting the inward shift due to the higher marginal costs of production.[31]

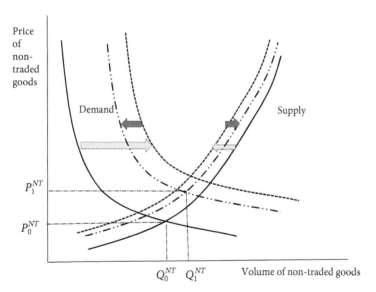

Figure 5.5. Effects of an oil price increase on the non-traded sector of an oil-exporting economy with a flexible exchange rate

---

[30] If capital were fully mobile, and the uncovered interest rate parity were thus to hold (see section 2.4.2.1), the sale of foreign currency by the government in the market would leave the exchange rate unchanged. For given domestic and foreign interest rates, as well as unchanged expectations of future exchange rates, any incipient appreciation of the currency would lead to capital outflows, restoring the initial level of the exchange rate.

[31] The exchange rate appreciation makes non-oil traded goods, whose price has decreased, more attractive, inducing substitution in demand away from non-traded goods. On the supply side, the less profitable traded goods sector has to reduce its workforce. This puts a downward pressure on nominal wages. For given prices and lower wages, the non-traded goods sector can afford to hire more workers and expand its output. Fig. 5.5 assumes that the resulting shift of the sector's supply curve will remain moderate, so that the marginal cost effects of the rise in oil prices will dominate.

The net effect is an increase in the price of non-tradables, which reinforces the real appreciation but also the initial inflationary effects of the oil price increase. The latter has however been dampened by nominal appreciation. The net inflationary effect of the oil price increase when the government spends the windfall is thus possibly less important than in the fixed rate regime.

This discussion leaves out the central bank's policy reaction. In a flexible exchange rate regime, the central bank is not required to buy the foreign currency sold by the government. It can, however, set its policy rates with maximal flexibility and react to the inflationary pressures by raising them. Inflation will be dampened by the combined effect of higher interest rates and a stronger appreciation of the domestic currency. This will come at the expense of output, both in the non-traded sector and in the non-oil traded sector.

Case B. The government does not spend the windfall. One observes, in this case, effects that are similar to those discussed in the fixed exchange rate, as there is no pressure towards exchange rate appreciation in the absence of foreign-exchange sales by the government. There is thus only the direct effect on CPI and on marginal costs, which affects the supply of non-traded and non-oil tradables. Global effects on aggregate demand will remain limited.

Whatever the reaction of government spending to the oil windfall, monetary policy has greater efficacy with flexible exchange rates. Unhindered by the need to maintain the parity exchange rate, monetary policy can pursue a stricter control of inflation, and aim at neutralizing the first- and second-round effects of positive oil price shocks on the CPI. This calls for a restrictive monetary policy, which will dampen aggregate demand and will limit cost-push pressures. The more the government spends the oil windfall, the more restrictive monetary policy will need to be, in order to keep the inflation rate on target, at the cost of decreasing the demand of all non-traded and traded goods. This will dampen aggregate demand, but may also entail output losses in those non-tradable sectors that do no benefit from the government's spending spree.

5.3.1.1.2 *Oil price shocks in oil-importing countries*

Many LFDC countries are oil importers rather than exporters. Increases in the price of oil will cause jumps in the CPI, directly through the presence of oil products in the consumer basket and indirectly through effects on the marginal costs of production of domestic firms, similarly to what has been discussed in the preceding section. However, contrary to the oil-exporting countries, the rise in oil prices causes, *ceteris paribus*, a deterioration in the terms of trade for oil-importing countries and therefore a fall in real income. Also, the import bill increases and aggregate output declines.

The price of non-oil traded goods also increases, following the rise in marginal costs of production of those goods across the world. This reinforces the rise of the CPI. The impact on the CPI may lead to 'second-round' increases in domestic input and labour costs. There will be a loss of competitiveness of the oil importer's tradable sector if the resulting increase in marginal costs is higher than that of its competitors.

In a system of *fixed exchange rates*, foreign prices fully determine the domestic price of tradables. The overall inflation rate will then be exclusively determined by the direct effect of the oil price increase on the CPI and by the behaviour of the prices of non-traded goods. The price of non-traded goods will decrease if aggregate demand and output decrease with the hike in oil prices. The loss of international reserves resulting from a larger oil import bill may contribute to deflationary pressures. Also, there is always the likelihood of second-round incremental effects on wages. If this is the case, controlling inflation through restrictive monetary policy might be costly in terms of lost output. If large emphasis is given to the welfare losses of unemployment, relative to those of price instability, monetary policy could become expansionary, to attenuate the decline in output. However, the monetary policy-induced decrease in the domestic interest will lead to additional and continuing losses in reserves. The expansion will be short-lived, just to buy time for adjustment. The scope for monetary policy is in any event very limited in a fixed exchange rate, unless capital mobility is quite low. Fiscal and income policies are therefore often mobilized in LFDCs to cushion, at least transitionally, the welfare impact of increased oil prices.

If *exchange rates are flexible*, there will be a nominal depreciation of the domestic currency, following the additional import expenses caused by the oil price increase, and given imperfect substitutability between domestic and foreign assets.[32] The depreciation feeds back into the CPI, via traded goods. Following the increases in the price of oil, the oil-importing country will suffer a decline in non-traded, and possibly also traded output. The change in the prices of non-traded goods will depend on the relative strength of two forces pulling in different directions. A decline in demand, caused by the negative income effects of the deterioration in the terms of trade, will lower *ceteris paribus* the price of non-traded goods; contrariwise, a rise in marginal costs will increase them. Whatever the net price effect, both factors contribute to the decline of non-traded output.

---

[32] When domestic and foreign assets are not perfect substitutes, the oil-induced current account deficit in the balance of payments cannot be financed by capital inflows without an initial depreciation of the exchange rate. With domestic interest rates unchanged, the domestic currency has to depreciate so as to generate a higher expected return on domestic currency assets in order to compensate the foreign investor for the increased risk taking (see section 2.4.2.2.1).

Monetary policy is potent in dampening inflation pressures and depreciations of the exchange rate. Rising interest rates will attenuate the depreciation of the currency and counteract, through its restrictive effects on aggregate demand, the cost–push effects of oil prices on domestic, non-traded goods. In addition, an initially restrictive monetary policy can limit the second-round effects of the oil price shock. This will be more effective if the credibility of the central bank is high. Indeed, second-round effects will be more subdued if inflationary expectations are well anchored. Nevertheless, the negative effects on output of this monetary policy strategy have to be taken into account by the monetary authorities, and assessed according to their optimal trade-off between price and output stabilization.

As already noted, oil price increases are usually compensated by government subsidies. Adverse price shocks then become a fiscal issue, particularly so for oil-importing countries.[33] With subsidies, both for consumers and for producers, there will be a lower decline in aggregate demand and in import volumes, unless they are paid for with higher broad-based taxes. If subsidies are paid for with taxes, the issue becomes more of a distributional skirmish than movements of aggregate demand. If subsidies fully compensate the increase in oil prices, no immediate effect of the oil shock on the CPI can be expected. However, if oil prices increase persistently and are subsidized, mounting pressures on the fiscal balance could end up in deficits so large that their monetary financing would be likely.

5.3.1.2 Food price shocks

As was the case with oil, the large weight of food on households' consumption and the limited substitutability by other goods implies that food price fluctuations can have a sizeable impact on overall consumer prices. The effects of oil price increases have deserved much attention, especially in the AEs. However, food prices are more closely correlated than oil prices with most indicators of global inflation.[34] Figure 5.6 illustrates, for Kenya, this strong correlation between the global CPI inflation rate and the rate of change of this index's food price component.

The increase in revenues of an export boom for *net food exporters* do not, as with oil, benefit the accounts of the government, except for a small fraction. Unlike oil and minerals, whose production is concentrated geographically and controlled by a handful of large enterprises that are administratively easier to tax,

---

[33] Although energy subsidies are pervasive in many LFDCs, it is striking that they are highest in oil-exporting countries, presumably because such countries can more easily afford their fiscal impact than oil importers. As reported in IMF (2013: 6), pretax subsidies (the difference between the retail price and the production/import cost) represented 0.8 % of GDP in 2012 for the median of SSA's oil exporters, while SSA's median oil importers actually did not subsidize but actually imposed taxes amounting to 1.6 % of GDP.

[34] Catao and Chang (2010: table 1) show that food price cycles correlate better than oil price cycles with different indicators of global inflation.

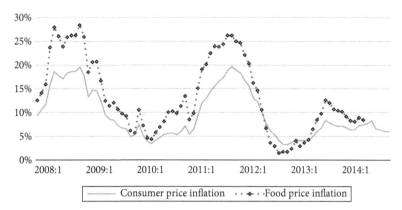

Figure 5.6. Kenya: consumer price and food price inflation
Source of data: FAO Statistics http://www.fao.org/faostat/en/#home

agricultural production is spread more widely and small farmers are responsible for large chunks of it, making taxation more difficult. The fiscal effects are minimal and the positive terms of trade effect is shared between the individual producers and the government, with the larger share accruing to the farmers.[35]

It is interesting to note that, for net food exporters, central banks can be expected to tighten their monetary policy in the case of a favourable shock in export prices. This is a reaction to the direct inflationary impact of food prices on the CPI and their indirect pressure on non-traded good prices, the latter resulting from higher aggregate demand fuelled by increased producers' income. With fixed exchange rates, central banks aim at sterilizing the monetary effects of increased international reserves. Domestic interest rates will be pushed up—to the extent allowed by a limited capital account openness. With flexible exchange rates, the monetary policy tightening will eventually lead to a nominal appreciation of the exchange rate. The higher policy interest rates and the ensuing nominal appreciation, which lowers the price of non-food tradables in the consumer's basket, will contain the inflationary pressures on non-traded good prices and on the CPI.

The effects of international price increases for *net food importers* will have positive output effects on the sector of agricultural tradables but negative demand effects on the non-tradable sector, especially since there is weak substitutability between food and other goods.[36] The effects on global output are more difficult to

---

[35] In some countries and on some occasions taxes have been levied on food exports. Such export taxes, in addition to raising revenue, are aimed at limiting the impact of the increases in international prices on the domestic prices of staples that are exported and are consumed domestically. The Argentinean export taxes (called *retenciones* in Spanish) on meat and grains are a classical example. This is an alternative way, outside of the reach of monetary policy, to stabilize the inflationary effects of increases in international food prices.

[36] Note that the effects of an increase in international commodity prices are not completely similar for net oil and for net food importers. First, oil price increases impinge on domestic firms' marginal

assess. If, as a consequence of higher international prices for food, there are second-round effects on wages, the CPI will experience persistent increases. Headline inflation is closely tracked by the labour unions; it is very visible, and hence becomes a clear issue in wage negotiations. Monetary policy will need to intervene in order to mitigate these second-round effects and keep inflationary expectations anchored close to the central bank's inflation target.

5.3.2 Monetary policy and exogenous price shocks: some lessons

5.3.2.1 The inflation–output trade-off

The discussion of the preceding sections shows that adverse supply shocks are huge challenges for monetary policy in LFDCs. Exogenous jumps in the price of oil or in the price of food directly lead to an upward push of the domestic price level, while simultaneously affecting output downwards. When monetary policy aims at price stability while also trying to mitigate variability in output, it faces a straightforward trade-off between these two targets when confronted with supply shocks (see section 4.2.1). To counter the inflationary consequences of an adverse supply shock, monetary policy needs to be restrictive, although this causes output to decline further. The more strictly price stability is pursued, the more negatively output will presumably be affected. Monetary policy's dilemma is about how to design its intervention so as to achieve the 'best' balance between these two negative effects of the supply shock.[37]

There are arguments that challenge the relevance of the supply shocks for the design of monetary policy. The essence of these counterarguments is that real shocks are reflected in relative price changes. Individual prices continually adapt to changing specific supply and demand conditions, but the resulting changes in relative prices need not to be a source of generalized inflation. Increases in the relative price of some goods or services are thus different from inflation, an increase in the *general* price level. Higher international prices for oil and food are in this view not necessarily conducive to higher inflation. One could indeed observe a rise in the relative price of food resulting from a combination of higher nominal prices for food and lower nominal prices for a variety of other goods and

---

costs, which is not the case for international food price increases. Second, even if the country is a net importer of food, domestic food producers have generally a more noticeable influence on domestic output, and thus on aggregate demand, than domestic producers of oil.

[37] Recall from section 4.2.1.3 that monetary policy's task is much easier when it faces adverse demand shocks. In this case, it can compensate by appropriate expansionary measures for the fall in aggregate demand, reversing simultaneously the decline in both price level and output triggered by the shock. This is possible because monetary policy is essentially a demand-oriented policy. Its reaction to a demand shock therefore necessarily affects *both* prices and quantities in the desired direction. There is no trade-off between price and output stability, contrary to the case with supply shocks. This general principle has to be somewhat mitigated, if possible supply effects of monetary policy measures through a 'cost channel' are taken into account (see section 2.2.1).

services recorded in the price index. There is no a priori reason, then, for the overall price level to rise. Why should the average level of prices be affected significantly by changes in the price of some goods relative to the price of others goods? Exogenous adverse shocks to the price of tradables, possibly exacerbated by globalization, cannot, according to this view, by themselves be responsible for recurrent inflationary episodes in LFDCs.

The above arguments do not hold, however, if account is taken of pervasive nominal price and wage rigidities. In this case, relative price increases can and indeed do lead to a higher price level. The price of food will rise, for example, but the price of other goods in the CPI index will not fall, especially those of non-traded goods, for which the nominal wage, one of the stickiest nominal prices, is a major determinant. The strict dichotomy of relative-price changes and inflation is therefore a theoretical construct that is of limited relevance for the practice of monetary policy. While the monetary authorities may not be able to achieve full control of the short-term dynamics of inflation provoked by relative-price changes, they are not freed of their responsibility to attenuate inflationary pressures with exchange rate and monetary measures.

5.3.2.2 Second-round effects

Another crucial responsibility for monetary authorities facing adverse supply shocks is to take control of second-round effects which may affect the price–wage nexus, directly triggered by the shocks' first-round effects on the price level. Higher food prices may creep into the prices of other goods and services and in wages. There can be a significant pass-through of food or oil prices into prices of other consumer goods. One simple way to gauge this pass-through is to examine the direct impact of food price increases on PPI inflation and on *core* inflation, two common alternative measures of inflation.[38]

A second pass-through mechanism is created by the relationship between actual or expected inflation and wages. The pass-through will be very significant if there is wage indexation, formally or informally. Higher food prices that rise the CPI may feed wage inflation, especially in the formal sector. This sets off a wage–price spiral. Rising wages raise the production costs of firms, thus putting upward pressure on prices of non-oil and non-food goods and services. There are, however, some countervailing forces at play which materialize over time, mitigating price pressures in the domestic economy, as a result of the negative output effects of the adverse supply shocks.

---

[38] Core inflation is given by the rate of change of consumer prices exclusive of food and energy prices. PPI inflation is given by the rate of change of the producer price index (PPI), which includes goods whose prices are on average stickier than consumer prices. Note that the definition of core inflation varies across countries. E.g. in Uruguay core inflation excludes changes in the prices of fruit, vegetable, and of goods and services whose prices are set or regulated by government bodies. See Portillo and Ustyugova (2015).

Second-round effects will depend very much on the reactions of monetary policy and on the exchange rate. While monetary policy may find it difficult to control food price rises on impact, its main challenge will then clearly be to avoid second-round effects. A clear, albeit prudent, tightening of monetary policy, may put a lid on second-round inflationary effect or strongly dampen them. This can be helped by letting the nominal exchange rate appreciate, if possible.[39]

Monitoring and controlling second-round effects of adverse price shocks will be the more important the more persistent the shocks are. If the shock is transitory, the danger of second-round effects will be limited, as the initial rise in the relative price will be more or less quickly reversed.[40] On the contrary, if the shock is very persistent or if the initial rise in the price of food or oil is followed by other recurrent rises, there will be a pressure on other prices and on wages, and the headline (CPI) inflation will be magnified. This second-round dynamic will continue as long as the real prices of food or oil continue to rise. The pressure will be heavier if the rise is left unchecked by monetary policy, as the price–wage spiral then feeds on itself and magnifies the shock's total effect on inflation. In this case, a central bank that does not want to see a persistent and protracted rise in core and PPI inflation needs to tighten monetary policy. Such a policy stance will help keep inflationary expectations anchored, and thereby also contribute to mitigate price and wage inflation.

5.3.2.3 The exchange rate regime

The efficacy of responses to exogenous shocks depends crucially on the exchange rate regime. Keeping the exchange rate fixed constrains monetary authorities' capacity to dampen the inflationary effects of the shocks. It is only if domestic and foreign currency assets are not close substitutes that monetary policy retains some clout despite the exchange rate peg. It can then be used restrictively to dampen inflation and possible second-round expected effects on wages and core inflation, at the cost of further losses in output.

Options are wider for central banks when exchange rates are flexible. Flexible exchange rates are to be preferred to fixed exchange rates when shocks are real— which is the case for oil and food price shocks. With flexible exchange rates, monetary authorities can, as discussed in sections 5.3.1.1.1.2 and 5.3.1.2, let the exchange rate appreciate with a tightening of monetary policy, which dampens the price shock's inflationary pressures. This enhances the efficacy of monetary authorities' actions, especially as the exchange rate is a crucial transmission channel of monetary policy in most LFDCs (see section 2.4). Céspedes and Velasco (2012) conclude, in their study of the macroeconomic effects of 117 episodes of

---

[39] See e.g. the case of Bolivia in 2008–11.
[40] This would be the case of international food price rises due to shortages caused by brief fluctuations of climate.

commodity price booms and busts, that output effects are less pronounced in economies with more flexible exchange rates.

5.3.2.4 CPI or PPI targeting

Central banks' reaction to adverse supply shocks may depend on the *particular inflation index* they wish to target when they aim at price stability (see IMF 2011). Should monetary policy remain accommodative with respect to external relative-price shocks as long as PPI inflation and core inflation remain on target? Or, instead, should it react forcefully to headline inflation, CPI inflation, the most visible effect of the adverse shock? This would imply aiming at much lower inflation (or even deflation) in the non-food (non-oil) domestic sectors.

Much will depend on the shock's expected persistence. A neutral or even an accommodative monetary policy is called for if the rise in food or oil prices is temporary. Headline inflation will exhibit a temporary spike. In any event, there is no need for the central bank to tighten its monetary policy. When the shock is persistent, the key decision for the central bank is how strong the tightening of monetary policy should be.

Frankel (2012) argues that targeting the CPI in the face of oil or food price increases is not recommended for an oil/food-importing country. Such policy induces a tightening of monetary policy and an appreciation of the exchange rate that erodes international competitiveness and enhances the recessionary effects of the terms-of-trade loss experienced by the country. Catao and Chang (2010) display an opposite viewpoint. Using a DSGE model, calibrated for a prototype small open EME, they find that CPI targeting dominates PPI targeting and exchange rate pegging in terms of welfare, for a volatility of food prices similar to what has been observed in the past.[41] In any case, the adverse effects of the stricter monetary policy required to target headline inflation in the face of external price shocks have to be weighed against the other possible advantages of choosing this index to target inflation, such as increased transparency and better understanding by the public of the central bank's monetary policy stance.

5.3.2.5 Coordination with fiscal policy

Finally, the reaction of monetary policy to exogenous price shocks has to take into account the stance of fiscal policy. Monetary authorities need to coordinate with fiscal authorities, as monetary policy needs to be underpinned by a sound

---

[41] Their argument is the following: if CPI targeting is pursued, a rise in food prices requires on impact a stronger tightening of monetary policy than under a PPI target. This causes, also on impact, a decrease, or smaller increase, in domestic prices other than food as well as a stronger reaction of foreign demand for home goods. All in all, therefore, output dynamics are in general more favourable under CPI targeting. This mitigates the decline in consumption. Relative to PPI targeting, consumers' welfare is increased as CPI targeting allows advantage to be taken 'of the so-called terms of trade externality i.e. to consume more per unit of domestic output' (Catao and Chang 2010: 35). One should however be somewhat careful and not take this conclusion as definite, as their DSGE model is based on a set of hypotheses which may not be fully appropriate for LFDCs, such as complete financial markets, rational expectations, and fully flexible real wages.

fiscal policy. When adverse shocks in oil or food prices trigger compensating consumer or producer subsidies in oil- or food-importing countries, monetary authorities need to insist on financing these subsidies by appropriate tax increases or budgetary austerity measures, and not by politically more attractive automatic monetary accommodation. One could at first sight argue that the use of subsidies initially lessens the need for restrictive monetary measures to check the inflationary impact of oil price hikes, and thus diminishes the intensity of the trade-off between price and output stability. However, the fiscal costs of subsidies will, over time, also lead to an adjustment of the domestic price to the international price, often in the form of a huge upward jump. Monetary policy will then be called upon for addressing the inflationary and output effects of what has now become a domestic price shock.[42]

Strict coordination with fiscal authorities is similarly needed from monetary authorities in oil-exporting countries or, for that matter, in any primary commodity-exporting country in which there is a strong connection between the commodity's externally set price and fiscal revenues. A key element in this respect is the extent of neutralization by the government of sudden increases in fiscal revenues on its expenditures. The lower the voluntary neutralization by the government, the more strongly monetary policy has to step in to dampen inflationary pressures and to avoid real appreciation. Failure to coordinate with fiscal authorities in good times, i.e. when commodity prices are above trend, may be costly for monetary authorities when the scenario is reversed. Sudden declines in international prices may have a huge impact on the fiscal deficit if neutralization has been absent in boom times. Government spending initiated in good times is then often difficult to dismantle in bad times, and political pressures on the central bank to 'temporarily' monetize the deficit may be stepped up, once more raising the spectre of fiscal dominance.

5.4 Summary

Monetary policy can be a potent tool to stabilize prices as well as output. However, its reach is often limited by fiscal constraints, and it is often challenged by unexpected changes in international prices. In this chapter we have examined how these two constraints impinge on monetary policy and hinder the achievement of its goals.

In the first section we discussed how persistent fiscal deficits can lead to inflation, now or in the future. Seigniorage becomes a natural adjustment variable

---

[42] The huge efficiency cost of maintaining over a long time a large discrepancy between domestic and international oil prices through administrative price caps will sooner or later lead to a steep hike in the domestic price of oil.

when the government fails to put a check on its primary deficits and when it is confronted with domestic and external borrowing limits. Monetary policy can also be constrained when there is no monetary financing of government deficits—if the government, for instance, pressures the central bank into keeping interest rates below what is required to maintain price stability. A high level of government debt may also generate destabilizing expectations on inflation and on the exchange rate. Lack of coordination between monetary and fiscal policy could result in the 'paradox of tight money'. Inflation is aggravated and put on an unstable path if fiscal policy disregards the requirements of government solvency, and if, simultaneously, monetary policy pursues strict inflation targeting. While such a scenario, as posited by the fiscal theory of the price level, should not be overstated, especially in the context of LFDCs, it draws attention to the importance of effective coordination between the government and the central bank. Such coordination can be facilitated by the setting of fiscal rules which, if effectively enforced, can avoid large budgetary deficits, limit their persistence, and thereby stabilize inflationary expectations.

The second challenge for monetary policy in LFDCs is presented by unexpected large external price shocks. These shocks, if not properly checked, hurt LFDCs more severely than AEs, because of their protracted effects and the absence of effective macroeconomic stabilizers. In the second section of this chapter, we examined how monetary policy can deal with the trade-off between price and output stability that such a supply shock inevitably implies. We have chosen to focus our analysis on oil and food price increases, distinguishing between net exporters and net importers. Several (selected) results stand out.

Optimal management of the inflation–output stabilization trade-off that external price increases imply is a key responsibility for LFDC central banks. The shock's second-round effects that threaten to prolong and reinforce its inflationary consequences need also to be addressed by the central bank with restrictive monetary policy.

Flexible exchange rates make it easier, relative to a fixed exchange rate regime, for monetary policy to achieve a good balance between controlling the inflationary effects of the shock and its adverse impact on output.

In oil-exporting countries, coordination between the government and the central bank is crucial to manage the windfalls brought by oil price hikes.

Government subsidies to cushion the effects of the shock for consumers may temporary facilitate the inflation–output trade-off faced by monetary policy, but their fiscal cost may increase the pressures for monetary financing of the budget deficit.

Targeting headline inflation, instead of targeting producer price or core inflation, calls for a more restrictive monetary policy, with additional adverse effects on output, to be weighed against the additional benefits of transparency.

APPENDIX 5A

Fiscal dominance according to the fiscal theory of the price level

Over the last two decades, a new approach of the interaction between monetary and fiscal policies has been developed (Leeper 1991; 2009; 2013; Carlstrom and Fuerst 2000; Cochrane 2011; Woodford 1995; 2001): the fiscal theory of the price level (FTPL). Although mainly oriented towards industrial countries, this approach has also found some echo in developing countries (Loyo 1999; Baldini and Poplawski-Ribeiro 2011). The main message of the FTPL is that fiscal dominance can occur through a channel that differs from the traditional seigniorage channel pioneered by Sargent and Wallace (1981) (see Box 5.2).

5A(1) The fiscal theory of the price level

The FTPL assumes firstly that the government issues nominal riskless debt, and not real or indexed bonds as in the Sargent–Wallace framework. The other key hypothesis is that the government is not expected to be strictly—i.e. in all times and in all circumstances— bound by its intertemporal budget constraint. This implies that some government actions may put the public debt on an explosive path, without the government immediately taking corrective steps, or credibly committing to act later, by levying more taxes or by reducing spending in order to satisfy its intertemporal budget constraint. This is called a 'non-Ricardian' assumption (Woodford 1995), and contrasts with the Sargent–Wallace framework, which holds that the government is credibly committed to strictly enforcing at all times its intertemporal budget constraint (the Ricardian assumption).

These two crucial hypotheses fundamentally change the way of looking at the interaction between monetary and fiscal policy and at its implication for the dynamics of inflation. To see this, consider the government's intertemporal budget constraint (GIBC):

$$\frac{B_{t-1}}{P_t}\left(1+R_{t-1}\right)=\left(\tau_t-g_t\right)+\frac{\left(\tau_{t+1}-g_{t+1}\right)}{\left(1+\rho_t\right)}+\frac{\left(\tau_{t+2}-g_{t+2}\right)}{\left(1+\rho_t\right)\left(1+\rho_{t+1}\right)}+\frac{\left(\tau_{t+3}-g_{t+3}\right)}{\left(1+\rho_t\right)\left(1+\rho_{t+1}\right)\left(1+\rho_{t+2}\right)}+\ldots \quad (A.1)$$

B_{t-1} is the nominal one-period debt outstanding at $t-1$, R_{t-1} the one period nominal interest rate set at $t-1$, τ_t real taxes and seigniorage receipts, g_t real government spending (excluding interest payments on debt), ρ_t the one-period real interest rate expected at t $\rho_t = \left(1+R_t\right)/\left(1+\pi_{t+1}\right)$. The government intertemporal budget constraint (GIBC) requires that, at t, the real value of the outstanding debt—the LHS of equation A.1—be equal to the present value of current and future primary surpluses. If only real debt is issued, as assumed by Sargent and Wallace (1981), the LHS of the GIBC is given, and any unexpected shock to primary spending, say in the form of larger transfers to households, needs to be sooner or later financed through higher taxes or, if not, through seigniorage generated by monetary accommodation and inflation—an increase in τ, current and future. The FTPL maintains that the dominance of fiscal policy over monetary authorities can arise through a mechanism other than seigniorage. With nominal debt given at t, an unexpected decrease in the present value of future primary surpluses will have a direct and immediate impact on the current price level P_t. The latter will rise, thus driving down the real value of outstanding nominal public debt until the GIBC is restored.[43]

This inflationary effect of the fall in the present value of expected surpluses (the RHS of equation A.1) which, in our example, results from the unexpected increase in transfers, is explained through a 'wealth effect'. At the initial level of prices, households feel richer as they benefit from the debt-financed transfer, and as they expect that the government will not finance that transfer by levying additional taxes. Feeling wealthier, they spend more, which drives up prices. The increase in the price level will cease only once the real value of debt coincides again with the lower present value of expected surpluses.

In the FTPL, the GIBC is thus an equilibrium relationship, not a strict constraint supposed to also hold 'out of equilibrium'. This matters especially when people expect that a 'fiscal limit' is about to be hit, indicating that the government is not ready to address a spiralling nominal debt by raising taxes or decreasing spending: 'A fiscal inflation [...] can occur based directly on expectation of future fiscal trouble' (Cochrane 2011: 6).

The FTPL type of fiscal dominance implies that fiscal policy is 'active', in the term used by Leeper (2009), in the sense that it is not constrained by the need to stabilize debt (i.e. by the GIBC). In such a situation, the stance of monetary policy is crucial for the dynamics of inflation. If monetary policy is also 'active', i.e. if monetary authorities set their nominal policy rates in order to achieve their inflation target, not only will they fail to reach their target, but inflation and nominal debt will possibly be put on an explosive path. This is Loyo's (1999) 'tight money paradox' interpretation of the Brazilian inflation experience of 1975–85: if monetary policy aggressively tries to contain an initial 'fiscal inflation', it increases real interest rates. The nominal debt issued to foot the higher interest bill on public debt will be considered as net wealth by households, convinced that fiscal policy will remain 'active' (i.e. that the government is non-Ricardian).[44] This will give a new push to inflation, accelerating it. If monetary policy is too aggressive, a hyperinflation dynamics may ensue. Only a 'passive' monetary policy is ultimately compatible with an 'active' fiscal policy. Such 'passive' monetary policy will no longer be able to control the actual path of inflation.[45]

In the FTPL, the inflation process is dominated by shocks to the expected present value of future budgetary surpluses. Inflation tracks the *nominal* growth of debt so as to prevent the real value of debt from growing, thereby satisfying the GIBC. In this sense, it is fiscal policy which provides the nominal anchor, not monetary policy. This may be termed *a strong form of fiscal dominance.*

---

[43] This is the key feature of the FTPL which is strongly contested by adherents of a more conventional monetary analysis of monetary and fiscal policy interactions. These insist that the price level cannot be determined by fiscal considerations—the intertemporal government budget constraint—alone, but that it ultimately depends on the dynamics of the money stock (see e.g. McCallum and Nelson 2006).

[44] The wealth effect arises as households expect future primary surpluses to remain unchanged, but now discount them at a higher real interest rate. This lowers the present value of expected future surpluses (the RHS of equation A.1) and, for a given initial nominal debt and price level, increases the household's real wealth.

[45] With passive monetary policy, the short-term interest rate is set, directly or by controlling the money supply, without concern for the actual inflation rate. Setting the one period interest rate in this way allows the central bank to control, for a given real interest rate, inflation expected for the coming period, but not actual inflation (Leeper 2009: 14).

5A(2) How relevant is the FTPL for LFDCs?

Beyond the side-questions on whether the benchmark models of the FTPL are 'realistic' for the LFDCs, a key issue is whether an LFDC government can be expected to act in a 'non-Ricardian' way, i.e. without much concern for its own solvency, as postulated by the FTPL.[46] The history of fiscal policy's performance in many LFDCs would probably point to accepting this possibility, at least for some periods in some countries. Note, however, that many LFDCs have been involved for long periods in IMF-sponsored adjustment programmes in which debt sustainability has been a crucial element. This should have contributed to minimizing opportunities for governments to adopt a 'non-Ricardian' behaviour, as pointed out by Christiano and Fitzgerald (2000: 9).

Two other characteristics of LFDCs are important when assessing the relevance of a FTPL type of fiscal dominance. First, the public debt of most LFDCs is an external debt denominated in foreign currency. Second, default on sovereign external debt is not a rare occurrence for LFDCs.

The market for nominal debt issued in domestic currency is in most of LFDCs either nonexistent or still in its infancy. Foreign currency debt is a form of indexed debt, or real debt. As explained above, the FTPL's channel linking inflation with fiscal policy only operates through the stock of nominal debt in domestic currency. The FTPL predicts that a larger share of foreign currency debt would magnify the inflationary effects of a fiscal shock (Loyo 1999: 18). As the foreign currency share is immune to unexpected inflation, the price level would indeed need to rise more to restore the initial real value of total debt if its domestic currency share is small. Such a prediction, however, raises the following question: would people still expect the government to be 'non-Ricardian' in the sense of the FTPL if the public debt is mostly in foreign currency? Or would they not, if convinced that there is a 'fiscal limit', either expect the government to resort to seigniorage to absorb unexpected fiscal shocks—as a 'Ricardian' government would act—or else default on their foreign-currency debt?

Default, or expectations of default, on public debt are usually not studied in FTPL models. It should however be easy to extend the reasoning of the FTPL to the specific, and relevant, case of foreign and domestic investors requesting a risk premium for holding a country's public debt. A negative fiscal shock to future surpluses would raise the risk premium, which would reinforce the decrease in the present value of expected future surpluses. The market value of the foreign currency part of the debt would fall as a result of higher discount rates. In addition, under FTPL's hypotheses, a rise in the domestic price level would also be needed to lower the real value of the nominal debt in domestic currency and thereby restore the real total debt to its initial value.

---

[46] FTPL models usually employ strong hypotheses (rational expectations, closed economies, nominal debt with floating rates, and no possibility of default on nominal debt). Some of these issues have been addressed: Loyo (1999) has developed an extension to an open economy, fully integrated in international goods and capital markets, as well as to an economy with indexed debt as a significant share of public debt. Cochrane (2011) enriches his model, introducing fixed interest rate long-term nominal debt along with short-term debt. Baldini and Poplawski-Ribeiro (2011) develop a model with a risk premium which rises with the level of domestic nominal debt.

FTPL clearly displays special characteristics in LDFCs, but its relevance cannot be rejected out of hand. Its message of a possible pure fiscal origin to inflation, and of the inflationary risks of debt instability, may probably be only relevant in specific countries and during specific episodes in which the main hypothesis of a 'non-Ricardian' government can reasonably be accepted. Strong institutions and credible fiscal rules as well as close monitoring of the budget can, however, contribute to minimize the risk of such a strong type of fiscal dominance.

On the empirical side, evidence in support of the FTPL is not easy to obtain, essentially because it seems difficult to directly discriminate between Ricardian and non-Ricardian fiscal policy regimes.[47] Indirect tests, based for example on the analysis of the dynamic interaction between primary surpluses and public liabilities, have been conducted, mainly for industrial countries. Baldini and Poplawski-Ribeiro (2011) apply such a battery of fiscal dominance tests, as well as complementary tests of 'monetary dominance', to a set of 22 sub-Saharan African countries. Noting that identification of regimes is fragile and that results should be interpreted with care, they conclude that, over the 1980–2005 period, a fiscal dominance regime could be identified for Botswana, Burundi, Tanzania, and Zimbabwe, and a 'monetary dominance' regime for Cameroon, Kenya, Nigeria, Rwanda, and South Africa.

---

[47] See Canzoneri et al. (2001: 1234) who note that they 'have not been able to develop a formal statistical test that would directly discriminate between Ricardian and non-Ricardian regimes. And indeed, since both regimes use exactly the same equations to explain the data, such tests may not exist'.

6

The Choice of Nominal Targets
in an Open Economy

6.1 Introduction

A central feature of modern monetary regimes is the use of a nominal anchor, i.e.
a constraint on a selected nominal domestic monetary variable, expressed in
numerical terms. According to Mishkin (1999), a nominal anchor of some form
is a necessary element of successful monetary policy regimes. Nominal anchors
set the conditions that make the price level uniquely determined. In addition,
they underpin price stability insofar as they contribute to tying down inflation
expectations. More broadly speaking, a nominal anchor is a constraint on
discretionary policy and helps to tone down its time-inconsistency problem. It is
closely linked to credibility issues and their institutional implications, as discussed
in Chapter 4.

An LFDC's decision to adopt one or the other nominal anchor will depend on
the country's history and its specific characteristics. To a large extent the choice of
the nominal anchor is path-dependent, and hence major changes in the policy
framework are often taken reluctantly. Also, many central banks in LFDCs do not
have an explicit nominal anchor but operate, in the best of cases, an assorted set
of several nominal anchors simultaneously. However, their monetary frameworks
are evolving, trying to emulate gradually the best practices of AEs. Many are in
the process of sharpening their targets as well as explicitly defining a nominal anchor.

Three types of nominal anchor are generally used in modern central banking:
exchange rate targeting, money targeting, and inflation targeting. Table 6.1 gives an
overview of the different monetary frameworks LFDCs adopted de facto in 2018 as
nominal anchors.[1] It appears that 47% of them have some form of exchange rate
targeting, of which more than half follow a conventional peg. Monetary aggregate
targeting and inflation targeting is pursued by 19% and 14%, respectively, of LFDCs.
Also, for 20% of countries no explicit anchor could be identified.

It can also be observed in Table 6.1 that many countries that use monetary aggregate targeting or inflation targeting still manage the exchange rate. The exchange rate

---

[1] The de facto monetary framework may differ from the de jure regime, especially in the case of
exchange rate anchors. A country may e.g. announce a floating exchange rate regime, while it heavily
intervenes de facto on the foreign exchange market to manage the path of the exchange rate.

Monetary Policy in Low Financial Development Countries. Juan Antonio Morales and Paul Reding, Oxford University Press.
© Juan Antonio Morales and Paul Reding 2021. DOI: 10.1093/oso/9780198854715.003.0006

Table 6.1. Monetary frameworks in LFDCs

	Exchange rate targeting	Monetary aggregate targeting	Inflation targeting	Other[b]	Total	%
No separate legal tender	6				6	5.4
Currency Board	6				6	5.4
Conventional Pegs	30			2	32	28.6
Stabilized and managed arrangements[a]	11	20	5	16	52	46.4
Floating		1	11	3	15	13.4
Free floating				1	1	0.9
Total	53	21	16	22	112	100.0
%	47.3	18.8	14.3	19.6	100	

Notes: [a] Crawling pegs, crawl-like arrangements, pegged exchange rates within horizontal bands and others. [b] With no explicitly stated anchor.
Source: Data from IMF (2019a).

has an overriding role in reducing the space of discretionary behaviour, and as such it is closely tracked or (as a minimum) taken into account in the set of monetary conditions monitored by authorities. It is to be noted that countries which combine different anchors may at times face problems of consistency.

A general observation which can be made at this point is that the choice of a nominal anchor is directly linked to the choice of the exchange rate regime and to the degree of actual openness of the capital account of the balance of payments. By the well-known Mundell–Fleming 'trilemma' there is no room for an independent monetary policy with a fixed exchange rate *and* free capital flows. Only flexible exchange rates would allow central banks to use monetary or inflation targeting to reach its domestic goals while keeping the capital account fully open. This view is, however, challenged. A more extreme view holds that with financial globalization, there is little room for an independent monetary policy, be it monetary or inflation-anchored, and this regardless of the exchange regime, as long as capital movements remain completely unhindered. The 'trilemma' reduces to a 'dilemma': an independent monetary policy is only possible if the 'global financial cycle' is tamed, i.e. if the disruptive effects of large global capital in- and outflows can be avoided.[2] This can be done by managing the

---

[2] The term 'global financial cycle' was coined by Hélène Rey. It refers to the cyclical co-movements of gross capital in- and outflows, of asset prices, and of credit growth observed across regions. These cycles are linked to changes in monetary conditions in the main financial centres, such as the USA, and to changes in investors' risk aversion. They are transmitted via global financial intermediaries, banks, and asset management companies. They have a capacity to profoundly affect the macroeconomic conditions of capital flows in recipient countries, irrespective of their exchange rate regime. They can lead to a build-up of foreign currency debt, excess credit creation, and asset bubbles, undermining financial stability and possibly paving the way for a financial crisis (see Rey 2018).

capital account directly and by resorting to macro-prudential instruments in order to cut off the transmission of international credit cycles to the domestic economy. Capital controls can shield domestic monetary policy and give it more space. The choice of instruments of capital control is, however, far from trivial. If chosen without adequate care, they can have high efficiency costs, as discussed in section 3.2.1.2. In any case, both targeted capital controls and macro-prudential instruments fall within the purview of the central bank's mandate to preserve financial stability (see section 4.2.2).

In sections 6.2 to 6.4, we discuss in turn each nominal anchor, pointing out their pros and cons. Section 6.5 is devoted to the special case of nominal anchors in dollarized economies. Section 6.6 offers a short summary. The chapter includes two appendixes: the first is devoted to the role played by international reserves; the second is a case study of monetary unions in sub-Saharan Africa.

6.2 Exchange rate targeting

6.2.1 Characteristics

Targeting the exchange rate has a long history. The targeting initially took the form of fixing the value of the domestic currency to a commodity, especially gold (or silver), or to a currency that was convertible to gold in the gold exchange standard arrangement. Since the suppression of convertibility to gold of the major currencies, for domestic transactions in the 1930s and for international transactions in the early 1970s, fixed exchange rate regimes are set with reference to the domestic currency of a low-inflation, large country. By fixing the value of the currency to the currency of a low-inflation anchor country, it is expected that domestic inflation will converge over time to that of the anchor country.

As shown in Table 6.1, exchange rate targeting comes in many different varieties, according to the degree of commitment to the fixed parity of the monetary authorities. Of the fifty-three LFDCs that had opted for exchange rate targeting in 2018, only about a quarter (23%) aimed at strict rigidity of their exchange rate through 'hard pegs', having adopted a currency board arrangement or using the anchor currency as domestic legal tender. A significant number of exchange rate-targeting LFDCs (56%) followed a conventional peg, in which the exchange is in principle fixed, but can be adjusted under specific circumstances of fundamental disequilibria in the balance of payments. A last category of exchange rate-targeting LFDCs (21%) had chosen a less constraining anchoring, for instance by allowing movements of the exchange rate in small steps around a specific, announced or unannounced target path ('crawling peg'), or within a target band.

Notice that exchange rate targets designed to anchor the price level concern only unified exchange rate regimes, which have become the standard. There are however some LFDCs that still use exchange controls, including multiple exchange rate regimes. These are propitious to the emergence of parallel markets.[3] Those have recently reappeared in selected LFDCs (see Box 6.1). Multiple exchange rates, with different rates for different categories of goods or services or for different accounts of the balance of payments, have many aims, mostly of a distributive nature or to protect given industries.[4] Some countries may have a dual exchange market imposing different exchange rates for current account transactions on the one hand and for capital account transactions on the other.

Box 6.1. Parallel exchange rates

Parallel unofficial markets for foreign currency develop when the availability of foreign currency is curtailed by exchange controls. Typically, in the case of a severe balance-of-payment deficit, originating either in the current or of the capital account, keeping the exchange rate fixed entails a persistent drain on international reserves. To address these disequilibria, countries are faced with a dilemma: abandon the peg or try to preserve it by adopting sufficiently restrictive monetary and fiscal policies. As both policies may produce severe negative consequences for domestic output and employment, authorities are inclined, in order to circumvent this dilemma, to resort to exchange controls. Countries on a flexible exchange rate regime face a similar dilemma when unbridled capital outflows threaten to lead to a too rapid depreciation of the currency.

Exchange controls are of various types (see section 3.2.1.2). Their function is to limit the demand of foreign currency at the official rate by rationing access of private-sector agents to foreign exchange on the official exchange market, as well as requesting them to surrender on this market their foreign exchange receipts. The excess demand for foreign currency that exists at the official rate spills over into a parallel black market, where the exchange rate rises relative to the official rate. Evasion of exchange controls becomes profitable and gives rise to the parallel supply of foreign currency. Importers have incentives to resell their foreign currency obtained at the official exchange rate in the parallel market. Exporters succumb to the temptation to evade the requirement to surrender their exports receipts on the official market, and sell them on the parallel market. Since the premium of the black rate over the

---

[3] IMF (2019a: 21) reports that in 2017 29 countries still maintained differentials between official, commercial, and parallel rates.

[4] A recent example is Venezuela in the early years of this century, whose exchange rate regime established a low domestic currency price for dollars to import 'essential' goods and for exports, and a higher exchange rate applied to imports of non-essential goods and services. A parallel ('black') market thrived alongside the official market.

official rate (or rates) can be very high, it should be obvious that this invites corruption.

The premium on the black market rate is an indicator of the degree of macroeconomic disequilibria. The higher the premium, the larger the disequilibria. The black market rate can be thought of as a shadow rate in the sense that it would be the rate at which the market clears in the absence of exchange controls. This is only partially true, as the parallel exchange market is an opaque and inefficient market, where information is limited to relatively few knowledgeable operators, on the supply as well as on the demand side. Black market transactions are, in principle, illegal, and operators face the risk of penal sanctions. This risk increases the premium. The latter nevertheless still usefully approximates the degree of overvaluation of the official rate, and nurtures expectation of future depreciations of the latter. As a result, domestic price setters frequently fix their prices in accordance with the parallel market exchange rate, thereby reinforcing, in a vicious circle, the degree of overvaluation and the expectations of depreciation. Inflationary expectations may thus lose their former anchor, which may lead the economy into a higher inflation path, even a hyperinflationary one.

Once the monetary authorities realize their powerlessness in controlling transactions in the parallel market, the black market becomes a grey market where the prohibition to deal in foreign currency is weakly enforced. In many cases, countries strive to unify their parallel exchange rates with the official rate by lifting exchange controls, as part of their package of measures to restore macroeconomic stability, pressured as well by the IMF. In most countries unification succeeded, and by the end of the 1990s parallel markets had almost vanished throughout the world. However, parallel markets are back in many developing countries. They have reappeared during the last decade, notably in countries, like Angola, Iran, Nigeria, or Venezuela, facing acute foreign currency shortages after international oil prices plunged, especially after 2014 (Reinhart 2016). In Nigeria, for instance, premiums on the parallel market started to rise in 2015, reaching levels up to 160% in 2016 and 2017, before falling to more moderate levels, as a result of easing of foreign shortages, within an exchange market still segmented by multiple currency practices (IMF 2019c: 7). In Venezuela, the premium became sizeable after 2012, even reaching levels up to and above 10,000% in 2018 when the official peg was abandoned, with the unified rate subject to rapid depreciation since (see e.g. Perrault 2020). In Egypt, where the foreign currency shortage was due to the consequences of political turmoil, a black market reappeared in 2013, with a premium that gradually increased to about 100% in 2016, when the decision to let the official rate float was taken, once more unifying the exchange market (IMF 2017: 5).

6.2.2 Advantages of exchange rate targeting

Exchange rate targeting has several advantages, not the least being its simplicity and clarity.

(i) The exchange rate nominal anchor fixes the inflation rate for internationally traded goods by equating the international inflation rate or closely approaching it. This directly contributes to *keeping domestic inflation under control*, given the weight these goods usually carry in the consumption basket. Also, if there is a high pass-through of the exchange rate on prices of non-traded goods and of wages (see section 2.4.3.3), fixing the exchange rate eliminates this external source of inflationary pressures.[5] In addition, if the exchange rate peg is fully credible, it contributes to fix inflation expectations to the inflation rate of the anchor country. These expectations of low inflation play a significant role in moderating the country's price–wage dynamics.

(ii) An exchange rate peg provides authorities with a disciplining device for fiscal and monetary policies, and therefore mitigates time-inconsistency problems arising from discretionary policy-making (see section 4.3.1). In a small open economy, the pressures against the exchange rate arise from imbalances between demand and supply of domestic money. Most often these imbalances are rooted in an over-expansionary fiscal policy and its monetary accommodation. However, with an exchange rate target, monetary policy (and fiscal policy) will be tightened as soon as losses of international reserves, pushed by devaluation pressures, become important. The viability of exchange rate targeting as nominal anchor thus crucially depends on the authorities' commitment, and effectiveness, in disciplining domestic monetary and fiscal policies ex ante in a way that is consistent with the fixed parity.

(iii) Exchange rate targeting has been an effective means of quickly reducing high inflation in LFDCs and EMEs. Most, although not all, inflation stabilization programmes began as exchange rate stabilization programmes. That is, the initial step was stabilization of the exchange rate (see Box 6.2 for a case study).

For an economy largely open to trade and to capital flows, anchoring the exchange rate to the currency of an important trade partner may be pursued in order to insulate the economy's real sector from unwanted volatility in the nominal

---

[5] The relationship between prices and exchange rate is not linear. The pass-through of exchange rates on prices usually increases with inflation, thus reinforcing the effects of exchange rate depreciation on inflation.

Box 6.2. Exchange rate-based inflation stabilization: the case of Bolivia 1985

In the trail of the external debt crisis of the 1980s, several Latin American countries suffered very high inflation. Bolivia suffered a true hyperinflation in 1984–5, starting, according to Cagan's (1956) characterization, when monthly inflation hit 50% and ending when the rise in prices fell below that number and stayed below for a year. Accumulated inflation from January 1985 to August 1985 was 8,000%. Inflation was quickly tamed in September 1985, and stabilization of the exchange rate, following the unification of the parallel and official rates, played a prominent role (Sachs, 1987; Morales, 2012: 37–66)

Indeed, exchange rate stabilization was a major component of the Bolivian stabilization plan. It had been used before, and would be used again, in other countries, e.g. in Argentina in 1991 or Bulgaria in 1997. It is true that stabilizations of high inflation have as necessary condition the narrowing of fiscal deficits, but often the first price that triggers the inflation stabilization process is the stabilized exchange rate. Bolivia adopted an administered floating rate that very shortly evolved into a crawling-peg arrangement, i.e. a fixed exchange rate regime with high-frequency adjustments in small steps. Stabilizing the exchange rate is often tantamount to inflation stabilization, particularly in countries that are de facto highly dollarized and where the pass-through from the exchange rate to domestic prices is very high.

When the credibility of an inflation stabilization plan is hard to obtain, e.g. because of previous failures or because political fragmentation is such that no agreement can be reached on the contents of a stabilization programme, exchange rate-based stabilization or even full de jure dollarization can be the only options. In the first case, as in Bolivia, exchange rate-based stabilization was supported by a fiscal policy package and buttressed by lifting the restrictions to freely operate with dollars. Operations with dollars had been previously forbidden. In the second case, full de jure dollarization, implying quasi-elimination of the domestic currency, substituted for a credible domestic stabilization plan. This happened in Ecuador in 2000, and to a large extent also in Zimbabwe in 2009.

Bolivian stabilization from hyperinflation in 1985 was not followed by large increases in the demand for domestic currency, as could have been expected from the theoretical models of inflation stabilization and from the experience of Central European countries in the 1920s. Instead, re-monetization took place in dollars. In fact the liberalization of the exchange market that accompanied the stabilization plan increased dollarization, and this despite the rapid and important drop in inflation. The incomplete convergence of expectations to actual inflation may be a factor that explains the feeble remonetization in domestic currency. Only recently, in the second decade of the twenty-first century, has dollarization receded.

exchange rate. Whether this reflects an optimal choice, however, depends on the nature of shocks faced by the country. The classic view is, broadly, that the exchange rate should be fixed when shocks originate in the monetary, financial sphere, while the exchange rate should be floating when shocks are mostly of real origin. This view reflects Poole's (1970) analysis on the optimal choice between the interest rate or the monetary aggregate as operating target, given that fixing the interest rate is tantamount to fixing the exchange rate (see section 1.3.3.3). Such a view, while clearly too simplified and blunt, nevertheless indicates that pegging the nominal exchange rate cannot insulate from all types of shocks. The many advantages of an exchange rate peg have to be assessed against its drawbacks.

6.2.3 Drawbacks of exchange rate targeting

The clear advantages of the exchange rate nominal anchor are, however, thwarted by strong drawbacks.

(i) The loss of an independent monetary policy, when substitutability between domestic and foreign currency assets is high, is an inevitable first draw-back. Monetary policy becomes fully subservient to the exchange rate target. With open capital markets, an exchange rate target causes domestic interest rates to be aligned to those of the anchor country. With a fully credible fixed exchange rate peg, uncovered interest parity will force equality of the domestic nominal interest rate with the foreign nominal interest rate (see section 2.4.2.1). Any deviation between domestic and foreign interest rates will be sanctioned by capital movements, forcing the central bank to intervene, by buying or selling foreign exchange and/or by adjusting its domestic policy rate (see section 3.5). The ability to use monetary policy to respond to exogenous, asymmetric, i.e. country-specific shocks is therefore lost. Also, shocks to the anchor country may be directly transmitted to the targeting country. However, substitutability between domestic and foreign currency assets in LFDCs can be deemed limited, although it is increasing in some countries. Therefore, the drawback of losing an autonomous monetary policy when opting for an exchange rate target as nominal anchor may be less damaging in LFDCs than in AEs and EMEs. Nevertheless, the scope of monetary policy narrows, and is constrained by the need to be consistent with what is required to maintain the exchange rate target.

(ii) The susceptibility to *speculative attacks* may be the greatest vulnerability of pegging the exchange rate. If the fixed rate exchange were to stay forever, there would be no speculation or vulnerabilities, but eternity of a fixed exchange rate is obviously not a realistic assumption. When there are recurring balance-of-payments deficits, the fall in international reserves may proceed at a moderate pace in the beginning, but after a threshold is reached the pace is hastened by expectations of devaluation that turn up in further capital outflows. These expectations may be 'self-fulfilling', in which case the exchange rate will be devalued (or even the peg abandoned) well before the stock of international reserves of the central banks is exhausted. Speculative attacks on the currency have become harder to resist with globalization, which has magnified the size of capital outflows relative to the amount of reserves central banks can mobilize to defend the peg. It is to be noted that even if the capital account of the balance of payments is only partially open, as is the case in many LFDCs, speculation against the exchange rate can occur. Capital movements can take the form of informal or illegal and unrecorded capital flight, which gives rise to a parallel exchange rate, therefore putting pressure on the official exchange rate (see Box 6.1). Probably as important if not more so in LFDCs, over-invoicing of imports and under-invoicing of exports, as well as postponing the repatriation of export receipts, constitute natural channels for speculating against the domestic currency in anticipation of a future devaluation.[6]

With hard pegs, currency board arrangements, and a fortiori full dollarization (see section 6.2.4.2), the possibility of currency crisis would, in principle, be barred, since all foreign exchange liabilities are fully backed by foreign exchange assets, explicitly or implicitly. Notwithstanding, there is always a non-zero probability (however small) attached to the rare event that the hard peg will be abandoned. This ultimately happened in Argentina in 2001. The spread of domestic interest rates vis-à-vis the interest rate of the anchor country reflects this probability.[7]

Doubts with regard to the strength and the willingness of the government to defend the peg, in particular about how much of its reserves it is willing to use to maintain parity, compound the peg's vulnerability. Various exchange rate models have addressed the dynamics of speculative attacks.[8]

---

[6] These so called 'leads and lags' may be responsible for huge losses of international reserves, especially for countries whose trade flows are important relative to their stock of international reserves.

[7] A tiny probability of a change in the peg over a given period, say a year, may generate a significant differential between the domestic and foreign one-year interest rates if the change is expected to be large if it occurs. This is a facet of the so-called 'peso problem'.

[8] A *first-generation* model of speculative attacks was formulated by Krugman (1979). In his model, the monetary financing of fiscal imbalances is the fundamental driver of currency crises. In the *second-generation models*, due to Obstfeld (1994), a rational government who has to react to a negative supply shock faces the following strategic choice: devalue, bearing a political cost and letting inflation rise, or keep the peg, accepting the unemployment costs resulting from the shock and the induced expectations of devaluation. The public holds rational expectations and understands the government's incentives. Multiple, self-fulfilling equilibria may arise from this confrontation. In

They concur in suggesting that a sufficiently strong exogenous shock can trigger speculative expectations of devaluation among rational investors. These will be reinforced if entrepreneurs in the tradable sector are led to lobby hard for a correction of the exchange rate to regain competitiveness and sometimes to alleviate the burden of their domestic currency debts. Such expectations of devaluation drive up domestic interest rates and may also feed into prices and wages, thereby compounding the problems of over-valuation and unemployment. The government may ultimately be forced to take action and devalue, well before international reserves are exhausted.

(iii) Even tiny annual divergences between domestic and foreign inflation rates cumulating over a sufficiently long period will be conducive to a sizeable overvaluation of the domestic currency. Such divergences may be brought about by the persistent effects of temporary exogenous shocks, as discussed in section 5.3. More generally, it cannot be expected that a fixed parity can be maintained for ever, even admitting that in some cases it can have a long life. Maintaining a nominal anchor which is overvalued poses, however, a dilemma for policy-makers. Keeping the peg reinforces its credibility but requires appropriate corrective measures, such as fiscal consolidation, restrictive monetary policy, and wage-moderating pol-icies. All these measures entail economic and political costs. The alterna-tive is to devalue, thereby temporally losing the country's nominal anchor and possibly also involving huge disruptions in the economy. Devaluation will in principle be more attractive if its expected positive effects on out-put in the tradable sector sufficiently mitigate the deflationary effects of the accompanying restrictive fiscal and monetary policies that in general will also be necessary to improve the country's external balance.[9] But it may also imply higher costs than keeping the peg, from both an economic and a political perspective, if the devaluation proves to be contractionary in its own, at least in the short run. For LFDCs, and more so for EMEs, this is often the case. On impact devaluations can be contractionary because of both demand and supply effects on the real side and because

particular, a high expected devaluation provides the incentive for the government to devalue, thereby validating the expectation, even if the actual shock it faces is small (see also Obstfeld and Rogoff, 1996: section 9.5.4). Finally, Chang and Velasco's (2001) *third-generation models* look at financial factors as the main cause of exchange rate crises, especially when troubled banks hit by illiquidity problems trigger panic among foreign creditors.

[9] As is well known, eliminating a current account deficit requires both expenditure-switching and expenditure-reducing policies. The former aims at increasing the relative price of traded vs non-traded goods. It shifts output to the traded sector and spending to non-traded goods. The latter directly targets global absorption, in order to reduce the traded-good component of domestic demand. A devaluation is mostly intended as an expenditure-switching policy, although it may also entail contractive effects, as discussed in Box 6.3. Fiscal, monetary, and nominal wage policies are employed more bluntly as expenditure-reducing policies but also, and importantly, to prevent excess demand in the non-traded sector that could annihilate, through wage and price increases in this sec-tor, the relative price effect in favour of the traded sector which the devaluation aims to improve.

of balance sheet effects, as argued by Krugman and Taylor (1978) and
Krugman (1999) and summed up in Box 6.3.

Even if devaluation is contractive in the short run, it can however have
positive medium- and long-run effects if it succeeds in rebalancing

---

Box 6.3. Contractive devaluations[a]

If there is initially a trade deficit, which is likely to be the case, a devaluation
will increase the price of imports on impact while the export response in the
tradable goods sector will still be sluggish. If there is a high pass-through of
the exchange rate to domestic prices, devaluation will cause a jump in the price
level, reducing gross domestic real income and aggregate demand. The ensuing
contraction of output, in turn, will compress imports and improve the balance
of payments. It is the contraction of output rather than the expected expansion
of tradables that produces the improvement in the trade balance.

In commodity-exporting LFDCs, devaluations have the fiscal effect of
increasing government revenue. Real income is redistributed from the private
sector to the government. Since in the short run the marginal propensity to
save of the government is very high, this increase in savings is contractive.

Devaluations may produce shifts in the distribution of income, as they increase
profits in the traded sector and reduce real wages. It penalizes the lower incomes
that presumably have a higher propensity to consume than consumers with high
income. Again, this is contractive.

As already discussed in section 2.4.3.2, the balance-sheet effects of devaluation
may also have a strong contractive effect on aggregate demand: this is especially
true when the fixed exchange rate regime has encouraged capital inflows and
excessive lending in foreign currency, leading to credit and asset price booms.
Devaluation raises the domestic currency value of foreign currency debts and
frequently triggers the burst of the asset price bubble. This may endanger the stability of the financial sector, while the reduction of net wealth will reduce current
spending by consumers. Devaluation may also decrease investment, as investors
will find it more difficult to borrow, given that the collateral they can post
against their loans will have melted away. This may imply negative consequences for output supply in the longer run.

Devaluation will also affect the supply side in the short run, if the production of non-tradables is very intensive in imported inputs. Devaluation raises
production costs and thereby constrains output in the non-traded sectors.
Notice that the possibility of contractive devaluations depends very much on
the initial conditions like the relative size of the non-tradable sector and the
degree of liability dollarization.

[a] Discussion based on Krugman and Taylor (1978) and Krugman (1999).

output towards the tradable goods sector and restoring the country's competitiveness. On the whole, therefore, it seems clear that theory cannot assess with certainty the net effect of devaluation on output. In practice, it will be the external and domestic contexts that surround and motivate the decision to devaluate that will largely contribute to determine the outcome, the latter obviously reflecting not only the effects of the devaluation itself but the combined consequences of concomitant exogenous shocks and induced policy responses.[10] Whatever the case may be, it is the potentially huge prospective costs of a devaluation that may lead authorities to procrastinate, even if postponing devaluation may ultimately compound their costs.[11]

6.2.4 Types of exchange rate targeting

There are two major types of exchange rate anchors: soft pegs and hard pegs.

6.2.4.1 Soft pegs

Exchange rates are fixed in soft pegs (*conventional pegs*) but they can be readjusted through devaluations or revaluations, as required by the need to correct lasting balance-of-payment imbalances. Such *conventional pegs*, currently used in 2018 by countries as diverse as Bhutan, Eritrea, Lesotho, Nepal, or Turkmenistan, are in the spirit of the Bretton Woods system set up in 1944, which gave birth to the International Monetary Fund and formed the backbone of the international financial architecture until the early 1970s.[12] International reserves are a crucial factor in this type of exchange rate arrangement, as they are a country's first line of defence of the peg, enabling the central bank to intervene in the foreign exchange market to maintain the targeted exchange rate (see section 3.5; see also Appendix 6A). On the other side, scant reserves or a rapid depletion of them endanger the targeted exchange rate.

Some countries, like Botswana, Honduras, Nicaragua in 2018, maintain another type of soft peg: *the crawling peg*, by which their currency is permitted to devaluate in small steps with high frequency. In doing so, they allow their inflation rate to be higher than that of the anchor country while maintaining the

---

[10] The empirical literature reports quite mixed results about whether the net effects of devaluations are contractionary or expansionary, as discussed by Vegh (2013: 383–5).

[11] The political costs can be very high, causing the fall of governments or at least the removal of the minister of finance after the measure is taken, as documented e.g. by Cooper (1971).

[12] The cited countries are from IMF (2019a: table 2). Note that there may be differences between de jure and de facto exchange regimes. For instance Bolivia's regime is classified as a stabilized arrangement although it is on a de facto peg, as the exchange rate has been kept unchanged since Nov. 2011, when its crawling peg was abandoned.

competitiveness of the real exchange rate.[13] Regular small devaluations have also been used to try to pre-empt speculative attacks against the domestic currency under the presumption that speculators would not act if the devaluation, if it occurred, could be expected to be small.

Crawling peg arrangements can be of the pre-announced type or not. In the first type, the path of the exchange rate is announced for a given number of days or weeks. This gives transparency and predictability to this exchange rate arrangement and brings it closer to that of a traditional peg. The crawling peg with no pre-announced path for the exchange rate (also called 'incomplete crawl') gives more freedom to the monetary authorities to cope with unexpected shocks.

LFDCs have also used exchange rate pegs, fixed or crawling, together with *horizontal bands*, an arrangement also called a *target zone*. For fixed pegs, upper and lower limits of the band are set simultaneously with the central, parity rate. For crawling pegs, the target zone takes the form of upward sloping bands around the central rate's path. In this arrangement, the monetary authorities intervene in the market whenever the exchange rate hits its ceiling, say $\bar{S}$ or its floor, say $\underline{S}$. Within the band, the exchange rate floats freely. As put by Obstfeld and Rogoff (1996: 575), 'the threat of intervention at the margin keeps the exchange rate confined between $\bar{S}$ and $\underline{S}$ for a wider range of fundamentals than would a free float. Thus the target zone buys some exchange rate flexibility with less variability than a free float would allow.' Obviously, the width of the band matters.

6.2.4.2 Hard pegs
Hard pegs are fixed exchange rates with (in principle) irrevocable parities or, at the minimum, parities that are institutionally difficult to change. Hard pegs, in all their varieties, constitute a mechanism to discipline the fiscal and monetary authorities, given the need to preserve at all times the credibility of the peg. Three types of hard peg can be considered: currency boards; unilateral currency unions; and common currency areas.

6.2.4.2.1 *Currency boards*
Currency board arrangements were used in the British colonies during the nineteenth and early twentieth centuries (and sporadically in the colonies of other colonial powers). More recent examples are those still operated by Hong Kong and Bulgaria, those of Estonia and Lithuania before the two countries joined the Eurozone (in 2011 and 2015, respectively), and that chosen by Argentina from 1991 to 2001.[14] However, with the exception of Djibouti, none of our LFDCs has

---

[13] Crawling pegs are usually intended, as indicated, for devaluations in small steps, but could be used for revaluations, should the need arise.

[14] Argentina is an EME. Schuler (2005) argues that neither Hong Kong nor the Baltic countries nor Argentina fit the orthodox model of currency boards, and would prefer to refer to them as 'quasi currency boards'.

adopted this form of hard peg. Currency boards exhibit two main characteristics: (i) de jure fixed exchange rates; and (ii) 100% backing of the monetary base
with foreign reserves. Within the currency board arrangement, the legal obstacles to readjusting the exchange rate are of paramount importance. Since the
exchange rate is fixed by law, devaluation needs the repeal of that law, which may
in most political scenarios be close to impossible. The 100% backing of the
domestic monetary base implies that additional domestic currency can be issued
only if there is a corresponding increment of foreign reserves.

Currency boards give, at least initially, high credibility to inflation control.
They are an effective means to stop short high inflation, as indeed happened in
Argentina when the currency board was introduced in 1991. However, they do
not by themselves necessarily prevent fiscal profligacy, as was initially believed.
As shown in the case of Argentina, the absence of a concomitant strict fiscal discipline ultimately led to the demise of the currency board, with dramatic consequences for the economy.[15] Also, currency boards leave the countries without a
lender of last resort, making it difficult for the central bank to honour its financial stability mandate.[16]

Finally, currency boards, like all fixed exchange rate arrangements, are unsuitable to cope with major external shocks. Also, they can be a straitjacket for international competitiveness. Intended to maximize credibility through making the
peg 'irrevocable', currency board arrangements make forced exiting, i.e. devaluing
the currency, especially painful because, along with the loss of the nominal
anchor, the credibility of the monetary authorities would be badly damaged. The
adjustment to the new uncertain environment and the enactment of necessarily
restrictive economic policies may throw the country into the worst possible
scenario: high inflation and at the same time a severe recession.

6.2.4.2.2 Unilateral currency unions

Unilateral currency unions are arrangements by which countries explicitly adopt
a foreign currency as legal tender, simultaneously abandoning their national
currencies. A foreign currency (the 'dollar') is used in all the functions normally
reserved to domestic currency. The country's currency disappears, except maybe
for very small denominations. We shall call this arrangement *full* or *de jure*
dollarization. For example Panama, Ecuador, and El Salvador have taken this step.
Full dollarization is to be distinguished from partial (or de facto) dollarization,

---

[15] In Argentina, fiscal deficits, which could not be financed with the central bank, were financed
instead by issuing dollar-denominated external debt. The resulting public and private debt build-up
led ultimately to a debt and foreign exchange crisis and to the abandonment of the currency board.
The ensuing devaluation of the exchange rate led to very high inflation, precisely what the hard peg
was intended to avoid. The Argentinean experience is consistent with the prediction of weak fiscal
dominance discussed in section 5.2.

[16] The Central Bank of Argentina had to use a series of conventional measures (decreasing reserve
requirements) and unconventional devices(reforming the central bank's charter) to perform this function when the need arose after the contagious Mexican financial crisis of 1994.

discussed in section 6.5, in that it is the result of an explicit decision by the country's government, whereas the latter occurs mainly as a decision of the public.

The main advantage of full dollarization is that, in principle, the domestic inflation and the domestic interest rates converge, under some conditions, to the inflation and interest rates of the anchor country. Also, de jure dollarization increases certainty, thereby reducing transaction costs and facilitating integration into the international financial system.[17]

Full dollarization completely precludes the country from using the exchange rate as an instrument to cope with exogenous shocks. Moreover, shocks in the anchor country, especially interest rate shocks, are directly and quickly transmitted to the dollarized economy. Very importantly, the management of public debt, if it is high, becomes even more problematic.

Is there still a role for a central bank with full dollarization? The answer is yes, but with dollarization the central bank is hamstrung, being devoid of most monetary responsibilities. Its monetary responsibilities of guaranteeing the liquidity of the financial system implies that it carries out monetary operations in dollars, as discussed in section 3.6.4.

As was the case for the currency board arrangement, the costs of leaving the currency union, even if this is adopted unilaterally, are very high, significantly higher than in the soft peg arrangements. Especially problematic is the unwinding of contracts agreed in dollars and their conversion to the new domestic currency. Also, in LFDCs where institutions are generally weak, the political costs of abandoning the unilateral currency union can be huge.[18]

6.2.4.2.3 *Common currency areas*

In a multinational common currency area, or monetary union (MU), members agree to irrevocably fix the bilateral exchange rates of their currencies, to adopt a common currency, and to set up common monetary institutions.[19] The pre-existing domestic currencies disappear after some time. As is, for example, the case in the Eurozone, the most recent and largest multinational MU currently in activity, the partner countries delegate common monetary policy to a supranational central bank. This implies that they give up monetary and exchange rate policy as tools to stabilize country-specific shocks. The loss of these instruments is deemed to be outweighed by the benefits of a common currency, particularly in strengthening trade and financial ties as well as in institution-building.

---

[17] De facto dollarization can also facilitate international integration, but less easily.

[18] In Ecuador, electoral promises of restoring the national currency that had been replaced by foreign currency did not materialize, despite of the nationalist policies followed by the government.

[19] Multinational MUs are to be distinguished from national MUs. The latter are characterized by an overlap of monetary and political sovereignty. National MUs have emerged in the 19th and 20th c. as outcomes closely associated with political unification. This has notably been the case for Germany and Italy in the second half of the 19th c. (Bordo and Jonung 1999). The 1990 German Monetary Union also coincided with the political reunification of West and East Germany.

The economic rationale of common currency areas has often been discussed with reference to the benchmark of an 'optimal currency area' (OCA). The theory behind this concept, developed in the early 1960s, focused on the gains in efficiency produced by the reduction of transaction costs that monetary integration would bring about. It also listed a number of conditions a common currency area would need to satisfy in order to be sustainable. Among these are a high degree of trade openness, a diversified production structure, and a flexible labour market, all of which could be expected to minimize consequences of the loss of the exchange rate as instrument of macroeconomic stabilization when asymmetric, country-specific shocks occur. While the OCA theory of MUs has initially nourished the discussions leading up to the European Monetary Union (EMU) project, later debate focused on other significant aspects which may affect the balance between benefits and costs of EMU. Among them is the opportunity to achieve at lower cost the price stability goal by putting monetary policy in the hands of an independent and fully credible central bank. Aside from the economic rationale, a main driver of a currency union is the political will to coordinate economic policies more closely and to abide by common rules. In a more extreme case, a monetary union could even be considered as a step towards political unification. Box 6.4 gives a short overview of an MU's main benefits and costs.[20]

Box 6.4. Common currency areas: benefits and costs

A. Advantages of a common currency

i) Efficiency gains: A reduction in transaction costs and a reduction in price uncertainty due to the elimination of exchange rate risk. These gains are proportional to the size of intra-union trade. Once the monetary union is in operation, these gains can be expected to increase together with stronger integration, with favourable effects on investment. Dynamic efficiency effects on growth can also result from the convergence of real interest rates among member countries: domestic nominal interest rates will converge as there are no changes to be expected in bilateral exchange rates and inflation rates will converge to the union-wide inflation rate.

ii) Policy coordination gains: A common monetary policy delegated to a common monetary authority has three major benefits: it eliminates competitive devaluations and harmful 'beggar-my-neighbour' monetary policy spillovers among member countries; it eliminates the threat of disruptive speculative attacks and exchange rate crisis; and it facilitates the setting up

---

[20] Box 6.4 points out the main elements developed by the vast literature on the costs and benefits of MUs. See e.g. Commission of the European Communities (1990), De Grauwe (1994), Obstfeld and Rogoff (1996: section 9.4.2), Beetsma and Giulodori (2010).

of a more independent central bank, thus mitigating the problem of 'inflation bias'. With enhanced credibility to resist pressures to accommodate government financing needs, the union's central bank can be expected to better fulfil its price stability mandate.

B. Costs of a common currency:

(i) Giving up monetary autonomy is the highest cost. Each member country forgoes the use of monetary and exchange rate policy to stabilize its output when facing asymmetric economic shocks, particularly real shocks, either on the demand or on the supply side. While the common monetary policy will take responsibility for dealing with union wide shocks, such a 'one size fits all' policy cannot address country-specific shocks. Other domestic and union-wide macro-stabilization and risk-sharing mechanisms (e.g. fiscal transfers) will be needed to compensate for the loss of monetary autonomy.

(ii) Aligning domestic preferences regarding the common monetary policy, as member countries may initially have diverging positions regarding the inflation–output trade-offs of the Union's central bank. Some members may give more weight to price stability, others to output stability. More inflation-prone countries, dependent on seigniorage receipts or on inflation tax to dilute high government debt, may have to face a painful adjustment of their public finances.

(iii) Transition costs, as convergence requirements for prospective member countries, usually include limiting the flexibility of the exchange rate, satisfying some constraints relative to fiscal deficits and public debt as well as an inflation rate below a given threshold. Such requirements may impose significant costs, which have to be borne before any benefit expected from the monetary union materializes. In addition, uncertainty about a country's capacity to join may lead to destabilizing speculative attacks.

With the crisis in the Eurozone in the second decade of the twenty-first century, the benefits and costs of an MU are under close scrutiny. The crisis demonstrated the stress and economic pain a huge asymmetric shock can impose on the affected countries.[21] It also emphasized the crucial need for centralized mitigation and risk-sharing mechanisms.[22]

---

[21] This asymmetric shock was the consequence of the Global Financial Crisis. Within the Eurozone, the periphery countries had built up, before this crisis, huge amounts of private and public debt, financed by capital flows from the centre countries. The crisis brought about a sudden stop and a reversal of these capital flows, followed by a crash in asset prices, a bank and a debt crisis in the periphery countries.

[22] These include among others strong cross-country fiscal transfers, high integration of financial markets and of the banking system, and effective coordination of macro-economic and macroprudential policies .

Several LFDCs have opted for an MU as exchange rate arrangement. The West African Economic and Monetary Union (WAEMU), the Central African Economic and Monetary Community (CEMAC), and the Eastern Caribbean Currency Union (ECCU) are the only MUs currently organized among LFDCs (IMF 2019a: 6–8). WAEMU and CEMAC were established in their current institutional form in the early 1970s, although their origin can be dated back to the creation in 1945 of the 'zone franc' in the French colonies in Africa. WAEMU's eight members share a common currency. So do the six CEMAC members. Each zone has its central bank and its currency—both called CFA franc pegged to the euro, with the same exchange rate. However, each currency only circulates in its own monetary zone. The peg to the Euro and the arrangements with the French Treasury that back both currencies are defining characteristics of the CFA franc (FCFA)[23]. ECCU, founded in the early 1980s, is an MU on a much smaller scale, with the Eastern Caribbean dollar as common currency. It regroups eight Caribbean islands, all former British colonies. The common currency area's external exchange rate is also pegged to the US dollar, specifically through a currency board. Appendix 6B discusses in more depth the issues encountered by a 'monetary-union-cum-fixed-external-peg' in LFDCs, taking WAEMU and CEMAC as case studies.

Three other groups of sub-Saharan African countries are engaged in an MU project (see Debrun et al. 2011; Berg and Portillo 2018b: 25–26): the West African Monetary Zone (WAMZ), the East African Community, and the Southern African Development Community (SADC), the largest group.[24] The three projects have faced serious problems in their regional economic integration process and in the building of a common institution. Given the huge heterogeneity among prospective member countries, large asymmetric shocks have repeatedly hampered convergence. Because of these difficulties, but possibly also because of weak political commitments, ambitious timetables for launching the respective MUs have been repeatedly rescheduled.

---

[23] The arrangements are being revised in the context of the announced change of CFA to ECO in the WAEMU (see Appendix 6B).

[24] The West African Monetary Zone (WAMZ) was initiated in 2001 among 6 West African non-WAEMU countries with the aim of establishing among them a single currency, and ultimately of joining WAEMU within the ECOWAS (Economic Community of West African States). ECOWAS already regroups the WAMZ and WAEMU countries. The 5-country East African Community launched in 2001 started with a custom union, was followed by a common market, and expects to evolve by 2023 into a monetary union. The Southern African Development Community (SADC) dates back to 1992, and began as a regional integration project in 2003, with the single currency as the ultimate aim of the process. Of the 15 countries of SADC, 4 participate already in a Common Monetary Area centred on South Africa. The latter's currency circulates as legal tender in the area.

6.2.5 Which exchange rate regime for LFDCs?

As already pointed out, the choice of a nominal anchor is directly linked to the choice of the exchange rate regime. Choosing the exchange rate as anchor implies that some form of fixed exchange regime is chosen. Fixing the exchange rate has, as discussed, clear advantages but also clear drawbacks. Both appear larger the 'harder' the peg. For example, a hard peg provides the strongest anchor for the price level but leaves the country completely (at times regrettably) unable to use the exchange rate as stabilizing instrument. The weight to be given to each advantage and each drawback when choosing an exchange rate regime will depend on many factors, such as the country's openness to trade and capital flows, the type and frequency of shocks it faces, the quality of its monetary institutions, the efficacy of the alternative price level anchoring policies, and political considerations. Choosing an exchange regime has therefore to be made on a case-by-case basis and, in general, not once and for all. Indeed, even if a fixed exchange rate regime has been a country's appropriate choice at some time, changes in its environment or reforms of its institutions may make alternative approaches to exchange rate policy more effective and more attractive.

Because of the weak integration of LFDCs with the world capital market, soft pegs may be more resilient to exogenous shocks for them than for EMEs. Fixed but adjustable pegs offer somewhat larger room for discretionary policy than hard pegs.[25] But as these countries modernize and hope to attract foreign investment, either direct or portfolio investment, the capital accounts of their balance of payments will become more open and, more importantly, more active. Therefore soft pegs may not survive in the medium term. Indeed, several LFDCs have opted for increasing exchange rate flexibility and switched to inflation targeting as a monetary policy framework (IMF 2015b). This does not, however, preclude that, within this new framework, managing the exchange rate will remain an important point of attention for monetary authorities, both because of its role as transmission channel and because of its impact on inflation expectations (see section 6.4.5.2).

---

[25] A 'corners hypothesis' about exchange regimes was popular in the late 1990s, before fading away (Frankel 2010). According to this hypothesis, arrangements anywhere between floating regimes and hard pegs were not sustainable in the long run because of globalization and attendant capital mobility (see e.g. Fischer 2001). The recommendation was that countries should adopt either a hard peg or a fully flexible exchange rate. However, not only are the actual choices of countries not aligned with this recommendation (see Table 6.1), but hard pegs have also been brought down, as evidenced e.g. by the 2002 Argentinian experience. In Frankel et al. (2019) it is shown that among de facto exchange rate regimes, the 'intermediate' regime is the most frequent within their sample of 145 countries. Exchange rate flexibility has increased over the years since the 1980s. Their regression analysis over 1975–2014 shows that there is a significant positive correlation between growth and an intermediate exchange rate regime, and that this relationship is more significant for lower-income than for higher-income countries.

6.3 Monetary targeting

As shown in Table 6.1, which reports the monetary frameworks declared in 2018 by the LFDCs of our set, 21 countries—close to 20%—used monetary targets as nominal anchor. In most cases, however, they also combine this intermediate target for their monetary policy with some form of exchange rate management. Monetary targeting consists in fixing targets for the rate of growth of the money stock. The targets for the next quarter or several upcoming quarters are announced by the central bank at the beginning of the fiscal year, or sometimes at the beginning of each quarter.

6.3.1 Principles of monetary targeting

Traditional monetary targeting is based on the time-honoured quantity theory equation, $Mv = PY$, with M the monetary aggregate, P the general price level, Y real GDP, and v the income velocity of M. Writing the equation in terms of growth rates, ignoring the double products of growth rates, we get $\hat{M} + \hat{v} = \hat{P} + \hat{Y}$ where the 'hat' superscript designates growth rates. For given forecasts of changes in velocity and output, respectively $\hat{v}^e$ and $\hat{Y}^e$, the monetary authorities choose as target growth rate $\hat{M}^T$, the rate that is compatible with $\bar{\pi} \equiv \hat{P}^T$, the desired inflation rate: $\hat{M}^T = \bar{\pi} + \hat{Y}^e - \hat{v}^e$. Sometimes the desired inflation rate and the projected change in output are combined into a target growth rate for nominal income, $\left(\bar{\pi} + \hat{Y}^e\right)$. The target rate for money growth is thus set as the difference between this target growth rate for nominal GDP and the forecast change in v, the income velocity of money.

Such a quantity theory-inspired choice of monetary aggregates as the intermediary target for monetary policy thus rests on the role that money is assumed to play as a key determinant of domestic spending and of the dynamics of inflation (see section 1.2.3). Money is in this view also considered as a 'synthetic' transmission variable of monetary policy that affects nominal spending through different channels, notably through the credit channel (see Chapter 2).

Monetary aggregates are, as intermediate targets, not directly under the control of the monetary authorities. Designing a monetary aggregate targeting strategy therefore implies that the central bank has to rely on an operating target, over which it has closer control and which displays a predictable relationship with the targeted monetary aggregate. The monetary base, or reserve (central bank) money, is usually the chosen operating target.[26] The monetary base B is connected to the target monetary aggregate M through the monetary multiplier m,

---

[26] Mexico and Peru, now both EMEs, employed banks' reserves as their operating targets before adopting inflation targeting.

according to the simple relationship $M = m.B$. The monetary base is the sum of sight liabilities issued by the central bank (currency held by the public and banks' reserves with the central bank—see section 1.2.3.3). Suppose the specific monetary aggregate targeted by the central bank is the narrow monetary aggregate, M_1, the sum of currency and of demand deposits with banks, held by the public. The ratio between M_1 and B, i.e. the corresponding monetary multiplier m_1, reflects in this case the public's preference for currency, relative to demand deposits, and banks' reserve holding behaviour, but also the impact of the central bank's required reserves and interest rate policies (see Box 6.5).

To implement its monetary targeting strategy, the central bank thus needs to translate the target growth rate of its monetary aggregate $\left(\hat{M}_1^T\right)$ into a target growth rate of the monetary base $\left(\hat{B}^T\right)$, taking into account the forecast change in the multiplier $\left(\hat{m}_1^e\right)$. Thus, $\hat{B}^T = \hat{M}_1^T - \hat{m}_1^e$

Box 6.5. The money multiplier

Many textbook descriptions of the money supply process take a somewhat mechanical approach: the central bank injects new reserves into the financial system through its open-market operations or by direct lending to banks. Banks use these reserves to provide new loans to their clients, in the process creating new demand deposits. Both bank credit and the money supply are thereby increased. Some of these new bank deposits will be converted into cash, as people wish to balance their total money holdings between currency and sight deposits, according to their payment habits and preferences. The expansion of bank credit and money is completed once all the additional reserves are converted into cash or are tied up in required or voluntarily held excess reserves to be held against the newly created deposits.

This process which links the (narrow) money supply M_1 (i.e. the sum of currency, C, and demand deposits held by the public with banks, D) with the monetary base, B (i.e. the sum of currency and bank reserves, R) is formally described by the following 'multiplier' relationship:

$$M_1 = m_1.B$$

where m_1 is the 'money multiplier'. Given that $B = C + R$ and $M_1 = C + D$, the multiplier is given by $(C+D)/(C+R)$ or, after rearranging, by:

$$m_1 = \frac{1+k}{k+r}$$

Continued

Box 6.5. *Continued*

where $k = C / D$ is the public's currency ratio, $r = R / D$ the banks' reserve ratio.

The multiplier thus reflects the public's preferences between cash and deposits as well as the banks' desired average reserve ratio, taking required reserves into account. It represents the contribution of banks and the public to total money creation, for a given supply of central bank money. It is larger than 1 (as $r < 1$) and rises when either k or r decline. Both ratios are behavioural ratios which are endogenous to the money and credit supply process.

The money multiplier will be affected not only by reserve requirements set by the central bank but also by interest rates. While a rise in the required reserve ratio will lower m_1, a rise in interest rates will increase it, as banks will strive to reduce their excess reserves. A decrease in the monetary base that leads to an increase in interest rates may thus simultaneously increase the multiplier, attenuating the restrictive effect of the reduction of B on M_1. Thus, far from being a mechanical process, the link between the monetary base and the money supply is deeply rooted in the broader functioning of money and credit markets.[a]

The above analytical representation of the money supply process is particularly useful when the central bank targets M_1. Projections of the multiplier are then an indispensable tool for helping the central bank set its target for the monetary base. However, the targeted monetary aggregates are often broader than M_1. Broader aggregates add time and savings deposits with banks. Still broader ones also add non-deposit liabilities, deemed sufficiently liquid like marketable bonds, issued by banks or by non-bank financial intermediaries, in domestic or in foreign currencies. Each aggregate has its corresponding multiplier: the broader the aggregate, the larger the multiplier. The relationship between the monetary base and broad aggregates is exposed to greater risks of instability. The larger multipliers are not only determined, as m_1 by the currency and the reserve ratios, but also by additional ratios, each reflecting the preferences between assets of different liquidity characteristics included in the aggregate (e.g. between savings and demand deposits, or between domestic and foreign currency demand deposits). This much more tenuous link between the monetary base and the broad monetary aggregates complicates policy-making. This has contributed to the demise of the monetary aggregate targeting framework in the AEs.

---

[a] This has been particularly stressed by Brunner and Meltzer (1968), who have done pioneering work in developing equilibrium models of the money and credit supply process.

For such a quantity-oriented monetary policy, focused on monetary aggregates, to be successful, three conditions need to be met: (i) there must be a strong and reliable relationship, between the growth rate of the monetary aggregate picked for target and nominal income growth and, ultimately, inflation; (ii) there must be a strong and reliable relationship between the monetary base and the targeted monetary aggregate; and (iii) the central bank needs to have at its disposal effective monetary policy instruments enabling it to closely control the growth of the monetary base according to its target path.

These are challenging conditions. Before turning to assessing them in the context of LFDCs, we briefly discuss the reasons which may have led LFDCs to adopt this particular monetary framework.

6.3.2 Reasons for selecting monetary targeting

While it may be often thought that LFDCs have a monetary anchor because of convenience, a more practical reason is that monetary targets correspond with the public's belief regarding the importance of restraints on the quantity of money.[27] Monetary targets can in general be easily understood by the public, especially when inflation is high.[28] Monetary targets are in this case used to send signals to the public of the intentions of the policy-makers to bring inflation down and, more generally, to keep it at low levels. These signals help to anchor inflation expectations. Monetary targets also have the advantage of holding central banks more accountable for the policies they pursue.

Monetary targeting has thus been implemented to lend more credibility to the central bank's anti-inflationary policy. This has been particularly important for countries where the central bank did not enjoy much independence and where fiscal dominance was a recurrent feature, with repeated central bank lending to the government. Putting limits on the central banks' domestic credit as part of the monetary targeting strategy helped them evade the threats of fiscal dominance and increase their credibility.

Closely related to this 'fiscal dominance' reason for selecting a monetary targeting strategy is the role played by the IMF's monetary and financial programming that borrowing countries implemented as part of the broad policy adjustment framework that went with the loan. Many LFDCs have over many years used the IMF's financial programming as their basic monetary framework (see Box 6.6).

---

[27] In opinion surveys, the public in LFDCs, after many years of being told this by economic authorities, consistently state that excessive money expansion and inflation are tightly associated. The governor of a central bank of a developing country told one of the authors of this book: 'in our countries the public is more monetarist than central bankers.'

[28] However, in countries where inflation has remained subdued over a long period of time, the public and even financial analysts pay much less attention to shifts in the quantity of money.

Box 6.6. The IMF's monetary programming

The IMF's analytical model for monetary programming basically relies on the quantity theory equation $M_t.v_t = P_t.Y_t.$[a] M_t is the monetary aggregate, P_t the general price level, Y_t real GDP and v_t the income velocity of money, observed at the start of the programming period. Projected values for the demand for money $\left(M_{t+1}^D\right)$ are obtained by combining the desired inflation rate $(\bar{\pi})$ with projections for GDP growth $(\hat{Y}^e)$ and for changes in $(\hat{v}^e)$ that are expected over the targeting period.[b]

$$M_{t+1}^D = \left(1 + \bar{\pi} + \hat{Y}^e - \hat{v}^e\right).M_t \tag{1}$$

Forecasting the money multiplier for next period $\left(m_{t+1}^e\right)$ gives the forecasted demand for the monetary base (reserve money) B.

$$B_{t+1}^D = \frac{M_{t+1}^D}{m_{t+1}^e} \tag{2}$$

The supply of base money at $t+1$ is given

$$B_{t+1}^S = NIR_{t+1} + NDC_{t+1} \tag{3}$$

where NIR denotes net international reserves, expressed in domestic currency, and NDC net domestic credit, the monetary base's two key counterparties.

Equilibrium between the supply of base money and its expected demand defines the central bank's target for the level of the monetary base to be achieved at $t+1$:

$$B_{t+1}^T = B_{t+1}^D \tag{4}$$

It is easy to see that if this target is met and if the forecasts for Y and v are correct, equilibrium between the supply and the demand for money will deliver a $t+1$ price level in line with the desired inflation rate.

It is thus the central bank's responsibility to keep the monetary base on its target path by closely monitoring the latter's two counterparties, NIR and NDC. For a given NIR, increases in NDC that imply an overshooting of the base target B_{t+1}^T will spill over into pressures on inflation and on exchange rate depreciation. If the central bank aims at keeping the exchange rate at some predetermined level and thus does not allow it to depreciate, the increase in NDC will cause a decrease in NIR^c. With capital controls or other impediments to the free flow of capital, the expansion of NDC would imply less exchange rate depreciation or a smaller decrease in NIR, but would still put pressure on prices.

In line with the model and the adjustment mechanisms outlined above, the IMF's monetary programming relies on two standard performance criteria (IMF 2014: 20): a floor on the stock of net international reserves $\left(NIR_{t+1} \geq \underline{NIR}\right)$ and a ceiling on net domestic credit $\left(NDC_{t+1} \leq \overline{NDC}\right)$. The floor target $\underline{NIR}$ will depend inter alia on the expected disbursements of foreign aid, net capital inflows, and forecasted changes in the current account of the balance of payments, based mainly on the anticipated changes in export volumes and prices. The ceiling $\overline{NDC}$ is set so as to be consistent with the floor for NIR and the reserve money target B^T_{t+1}. The NDC ceiling also reflects the fiscal side of the IMF's financial programming exercise, as NDC mostly consists of lending to the government. A reserve money target is often added, within the assessment process of the Fund's monetary programme conditionality, either as a third monetary performance criterion or as an indicative target only (IMF 2014: 14). While the performance criteria on NIR and NDC are specifically designed to address the country's external sustainability, the reserve money target criterion aims at keeping a check on inflation.[d] The technical memorandum of the Fund's country programme also determines the conditions under which the performance criteria are to be adjusted upwards or downwards. More generally, monetary conditionality of the Fund's programmes is evolving towards more flexibility for countries that have moved to flexible monetary targeting or are considering outright inflation targeting (IMF 2014: 7).

[a] On the IMF's programming model, see also Agénor and Montiel (1999, chapter 13) and Vegh (2013, pp. 279–280)

[b] Equation (1) neglects the double products of growth rates.

[c] If the exchange rate is fixed and capital freely mobile, the change of NIR is equal to the opposite of the change in NDC. This adjustment of the money supply to money demand through changes in NIR is a basic tenet of the monetary approach to the balance of payments in a fixed exchange regime. This approach was partly developed in the Fund and has inspired the monetary conditionality of its adjustment programmes.

[d] For a critique of the strong hypotheses of the framework that underlies the IMF's monetary and financial programming, see Easterly (2004).

The framework was initially aimed at promoting balance-of-payments adjustment in regimes of fixed but adjustable exchange rate, but has been applied more widely. With predetermined exchange rates, the key policy variable for restoring balance-of-payment imbalances or preventing them is domestic credit creation.[29]

[29] This goal of the programming exercise underlines the importance of avoiding a balance-of-payments crisis that could end in catastrophic and disorderly devaluations of the exchange rate. This

The programme provides for a ceiling target on domestic credit (NDC), together usually with a floor target for the level of net international reserves (NIR), the two components of the central bank's monetary base (reserve money). A ceiling on base money is also sometimes included. Those targets relating to the central bank's balance sheet are set on a quarterly basis and are regularly monitored as performance criteria within the programme's conditionality framework. Note that IMF adjustment programmes also usually entail a broad array of other measures, especially in relation to the government's fiscal accounts.

A last aspect which may account for the choice of a monetary aggregate targeting strategy in LFDCs is the informational context in which monetary policy has to be conducted. Central banks in LFDCs have timely and precise information on the money base, while information on interest rates that is relevant for private-sector decisions is either not available at relevant frequencies or is insufficiently informative, as observed interest rates are often not market-clearing. With interest rates being an unreliable and weak channel of monetary policy transmission (see section 2.2.3), the monetary authorities of many LFDCs, if not most, lack a clearly spelled-out interest rate policy. As importantly, the public and even the domestic financial sector pay scant attention to the interest rate policies of the central bank. The effective and shadow rates employed by the private sector are determined more by the overall financial conditions of the country, including the state of liquidity of the banking sector, and by the risk perceptions of the lenders. The low relevance of the policy interest rate for the decisions of economic agents originates in the LFDCs underdeveloped financial markets. This structural weakness reduces the impact of policies that target the interest rate or that have the interest rate as instrument. On the other hand, easily observable monetary aggregates embed valuable and timely information on the state of the economy, the tightness of credit, and liquidity conditions, as well as on inflationary pressures (IMF 2015b: 37).

6.3.3 Challenges of monetary targeting

As already noted, the efficacy of monetary targeting depends on three crucial conditions.

First is a strong and reliable relationship between targeted monetary aggregates and nominal income. This raises the issue of the stability, i.e. the predictability of the demand for the monetary aggregate chosen as target or, equivalently, of its income velocity, as the behaviour of the latter directly reflects changes in the demand for money. One could a priori argue that money demand in LFDCs can

---

would ultimately lead to financial crisis and produce a jump in the inflation rate. It does not, however, exclude the possibility of a devaluation of the exchange rate if carried out in an orderly way.

be expected to be more stable than in AEs or EMEs, precisely because of fewer opportunities of financial diversification and a lower substitutability of money with other assets. The increasing substitutability of money with other liquid assets, driven by financial innovation, was indeed a major factor in the breakdown of the relationship between the narrow monetary aggregate M_1 and nominal income in the AEs during the 1970s.[30] Yet similar effects of financial innovation on the stability of the demand for M_1 can also be observed in LFDCs. Indeed, a panel study by Dunne and Kasekende (2016) documents for 34 sub-Saharan Africa countries, many of which used monetary targets, that financial innovation—the introduction of ATMs, of debit cards, and of mobile money—had a significant negative impact on the demand for M_1 over 1980–2013. IMF (2014:17) reports that, for 38 Fund-supported programmes with explicit targets on reserve money over 2002–2012, projections of annual changes in velocity in programme countries have over the period shown significant discrepancies with actual outcomes, with a root-mean-square error of 9%. The consequences of over- or under-estimating the change of velocity are that monetary policy will be too restrictive or too expansive, respectively, if strict adherence to the target is pursued.[31] To avoid such unintended effects on output and inflation of velocity shocks, the central bank may prefer to miss its monetary aggregate target.

The second condition for an efficient monetary aggregate targeting framework is the stability of the relationship which links the intermediate target, say M_1, and the operating target, the monetary base, B. The target growth rate for the monetary base is given by $\hat{B}^T = \hat{M}_1^T - \hat{m}_1^e$. Keeping the monetary aggregate on target by adhering to the base money target implied by the forecast of the multiplier will be effective if this forecast is sufficiently precise and reliable. This is a challenge, as shocks to the multiplier may have multiple origins (see Box 6.5). While the efficacy of forecasts may differ from one country to the other (see e.g. the case of Rwanda in Box 6.7), the stability of the money multiplier is likely to be a difficult issue in several countries. Indeed, the above-mentioned IMF (2014) study for 38 programmes in reserve targeting countries also reports a 9% root-mean-square error in projecting annual changes in the money multiplier (p.17). As importantly, the broader the monetary aggregate to be targeted (M_2, M_3,...), the more tenuous will be the link between the latter and the monetary base,

---

[30] This breakdown was identified early on by Goldfeld (1976), who observed a huge negative shift in the US demand for M_1, which he dubbed 'the case of missing money'. The large unexpected decrease was due to the emergence of money market fund shares, a new financial instrument, very liquid and interest-bearing. Successive waves of financial innovation continued to undermine the stability of the demand for money, actually also undermining the monetary aggregate targeting strategy.

[31] Recall that the central bank sets its target according to $\hat{M}^T = \bar{\pi} + \hat{Y}^e - \hat{v}^e$. Actual changes in these variables conform to $\hat{M} + \hat{v} = \hat{P} + \hat{Y}$. If $\hat{M} = \hat{M}^T$ (strict adherence to target), then $\left(\hat{P} - \bar{\pi}\right) + \left(\hat{Y} - \hat{Y}^e\right) = \hat{v} - \hat{v}^e$. Overestimating changes in velocity $\left(\hat{v} < \hat{v}^e\right)$ implies that inflation or output growth, or both, are below their target or forecast, the consequence of an over-restrictive monetary policy.

implying greater difficulties in achieving a good and reliable forecast of the corresponding money multiplier (see Box 6.5).

The last challenge for efficient monetary targeting is for the central bank to have the actual capacity to keep the reserve money aggregate on target. This implies that it has at its disposal an efficacious set of monetary policy instruments to manage on a daily basis the volume of central bank liquidity, as well as good capability of forecasting banks' liquidity needs (see sections 3.2.2.2 and 3.4.3).

6.3.4 Flexible monetary targeting

Responding to these different challenges has been a difficult task for most central banks that have adopted a monetary targeting framework. As a result, target misses have been frequent, with likely damaging effect on the credibility of the central bank.[32] These difficulties led most AEs to abandon this strategy in the 1980s and to scale down the role of monetary aggregates, from that of a precise target to comply with to that of an important forward-looking indicator of the medium-term monetary policy stance.[33]

While many LFDCs have monetary targeting as their basic monetary framework, few of them implement it strictly. Strict implementation in the face of exogenous shocks to the demand for money will give rise to undesired large fluctuations in interest rates. This has for example been documented for Tanzania and Uganda during the periods during which targets were strictly enforced (IMF 2014: 18). Wide variations of interest rates not only hamper the development of the interbank market and thus hurt the transmission of monetary policy, but also produce macroeconomic volatility. Andrle et al. (2018: 335) conclude their analysis of monetary targeting in Kenya by observing that weak compliance with formal monetary targets has, a posteriori, actually been fortunate, as the target misses were mostly driven by money demand shocks, and as excessive interest rate volatility was thus avoided.

In actual practice, central banks thus allow deviations from the broad money targets, often for good reasons. According to IMF (2015b: 51) deviations from

---

[32] Deviations from targeted growth rates have, in addition, usually not been corrected with measures designed to bring the aggregate back on its target path. A severe assessment of this policy framework is given by Bernanke (2006: 2), who notes that, for the Federal Reserve, 'the adoption of targets for money and credit growth was evidently not effective in constraining policy or in reducing inflation, in part because the target was not routinely achieved'.

[33] The German Bundesbank continued, however, with a medium-term monetary targeting strategy, pragmatically implemented, until the country entered the Eurozone in 1999. The European Central bank maintained a medium-term target path for a broad monetary aggregate, M3, until 2003. It then discontinued this targeting approach and opted for a strategy in which the risks to price stability are assessed on the basis of 'two pillars', an economic analysis and a monetary analysis. The latter includes the monitoring of several monetary aggregates, assessing their information content for future inflation and economic growth.

target were in general not indicative of over-loose monetary policy but mostly reflect accommodation of shocks to money demand. One thus observes de facto a flexible approach to monetary targeting, even at the risk of blurring information to the public and of losing credibility. Berg et al. (2018c) advocate such a flexible approach. They propose, in the spirit of the original analysis of Poole (1970), combining a monetary-targeting rule with an interest rate-targeting rule, allowing for an optimal degree of adherence to each rule. Adherence to money targeting will, among other factors, depend on the relative volatilities of real and financial shocks, as well as on how accurately observed interest rates and output inform the central bank on the actual state of the economy. Simulations results of their model show that noisier, less informative measures of both variables push towards greater adherence to money targets (Berg et al. 2018c: 159–60).[34] Maehle (2020) spells out how flexible monetary targeting can play a role as a transitional arrangement for countries wishing to progressively move to a formal inflation-targeting framework. A quantity-based operating framework, based on longer-term targets for average reserve money (possibly with a band), could be combined with an interest rate corridor. The latter, set by the central bank's lending and deposit standing facilities, would soften the volatility of interbank interest rates. It would be periodically repositioned, so as to remain consistent with the targeted path for the monetary aggregate. Gradually, therefore, quantitative targets for monetary aggregates would be monitored more as indicators of monetary conditions, as is the case in AEs, than as targets to which policy should strictly adhere. Box 6.7 describes the experience of Rwanda with monetary programming. Flexible monetary targeting plays thus an important role in the transition to inflation targeting, which we discuss in the next section.

6.4 Inflation targeting

Since 1990 a significant number of AEs and, less than a decade later, EMEs have adopted inflation targeting (IT) as their framework for monetary policy. The

---

[34] Berg et al. (2018c) derive, within a simple New Keynesian macromodel under incomplete information, an optimal revision strategy of both monetary targeting and interest rate targeting, in response to new information. Also, they derive an optimal degree of adherence to the first target, relative to adherence to the second, when the economy is exposed to contemporaneous shocks in money demand, in aggregate demand, and in potential output. They first assume that the central bank accurately observes the data for output and interest rates that are relevant to the private sector. The optimal degree of adherence to the monetary targeting rule will in this case be *weaker* if, for instance, the volatility of money demand or the volatility of potential output is high. It is similarly weaker if the interest elasticity of money demand is low or if the central bank is less 'hawkish', i.e. less keen to meeting its inflation target. In a second step, the authors assume that the central bank can only observe noisy measures of both interest rate and output variables. This introduces an additional dimension, when deciding on the optimal degree of adherence to the rules, and tilts it towards greater adherence to the monetary target.

Box 6.7. Monetary targeting in Rwanda

Rwanda exemplifies well the monetary targeting policies followed by many LFDCs for many years. It also exemplifies how monetary frameworks evolve, as the National Bank of Rwanda (NBR) adopted a money target in 1997 and then switched in 2019 to an inflation targeting-type strategy, after a transition period of several years.

For more than 20 years Rwanda has practised monetary targeting, with price stability over the medium to long term as the central bank's ultimate target. During this period, broad money (M_3) was the intermediate target and base money the operating target. Targets for the latter were set on a quarterly basis and sometimes at a higher frequency. They were usually combined with a floor on the central bank's net foreign assets and a ceiling on net financing to the government as part of performance or indicative criteria linked to the monetary conditionality of IMF programmes. Targets for M_3 were not clearly announced to the public, lending some opacity to the strategy. To meet its targets for the monetary base, the NBR used an increasingly rich array of the monetary instruments described in Chapter 3.

Judging from the record of moderate inflation and high growth, the policy has been satisfactory, with an average yearly inflation of 6.5% and an average annual rate of growth of GDP of 7.8% over the period 2000–2018 (S: WDI data). The NBR aimed informally at an inflation rate of 5% (Charry et al., 2018: 377). Inflation has been mostly within the single-digit range, with some spikes above, the result of international food and oil price shocks in 2008.

Rwanda's monetary targeting strategy has benefited for many years from a relatively stable money multiplier and stable demand for money according to econometric evidence (Hauner and Di Bella 2005; Rusuhuzwa and Irankunda 2012; Rusuhuzwa and Mutuyimana 2016). The latter two studies, however, report structural breaks and greater instability since 2011 for these crucial relationships, the consequence of financial deepening and technology-driven financial innovation.

Deviations from base targets have frequently occurred, mostly in response to money demand shocks but also to accommodate exchange rate shocks. According to IMF (2015b: 54) target misses have usually been kept within a limited range—narrower than what has been observed for comparator countries, Kenya, Tanzania, and Mozambique.

The increasing unpredictability of the multiplier and of the income velocity of money has encouraged the NBR to gradually adapt its monetary framework. Initial steps in 2012 focused on giving more flexibility to its quantity targeting by adopting a ±2% band around the monetary base target, the latter expressed as a quarterly average instead of an end-of-period value. To check volatility of short-term interest rates, NBR introduced lending and deposit standing facilities, with rates set so as to keep interbank rates within a ±2% band around the NBR's repo policy rate. This corridor was reduced to ±1% in 2017. The observed improvement in the functioning of the interbank market and in the transmission of NBR's interventions on money market rates led the NBR to a price-based monetary policy at the start of 2019. The new framework features a medium-term headline inflation target of 5%, with a target band of ±3 percentage points. The NBR's operating target is now the short-term money market interest rate, with rates for the lending and deposit standing facilities set respectively at +100 and −200 basis points around the policy rate (Rusuhuzwa 2019).

switch towards this framework was motivated in AEs, as e.g. in the UK, by the failure of both monetary and exchange rate targeting to deliver price stability. In EMEs, IT was mostly adopted when the exchange rate peg had to be abandoned, sometimes abruptly, as in Brazil in 1999, or more progressively, as in Chile, with the aim of consolidating ongoing disinflation efforts by a move towards a new credible anchor. As reported by IMF (2019a: 7), 41 countries (21%) were using fully-fledged IT as a monetary framework in 2018—fully-fledged in the sense that, in principle, all the defining characteristics of IT, as presented in section 6.4.1, supposedly guide monetary policy decisions. Among them, there are 16 LFDCs, representing 14% of our set (see Table 6.1). As shown in Table 6.2, adoption of IT has in many of these countries been relatively recent. Note that some LFDCs considered as IT a simple announcement of targets for the inflation rate by their central bank, without complying with the whole set of rules and practices aimed at anchoring inflation to this target, as conventionally applied in AEs and EMEs.[35] In what follows, we shall not consider as IT the loose adoption of inflation targets.

IT comes in different varieties. The strict type of IT exclusively aims at reaching the inflation target in order to establish the crucial credibility of the commitment of monetary authorities to low inflation. However, experience has shown that central banks could not avoid paying attention to other goals as well. These includes economic activity and, especially since the financial crisis of 2007–8, financial stability, as discussed in section 4.2.2. Thus emerged the concept of 'flexible IT', a concept that underlies the current practices of most inflation-targeting central banks. It is, however, as discussed in section 6.4.5.1, a challenging task for

---

[35] It has often been observed that countries which intend to stabilize inflation, especially when it is high, announce an inflation target as part of their stabilization package. Yet the latter may be closer to exchange rate targeting or to monetary targeting than to an explicit IT policy framework.

a central bank to manage policy trade-offs and keep the 'flexibility' aspect of IT in line with its fundamental aim, price stability.

6.4.1 Principles of inflation targeting

The main elements of a fully-fledged inflation targeting framework consist of:

(i) *An institutional and binding commitment to price-stability as the primary goal of monetary policy.* This implies that, in principle, no other monetary policy goal fundamentally interferes with this primary goal of price stability.

(ii) *Public announcement of a numerical medium-term target (sometimes a range) for the inflation rate.* The announcement of the inflation target clarifies to the public the central bank's strategy with respect to its price stability goal. The target inflation rate itself can be set either by the ministry of finance or by the central bank. Most frequently it is set by agreement between both institutions. LFDCs generally set a relatively ample time horizon to meet the announced goal. Also, a numerical range is in most cases preferred for the inflation target (see Table 6.2). Announced targets are usually not set once and for all, but may be periodically changed. As part of a realistic inflation-reduction strategy, they may for example be lowered progressively, as has often been the case. They may however also exceptionally be raised, under the pressure of exogenous events, as Ghana did in 2008–9 following the strong rise in imported food prices (Bleaney et al. 2020b). Most central banks opt for targeting headline inflation, measured as the increase in CPI (Hammond 2012). The Central Bank of Uganda, however, targets core inflation, i.e. CPI inflation after excluding changes in its most volatile components, in general changes in oil and food prices.

(iii) *Central bank independence.* In an IT framework, the central bank is held responsible for achieving the publicly announced inflation rate objective. Central banks thus need not only to be given a clear mandate of price stability but also to enjoy, as a minimum, 'instrument independence', the ability to set freely their policy instruments in order to efficiently pursue their mandate (see section 4.3.2). At the same time, the central bank needs to be accountable with regard to the attainment of the inflation target as well as of the other objectives, such as economic activity, that are part of its remit.

(iv) *An intermediate target of monetary policy defined as the central bank's own forecast of the path of inflation towards its medium-term goal.* Using actual inflation as an intermediate target would not be an efficient policy

Table 6.2. Inflation-targeting LFDCs

Country	Date of adoption	Inflation target at year of IT adoption (%)	3 year average inflation rate before IT adoption (%)	Average inflation rate since IT adoption (up to 2019) (%)	Standard deviation of inflation since adoption (up to 2019) (%)	inflation target 2020 (%)
Philippines	2002	4 ± 1	5.1	3.7	1.9	3 ± 1
Guatemala	2005	5 ± 1	7.1	5.1	2.5	4 ± 1
Indonesia	2005	5 ± 1	8.2	6.1	3.0	3 ± 1
Armenia	2006	4.5 ± 1.5	4.1	3.9	2.9	4 ± 1.5
Serbia	2006	4 – 8	12.3	5.9	4.0	3 ± 1.5
Ghana	2007	8.5 ± 2	12.9	12.6	4.1	8 ± 2
Albania	2009	3 ± 1	2.9	2.1	0.7	3 ± 1
Georgia	2009	3	9.5	3.5	3.0	3
Paraguay	2011	5 ± 2.5	5.8	4.1	1.7	4 ± 2
Uganda	2011	5	9.7	6.4	4.4	5 ± 2
Dominican Republic	2012	3 – 5	5.4	2.8	1.3	4 ± 1
Moldova	2013	3.5 – 6.5	6.6	5.7	2.1	3.5 – 6.5
Kazakstan	2015	4	5.9	8.0	3.8	4 – 6
Costa Rica	2016	3 ± 1	3.5	1.5	1.0	3 ± 1
Ukraine	2016	5 ± 1	20.2	11.8	3.0	5 ± 1
Jamaica	2017	4 – 6	4.8	4.0	0.3	4 – 6

Sources: IMF (2019a) for IT countries in 2018; Jahan (2018); De Gregorio (2019) and central bank websites for year of adoption and IT target; 2020 target from 'Central Bank News' website; average inflation rates and standard deviations computed from World Bank's WDI data.

because of the lags involved between actual inflation and monetary policy decisions taken by the central bank. Focusing on the central bank's inflation forecasts instead implies that the central bank has to include in this forecast all relevant informative variables, but also its own policy reaction to deviations of inflation, current and expected, from its medium-term target. Moreover, in the context of flexible IT, the projected evolution of output, of exchange rates, and of asset prices may matter, not only as key variables for forecasting inflation, but also to assess to what extent they deviate from their own explicit or implicit targets. When forecasting inflation, the central bank will thus take into account how it plans to react to expected deviations of output from its potential level, or of asset prices and exchange rates from their respective equilibrium levels, fully aware of the involved trade-offs with its inflation target.[36] Spelling out these crucial inflation forecasts necessitates very intensive economy-wide analysis and projections, and represents a challenging task for the central bank.

(v) *Short-term interest rates are monetary policy's operating target.*[37] The central bank sets accordingly its *policy rates*, e.g. its overnight or seven-day repo rates and the rates of its standing facilities, which directly guide short maturity interbank rates (see section 3.3.2.3). A flexible inflation-targeting central bank thus sets its current and expected future key policy rate in such a way that the forecasts of inflation and of the other targeted variables, especially output, move in an appropriately balanced way toward their respective medium-term target. Box 6.8 briefly elaborates on such a policy interest rate reaction function, the Taylor rule.

(vi) *High transparency of the monetary policy strategy.* The central bank needs to communicate efficiently with the public and financial markets about its policy-making in an uncertain environment. Communication is necessary because the central bank's legitimacy implies accountability. Because communication decreases uncertainty about monetary strategy, it is also a way for the central bank to build confidence in its policy, to enhance its credibility, and ultimately to better anchor inflation expectations to its inflation target (see section 4.3.2.3). A key instrument of transparency is the Inflation Report (or Monetary Policy Report). Regularly issued, it informs the markets of the attainments and the failings of past policy decisions, e.g. explaining to what extent past deviations from targets were

---

[36] Such forecast targeting can be described, according to Svensson (2010: 1240), as 'setting the policy rate (more precisely, deciding on a policy-rate path) such that the forecasts of the target variables conditional on that policy-rate path "look good", where "look good" means that the forecast for inflation stabilizes inflation around the inflation target and the forecast for resource utilization stabilizes resource utilization around a normal level.'

[37] However, when the interest rate hits its zero lower bound, as has been the case in AEs, the exchange rate can be used as an instrument to achieve the inflation target (Adrian et al. 2018: 5).

Box 6.8. Setting the policy interest rate

With short-term interest rates as the operating target, the setting of interest rates is the central bank's key monetary policy decision in an IT framework. In a flexible IT regime, in which the central bank targets not only inflation but also output, it sets its policy rates in such a way that their expected effects on the domestic economy bring both variables closer to their target. In setting its rates, it takes into account the extent to which inflation and output currently deviate from target, as well as the relative priority it assigns to correct these respective deviations. Such a monetary policy reaction function for setting the short-term interest rate i_t is known as the Taylor rule, originally developed by Taylor (1993) and given, in its simplest and widely used form, by:

$$i_t = \overline{\pi} + \overline{r} + a_\pi \left(\pi_t - \overline{\pi} \right) + a_y \left(y_t - \overline{y} \right) \tag{1}$$

$\overline{r}$ is the steady state real interest rate, π_t and $\overline{\pi}$ are the current and target inflation rates and y_t and $\overline{y}$ are current and target real output, expressed in logs, their difference representing the percentage output gap. a_π and a_y, both positive, are the policy reaction coefficients. The larger a_π, the stronger the central bank will rise the short-term interest rate in reaction to any given deviation of inflation from target.

Alternative formulations take into account that the IT framework focuses on inflation forecasts as monetary policy's intermediate target. Interest rate smoothing by the central bank is also often considered. This leads to the following inflation forecast-based Taylor rule, often used for modelling monetary policy (see e.g. Charry et al. 2018: 382). π^e_{t+1} is the one-year ahead expected inflation rate and γ the interest rate-smoothing parameter.

$$i_t = \gamma i_{t-1} + \left(1 - \gamma \right) \left[\overline{\pi} + \overline{r} + a_\pi \left(\pi^e_{t+1} - \overline{\pi} \right) + a_y \left(y_t - \overline{y} \right) \right] \tag{2}$$

When the central bank has additional auxiliary targets, the Taylor rule may be augmented by including additional terms, such as deviations of nominal (or real) exchanges rates or asset prices from their respective estimated equilibrium values. In any case, one should be aware that such monetary policy reaction functions are to be considered as benchmarks used for evaluation of past policies or as inputs for current policy-making, clearly not as a rule a central bank would strictly adhere to.

the result of exogenous shocks and not of policy mistakes. It also explains current as well as future monetary policy orientation. Usually the report includes detailed forecasts of inflation as well as of other targeted variables.

(vii) *Abandoning the targeting of exchange rates or of monetary aggregates.* Combining IT with the pursuit of another nominal anchor carries the risk of blurring IT's main tenet, that of credibly conveying the central bank's commitment to price stability. Floating exchange rates are the norm, though nominal or real exchange-rate movements may still be a concern for central banks in LFDCs (see section 6.4.5.2). IT also implies a reduced role of traditional intermediate monetary targets such as money or credit growth and the level of international reserves. At most these appear in the set of indicators of monetary conditions used to forecast inflation.

6.4.2 Advantages and disadvantages of inflation targeting

6.4.2.1 Advantages

Inflation targeting has several advantages. First, it provides for a central bank a good compromise between the credibility of its inflation target and the discretion needed to mitigate the domestic effects of exogenous shocks. Because of its forward-looking characteristic, it attenuates the time-inconsistency problem that leads to inflation bias, and improves the trade-off between inflation and output stabilization that arises when the central bank has to deal with exogenous shocks.[38] Second, in contrast to exchange-rate targeting, and like monetary targeting, it enables monetary policy to focus on domestic considerations and to respond to shocks to the domestic economy with the necessary flexibility. Third, inflation targeting has also the advantage that shocks to the demand for money are largely irrelevant, because the monetary policy strategy no longer relies on a stable money–inflation relationship, in contrast with monetary targeting. Fourth, inflation targeting has, like exchange-rate anchoring, the important advantage that it is readily understood by the public.

6.4.2.2 Disadvantages

There are for LFDCs three main disadvantages to IT. The first one is that it necessitates a set of demanding preconditions that are for LFDCs often not easy to meet (see section 6.4.3). The second is that it is not easy to manage IT when shocks to the supply of output are frequent and sizeable, even when the IT regime

---

[38] The IT framework consists of a balanced mix of rules and discretion, and was labelled 'constrained discretion' by Bernanke and Mishkin (1997: 104). See also section 4.3.1.

is of the flexible type. Adhering too strictly to the inflation target leads to excessive volatility of output, while smoothing output by accepting wide deviation from the inflation target damages the credibility of the latter. Frankel (2010: 19–20) notes that, because IT is not robust to supply shocks, authorities face two difficult options to manage the credibility of the inflation target: (a) target 'core CPI inflation', which excludes the effects on the domestic price level of its most volatile components (food and energy price shocks); this allows the central bank to more easily stick to its inflation target commitment when supply shocks materialize; (b) target 'headline CPI inflation' and explain ex post to the public why the target has not been met because of adverse supply shocks. Both, however, are likely to make it harder for the central bank to achieve and preserve credibility. Core inflation may indeed be a difficult concept for the general public to grasp. Alternatively, ex post explanations of target misses by the central bank carry the risk of being difficult to understand and to accept.

The third reported disadvantage of IT is that it sidelines financial stability. In AEs, inflation targeting has been criticized in the wake of the 2007–8 financial crisis for having led central banks to pay too little attention, despite warnings, to the behaviour of asset prices and to credit growth. Since IT leaves aside concerns regarding the price of financial assets, it could not prevent and, worse, may have fostered financial instability and the emergence of 'credit bubbles'. Low inflation and low nominal interest rates led to imprudent credit expansions by banks, and to excessive leverage of households and firms. Moreover, in EMEs and in some LFDCs, increases in the interest rate to quell inflationary pressures may have induced strong and worrisome capital inflows whose reversal led to exchange rate depreciations, leading to an additional threat to financial stability. Combining concerns for financial stability with price stability as well as with output stability is thus the utmost challenge for flexible IT (see section 6.4.5).

6.4.3 Prerequisites for adopting inflation targeting

The adoption of IT as monetary framework requires a set of initial conditions. LFDCs that have adopted IT have only rarely done so immediately; they have proceeded in steps, sometimes over several years, evolving progressively towards the new monetary anchor.

6.4.3.1 Initial conditions
Several initial conditions should be met when putting an IT framework in place, in order to increase its chances of success. However, few EMEs and a fortiori LFDCs that are now inflation targeters have met the initial conditions set out below, though they have been able to establish them over time.

(i) Price stability has to be the overarching concern of monetary policy, and this has to be conveyed both to the public and the government. The banking system as well as the business community have to internalize the idea that the central bank will aim at this target as its top priority. Also, the lessening of the central bank's attention to previously targeted variables like the exchange rate and the level of foreign reserves needs to be well understood by the public. This is challenging. Political support and cooperation of the domestic financial system, especially the banking system, with the central bank appear as crucial ingredients for the success of IT in LFDCs.

(ii) Absence of fiscal dominance. To be effectively independent and fully focused on its price stability mandate, the central bank needs to be able to resist pressures to monetize fiscal deficits and generate seigniorage (see section 5.2.3). It must also be able to manage interest rates without the constraints imposed by a government wishing to minimize the costs of a high public debt. To guarantee this, the price stability goal must be a goal fully accepted by the government. Also, a sufficiently strong and transparent institutional framework has to detail the respective responsibilities both of the central bank and of the government, and establish effective accountability mechanisms.

(iii) Reliable transmission channels of monetary policy, like sufficiently deep financial markets—especially the money market, where the direct interaction between the central bank and financial intermediaries is organized. A sufficiently rich array of refinancing and open-market operations by the central bank needs to be in place, so that a sizeable interbank market emerges and develops. In particular, the open-market operations must be instrumental in aligning the rate of the interbank market with the central bank policy rate (or rates).

(iv) A sound financial system, so as to minimize potential conflicts between financial stability and monetary stability. Similarly to a high initial public debt that puts fiscal dominance type pressures on the central bank, an unhealthy financial system may also constrain the central bank's policy-making. Providing liquidity to ailing banks and keeping interest rates low to avoid their failing may jeopardize the country's inflation-targeting policy.

(v) Low dollarization. While the IT framework in principle implies floating exchange rates, high dollarization makes the domestic economy particularly vulnerable to large depreciations of the exchange rate, mainly because of the adverse balance-sheet effects that put financial stability at risk.

(vi) Sufficiently low initial inflation. IT cannot be adopted in a context of very high inflation, which is very often also the consequence of significant fiscal dominance. Adopting IT in such circumstances would profoundly question the credibility of the new framework. How low the inflation should be is, however, a question of judgement. Agénor and Pereira da Silva (2019: figure 2.1) report that all middle-income countries which adopted IT had inflation rates below 17%, with one exception (Argentina, with 35%). Table 6.2 shows that LFDCs which adopted IT had, three years before adoption, an average rate of inflation that was mostly below 10%, with some exceptions.

(vii) Finally, there is a need for a solid and experienced technical staff in the central bank, in possession of adequate data and familiar with handling econometric models and other techniques of forecasting. The technical staff must be able to prepare forecasts of the target variables, with low margins of error, relying on sufficiently informative models, adequately tailored to the specificities of the country's economy. Since the central bank's forecasts of inflation are the intermediary target of monetary policy in the IT framework, their quality and reliability are of crucial importance and require utmost care. They are an input in the monetary policy decision-making process, as well as, a posteriori, the benchmark against which actual outcomes will be assessed.

6.4.3.2 Evolving towards IT

Adopting IT requires LFDCs to take multiple preparatory steps in order to meet the most important initial conditions discussed above, before adopting IT or as soon as possible afterwards. Evolving to the new regime may, in addition, involve specific issues for LFDCs which adhered to targeting monetary aggregates and for those which embraced some form of exchange rate targeting.

For LFDCs leaving monetary targeting, the transition may occur gradually and relatively easily by first adopting 'flexible monetary targeting' (see section 6.3.4). In such 'evolving monetary regimes' there is a mix of elements of monetary targeting and IT with 'more focus on analysis than on a pre-set money rule' (Laurens et al. 2015: 27). The monetary base aggregate would be downgraded as operating target, and the significance of the broader aggregates as intermediate targets would be progressively attenuated. The latter would however continue to be monitored, mostly as valuable inputs for economic forecasting and analysis. Short-term liquidity management by the central bank would be strengthened, with the very explicit aim of reducing the volatility of short term interbank rates. As central banks strengthen their analytical capabilities, including their proficiency in risk-analysis, and their forecasting prowess, they would gradually move towards inflation forecasts as intermediate targets of their monetary policy. Concomitantly, the interbank market needs to acquire a more important place in the domestic financial landscape. Its short-term interest rate should align itself with the central bank policy rate. At this stage, built over time, the fully-fledged IT monetary framework would have been reached. Box 6.9 describes the experience of Paraguay.

Box 6.9. Inflation targeting in Paraguay

South American countries have a long history of high inflation. However, Paraguay was an exception. While its inflation rates were relatively high until 2000, they never reached the levels of some of its neighbours. Average annual inflation was 17.9% between 1980 and 2000.

In the 1990s broad disinflation occurred across the world, and South American countries followed the trend. Disinflation was partly spanned by productivity gains in AEs as well as by the insertion and the increased participation of China, a low-cost producer, in the world economy. Also, the South American countries had learned from their past mistakes and improved their governance and management of the economy. In this setting, Paraguay performed as well or better than its neighbours, with inflation dropping to 7.8% in the decade preceding the adoption of IT. Inflation thus came down in Paraguay, as elsewhere, before the adoption of the IT framework. But with IT, there was an improvement in the conduct of monetary policy that consolidated the gains in controlling inflation. The level of inflation was lowered and, as importantly, the volatility of inflation was reduced.

In 1995 the Central Bank of Paraguay was granted de jure independence—a crucial factor in gaining credibility of its anti-inflationary stance. IT was announced in 2004, and preparatory work for the adoption of this strategy started that year. Before and during the transition to full IT, the Central Bank of Paraguay targeted monetary aggregates. Fully-fledged IT came in 2011. Paraguay joined the eight Latin American countries that had adopted IT as their monetary framework. A medium-term (two-year horizon) target range centred on 5% and a band limit of ±2.5% was then established for CPI inflation. The exchange rate is flexible, but in times of turbulence the Central Bank intervenes in the foreign exchange market. While there is currently no explicit target for the exchange rate, its path follows a de facto crawling peg band (De Gregorio 2019: 7).[a] The main exogenous shocks arose from repercussions of turbulences in Paraguay's large neighbours, Argentina and Brazil.

The main instrument of monetary policy is the Interest Rate of Monetary Policy (TPM, its acronym in Spanish), set at meetings of the executive committee of monetary operations of the Central Bank of Paraguay. TPM is the pivot for interest rates of standing facilities and for benchmark rates in open-market operations. It is also managed in a framework of 'flexible' IT. It is lowered, as in 2019, when there are threats to employment and the level of activity, so as to mitigate the slowdown in a way that is consistent with the inflation target. The policies of the Central Bank of Paraguay and its view of the economy are communicated to the financial system, mainly the banking system, in its report of monetary policy, published on a quarterly basis.

Actual inflation as well as expectations of inflation have very quickly converged to the Central Bank's target at IT's adoption, and have remained within the target band since, pointing to a significant credibility effect of IT (Alonso 2018: 6–7). The target's central rate was lowered twice and its band narrowed. As of 2020 the target range is of 4% ±2%.

> [a] IMF (2019a) does not, however, classify Paraguay's exchange rate regime as a 'crawling' arrangement, but as 'floating', though not as 'free-floating'.

For LFDCs which have exchange rate targeting as their monetary anchor or which seek exchange rate stability, although not necessarily fixity, through a managed float, the transition to IT necessarily implies that the central bank loosens its grip on the exchange rate. This applies also to those LFDCs without an explicit nominal anchor, but whose central banks track a set of monetary indicators along with the exchange rate. In its transition to IT, the central bank's exchange rate policy should be geared to avoid abrupt changes in the rate, but not to the defense of a given target value, that moreover can be expected or guessed by the public, even if this is not announced. Interest rates must aim at stabilizing inflation, not the exchange rate. A clear and credible communications strategy on the primacy of the medium-term inflation target can substitute for frequent interventions in the foreign exchange market. Transparent and clearly explained interventions rules can be useful to convey the message that interventions are consistent with inflation-targeting priorities (IMF 2015b: 40). Also, the development of a sufficiently deep private market for foreign currencies, for spot transactions as well as for operations with derivatives, supplemented by the appropriate infrastructure of rules, regulations, and supervision, would lessen the need for central bank interventions.

Central bank inflation forecasts are a key ingredient of an IT framework. An IT central bank needs to regularly assess whether the current stance of monetary policy is still well aligned with the desired convergence path of inflation toward its target rate. The long lags between policy decisions and actual inflation outcomes imply that this assessment has to be carried out with inflation forecasts. The latter are the central bank's best conditional forecasts of inflation outcomes over a one- or two-year policy horizon. Inflation forecasts are regularly announced by the central bank, often immediately after the meetings of the monetary policy committee and in any case in regular inflation reports. This directly contributes to the transparency and accountability requirements that are important tenets of IT.

Official inflation forecasts published in the inflation reports are usually a baseline forecast. The forecast is accompanied by a thorough discussion of the risks that inflation outcomes will diverge from the baseline forecast under alternative

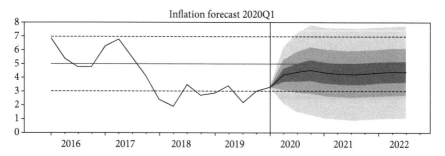

Figure 6.1. Inflation forecast fan chart

Note: The figure is based on a forecast exercise with actual inflation data and a simple linear autoregressive model. Horizontal lines reflect the hypothetical center and band limits of the inflation target.

scenarios, and of possible policy responses should these risks materialize. Box 6.10 discusses some methodological aspects of inflation forecasts. Fan charts are used to show in a synthetic manner the central bank's view of the probability distribution of inflation outcomes over the policy horizon. Figure 6.1 is an example of such an inflation forecast fan chart for a hypothetical central bank whose target range is 5 ± 2%. The central, darkest shaded area around the point forecasts indicates the range of inflation rates expected to occur with a 30% probability. Similarly, outcomes in each pair of lighter shaded areas are also assigned a 30% probability. The fan thus spans, for any given quarter, outcomes that are expected to occur with a 90% probability. The fan becomes larger the further ahead in time the inflation rate is projected, reflecting increased uncertainty about the future.[39]

6.4.4　Performance of inflation targeting

Since IT has been embraced by a number of countries in the 1990s, empirical evidence on its performance has always been a question of high interest, particularly for policy-makers of countries planning to adopt it. Empirical research has been abundant, using different methodologies and econometric techniques and focusing mostly on the performance of IT adopters, compared to non-adopters, in terms of inflation and output levels, of inflation and output variability. Among those, the study by Samarina et al. (2014) is representative of the two most

---

[39] While most AE and EME IT central banks publish fan charts of forecasts for both inflation and output growth, this is not always the case in LDFCs, possibly because of poor data quality on aggregate economic activity.

Box 6.10. Inflation forecasts

Inflation forecasts are produced conditional on the current state of the factors that determine inflation, and on their expected future developments. The process relies on forecasts from various types of econometric model as well as on policy-makers' informed judgement.

LFDCs' central banks to a large extent use time-series models. Unrestricted vector auto-regressions (VAR) are linear models that involve current and lagged variables of inflation and of the latter's main determinants, like the exchange rate, real activity, and a domestic interest rate. The simultaneously estimated dynamics of these variables allows inflation forecasts for a few quarters ahead. More elaborate VAR models of many types offer useful refinements. Structural VARs (SVARS), the most popular, impose some economic structure on contemporaneous or long-term interactions between the variables. Bayesian VARs allow some priors to be incorporated into the estimation of the VAR parameters. VARs with time-varying parameters better capture structural changes in the interaction between determinants of inflation. VAR models may also include exogenous variables, like international commodity prices or interest rates. In this case, the projection of the inflation rate requires an exogenous projection for the path of these variables. Inflation forecasts are then also conditional on the chosen projection, for instance a 'no change' scenario.

Inflation-targeting central banks of LFDCs have also developed, or started to develop, semi-structural projection models, mostly within the Forecasting and Policy Analysis System (FPAS) advocated by the IMF for middle- and low-income countries. Such theory-based models, which we discuss in section 7.4, can be expected to be, by construction, more coherent than data-driven VAR models and therefore more efficient in producing projections for the medium term. Inflation forecasts produced with these models also rely, like those of VAR models, on scenarios bearing on the projected path for the model's exogenous variables. Also, the projected path of the short-term interest rate, the IT central banks' operating target, critically shapes the inflation forecasts. Some central banks postulate a constant interest rate, others use a Taylor-type reaction function that is endogenous to the forecasting model used, still others a judgement-based path. Whether the central bank should, for transparency reasons, fully disclose the projected interest rate path, as is the case in some AEs, is still a much-debated issue (Hammond 2012: 12–4).

IT central banks' official inflation forecasts are not a mechanical output of a particular model but forecasts in which policy-makers' judgement plays a significant role. The forecast may combine the outcome of several models, as well as taking into account information that is not embedded in them, such as survey-based inflation expectations from consumers and businesses or high-frequency indicators of economic activity.

common empirical approaches used.[40] The results of their study bearing on a sample of 25 advanced and 59 emerging and developing countries over 1985–2011, point to strong evidence that IT reduces inflation in emerging and developing countries, though not in AEs. Balima et al. (2017) perform a meta-regression analysis of 113 studies relating to the effects of IT on different performance variables.[41] They conclude that 'studies based exclusively on a sample of developing countries are more likely to conclude in favor of IT's effectiveness in bringing down inflation and its variability' (p. 17). More broadly, their findings suggest that 'the beneficial effect of IT on price and output stability is stronger in developing countries' (p. 22), and also that those effects are strongest in countries that have implemented full-fledged IT. Agénor and Pereira da Silva (2019: 40–1) also conclude from their survey of empirical IT studies of a representative group of upper middle-income countries that IT has been successful in reducing inflation and inflation expectations, more so than in AEs. IT adoption also led to lower variability and lower persistence in inflation expectations, as well as to a lower output cost to reduce inflation. Such positive assessment of IT performance for developing countries is in general attributed to its credibility effect, the adoption of IT signalling decisive commitment of the authorities to price stability.

Most IT targeters in the low-income countries group have been late adopters, which gives little hindsight to reliably assess IT's performance. Recently, Bleaney et al. (2020a), however, address this question by carrying out a cross-country panel study over 1980–2016. They evaluate whether IT's performance in reducing inflation has been different across three categories of IT adopters: LICs, EMEs, and high-income countries. It is interesting to note that the 11 inflation-targeting LICs they consider overlap, with one exception (Peru), with the IT-targeting LFDCs of our set (Table 6.2). Their study's results indicate that 'IT has been far less effective in LICs than in EMEs, highlighting the presence of significant heterogeneity in IT effects within non-advanced countries' (p. 22). Exploring the role played by differences in institutional quality, as measured by an indicator of government accountability, the authors point out that IT is more effective when institutional quality is high. The smaller effect observed for IT on inflation in LICs, relative to EMEs, can thus presumably be attributed to lower institutional

---

[40] The two approaches are the difference-in-differences (dif-dif) and the propensity score methods. In the first one, the sample period is divided between two sub-periods, before and after IT adoption, using a benchmark cut-off date. The difference in the average inflation rates of IT targeters before and after adoption is then compared to the difference between the inflation rates observed for these two sub-periods in a control group of non-adopters. The second, propensity score method also compares IT versus non-IT adopters, but after correcting for a selection bias that may affect the diff-diff method. The latter could indeed produce a biased result of IT's efficacy if countries with past experience of low inflation were more likely to adopt IT.

[41] For a brief discussion of the methodology of a meta-regression, see Ch. 4, n. 40.

quality and, consequently, to a greater likelihood of the central bank being exposed to the risk of fiscal dominance. Loose constraints on the executive branch of the government lift the roadblocks to monetary financing of fiscal deficits.

Very cursory evidence on the heterogeneity in IT experiences in LICs can also be found in Table 6.2. While all LFDCs have, with one exception, decreased their average inflation rate since IT adoption, relative to its three-year average before adoption, the variability of the inflation rate relative to the central target rate at adoption has been low in some countries, high in others.[42]

Heterogeneity in the experiences of IT targeters among LICs is also borne out by individual country studies. Brownbridge and Kasekende (2018) discuss, in a broad-based analysis, the Ugandan five-year experience (2011–16) with IT, and conclude that it has largely been successful. They attribute this success to the central bank's strong and unambiguous commitment to controlling inflation and to a clear and transparent framework for setting monetary policy (p. 51). A different conclusion is drawn by Bleaney et al. (2020b), who review 10 years of IT in Ghana. They evaluate it as unsuccessful, given that the relatively high and varying inflation target has been persistently exceeded by a large margin. Inflation expectations have also been persistently above the target rate, suggesting low credibility of the latter. They conjecture that this lack of success is the result of a latent fiscal dominance that emerged under the pressure of mounting fiscal deficits.

6.4.5 Challenges to inflation targeting in LICs

6.4.5.1 Credibility
The IT framework has been embraced by central banks that wished to enhance the efficacy of their monetary policy in achieving price stability. The forward-looking and commitment-based nature of the framework and the transparency and communication strategy that it requires are expected to bring the necessary expectations anchoring credibility benefits. A solid credibility reputation also allows the central bank to use discretion to smooth the effects of exogenous shocks on economic activity without being quickly 'punished' by inflation expectations straying from the medium-term target rate.

The principal challenge of IT is therefore to maintain credibility—more precisely, given the long lags between policy decisions and actual inflation, the 'credibility of a promise to reach the inflation target in the future' (Agénor and Pereira da Silva 2019: 22).

---

[42] The standard deviation of inflation post-IT adoption has varied between 7% and 100% of the initial target rate (the centre of the target band) among the 16 LFDCs of Table 6.2. This may suggest, at first glance at least, that in countries with a high ratio the central target for the inflation rate has often been missed.

Reinforcing and preserving the institutional guarantees on which the commitment to price stability is grounded clearly is the foremost challenge. In many IT-adopting LFDCs, this often amounts first to keeping fiscal dominance at arm's length.

The other important challenge for LFDCs is to maintain credibility of their commitment to price stability when they are also tempted to use monetary policy to simultaneously pursue other targets, such as output stability, real exchange rate stability, and financial stability. Such practice is not in principle incompatible with a broad version of flexible inflation targeting, under the condition, however, that the pursuit of these other targets remains strictly consistent with the medium-run inflation target.[43] Any public doubt about such consistency endangers the central bank's credibility. The flexible version of IT, of stabilizing output alongside inflation, has been widely accepted and practised by most if not all inflation-targeting countries.[44] Financial stability has also been added to the central bank's price stability mandate in the wake of recurrent financial crises, and especially the 2007–8 global financial crisis (see section 4.2.2). To manage this additional trade-off efficiently, central banks have in all countries resorted to macro-prudential instruments, in close cooperation with prudential supervisory bodies, as discussed in section 3.6.

6.4.5.2 Exchange rate, output, and financial stability

In contrast with AEs, there is in EMEs and LFDCs a close connection between the traditional targets on price, output and financial stability that runs through the exchange rate. For this very reason, exchange rate stabilization occupies a place of choice in the policy menu of many LFDCs, receiving the same priority as inflation stabilization, regardless of the monetary anchor. Indeed, the stabilization of inflation often goes hand in hand with exchange rate stabilization, because of the possibly still high pass-through of exchange depreciation on inflation. Inflation stabilization is almost an impossible task in face of rapid exchange rate depreciation. Limiting exchange rate depreciations may also protect financial stability when it is threatened by currency mismatches in agents' balance sheets. On the other hand, a sharp appreciation of the real exchange rate, resulting from booming international prices for LFDCs' commodity exports or from capital inflows, has high costs in terms of forgone output because of the general loss of competitiveness in the non-commodity tradable sector (see section 5.3).

---

[43] Actually, 6 out of the 16 IT LFDCs reported in Table 6.2 are defined in IMF (2019a: 6–7) as inflation targeters with stabilized or crawl-like exchange rate arrangements.

[44] Note that Nominal Income Targeting (NIT) has received significant attention as an alternative to the flexible version of IT that involves both inflation and output stabilization. NIT modifies trade-offs between both targets but does not necessarily do better than IT when welfare effects of both regimes are compared in a standard New Keynesian model (Agénor and Montiel 2015: 246). It has also been argued that, for EMEs and developing countries specifically, targeting nominal GDP would not be of any help, essentially as it neglects, like IT, exchange rate and financial stability issues (see e.g. Velasco 2013).

Dealing with unwarranted fluctuations of the exchange rate by adjusting the domestic interest rate is, at first glance, an option to be considered. It has been suggested that inflation-targeting LFDCs incorporate changes in the real exchange rate as an additional argument in a modified-interest-rate Taylor rule, as noted by Agénor and Montiel (2015: 253). However, it is unlikely that this will be effective in dealing with large shocks to the real exchange rate while simultaneously preserving the inflation target. If, for instance, the central bank raises the short-term interest rate to absorb the liquidity brought about by the expansion of commodity exports, it will induce capital inflows that strengthen the exchange rate, defeating the intended effect. If it leaves unchanged or reduces the policy interest rate to limit capital inflows, overheating of the economy will continue or even increase. This will not avoid real exchange rate appreciation.

Central banks in developing countries, especially in EMEs, where large capital in- and outflows are most frequent, thus intervene in the foreign exchange market, both in the upswing and in the downswing. EMEs and LFDCs which have adopted IT do so to dodge large fluctuations in the nominal exchange rate rather than to defend a given rate level, directing their attention to the trajectory of the real exchange rate while aiming simultaneously to lower inflation. To this end, central banks frequently sterilize their FX interventions by implementing domestic monetary operations that partially or totally cancel the effects of interventions on domestic liquidity. Thus, in principle, sterilized interventions allow the central bank to keep the real exchange rate close to its medium-term equilibrium value and, separately, to assign the short-term interest rate to its domestic targets.[45]

Inflation-targeting LFDCs may thus employ sterilized FX interventions and macro-prudential instruments to maximize their chances to achieve output stability and preserve financial stability without endangering their commitment to medium-term price stability.[46] In this regard, however, transparency and communication should be key preoccupations for an inflation-targeting central bank, as stressed in section 6.4.3.2. Clearly explaining its multi-target policy, and the use it makes of its different instruments, interest rates, FX interventions, and macro-prudential instruments, is indispensable to avoid sending confusing

---

[45] As discussed more thoroughly in section 3.5.2, sterilized interventions allows separate targeting of exchange rate and inflation, especially when capital mobility is not too high. But they are not without limits or without costs. Also, assessing the equilibrium level of the real exchange rate is not an easy task and is open to much uncertainty, calling for caution in managing FX interventions and for assigning them mostly to mitigating gross misalignments.

[46] Céspedes et al. (2012: 52) define such approach as a new, expanded, and enriched version of the IT framework, adopted by EMEs. Agénor and Pereira da Silva (2019: 2) use the term 'Integrated Inflation targeting' (ITT) for a monetary framework that optimally combines monetary and macro-prudential policy. They include in the latter the use of foreign exchange rate interventions, as well as of temporary capital controls, that are motivated by financial stability considerations. Hofman et al. (2020) also acknowledge that sterilized FX interventions may be justified within an IT framework as an additional instrument for managing financial stability risks when the use of the domestic interest rate to this end is counterproductive.

signals to the public (Agénor and Pereira da Silva 2019: 56; Hofman et al. 2020: 14). Not to do so would blur its commitment to price stability, threaten its credibility, and ultimately endanger the IT framework itself.

6.5 Nominal anchors in dollarized economies

While the cases of full dollarization discussed in section 6.2.4.2.2 are rare, partial or de facto dollarization is frequent.[47] In many LFDCs, foreign currencies circulate to a significant extent side by side with the domestic currency. Because of this, LFDCs face specific difficulties and policy challenges. We have already discussed, in section 2.4.2.2.2, how dollarization affects the exchange rate channel of the monetary policy transmission mechanism, making it stronger but also less reliable. In section 3.6.4, we examined how central banks have to adapt their policy instruments when the country's banking system is heavily dollarized, in order to fulfil their LOLR function. In this section, we first briefly discuss the extent of dollarization in LFDCs and its characteristics, before exploring how it complicates the choice of a nominal anchor.

6.5.1 Characteristics of dollarization

Dollarization arises in countries with high inflation and where other institutions designed to cope with high inflation, like wage and price indexation to the domestic consumer price index, are absent. It should be noted that dollarization not only protects from high inflation but also helps to sustain the inflation stabilization effort in its initial stages.[48] It is only later that it becomes a problem. Also, when high inflation has destroyed the domestic banking sector, as happened in many Latin American countries in the 1980s, dollarization facilitated its reconstruction. It is to be noted again that partial dollarization is a decision of the public rather than of the authorities, as is the case of full dollarization. However, authorities may play a significant role once dollarization has become widespread, stepping in to legalize it and even to facilitate operations in dollars in the domestic economy. Many LFDCs went through this experience. Also, globalization of financial markets has broadly contributed to reinforce dollarization. Figure 6.2

---

[47] As already mentioned, 'dollarization' is used as a generic term, referring to the use, on a significant scale, of a foreign currency in functions normally reserved to domestic currency in an economy. In some countries, like Albania, it is the euro which is used as a parallel currency. In other countries the currency of a neighboring country may be widely used (e.g. the South African rand in Zimbabwe).

[48] The stabilization from hyperinflation in Bolivia in 1985 produced a re-monetization in dollars rather than in domestic currency, as described in Box 6.2. In fact, the liberalization of the exchange market that accompanied the stabilization plan increased dollarization, despite the rapid and important drop in inflation.

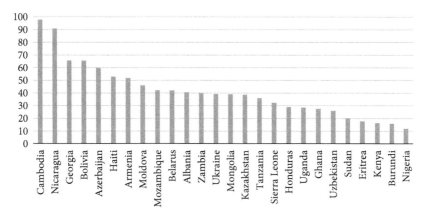

Figure 6.2. Deposit dollarization in selected LFDCs (average 2006–9 ratios, %)

Source of data: Mwase and Kumah (2015: 25, table A.1)

reports deposit dollarization ratios that were observed a decade ago for a selection of LICs.[49] Significant dollarization is encountered in a number of LFDCs, with very high levels observed in some, as in Cambodia and Nicaragua. Since then, the domestic impact of the international financial turmoil of 2007–9, as well as the commodity export boom that lasted from 2004 to 2014, somewhat reduced the appeal of dollarization in LFDCs and stimulated policy efforts to contain it. Bannister et al. (2018: 10–1) report that the average rate of dollarization in emerging and developing countries was on a declining trend over the 2000–2015 period, but that cross-country experience was uneven. The reduction was strong in some countries, (e.g. Bolivia and Angola), but more mitigated or even nonexistent in others (e.g. Cambodia, Nicaragua).

There are several varieties of dollarization, each closely associated with specific functions of money in the economy.[50]

- Currency substitution. Dollars are used as means of payment, in cash and current account bank deposits.[51] This is especially, although not only, the case for purchases of investment goods and of investment-type consumer goods, like houses, cars, appliances, and furniture.

---

[49] The dollarization ratio is defined as the ratio between FX deposits and the total of FX and domestic currency deposits. Fig. 6.2 is based on data reported by Mwase and Kumah (2015: 25) for a set of 42 LICs with some dollarization of deposits. The 26 LFDCs included in the figure have a ratio above 10%.

[50] Detailed studies of dollarization can be found e.g. in Levy Yeyati and Sturzenegger (2002), Levy Yeyati (2006) and in Armas et al. (2006).

[51] Currency substitution is strengthened by network effects. The larger the network, the smaller for an individual user the transaction costs of using the foreign currency. Reding and Morales (2004) show how such network effects are shaped by the inflation rate, and how they can generate a persistent economy-wide currency substitution.

- Financial dollarization. Dollars are used to maintain the real value of domestic financial assets and liabilities. Financial contracts are denominated in foreign currency, in particular for bank deposits and loans. The amounts of banks' liabilities and assets in dollars are determined simultaneously. Banks accepting dollars in deposit will also lend in dollars, in order to minimize their foreign exchange exposure, as requested by good risk-management practices as well as by specific prudential regulations on foreign exchange positions. Often, prudent depositors prefer dollarized deposits for fear of large losses in case of devaluation, however small the probability of this happening. Borrowers accept dollar loans because they consider them cheaper. Indeed, loan rates are in general higher for domestic than for foreign currency loans. In adopting such a myopic attitude, borrowers abstract from the effects of a possible devaluation on the domestic currency cost of their dollar loan. This may happen if the parity of the exchange rate has been maintained over a long period, leading people to assign a low probability to the occurrence of devaluation.
- Real dollarization. The *pricing* of goods and services is done in dollars, although payment may be accepted in local currency. Wages are generally fixed in domestic currency, except maybe for the upper end of the wage scale. Fees charged by practitioners of liberal professions, like doctors and lawyers, are usually quoted in dollars.

Table 6.3 illustrates different forms of dollarization in four LFDCs in 2019. The extent of currency substitution may be measured by the dollarization ratio of residents' demand deposits, that of financial dollarization by the dollarization ratio of time/savings deposits and of bank loans. Referring also to Figure 6.2, one notes that dollarization has decreased since 2006–9 in Bolivia and Mozambique, while it has remained virtually unchanged in Armenia and in Cambodia, a country with almost full dollarization. Table 6.3 also illustrates that dollarization generally, though not always, affects to a similar extent demand deposits, savings/time deposits, and bank loans.[52]

Table 6.3. Dollarization indicators in selected LFDCs (2019)

	Demand deposits	Savings/time deposits	Loans
Armenia	40%	48%	51%
Bolivia	27%	23%	1%
Cambodia	90%	94%	97%
Mozambique	30%	20%	15%

Source: National central banks or supervisory authorities: Dec. 2019 data.

[52] A strong correlation between loan and deposit dollarization is to be expected as a result of banks' currency risk management. Bannister et al. (2018: 11) indeed report for their 2000–2015 sample period a correlation coefficient of 0.82 between the two dollarization ratios, but also note that there are many variations across countries.

Dollarization is also characterized by hysteresis: even when inflation fades, it does not necessarily decrease. The upper limit to partial dollarization is given by regulations bearing on taxes, wages, and foreign exchange positions in the banking sector. Also, there will in general remain a demand for domestic currency in small denominations, for instance to pay for groceries and for similar low-value transactions. As mentioned above, wages and salaries, except for the upscale ones, are paid in domestic currency. As a general rule, current taxes of domestic taxpayers are paid in domestic currency, but overdue taxes are indexed to the dollar (implying a case of real dollarization). Also, sometimes foreign corporations are allowed to pay taxes in dollars.

Summing up, partial dollarization has several advantages, the main one being that it responds to public demand to cope with high inflation. This point cannot be underestimated. Also, allowing operations in dollars has been instrumental in the inflation stabilization efforts of many countries and in the ensuing reconstruction of their banking systems.

6.5.2 Challenges raised by dollarization

Dollarization can give rise to severe problems and significant vulnerabilities. The drawbacks of dollarization loom large, as it deprives domestic authorities of the control they would otherwise have on their currency. The loss of seigniorage revenue is one of dollarization's typical consequences. It may significantly weigh on the country's budgetary balance, specifically for those who find it difficult to mobilize resources through taxation.[53] Also, as discussed in section 3.6.4, the central bank cannot fully exercise its LOLR function to the extent that banks' liquidity shortages are expressed in foreign currency. This obliges it to address systemic liquidity problems in other ways, in particular forcing a high accumulation of foreign exchange reserves.[54] This can be very costly, hurt the net income of the central bank, and ultimately weaken the financial health of the government.[55]

Many of those drawbacks are observed whichever monetary anchor the central bank choses, although there may be specific twists to it that depend on the chosen anchor. However, and as importantly, dollarization very much complicates the

[53] Seigniorage arises from the issuing of monetary base (see Box 5.1). Dollarized economies forgo seigniorage to the extent that the demand for domestic currency base money is reduced. The seigniorage on the foreign currency bank notes in circulation in the country is indeed captured by the issuing foreign central bank.

[54] Unless the central bank can access readily credit lines and swaps with international creditors. This is not a realistic option for most LFDCs.

[55] On the cost of international reserves, see Appendix 6A.

actual choice of a nominal anchor for the domestic price level. We briefly explore this aspect.

6.5.2.1 Dollarization and exchange rate targeting

When dollarization is sizeable, the pass-through of the exchange rate to the domestic price level can be expected to be quick and large. Superficially, this would suggest *exchange rate targeting* as a good choice for anchoring the price level. However, dollarization exacerbates the conflict between price and output stabilization that characterizes fixed-exchange regimes. With dollarization, moreover, financial stability becomes a major additional dimension that authorities have to take into account when devising their exchange rate policy. Dollarization increases financial fragility, insofar that it may cause solvency and liquidity problems (see section 3.6.4).[56] Output stabilization may require a devaluation to help the tradable sector, but that may weaken the financial sector, given the foreign-currency loans made to households and to firms that obtain their income in the sector of non-tradable goods. The balance sheet effects of devaluation in countries with financial dollarization have severe consequences on the level of activity and may propel the economy into recession. In this setting, devaluations may be contractive, as discussed in Box 6.3. As a consequence, the exchange rate cannot be moved as would be necessary to redress macroeconomic imbalances, because of its effects on credit risk and on the soundness of the banking sector. Adjustment is postponed or, in crawling-peg countries, slowed. In addition, expectations of a forthcoming devaluation, however small, can reinforce dollarization.

6.5.2.2 Dollarization and monetary aggregate targeting

With dollarization, anchoring the price level through the *control of monetary aggregates* is also made significantly more difficult. To start with, should dollar liabilities of the domestic banking sector be included in the aggregates monitored by the monetary authorities? In principle not, as monetary targeting is about

---

[56] The conventional view that financial dollarization enhances the risks to financial stability has been recently challenged by Christiano et al. (2019). They argue that deposit dollarization mainly reflects a demand for insurance by households against exchange rate depreciations that are associated with recessions. Such insurance is (mostly) provided by domestic dollar borrowers, firms or banks. The difference between domestic dollar and local currency interest rates reflects the insurance premium paid by households to domestic non-financial firms. The latter appear to be the ultimate insurers when banks adequately control their foreign exchange exposure. Non-financial firms can diversify their risks broadly, especially when they are large and their borrowing in dollars is long-term. Over the long-run benefits of expenditure switching of a devaluation partially reverse the negative effects on their balance sheets. The authors also empirically assess whether such useful business-cycle insurance role of dollarization comes at the cost of increased financial fragility. They conclude from an empirical study of banking crises that there is little support in the data that higher deposit dollarization is associated with an increased frequency of increased severity of banking crises, adding that remaining concerns can be managed by appropriate regulations of banks' currency mismatches and of capital requirements on their foreign currency loans.

anchoring the *domestic currency* price level. Yet banks' domestic dollar liabilities held by residents form part of the economy's global liquidity—an argument to include them in the broader monetary aggregates. Sight, savings, or time deposits in dollars easily substitute for domestic currency holdings, or can easily be converted into domestic currency (see section 1.2.2). The same holds for dollar notes in circulation in the economy. The latter posit, additionally, a measurement problem. Monetary authorities therefore frequently publish and monitor two separate types of monetary aggregate—those encompassing only domestic currency monetary liabilities and those including domestic banks' dollar liabilities held by residents.

'Domestic dollar' liquidity also arises from credit operations made by the domestic banking system. These operations, initiated on the asset side of the banks' balance sheet, generate new 'domestic dollar' deposits: a 'money multiplier' is at work, similarly to what is observed for domestic currency bank credits and deposits. Since 'domestic dollar' liquidity may affect spending and aggregate demand, the monetary authorities would wish to have a handle on them, but this task is very difficult, if not impossible. Some control can be gained by imposing high compulsory reserve requirements on banks' dollar deposits, which decreases the broad money multiplier. However, the 'domestic dollar' component of the monetary base and 'domestic dollar' interest rates, regardless of their maturity, largely escape the control of the central bank. The open-market operations of the central bank, when conducted in dollars, have a limited reach in the banks' asset composition and on the rates they quote for their dollar deposits and loans. Although not perfect substitutes, domestic dollar and genuine US dollar deposits of sufficiently large size command interest rates which in principle cannot diverge beyond a country/banking risk spread. This spread cannot be influenced very much by the central bank's refinancing and open-market operations. The central bank can, however, to some extent use its policy of specific reserve and liquidity requirements on domestic dollar deposits to decrease their attractiveness for the less internationally mobile depositors. This central bank policy limits the liquidity effects of dollar deposits and simultaneously encourages banks to raise the cost of domestic foreign currency loans. Figure 6.3 illustrates for Bolivia, over 1994–2019, the degree of dependence of dollar deposit rates relative to US rates.[57] With the exception of a short period in 2005–8, interest rates on domestic dollar deposits have been higher than US rates but have followed them closely. After 2010, the domestic dollar rate follows the strong decline in US rates and has remained at low levels.[58] Dollarization thus limits—and very significantly so if it severely

[57] The figure also shows the positive effects on domestic currency rates of three concomitant factors: declining inflation, declining exchange rate depreciation, and decreasing dollarization.
[58] The very active policy of reserve requirements undertaken in 2005–8 which penalized deposits in dollars explains the negative spread observed then between the two rates. Banks shifted the cost of the reserve requirements to the depositors instead of the credit-takers, as is usually the case. In

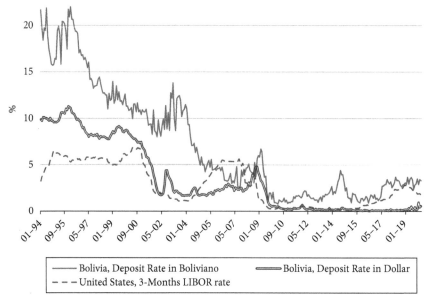

Figure 6.3. US interbank rate and Bolivian deposit rates in domestic and foreign currencies, 1994–2020

Source of data: IMF, Internationa Financial Statistics

affects banks' domestic liabilities—the influence of the central bank on the domestic financial system, and hence impairs the interest rate and credit channels of monetary policy transmission mechanisms on which a monetary aggregate targeting policy relies.

6.5.2.3 Dollarization and inflation targeting

The implementation of IT in financially dollarized economies is also challenging, since the main tenets of this framework are flexibility of the exchange rate and strong reliance on domestic interest rate management. Sharp variations in exchange rates can jeopardize the inflation target, besides having undesirable balance sheet effects, with contractive consequences for economic activity. Also, in a highly dollarized economy the instruments of monetary policy are, as indicated above, considerably weakened. Because of this weakness, the pass-through from policy rates to lending and borrowing rates of the banks may not be as significant as the monetary authorities would wish.

particular, small deposits are 'captive' deposits that could not flee the country because of lack of information and also because of minimum deposit requirements in the foreign banks. The same factors explain the low and quasi-constant level of the domestic dollar deposit interest rate after 2010, as banks, which had already strongly decreased the dollarization rate of their loans, discouraged dollar deposits (see Table 6.3).

Only a few dollarized LFDCs have opted for IT as their nominal anchor framework, and most only recently so.[59] An interesting parallel case is Peru, a country that was highly dollarized but which adopted early on an inflation-targeting framework. This framework has been coupled with explicit control of the risks posed by the financial system's extensive dollarization.[60] Inflation targeting has met with considerable success there: inflation has been checked, dollarization has receded, and the overall performance of the economy has been remarkable.[61] Box 6.11 shows how Peru has successfully adapted the basic framework of inflation targeting.

As discussed in section 6.4.5.2, inflation-targeting LFDCs also face the specific challenge of avoiding, for financial stability reasons, disruptive changes in the exchange rate. They do so partly by relying on sterilized foreign exchange interventions. Dollarization complicates the task, essentially because it increases the substitutability between domestic and foreign currency, making sterilized interventions less effective.

6.5.3 De-dollarization

Given the pitfalls of dollarization, many countries, particularly in Latin America, have proceeded with gradual de-dollarization.[62] Sustained low inflation that triggered confidence in the commitment to price stability, big improvements in the international reserves position, and long periods of exchange rate appreciation overcame the reluctance of the Latin American public with regard to their own currencies.[63] In addition, deposits in domestic currency have been subjected to more benign regulations than deposits in foreign currencies. For instance, the interest income on deposits in domestic currency is being less taxed than that on deposits in foreign currency. Also, required reserve ratios have been higher for

---

[59] Albania, Armenia, Georgia, Paraguay, and Ukraine are IT countries that exhibit the largest rates of loan dollarization among the 16 IT LFDCs identified in Table 6.2. Their loan dollarization rates ranged between 47% and 57%. All, except Paraguay, were on a declining trend over the previous decade (source: IMF Financial Soundness Indicators Database).

[60] Peru is now an upper-middle-income country and has not been included in our set of LFDCs. However, its domestic financial markets are still shallow, and its experience with IT under dollarization illustrates very well the challenges faced by monetary authorities. Peru's dollarization rate is sizeable but not extreme, with residents' foreign currency deposits currently accounting for around 40–45% of total deposits.

[61] See the discussion of the challenges posited by dollarization to inflation targeting in Peru in Armas and Grippa (2005) and in Armas et al. (2014).

[62] The abrupt and forced de-dollarizations of the 1980s in Latin America (e.g. Bolivia, Ecuador) failed miserably. Not only did dollarization continue, albeit underground, but these measures prompted capital flight, which in turn fuelled ongoing inflation. De-dollarization became widely unpopular, and was wrongly blamed for the high inflations that plagued many Latin American countries in that period.

[63] Long periods of exchange rate appreciation raise the awareness of the public that the exchange rate can move in two directions, and that holding dollar deposits is thus a two-way bet.

Box 6.11. Inflation targeting in a dollarized economy: the case of Peru

---

Peru has operated an IT framework since 2002. A first key characteristic is that the target inflation rate is set to 2%, with a tolerance range of ± 1%. It is aimed to be close to the US inflation rate, and stands at a level lower than the rate used by other inflation targeters. The driving idea is that the public should not find differences in terms of purchasing power between holding domestic currency and holding dollars.

Second, the analytical and forecasting framework used for setting the monetary policy rate within the IT framework incorporate crucial 'dollarization variables' that interact with domestic credit conditions, such as the 'domestic dollar interest rate', the balance sheet effects of exchange rate depreciations, and the central bank's foreign-exchange interventions and active policy of required reserves (see Armas and Grippa 2005).

The third characteristic of Peru's IT framework is that it is operated within a set of prudential policies designed to prevent disruptions caused by dollarization, which could magnify the effects of external shocks. Such policies include maintaining a high level of international reserves as an insurance for liquidity risks in the domestic financial system, and intervening in the foreign exchange market to pre-empt wild fluctuations of the exchange rate; it also includes setting required reserves on banks' foreign-currency liabilities at a level higher than for domestic currency liabilities and of using such reserves in a countercyclical way to attenuate the effects of capital in- and outflows on domestic financial markets. To further encourage de-dollarization, the central bank helped banks avoid the currency mismatch they would face if they financed loans in domestic currency with deposits in domestic dollars. To this end, the central bank offered banks attractive long-term cross-currency repos, lending domestic currency against the banks' dollar assets. The availability of a long-term domestic currency funding gave banks a strong incentive to de-dollarize their loan portfolio (Castillo et al. 2016).

It is interesting to note that, while the features of inflation targeting in Peru take into account dollarization, inflation targeting has in turn reduced dollarization and has been conducive to financial deepening in domestic currency, in fact to the creation of a financial market in domestic currency that was hitherto inexistent or, to put it more accurately, had been destroyed by decades of macroeconomic instability.

dollar deposits than for domestic currency deposits.[64] Prudential measures, such as higher liquidity requirements on dollar deposits, stronger provisioning of banks' foreign currency lending, limits and higher capital requirements on specific FX exposures, were designed to induce banks to internalize the risks carried by dollarization (García-Escribano and Sosa 2011: 11–2). In some cases, central banks took additional measures to help banks increase domestic-currency lending without having to worry about the currency mismatch entailed by funding in dollar deposits (see Box 6.11 on Peru). Similar regulatory measures were taken by dollarized economies outside Latin America, including by LFDCs like Armenia, Albania, and Kazakhstan.

Experience shows that de-dollarization is at best a gradual process. It is exposed to the risk of reversals, and its ultimate success is not necessary guaranteed. Maintaining for a long period an environment of stable, low inflation is a critically necessary condition for de-dollarization to succeed, but it is not sufficient. Gradualism in de-dollarization appears inevitable if factors that have given rise to dollarization and allowed it to take deep roots are still active. Gradualism may even be desirable if a sufficiently strong and efficient local currency financial intermediation is not yet available.[65] To the extent that de-dollarization is driven by a policy-induced increase in the relative cost of foreign currency intermediation, it is important that it be accompanied by sufficiently strong improvement in the efficiency of domestic currency intermediation. Indeed, if the extent and quality of financial intermediation, whether in foreign or domestic currency, were to globally decrease, disintermediation may occur, which could slow down or possibly reverse financial deepening.

6.6 Summary

Monetary anchors have a central role in the modern practice of monetary policy. In this chapter we have discussed the nominal anchor choices open to LFDCs.

---

[64] Widening these differences in reserve ratios increases the cost of dollar intermediation for banks, relative to domestic currency intermediation. Banks will pass on this larger cost by posting lower rates for dollar deposits and higher rates for dollar loans. This encourages de-dollarization of both deposits and loans.

[65] Della Valle et al. (2018) consider that there is some optimal dollarization level below which the costs of de-dollarization—financial disintermediation due to a possible worsening in quality and cost of financial intermediation—become larger that its benefits. They estimate such benchmark levels for various countries, using a worldwide panel data analysis of the determinants of deposit dollarization. A country's benchmark level takes into account its structural characteristic (e.g. size, openness, importance of remittances), and is based on a counterfactual of 'good macroeconomic performances' (e.g. low and constant inflation). Estimated benchmark dollarization rates can be as high as 40%, for countries like Albania, Armenia, or Georgia.

They fall into three categories: exchange rate targeting, monetary targeting, and inflation targeting. Identifying with some precision the nominal anchors to which LFDCs adhere is not as straightforward as it is for AEs and even EMEs because of the multiplicity of LFDCs' monetary policy objectives; in some cases these are not even not explicitly stated.

Exchange rate targeting and money targeting are the preferred anchors in LFDCs. Exchange rate targeting has many attractive features, especially because it provides an easily understood anchor for the domestic price level as well as a disciplining device for monetary and fiscal policies. Through history, many stabilizations of high inflations and hyperinflations were initially exchange rate based.

Exchange rate targeting suffers, however, from several drawbacks, like the impairment of monetary policy's scope, and from vulnerabilities, like the risk of speculative attacks when credibility of the anchor is incomplete. Exchange rate targeting regimes in LFDCs range from hard pegs—as in the two monetary unions in Africa whose common currencies are pegged to the euro—to various forms of soft peg.

Each type of exchange rate targeting commands a different balance of advantages and drawbacks. In addition, LFDCs share with EMEs the general characteristic that monetary authorities closely monitor the exchange rate as a key nominal variable and frequently intervene in the foreign exchange market even if they do not recognize themselves as exchange rate targeters.

The choice to target monetary aggregates has sometimes been used as an alternative to exchange rate based stabilisations or, in any event, as complement to it in countries that have suffered high inflations and hyperinflations. Also, it has been employed where financial markets were shallow. In announcing targets for monetary aggregates, authorities signalled their commitment to price stability to a public convinced of the monetary roots of inflation. Monetary aggregates are closely and easily tracked, and have a clear informational advantage vis-à-vis interest rates when the market clearing level of the latter is difficult to observe. Domestic credit targeting, following the programming models of the IMF, has also often preceded the adoption of monetary targeting. The greatest challenge for money-targeting countries is that the link between the central bank's operating target, the monetary base, and nominal income, its ultimate target, has become less and less reliable, as a result of financial innovation and changes in the structure of the financial sector. Also, strict monetary targeting may produce unwarranted fluctuations in interest rates. Given the contingency of these outcomes, monetary targets are not usually implemented very strictly. There are many target misses, often for good reasons. Despite the risk this may carry for the central bank's credibility, practice of such a flexible type of monetary targeting has been widespread. Also, flexible monetary targeting can be a stepping-stone to inflation targeting.

A still small, though increasing, number of LFDCs has inflation targeting as their monetary framework. Adoption of IT usually proceeds in stages, as there are many prerequisites to successful implementation, such as central bank independence to back up a strong commitment to price stability, institutional accountability, and absence of fiscal dominance. Flexible inflation targeting is the norm. In LFDCs, as in EMEs, flexible inflation targeting has been widened, beyond the goals of price and output stability, to also encompass financial stability. In particular, risks arising from excessive swings in exchange rates (nominal and real) are of concern in this enlarged approach. Experience of IT in most LFDCs is as yet short and quite heterogeneous in its performances. Inflation-targeting LFDCs' main challenge is to keep the credibility of their commitment to the announced medium-term inflation target. Such commitment could be quickly questioned if fiscal dominance threatened to return. Doubts could also arise if authorities failed to convince the public that the large short-term deviations from the inflation target were consistent with the authorities' optimal response to severe shocks to output or to financial stability, and not an abandonment of their price stability goal.

De facto dollarization and, more rarely, de jure dollarization are features of the monetary landscape of LFDCs. Dollarized economies face specific challenges, whichever the nominal anchor they choose. The high substitutability between domestic and foreign currency that characterizes dollarization imposes heavy constraints on the monetary policy authorities can implement. Dollarization also increases financial fragility and makes trade-offs between price, output, and financial stability more acute. Many central banks of dollarized economies have thus complemented their domestic-currency monetary policy instruments with similar instruments in foreign currency, to better manage systemic liquidity risks. They have also implemented specific macro-prudential instruments to discourage dollarization. While some countries have largely succeeded in de-dollarizing their economy, others have not. De-dollarization is a gradual process that, to be successful, needs to restore an enduring environment of low inflation and, in parallel, to increase the attractiveness of financial intermediation in domestic currency. For a central bank, there is an appealing reward—to regain control of its monetary policy. Indeed, a genuine monetary policy can be conducted only in domestic currency.

APPENDIX 6A

International reserves in LFDCs

The nature, role, and management of international reserves (IR) has already been discussed in section 3.5.4, in the context of foreign-exchange interventions by the central bank. In this appendix we briefly return to the precautionary aspects of the stock of foreign reserves, before focusing on international cooperation arrangements designed either to attenuate the effects of foreign exchange shortages or reduce the costs of holding large stocks of reserves domestically as a self-insurance.

6A(1)   Stocks of IR in LFDCs

LFDCs, like EMEs, are more vulnerable to exogenous shocks than AEs, and one of the main functions of foreign reserves is to cushion them. In contrast to EMEs, where balance of payments crises arise mainly in the capital account, LFDCs mostly experience shocks to the current account, either from terms of trade, natural disasters, remittances, or delays in the disbursements of foreign aid. However, capital account shocks may also happen in LFDCs, like episodes of capital flight nurtured by expectations of a devaluation of the fixed peg or banking and liquidity crises in heavily dollarized economies. Any of these shocks puts a drain on the stock of IR, threatening a shortage that, for credit-constrained LFDCs, may have severe consequences for their economy.

For LFDCs, the insurance aspect of foreign reserves against foreign shocks is crucial. Given that LFDCs are prone to such adverse balance-of-payment shocks, one would expect them to hold a sufficiently large precautionary stock of international reserves. However, the country-specific optimal level of reserves is difficult to calculate. The country needs to strike a balance between the benefits of holding additional reserves—more absorption-smoothing by lowering the probability of a crisis and decreasing its severity—and their opportunity costs.[66] Figure 6.4 illustrates this insurance aspect of reserves for 94 LFDCs of our set, using as indicator for each country the ratio of reserves to monthly imports, averaged over 2014–18.[67] The median value of the ratio stands at 4.0 months, above the 3-month norm recommended by the IMF. However, a third of countries in the set are below this 3-month norm, while only 40% abide by the more prudent 5-month threshold.[68] It is thus doubtful that the protection provided by the stock of IR is adequate for a significant part of LFDCs. Crispolti et al. (2013: 13–15) report that countries whose IR were higher than three months of imports during the year preceding an external shock experienced almost no decline in real GDP, whereas growth performance was severely affected in those countries with reserves below this threshold.

The main characteristics of international reserves are their liquidity and easy availability. Other external assets may supplement reserves, but they are not generally as liquid or as

---

[66] For credit-constrained economies, the opportunity cost of IR could be approximated by the marginal product of capital, the cost of forgone fixed investment, as implied by the evolution of the output-to-capital ratio in the economy (IMF 2016a: 21).

[67] Data are from the World Bank's WDI. The countries reported in the graph exclude 3 oil-exporters (Libya, Algeria and Uzbekistan) whose ratios are above 15%. Also excluded are the SSA countries engaged in a monetary union in which reserves are pooled (see Appendix 6.2).

[68] The recommended 3-month import rule is complemented by a 20% broad money coverage ratio and a 100% short-term debt coverage ratio. These norms are to be adjusted by taking country-specific characteristics (e.g. the exchange rate regime) and vulnerabilities (e.g. dollarization) into account (IMF 2016a: 18–19). For example, IMF (2019h: 43) mentions a 5-month norm for a resource-rich currency union like CEMAC, and even a 9-month norm for a resource-rich economy with fixed exchange rates.

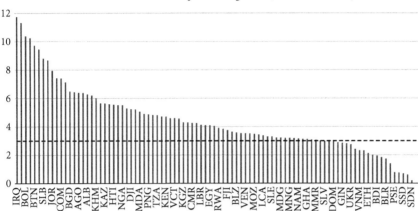

International reserves -Import coverage ratio (number of months)

Figure 6.4. International reserves: import coverage ratio (number of months)
Source: World Bank WDI database, 2014–18 average. The horizontal line shows the 3-month informal norm.

available. Conversely, when a balance-of-payment crisis arises, external assets that are considered reserves may not be as liquid as was thought before the crisis. Also, reserves like monetary gold may not be readily available because of legal impediments or because they have to be converted first into hard foreign currency at significant cost.[69] Therefore, not only the amount of reserves but also their composition and their actual degree of liquidity have to be factored in when evaluating the optimal level of reserve holdings.[70]

6A(2) International reserve borrowing arrangements

International cooperation can lessen the costs of holding reserves. If countries can borrow at reasonable cost in international markets or from international finance institutions when they are in need, some cost reductions can be reaped.

[69] E.g. in Bolivia, the pledging of gold as collateral and a fortiori its sale by the central bank requires a previous legislative authorization.
[70] Management of foreign assets is an important responsibility of central banks. Foreign exchange (and sometimes monetary gold) held by LFDCs is normally invested in safe and liquid assets in AEs' financial markets, exceptionally in EMEs. The management of reserves can be outsourced to specialized asset managers from abroad, but in this case usually with contract clauses that tightly specify the eligible foreign assets and the currencies of their denominations, paying attention to their safety, their liquidity, and, finally, their returns.

6A(2.1) The IMF

The International Monetary Fund (IMF) has the largest pool of reserves. These resources are provided by the subscriptions (quotas) of its 189 member countries or by borrowing from a subset of its members and from institutions. The IMF also has the capacity to issue new, additional international liquidity through the allocation of a specific reserve asset, the Special Drawing Right (SDR).

Standby loans to help countries with transitory problems of balance of payments have been available almost since the beginning days of the IMF.[71] They are supplied at non-concessional terms, within the limits given by a multiple of a country's quota. Contingent credit lines of the IMF can supplement reserves held domestically in order to meet external shocks at short notice. For LICs, special facilities exist with a similar purpose, featuring concessional terms and providing some flexibility in terms of the conditionality that gives access to these loans. The Rapid Credit Facility (RCF) and the Precautionary Credit Line (PCL) have been set up specifically for LICs to help address (respectively) urgent or potential balance-of-payment needs.[72]

Heavy conditionality is often attached to stand-by loans. IMF-supported programmes usually insist on fiscal austerity that hits consumption at the worst possible time. Because of this, in some LFDCs (more so in EMEs) there is often a stigma attached to the IMF stand-by assistance. No programme with the Fund is required for accessing the two contingent credit lines, but an applicant country needs to have a track record of sufficiently strong policies. Ex post conditionality may be imposed. The conditionality that goes with the IMF loans is frequently resented by the borrowers. Some LFDCs may for this reason wish to keep high levels of reserves so as to give themselves more breathing space vis-à-vis the IMF.

Note finally that the IMF's lending capacity is specifically called for in times of regional or global financial crisis when many countries simultaneously face urgent and severe balance-of-payment problems. In these instances, the IMF is actually called to intervene as a de facto lender of last resort of the international financial system, lending to countries as a central bank would lend, as LOLR, to its domestic banks in times of crisis.[73] While these interventions have in the past mostly targeted EMEs in Latin America and Asia or, more recently, AEs, they have also indirectly benefited LFDCs by mitigating the consequences of these crises on the latter's international trade flows.

---

[71] We only refer here to the IMF's financing windows with relatively quick disbursements, to be accessed for transitory balance-of-payments problems. The IMF also provides LICs with longer-term lending facilities to accompany (at concessional terms) the necessary structural transformations of their economies.

[72] The importance of the RCF has become particularly evident during the outbreak of the 2020 coronavirus pandemic.

[73] However, contrary to a central bank, which has the capacity to issue its monetary liabilities in unlimited amounts, the IMF can only lend out of its available or borrowed resources. Although it has the capacity to issue new international liquidity in the form of Special Drawing Rights (SDRs), this can only occur through a global allocation, to be distributed to all member countries in proportion to their quota. This is a protracted process. The last allocation dates back to 2009, in the wake of the global financial crisis. There are currently calls for a new SDR allocation to help countries, especially poor countries, to cope with the consequences of Covid-19.

6A(2.2) Regional arrangements

Inter-country arrangements can also help reduce the costs of IR, while providing the same benefits as would accrue from keeping reserves nationally. Regional agreements for the pooling of reserves would, in theory, have a double benefit: access to reserves when needed and with lower conditionality than that of the IMF; and reducing the costs of maintaining domestically high levels of reserves.

Regional arrangements coexist with IMF, but they usually have a more modest scope, and the resources at their disposal are significantly smaller than those of the IMF. Two regional agreements potentially allowing the pooling of reserves are worth mentioning: the Chiang Mai Initiative (CMI) and the Latin American Reserve Fund (FLAR, its Spanish acronym). Both CMI and FLAR have evolved considerably since their creation. In addition to these two, one should also mention the West and Central African Monetary Unions, where the pooling of reserves is the rule. We discuss these in depth in Appendix 6.2.

CMI was set up after the 1997–8 Asian crisis. It regroups the ASEAN+3 countries (10 South-East Asian countries, China, Japan, and South Korea). The core mechanism in the CMI is its swap network of central banks. Initially based on bilateral swaps, this network has evolved into a multilateral liquidity support facility.[74] Given the size of the economies participating in the CMI, the resources that the agreement can quickly mobilize among the member countries are higher than would be available to many of them when borrowing from international financing institutions. CMI is not, strictly speaking, a fund; rather, it is a 'pool' of promises to provide financing up to an agreed amount. If there is a balance-of-payments or liquidity crisis, a central bank of a member country can swap its national currency for US dollars from this pool. Lending is subjected to multilateral surveillance and conditionality. An IMF programme is also required if the amount drawn exceeds 30% of a country's maximum swap quota. Further strengthening of CMI has been repeatedly called for, mostly for two reasons. First, to increase the amount of available resources: should a crisis hit a large country or several countries simultaneously, CMI's resources would clearly be insufficient. Second, to increase the resources that are accessible without being subjected to IMF conditionality (Kawai 2015).

FLAR is older than CMI.[75] It is a true reserve fund that has provided balance-of-payments financing for over four decades. Five of the current eight members are LFDCs. FLAR has been able to support a set of countries with limited financial capacity. Against all odds, it has been one of the most successful institutions of financial cooperation. In addition, since FLAR enjoys a higher credit rating than its members taken individually, it can channel outside resources at a lower cost. Member countries acting individually would face higher risk premiums. FLAR competes well with the IMF in the scale of financing, as the IMF's credits are small for the type of LFDC that is a member of FLAR. Lending by FLAR is without conditionality, and yet it has never suffered delinquencies. The main beneficiaries of FLAR loans have been Bolivia and Ecuador, the two smallest economies of

---

[74] For a recent account of CMI, see Kawai (2015). Cooperation in the CMI involves, in addition to the swap network, the monitoring of capital flows, regional surveillance, and capacity-building in crisis prevention.

[75] FLAR was created in 1978 as the Andean Fund of Reserves (FAR). In 1991 it extended its membership and became the Latin American Reserve Fund (FLAR). Current members are Bolivia, Colombia, Costa Rica, Ecuador, Peru, Uruguay, and Venezuela. FLAR (2015) gives an interesting chronology of the evolution of the institution as well as a complete description of its operations.

the association. FLAR has also acquired substantial experience in IR management. Given this, it helps central banks of the member countries not only in handling their reserves but also with technical assistance and guidance.

APPENDIX 6B

The West and Central African Economic and Monetary Unions

The West African Economic and Monetary Union (WAEMU) and the Central African Economic and Monetary Community (CEMAC) are monetary unions (MU) of respectively eight and six LFDCs. As MU, their members share a unique currency, in both cases the CFA franc. A specific and crucial characteristic is that the two MUs peg their common currency to the Euro. The peg dates back to their creation in 1945, when their currencies were tied to the French franc, the currency of the former colonial power.[76] The CFA franc has been devalued only once, in 1994, since its inception in 1945.

WAEMU and CEMAC are separate and independent monetary unions, but share many common features.[77] The Central Bank of West African States (BCEAO) is the central bank of WAEMU, and the Bank of Central African States (BEAC) is the central bank of CEMAC. The arrangements of these two MUs with France, the anchor country, are crucial. They date back to the start of the two MUs and have not undergone major changes since then. Some changes may, however, be in the offing, as briefly discussed below. A cornerstone of the arrangements is that the French Treasury guarantees convertibility between the euro and each CFA currency, at the fixed CFA franc/euro exchange rate. As counterparty to this unlimited guarantee of convertibility, the member countries' foreign exchange reserves are centralized with the two central banks, BCEAO and BEAC, which in turn deposit a fraction of those reserves (currently 50%) in a remunerated account at the French Treasury. A key provision is that BCEAO's or BEAC's balance on this account can be negative for an amount which is in principle unlimited. However, there are specific rules in order to prevent any critical debtor position to become long-lasting.[78]

The rules and institutions governing WAEMU and CEMAC provide for free capital mobility among member states in each union and with France.[79] They also include guidelines for fiscal discipline and for monitoring economic convergence among member states.

---

[76] The entry of France into the European Monetary Union in 1999 redefined the parity of the CFA franc in term of Euros.

[77] The monetary unions of WAEMU and CEMAC are also customs unions. The custom unions, including a common external tariff, were however only fully implemented well after the start of the monetary unions—for CEMAC from 1994, for WAEMU from 2000 (Banque de France 2015).

[78] These comprise, besides a high interest rate on the liability position, the obligation of the WAEMU or CEMAC central bank to prevent as much as possible a negative position on its account at the French Treasury. This includes depositing in this account foreign exchange reserves held in their own accounts, or even collecting foreign exchange held by various public or private organizations in member countries, or inviting member states to make use of their drawing rights with the IMF (Banque de France 2015).

[79] Fielding (2005b: 2) observes 'a reasonable degree of capital mobility across the frontiers of each of the two monetary unions'. Note the use of the word 'reasonable' rather than 'perfect' applied to capital mobility. IMF (2019a) indeed reports surrender requirements of exports receipts as well as several restrictions on external capital mobility for WAEMU and CEMAC member countries.

Monetary financing of member states by the common central bank has been limited since the beginning to a maximum 20% of any country's fiscal receipts. However, since 2013, such direct financing of member states is no longer authorized in WAEMU, and is being progressively reduced in CEMAC. Stronger economic convergence between member states is fostered through regular meetings of the respective regional commission. The latter monitors the union's convergence criteria: an inflation rate of less than 3% and a public debt/GDP ratio of less than 70% for both MUs, a budget deficit below 3% for WAEMU and, for CEMAC, a country specific fiscal balance norm that stipulates partial savings of government's oil revenue. Appropriate policy recommendations are made by the commission, which may include sanctions against non-compliant member countries.

A large literature exists that evaluates the costs and benefits of WAEMU and CEMAC.[80] Pegging to the euro has implied that average inflation has not been significantly higher than in the Eurozone, and well below the average observed for other sub-Saharan African countries. This has been clearly to the advantage of the member states, but has not prevented the build-up of other macroeconomic imbalances, as witnessed by the 1994 need to devalue. The credibility of the peg, as guaranteed by the anchor country, France, is also thought to be a significant advantage for external trade and for attracting foreign direct investment. Another clear advantage of the common currency is the saving in transactions costs and reduction in uncertainty offered by fixed bilateral exchange rates between member countries. These efficiency gains (see Box 6.4) are often downplayed for advanced countries, but this advantage may be sizeable for LFDCs. Indeed sub-Saharan African countries that do not belong to either of the two monetary unions cannot rely on direct bilateral exchange rates for trading with neighbouring partners, but instead have to use costly two-way currency transactions through the US dollar. Concerning potential costs faced by WAEMU and CEMAC as 'monetary-unions-cum-fixed-external-peg', four important issues need to be considered.

First, neither MU comes close to being an optimal currency area. Although the OCA criteria are not really fully achieved by any currency union, they are still less so for WAEMU and CEMAC. Trade among the member states in both MUs is still modest, production structures are divergent, factor mobility is low, and economic convergence is far from accomplished. Not surprisingly for LFDCs, financial integration is still limited, although there is progress in the devising of common rules and processes for the financial sector. Risk-sharing mechanisms at the union level are absent.

Second, monetary policy is mainly focused on keeping the peg. Bank credit to the private sector may be truncated by the central bank when the level of international reserves threatens to fall below target.[81] The countries in the two MUs are by and large commodity exporters, in the agricultural or extractive sectors. Terms-of-trade shocks, both positive and negative, can be large, and moreover are rarely synchronized across member countries. The consequences of asymmetric shocks on economic activity cannot be dealt with

---

[80] Debrun et al. (2011) present a brief survey. See also Fielding (2005a), Laskaridis and Toporowski (2016), and African Development Bank (2019: 34–8; 92).

[81] The CFA arrangement stipulates that central bank gross reserves have to be above a threshold of 20% of the central bank's monetary liabilities. Even if the amount of reserves satisfies this threshold, which is usually the case, it may fall below another norm for LFDCs, a minimal number of months of import coverage (3–5 months). In this case, monetary policy needs to remain restrictive. The central bank may even take capital flow management measures (foreign exchange repatriation and surrender requirements), as is e.g. the case in CEMAC (IMF 2019h: 13).

by monetary policy, because of its 'one size fits all' character on the one hand and the peg to the euro on the other.[82]

Third, the peg to the euro implies that monetary policy cannot properly deal with shocks that are common to the MU but asymmetric to the Eurozone. The peg exposes the two MUs to exogenous shocks originating in the euro's bilateral exchange rates, notably in the euro/USD rate. For example, an appreciation of the euro relative to the USD will depress domestic currency prices of commodity exports, whose international prices are set in USD. It has been observed over the last two decades that such cycles of appreciation/depreciation have low frequency but are persistent. Such swings in the euro/USD exchange rate can thus contribute to long periods of overvaluation in the CFA zone, with a depressing effect on growth.[83]

Fourth, whether shocks originate abroad or domestically, it is ultimately with fiscal policy that any countercyclical policy mainly rests. Fiscal policy is, however, burdened by many tasks, as is the case in all LFDCs. This translates into differences in spending patterns, in tax collections, and in seigniorage, since in most countries expenditures are larger than tax revenue. Most countries in both MUs exhibit chronic fiscal deficits financed partly with foreign aid but also with seigniorage and the inflation tax.[84] The risk of fiscal dominance is in general still present in member countries that are unable to raise taxes or to apply checks on expenditures with low social value. WAEMU's and CEMAC's fiscal rules and convergence criteria have clearly helped to attenuate fiscal dominance, but there have been many lapses, with often only a slow return to compliance.

Assessing the balance between the benefits and costs of WAEMU and CEMAC is a difficult exercise, especially as it combines two separate aspects, the MU per se and the fixed peg, which both affect its performance. However, it is clear that WAEMU and CEMAC over the long run produced better results in terms of price stability, relative to comparable sub-Saharan countries. Such a clear conclusion cannot however be drawn as regards the incidence of this type of exchange rate arrangement on real growth dynamics. Measuring the incidence of a specific monetary institution on comparative growth performances among very heterogeneous countries is a trickier exercise than comparing inflation rates. Reviewing several econometric studies addressing this question, Fielding (2005a: 17) notes that the 'link between long term growth and Franc Zone membership is rather weak'. More recent empirical studies of this type are to our knowledge not available.

The net benefit of the two CFA monetary arrangements has often been questioned in member countries' economic and political circles. The specific relationship with France, the anchor country but also the former colonial power, has often been resented as an outdated relationship, sometimes very strongly so by opinion leaders. Globally, however, a political consensus on these arrangements continues to exist, but some changes are about to be introduced to the CFA arrangement. In December 2019, it was announced that WAEMU would introduce a new common currency, the ECO, thereby ditching the CFA franc. This symbolically important measure was to take place in principle by July 2020, but has been postponed, and no new deadline has been announced. The link with the euro

---

[82] Houssa (2008) documents that supply shocks display a negative or weakly positive correlation in WAEMU, and points to larger asymmetry than what is observed in the Eurozone.

[83] Owoundi (2016) focuses on the growth effects of real-exchange misalignments in sub-Saharan African countries in general, and in CFA-zone countries in particular, over 1980–2011. An overvaluation is shown to have a negative effect on growth which is larger for CFA zone countries.

[84] Seigniorage is collected at the union level and then retroceded to member countries. The inflation tax is constrained by the fact that a large part of countries' public debt is denominated in foreign currency (see Baldini and Poplawski-Ribeiro 2011: 429).

would be preserved, as would be the guarantee of full convertibility given by the French government. Also, the BCEAO would be no longer obliged to deposit part of its international reserves with the French Treasury. Representatives of the French government would also cease to participate in the BCEAO governing bodies that manage monetary policy. No such institutional change has yet been announced for CEMAC.

Whether these institutional changes would actually give the BCEAO an enlarged autonomy in formulating its monetary policy is doubtful as long as the peg with the euro is maintained unchanged. In this case, its current level may come under review and a devaluation of the ECO with respect to the euro envisaged. Such a move would need to carefully assess the balance between its costs and benefits, as well as the distribution thereof across member countries. Particularly negatively impacted at the outset would be those that have built up sizeable positions in foreign-currency (see S&P Global Ratings 2020).

Finally, it has to be noted that WAEMU's move to the ECO is, in principle, part of a political process with the aim of setting up the West African Monetary Zone (WAMZ), which earlier had already chosen the ECO as common currency. This unilateral move of WAEMU has raised some questions among non-WAEMU members of the WAMZ. This has put further political strain on a very ambitious and challenging project.[85]

---

[85] The WAMZ would be a much more heterogeneous grouping of countries than WAEMU. Nigeria, an oil-exporting country, would be the dominant player, the other members being much smaller, oil-importing countries.

7

Modelling Monetary Policy

A Brief Overview

7.1 Introduction

Informed, well-thought-out monetary policy decisions are crucial for leading the economy on a smooth and consistent path towards the goals society has entrusted to its central bank. However, achieving these goals in the face of adverse domestic or external shocks is a daily, often difficult, challenge for central banks, particularly so in LFDCs.

In the not too distant past, central banks were seen mainly as providers of fiduciary money to the government and to the public.[1] But the role of central banks and the environment in which they operate has been evolving, as discussed in the preceding chapters of this book. Equipped now with a broad set of policy instruments, central banks have seen their mandate enlarged and more clearly specified, with the support of a broad consensus within society. The goals they are expected to achieve confront them with difficult decisions about how best to arbitrage among them. In this regard, achieving and preserving high credibility for their policy-making and taking decisions in a context of strong institutional transparency and accountability offers central banks the best chance to fulfil their mandate efficiently.

Central banks' decisions cover a wide range, from the fundamental one of which nominal anchor to select to those related to the day-to-day management of monetary policy, like deciding when to raise the policy rate and by how much. Any such decision has to be taken in an environment of pervasive and often huge uncertainty: about the current state of the economy and the developments of its domestic and foreign determinants, about the structural relationships that shape the economy, about the behavioural interactions of agents and their impact on asset and goods markets…Uncertainty as well concerning how quickly and how strongly monetary policy decisions affect output and prices.

To take decisions that rest on the best-informed assessment of the environment in which they operate, central banks first rely on a regularly updated battery of key macroeconomic and financial indicators that are expected to describe, as precisely as possible, the current economic situation. This represents a first and

---

[1] See sections 1.3.2.1 and 5.2.1.

Monetary Policy in Low Financial Development Countries. Juan Antonio Morales and Paul Reding, Oxford University Press.
© Juan Antonio Morales and Paul Reding 2021. DOI: 10.1093/oso/9780198854715.003.0007

essential input for the central bank's decision-makers in forming their judgement about the state of economy and, equally importantly, about the implications thereof for monetary policy. Such an indicator-based approach has shortcomings, however, as decisions would mostly be taken on the basis of past experience within the confines of the country or from lessons drawn from abroad. In this setting, there is the risk that many decisions will be based on hunches rather than on a systematic exploration of available policy options.

Central banks in many countries have therefore adopted a modelling approach as an essential feature of their monetary policy decision process. Central banks of AEs, EMEs, and more and more those of LFDCs rely on various types of formal quantitative model to help evaluate and forecast the effects of their policy decisions. Though these models are simplifications of reality, they have the merit of bringing to the decision-makers the main implications of their policies as well as the risks embodied in each measure that is considered.

We briefly describe in this chapter the main characteristics of the models that are currently part of the standard toolkit of central banks, including those of LFDCs, and assess to what extent they contribute, with their strengths and despite their limitations, to improving the quality of monetary policy decisions. In section 7.2 we discuss at a general level how models can usefully be combined with judgement when policy-makers have to choose the optimal stance of monetary policy. Section 7.3 is devoted to full-scale structural models, mostly of the DSGE—dynamic stochastic general equilibrium—type, the variety pioneered by central banks in AEs. Section 7.4 reports on smaller, semi-reduced form models tailored to the context of LFDCs, often developed with the support of the IMF's technical assistance. Section 7.5 concludes with a short summary.

7.2 Judgement and models in monetary policy-making

7.2.1 Central banking and models

According to Taylor (2016: 2), the use of models for policy-making dates back to 1936, when Jan Tinbergen used simulations of his econometric model of 36 equations to assess the effects on the Dutch economy of a devaluation of the exchange rate—actually the abandonment of the gold standard. Since then, considerable academic research effort has been invested in building, estimating, and simulating econometric models of various sizes, of Keynesian or monetarist inspiration, models that were, from the 1960s on, progressively adopted by the research departments of leading central banks (Taylor 2016: 3). The generalized abandonment in the early 1970 of the Bretton Woods system of fixed exchange rates gave central banks that adopted floating exchange rates much more independence, as well as responsibility, in managing their monetary policy. Monetary policy-making became a richer, though more complex, exercise. This encouraged central bank economists to join the academic debate on key conceptual issues, such as the role of monetary aggregates, the transmission mechanism of monetary policy, and the choice of monetary policy instruments, as well as on the contribution of macroeconomic models to policy-making under uncertainty.[2]

The rational-expectations revolution in macroeconomics brought about a profound rethinking on the way to model agents' behaviour. Expectations about the future evolution of key variables, such as income, inflation, and exchange rates, were no longer to be considered as exogenous or adaptive, but as fully endogenous and therefore directly dependent on policy choices and regimes. This implies that macroeconomic models whose behavioural equations are estimated over a period characterized by a specific policy regime cannot be used to simulate policies that change this regime (Lucas 1976). Because forward-looking agents adapt their expectations and their behaviour to policy changes, the parameters of the behavioural equations estimated under the past policy regime will no longer be valid, and using the model for evaluating the effects of the new policy will give misleading results. To overcome this fundamental critique—the 'Lucas critique'—a new generation of macroeconomic models emerged, based on microeconomic foundations. Such models' key relationships reflect the behaviour of optimizing agents, whose preferences are characterized by 'deep parameters' that are independent of the policy regime. The models have been mostly developed as successive generations of 'dynamic stochastic general equilibrium' (DSGE) models. They now prominently feature in the tool box of the central banks of many AEs and EMEs.

The use of models for monetary policy-making has been much more limited in LFDCs. In many of these countries, IMF-inspired monetary programming within a fixed exchange rate regime provided, for many years, the first basic analytical tool for elaborating monetary policy (see Box 6.6). While relevant for key issues, such as central-bank financing of budgetary deficits, the framework involved a limited number of behavioural relationships, and was not conducive to developing in the central banks a strong analytical capacity for assessing crucial monetary policy issues (Berg et al. 2006: 5–7).[3] In addition, the space for an independent monetary policy is very thin with exchange rate targeting, even nonexistent at the limit.

Over the last two decades, some countries have abandoned the fixed peg and moved to inflation targeting (see section 6.4). Given the forward-looking perspective of this approach, the discussion of monetary policy needed to be significantly enriched, as forecasts of key variables became crucial inputs for policy formulation. To guarantee a sufficient quality of their forecasts, of their policy

---

[2] See e.g. Goodhart (1989b: 349–50) about the difficulty for policy-makers in interpreting diverging quantitative estimates produced by various models of Keynesian or monetarist inspiration.

[3] Governments and central banks would also often try to circumvent in their execution the provisions of such monetary programmes. The issue of ownership of the programmes was a major concern during the 1980s and 1990s.

discussions, and ultimately of their ensuing policy decisions, central banks of inflation-targeting LFDCs had to undertake a significant modelling effort. Other central banks in LFDCs also strove to modernize their monetary policy framework and develop their analytical capacities. Many benefited in this respect from the specific expertise and technical assistance of the IMF, and its FPAS (Forecasting and Policy Analysis System) (Anand et al. 2018: 250–52). The FPAS is designed to help monetary-policy decision-making in middle- and low-income countries by (among other prescriptions) 'employing a macroeconomic model with standard properties that broadly accord with the view of the monetary policy committee on how the economy works' (Al-Mashat et al. 2018: 45). The model, kept relatively simple in the initial stages so that its lessons can be easily understood and communicated, is open to future expansion and expected to increase in complexity to better fit the economy's structure, in parallel with the technical staff of the central bank acquiring more experience.

7.2.2 Models and judgement as complements

Models and judgement are not substitutes but are complementary. Models are used for two main purposes in the decision-making process: forecasting and policy analysis. In each case, their contribution consists in offering the decision-maker a coherent analytical framework, within which he/she can confront the model's output with his/her own judgement.

7.2.2.1 Forecasting

A fundamental, primary aim of models is to forecast, at selected time horizons, the evolution of macroeconomic and financial variables, conditional on a particular policy path.

For short-term horizons, simple time-series models do a good job. Multivariable vector auto-regressive (VAR) models, which comprehensively capture the historically observed dynamics of a set of variables, are known to have a good forecasting performance for one or two quarters ahead, especially for variables that, like inflation and output, generally display significant persistence. Such models provide point estimates as well as confidence intervals for the variables' likely evolution. VAR models, however, lose reliability when they become larger, as the number of parameters to be estimated becomes important. Bayesian VAR models deal with over-parametrization and over-fitting issues by imposing priors on the probability distribution of the parameters. They are known to have a good performance record for policy forecasting (Assenmacher 2017: 26). Dynamic factor models allow forecasters to draw on the information included in a large set of data series, as the latter are summarized in a limited number of synthetic 'common factors'.

For a longer-term horizon, there is the need to impose structure on the joint evolution of the forecasted variables. Structural or semi-structural economic models, of various complexities (see sections 7.3 and 7.4) impose a stronger structure. Such models are a simplified (often drastically simplified) representation of the interactions and constraints at work in the economy. However, they are grounded in economic theory and are expected to fit sufficiently closely the economy's actual functioning, as observed in the data. They are used to project the future path of policy goal variables, like inflation and output, under alternative hypotheses about future developments of the model's exogenous variables, like commodity prices or export demand, or alternative hypotheses of the path of the monetary policy rate. Stochastic simulations of such models provide 'confidence bands' around central projections.

Model forecasts are very valuable, but policy-makers cannot rely mechanically on them. They are to be confronted with judgement forecasts. The latter are based on a careful analysis of all information, quantitative as well as qualitative, available at the time of forecast. Prepared by the central bank's staff and drawing on the monetary policy-maker's own experience and expertise, judgement forecasts take into account a much larger set of information than what forecast models can handle. They are also very reactive to the most recent information about the economy, either found in readily available high-frequency indicators, such as daily data on oil and other commodity prices, exchange rates, interest rates, or stock market prices, as well as in regular market sentiment surveys, or directly collected through (formal and informal) contacts with the business and financial community.

While the models' forecasts offer the advantage of analytical consistency, policy-makers need to use their judgement to critically assess them in light of their own experience. As expressed by Svensson (2005: 4): 'All models are drastic simplifications of the economy, and data give a very imperfect view of the state of the economy. Therefore, judgemental adjustments in both the use of models and the interpretation of their results—adjustments due to information, knowledge, and views outside the scope of any particular model—are a necessary and essential component in modern monetary policy.'

7.2.2.2 Policy analysis

Models are used to analyse monetary policy issues and to assess policy options. Simulations of properly estimated or calibrated models are used to study the effects of exogenous variables or of policy variables on the dynamics of endogenous variables of interest, for example to better understand the monetary transmission mechanism (see section 2.7). Scenario analyses, in which many exogenous variables are altered simultaneously, have various purposes. As already mentioned, the forecast exercise produces model projections under different scenarios relating to the external environment in which the economy will evolve over the forecast horizon and/or under different monetary policy settings.

The analytical strength of models can also be exploited to better understand how monetary policy works by exploring counterfactual, 'what if' scenarios. For instance, what would have happened to inflation and output if monetary policy had reacted more quickly and more stringently during a past, significant episode of inflationary pressures? Model simulations can also be used to evaluate different policy options, comparing for instance different mixes of monetary and fiscal policies when dealing with oil windfall gains, assessing the differential effects of CPI and core inflation targeting, or evaluating how to combine monetary and macro-prudential policy instruments.

The right model needs to be used for the right purpose. For example, large-scale models have low flexibility, which makes them unsuitable for short-term forecasting. Or, with the 'Lucas critique' in mind, a model in which expectations are not endogenous, not model-consistent, cannot properly be used to evaluate the effects of important changes in policy regimes. Central banks thus usually rely on a suite of models. Blanchard (2018) draws attention in this respect to the fundamental distinction to be made between theory and policy models. Theory models should have a deep and tight theoretical structure, reflecting the essential features of agents' behaviour, and be dedicated to clarify policy issues in a general equilibrium setting. Policy models should focus on policy issues and explore alternative policies. To this end, they should mainly aim at fitting the data well, including their dynamics, even at the cost of a less rigorous theoretical structure.

Central banks' suite of models also usually contains a series of 'ancillary models', designed, for instance, to analyse the implications of forecasts of the main model for the labour market or for other crucial sectors of the economy. Alternatively, their output may be used as input for scenario analyses with the main model. This is for example the case when expected inflation and expected output in the main model are captured by inflation and output forecasts obtained from a small-scale VAR model.

7.3 Structural models: dynamic stochastic general equilibrium models

Many central banks of AEs and EMEs use large or medium-sized structural macroeconomic models to research monetary policy issues, to elaborate monetary policy strategies, and to assist policy-making.[4] Many of those structural models (though not all) are dynamic stochastic general equilibrium (DSGE) models. A structural model is a system of simultaneous equations that describes

---

[4] Christiano et al. (2018: 132) provide references to several central bank DSGE models.

the behaviour of agents who interact within a given economic structure. The model describes the dynamic interactions of the endogenous variables among themselves and with exogenous variables. The model is characterized with cross-equation constraints that need to be taken into account when it is brought to the data. The basic DSGE model is a structural model that has distinctive features: it has solid theoretical microeconomic foundations within a general-equilibrium setting; it displays prominently rational agents who are intertemporal optimizers and hold endogenous, model-consistent, forward-looking expectations; it is stochastic, in the sense that, given the rational expectation assumption, its equilibrium can only be disturbed by random shocks to its exogenous or to its endogenous variables. Current DSGE models used in central banks are usually referred to as a 'New Keynesian' (NK) DSGE models because, unlike their direct predecessors, the Real Business Cycles (RBC) models, they take into account nominal rigidities and thereby allow monetary policy to play an important role. The aim of this section is to give a short introduction to the main properties of DSGE models, to their uses in exploring monetary policy, and to their limitations. However, its intention is not to survey the vast literature about them. We start illustrating the intrinsic characteristics of a DSGE model by referring to one of its very basic versions.

7.3.1 The simple canonical DSGE model

In its simplest, closed-economy version, the NK DSGE model describes the behaviour and interactions of households and firms and the central bank's policy reaction function.[5] We first discuss the model's three main building blocks, then its reduced form, which is presented in Box 7.1.

(i) The representative infinitely lived household maximizes the expected present value of its lifetime utility, which depends on the sequence of its consumptions of a bundle of different goods as well as on the sequence of the hours of labour supplied. In this simple version there are no constraints on borrowing and lending, allowing the consumer to optimize under a single intertemporal budget constraint.[6] The household's decisions take into account the prices of goods, as set by firms, and the equilibrium wage and interest rates. Dynamic optimization determines the optimal values for its consumption bundle, its labour supply, and its savings/borrowings

---

[5] See Galí (2008: ch. 3). Agénor and Montiel (2015: ch. 12) provide a slightly extended version of the basic model.

[6] The household's intertemporal budget constraint is completed with a solvency condition that precludes a 'Ponzi game', i.e. the possibility of infinite indebtedness.

in the form of bonds. Given a specific form for the household's utility function, the optimal consumption bundle is given by a forward-looking dynamic equation: current consumption depends negatively on the expected real interest rate and positively on expected future consumption. The optimal relationships are shaped by three parameters describing the household's preferences: the subjective discount rate, the disutility of labour supply, and the intensity of the intertemporal substitution of consumption.

(ii) Firms each produce a differentiated good and are monopolistic price-setters. All have identical Cobb–Douglas production functions that depend only on labour input and are subject to technological shocks. Each firm faces a demand for its product as well as the equilibrium nominal wage rate. Nominal rigidity is introduced in the model by assuming that, each period, a given fraction of firms keep their price unchanged.[7] These firms serve the demand addressed to them at that fixed price. Each period, a firm has a constant probability of keeping its price unchanged. When the firm gets the opportunity to change the price, it sets it so as to maximize the value of the current and future profits that it can expect while its price remains fixed, i.e. until it can re-optimize. The price is optimally set as a mark-up over the weighted average of the current marginal costs and of the sequence of future marginal costs that are expected over the whole period during which the firm will not be able to adjust its price. The firm's equilibrium prices, output, and labour demand depend essentially on three parameters: intensity of the decreasing returns to labour in the production function, price elasticity of the demand for the good it produces, and degree of price rigidity—i.e. the probability that it will not be able to change its price in any given period.

(iii) Monetary policy is set according to a rule, a policy reaction function. The most common one, which is used for this canonical DSGE model, is the Taylor rule in which the central bank sets the nominal interest rate as a function of current inflation and of the output gap, the difference between current and natural output.[8] The respective weight that the central bank attaches to each goal reflects its preferences concerning inflation and output stabilization. Deviations from the rule are modelled as shocks. These shocks describe discretionary monetary policy interventions. The interest rate is the model's sole channel of monetary policy transmission.

---

[7] This nominal rigidity hypothesis proposed by Calvo (1983) with regard to price-setting has been briefly discussed in section 4.2.1.1. An alternative hypothesis to introduce nominal price rigidity is to allow for non-linear adjustment costs in changing prices.

[8] See Box 6.8. Note also that his specification implies that monetary authorities do not target an output that is higher that the natural rate. The monetary policy implications of an alternative specification in which authorities aim at an output level higher than the natural level are briefly discussed in section 4.3.1.1 and Appendix 4.A.

The model's general equilibrium implies that all markets for goods and labour clear. Firms' aggregate supply matches consumers' aggregate demand. Firms' prices are aggregated into the general price level. Equilibrium in the labour market determines the nominal wage and aggregate employment. There is no involuntary unemployment.

In this simple model, dynamics are driven by three types of shock: an aggregate demand shock, a cost-push shock, and a monetary policy shock.[9] Each one is characterized by its volatility and its persistence. In the absence of shocks, the model is at its steady state, with inflation on target and output at its natural level—its equilibrium level under flexible prices. Although monetary policy has a nontrivial impact on real activity in the short run, money is neutral in the long run.[10]

Although very simple, the fully specified model cannot be analytically solved, as it is highly non-linear. Even before considering estimating such a basic model, exploration of the model's behaviour can be carried out numerically. This involves calibration of the model's parameters, i.e. selecting numerical values that are acceptable from the point of view of theory and are guided by empirical observation. Such numerical simulations are greatly simplified by log-linearizing the model around its steady state. The model is then reduced to a system of linear equations.

For the simple model described above, log-linearization around the steady state makes it possible to reduce the model to a system of three linear dynamic equations. This reduced-form model is often referred to as the 'core' NK DSGE model, and is presented in Box 7.1.[11]

Equation (1) is referred to as the dynamic IS schedule, equation (2) as the New Keynesian Phillips Curve (NKPC), and equation (3) as the Taylor rule.[12] This reduced form of the model makes the role of expectations very clear. Current aggregate demand and current inflation depend on their expected future values. This implies that not only current but also expected future monetary policy will have an effect on current inflation and output.

---

[9] The aggregate demand shock may originate in a change in consumer preferences or in the exogenous natural real rate of interest. Cost-push shocks are price or wage mark-up shocks. Technology shocks do not directly appear in this list of shocks, but can be traced, in the model's specification presented in Box 7.1, through their effects on the natural interest rate—a positive technology shock decreases the natural rate—which appears in equation (1). See Galí (2008: 49).

[10] Actually, the money stock is, in the version of the basic model described in the text, a missing endogenous variable, as monetary policy is modelled as targeting the interest rate. Adding an ad hoc demand for money allows the dynamics of the money stock to be made explicit.

[11] Galí (2008: ch. 3) gives a detailed presentation of the micro-foundations of this reduced-form model.

[12] Contrary to the IS of elementary macroeconomics, this dynamic IS expresses the current level of aggregate demand as a function not only of the real interest rate but also of expected future output. The NKPC and the Taylor rule have been discussed earlier, respectively in section 4.2.1.1 and Box 6.8.

Box 7.1. The core New Keynesian DSGE model

Aggregate demand

$$\tilde{y}_t = E_t(\tilde{y}_{t+1}) - \frac{1}{\sigma}\left[i_t - E_t(\pi_{t+1}) - r_t^n\right] + \varepsilon_t^D \tag{1}$$

Aggregate supply

$$\pi_t = \beta E_t(\pi_{t+1}) + \kappa \tilde{y}_t + \varepsilon_t^S \tag{2}$$

Monetary policy

$$i_t = \bar{\pi} + \bar{r} + a_\pi\left(\pi_t - \bar{\pi}\right) + a_y \tilde{y}_t + \varepsilon_t^M \tag{3}$$

$\tilde{y}_t$ is the output gap (the percentage difference between current and natural output), π_t the inflation rate, i_t the nominal interest rate, r_t^n the exogenous natural (flexible price) real interest rate, $\bar{r}$ its steady state level, $\bar{\pi}$ the target inflation rate, a_π and a_y the central bank's policy reaction coefficients with respect to inflation and output, both positive. ε_t^D, ε_t^S and ε_t^M are uncorrelated demand, supply and monetary policy shocks, respectively. E_t is the expectation operator, based on information available at t.

All the parameters of the three equations in Box 7.1 are positive. They are either the parameters that characterize the model's structural form—the 'deep' parameters—or an explicit function of them. This is, for instance, the case for the slope of the NKPC, the parameter κ, which describes the impact of output on inflation. This reduced-form parameter is decreasing in the firms' price-rigidity parameter and increasing in the households' disutility of labour supply parameter, two 'deep' parameters of the underlying structural model. Calibration of the model involves attributing a value to all the model's deep parameters so as to obtain the values for the reduced-form parameters.[13] Once properly calibrated, the model can be used to study the effects of monetary policy or of other shocks through impulse response functions (IRF). IRFs describe the dynamic response of the system's endogenous variables to the specific shock.

---

[13] As the model features an interest rate rule, a constraint needs to be imposed on the parameters of the central bank's policy reaction function for a determinate steady equilibrium to exist. This constraint implies in particular that the central bank has to be sufficiently reactive to deviations of inflation from target.

7.3.2 Main extensions

The basic model, in its simplicity, has mostly pedagogical virtues. It has given rise to many extensions, all endeavouring to bring the model closer to reality by correcting its shortcomings and omissions. The aim is to improve its capacity to serve as support for policy analysis without sacrificing its theoretical consistency. Some extensions were straightforward, such as small open-economy models with international trade in goods and assets, or the introduction of endogenous investment and capital accumulation by firms. More fundamentally, research strove to improve the structure of DSGE models by addressing their most restrictive hypotheses about the behaviour of agents or the functioning of markets. This research effort was strengthened when strong criticism was voiced against DSGE models on the ground that they had not been able to forecast the 2007–8 financial crises. Extensions focused particularly on the following fields (Galí 2018; Pereira da Silva 2018):

(i) Labour market frictions: involuntary unemployment becomes a possible outcome in DSGE models that combine nominal price rigidities with search and matching frictions, wage bargaining, and real-wage rigidity in the labour market (Blanchard and Galí 2010).

(ii) Imperfect financial intermediation: frequent empirical observations like credit rationing, risk premiums to be paid by borrowers or financial crises, belie the basic model's hypothesis of complete financial markets. DSGE models' nominal rigidities were thus progressively complemented with credit market frictions, mainly agency costs related to the monitoring of moral hazard and asymmetric information aspects. The collateral that households, firms, or governments need to put up to get a loan were given a crucial role in constraining access to credit or in determining the endogenous external risk premium to be paid.[14] Borrowers' net worth became an important driver of the economy's dynamic response to monetary and financial shocks. When this financial-friction framework was complemented with a full specification of the banking sector, DSGE models were ready to be used to explore financial cycles, the role of bank credit in the transmission of monetary policy, the mechanism of the financial accelerator and the interactions between monetary and macroprudential policies (see e.g. Christiano et al. 2018: 134–5; Agénor and Montiel 2015: 473–4).

---

[14] This is particularly crucial for LFDCs, where is has been frequently observed that the collateral posted by the main shareholders and owners of the enterprises is of the real estate that they own. This runs against the concept of limited liability. This happens also in AEs and EMEs, but to a lesser extent than in LFDCs.

(iii) Heterogeneity of agents: Although consumption is a fundamental component of aggregate demand, the behaviour of consumers is cast, in many early DSGE models, in the very simplified framework of a single, representative agent, with rational expectations, who optimizes his intertemporal consumption flow under the constraint of his expected permanent income. This neglects many aspects of actual consumer behaviour, especially credit and liquidity constraints, uninsurable income uncertainty, and short-term decision horizons (Muellbauer 2016). More recent DSGE models address this issue by considering two-agent or multiple-agent frameworks: patient consumers (savers) vs impatient ones (borrowers facing collateral constraints); intertemporal optimizers versus 'hand-to mouth', financially excluded, households; or, more generally, households that differ by the amount of liquid and illiquid assets they hold and by the idiosyncratic shocks they face (Kaplan et al. 2018). Such alternative micro-foundations, particularly appropriate for developing countries, alter and enrich the monetary transmission mechanism and the interaction between monetary and fiscal policy.[15] They also allow DSGE models to go some way towards exploring the distributional effects of shocks and policies on the welfare of different categories of agents.

(iv) Expectations: Rational expectations (RE), also termed 'model-consistent expectations', are a cornerstone of DSGE models and emerged as a response to the 'Lucas critique'. In early DSGE models, RE were also combined with the full-information hypothesis. Both hypotheses, however, assume too much about the actual cognitive and forecasting capabilities of individuals. RE are also at odds with experimental evidence showing that agents have 'bounded rationality' and are subject to beliefs and emotions, as stressed by the behavioural approach to economics and finance. The introduction of imperfect information and adaptive learning as a way to form expectations about the future has been one way for DSGE models to attenuate somewhat the unrealistically strong full-information RE hypothesis.[16] Information lags about the current state of the economy have been used to rationalize the introduction in DSGE models of agents who hold backward-looking, adaptive expectations, or act according to 'rules of thumb', while others are RE optimizers.[17] Some efforts have also been devoted to introducing selected behavioural features in the agent'

---

[15] Financially constrained households react more to monetary policy-induced changes in aggregate income, as Ricardian equivalence no longer holds for them. Monetary policies have distributional consequences in this case. See e.g. Kaplan et al. (2018).

[16] See our brief discussion in section 2.5.

[17] This underlies the 'Hybrid New Keynesian Phillips Curve' which features, along with the output gap and future expected inflation, also past inflation as a determinant of current inflation (see section 4.2.1.1).

optimizing framework (De Grauwe and Ji 2019: 18; Galí 2018: 97). However, the forward-looking RE paradigm still remains a key characteristic of DSGE models.

These extensions, as well as many others, are part of a continuing effort to increase the realism of DSGE models while keeping them on solid theoretical ground. As a consequence, however, DSGE models have become more complex in their structures. Also, the methods to compute their solutions have become more complex.[18] Finally, bringing the model to the data has raised additional challenges.

To give a DSGE model an empirical content, i.e. to bring it as close as possible to the observed reality, its behavioural and structural parameters need to be given numerical values. This is done though estimation or calibration, or through a mixture of both. When the model is large, one has to resort to Bayesian estimation of the set of simultaneous equations it contains. This allows the use of priors, based on external information, that restrict the space of likely parameter values. Calibration is based on observed data, on estimates obtained by other studies, or on values that are thought to be consistent with theory. It is used when estimating the parameters directly is not possible, due to the paucity of data, which is most often the case in developing countries.

The empirical validity of a calibrated or estimated DSGE model is usually assessed by comparing the impulse response functions (IRF) generated by the model for a given shock with those obtained from a Structural-VAR model estimated from the relevant data, for the same shock and the same variable. Additional comparisons may serve to check whether the stochastic simulations of the model reproduce for its key endogenous variables (e.g. inflation, output) patterns in their second moments—in their auto-correlations, variances, and co-variances— that broadly match those observed in the data for the same variables.[19] In-sample forecast errors for the main variables of interest are also used for validation purposes.

7.3.3 DSGE models and monetary-policy issues in developing countries

As already mentioned, DSGE models have become for central banks, mostly in AEs but also in some EMEs, an important tool for policy analysis and forecasting.

---

[18] Resolution methods for models with rational expectations have, for example, to deal with the possibility of self-fulfilling multiple equilibrium paths.
[19] As recalled by Assenmacher (2017: 27), SVAR models are useful for evaluating DSGE models if their identification restrictions are consistent with those in the latter model.

Equally important, structural DSGE models have been used to explore, at a fundamental, theoretical level, monetary policy issues that are specific to developing countries. Efforts have been deployed to incorporate the specific structural characteristics of developing countries. We illustrate this in some detail by presenting in Box 7.2 and Box 7.3 two such studies that are based on fully-fledged DSGE models. In the first study, Agénor et al. (2018) explore the effects, for a middle-income country, of an external financial shock that generates unexpected capital

---

Box 7.2.   Analysing external financial shocks in a middle-income country with a DSGE model

Agénor et al. (2018) examine in an open-economy DSGE model how monetary and macro-prudential policies can be optimally combined in a small open developing country. The real sector is modelled in the standard way: a representative household, flexible nominal wages, three domestic goods—final, intermediate and capital—and an imported intermediate one, with monopolistic price-setting by the producers of domestic intermediate goods and with nominal rigidities. The model's main focus is on financial frictions and on the authorities' instruments to manage capital inflows. The financial sector features deposit-taking banks that may borrow from the central bank, at an endogenous penalty rate, and are subject to reserve requirements. Households and banks may borrow abroad, where they face an endogenous spread that increases with the amount they borrow. Banks monopolistically set the rate on their risky loans to capital goods-producing firms as a function of repayment probabilities. The latter depends on the ratio between the loan amount and the housing stock pledged as collateral by households, the firms' owners. The central bank policy is described by four rules: (i) a Taylor-type policy rate reaction function, with a smoothing effect; (ii) a reserve targeting rule for interventions in the exchange market to smooth the exchange rate and to guarantee a sufficiently high level of international reserves—with the latter a function of the total amount of private sector's foreign liabilities; (iii) a sterilization rule, describing to what extent foreign-exchange interventions are sterilized by open market operations; and (iv) a countercyclical bank reserve requirement rule. The model's parameters are calibrated so as to reflect the main characteristics of an average middle-income country.

In a first step, the authors use the model to investigate how the economy reacts to a temporary decrease in world interest rates and to the ensuing capital inflow when required reserves are kept constant and sterilization is partial. The model's impulse response functions are in accord with the main stylized facts produced by a drop in the world interest rate. One observes inter alia a capital inflow, a nominal and real exchange rate appreciation, an increase in bank credit, an increase in real house prices, a fall in loan and bond rates, a boom in domestic activity, reinforced by the financial accelerator mechanism, and an inflation rate whose increase is mitigated by the currency's nominal appreciation and the rise in the central bank's policy rate.

In a second step, the authors apply a welfare analysis to discuss optimal policy rules. The central bank in this set-up chooses the values of the parameter of its countercyclical reserve requirement rule and the parameter of its sterilization rule that best preserve both macroeconomic stability and financial stability after a world interest rate shock. To this end, the central bank minimizes a composite loss function that is a weighted average of the volatility of inflation, the volatility of domestic real activity, and the volatility of a composite financial stability indicator. The latter is based on volatilities of capital inflows, credit-to-output, interest rate spreads, real house prices, and real exchange rates. Countercyclical reserve requirements improve macroeconomic stability by decreasing the volatility of credit, investment, and domestic demand. However, at too aggressive levels these measures weaken financial stability, as they make interest rates become more volatile. Sterilization contributes to stabilizing interest rates, asset prices, and capital flows, which benefits both macroeconomic and financial stability. Also, combining both instruments—countercyclical reserve requirements and sterilization of foreign-exchange interventions—improves welfare, as measured by the central bank's loss function, relative to using only one instrument. As countercyclical reserves may become counterproductive at some point, the sterilization of foreign-exchange interventions is a welcome additional instrument to achieve global stability. To optimally react to external financial shocks, the two instruments should be used as complements.

inflows, and discuss how to coordinate monetary and macro-prudential policy to mitigate those effects.[20] In the second study, Dagher et al. (2012) analyse the effects of an oil—or a foreign aid—windfall in a low-income country, and examine how these effects are shaped by the reactions of fiscal and monetary authorities.[21] The authors calibrate their model in order to match, as closely as possible, the characteristics of the country studied. Both studies use model experiments to explore the transmission mechanisms of the shocks and of mitigating policies.

[20] We discussed several aspects related to this issue in sections 3.6 and 4.2.2.
[21] Some aspects related to this issue were discussed in section 5.3.1.1.

Box 7.3. Analysing oil or aid windfall shocks in a low-income country with a DSGE model

Dagher et al. (2012) analyse the short-term effects of windfalls in an open-economy DSGE model that reflects the characteristics of a low-income country. They focus on how such unexpected foreign-exchange earnings, whether originating in oil revenues or aid flows, are managed by the government and the central bank. As a short-cut to describing the economy's low financial depth, the DSGE model features two types of household, the intertemporal optimizers and those who have no access at all to financial intermediation. Financial frictions also constrain the economy's capital account: households that are dynamic optimizers—the only agents that can operate in international capital markets—face portfolio adjustment costs that limit capital mobility. Local financial markets, in which intertemporal optimizing households, the government, and the central bank are active (there are no banks), operate without friction.

The real economy is organized around a traded goods sector, where firms are price-takers, and a non-traded goods sector, where firms are monopolistic price-setters and where price rigidity results from the cost of adjusting prices. The firms' production function embodies sector-specific labour and its own endogenous capital stock, as well as public infrastructure capital. Labour supplied by households in the traded and non-traded sectors are imperfect substitutes, with the implication that labour market equilibrium exhibits wage differentials between the two sectors. Households consume both traded and non-traded goods.

The government that benefits from the windfall faces a standard intertemporal budget constraint. It is confronted with two simple fiscal rules: (i) increase its spending on consumption and investment goods; (ii) follow a smooth forward-looking rule, linking growth in spending to GDP growth and using a sovereign wealth fund to accumulate its temporary savings. The central bank has two rules: (i) a simple Taylor rule, to set its policy rate as a strict inflation targeter; (ii) a rule to adjust its international reserves to a long-term stock target and, in the short run, to accumulate as reserves a portion of the oil- or aid-induced windfall foreign exchange inflow. Consistency between the two rules is maintained by appropriately sterilizing the accumulation of reserves. The authors calibrate the model to broadly match the economy of Ghana—a country expected to benefit from an oil boom, at the time the paper was written.

The authors conduct first a baseline simulation that assumes that, following the windfall gain shock, the government does not save the unexpected revenues but spends them, while the central bank does not intervene on the foreign-exchange market. The effects of the windfall are a real exchange rate appreciation, a short-lived boom in GDP, reflecting an expansion in the non-traded sector, partly compensated by a decline in the traded sector, higher inflation in the non-traded sector, and, as a result, a non-oil trade deficit close to the windfall income. Macroeconomic volatility is magnified when specific LFDC characteristics are accentuated—limited capital account openness, a large share of financially constrained households, weak labour mobility between the trade and non-traded sectors. These characteristics lead to amplified inflationary pressures of the windfall, inviting a stronger stabilization response of monetary authorities.

Experiments with other rules lead to the following lessons: using a 'permanent income' rule to accumulate savings in a sovereign wealth fund and smooth government spending induces less macroeconomic volatility than in the benchmark scenario, and increases aggregate welfare. Welfare also increases because the smoothing policy allows the government to finance over time higher investment in public infrastructure, which permanently increases global output. The global increase in welfare, however, hides differences across households: optimizing households dislike volatility, and gain from expenditure smoothing by the government, while credit-constrained households most value the short-run income booms associated with the full-spending policy, and are penalized by a smoothing policy. The experiments also indicate that coordination between fiscal and monetary policy is necessary to manage the effect of a windfall. If the government fully spends the unexpected revenue while the central bank, independently, accumulates reserves to limit real exchange appreciation, the welfare gains are reduced. Sterilization of the accumulation of reserves leads to an increase in the real interest rate, crowding out private consumption and investment, with negative consequences on medium-term output. Coordination with the central bank is required to align accumulation of reserves by the central bank with the amount of windfall revenues that the government wishes to temporarily save.

Both also develop a normative approach by comparing the welfare effects of different policies.[22]

Structural DSGE models that are designed to capture the essential specific characteristics of low-income countries are not numerous. Some closed-economy DSGE models explicitly incorporate the duality of the labour market.[23] Castillo

---

[22] The DSGE models' microeconomic foundations allow a welfare analysis. Shocks and policies ultimately affect households' utility. Aggregating these effects on utility would give a true measure of global welfare effects. A second-order approximation is, however, often used. It expresses induced welfare losses as a function of the volatility of consumption around its steady state. In the basic NK model, the latter depends directly on the volatility of inflation and on the volatility of the output gap (Gali 2008: 86–9). This approach underlies the loss functions approach such as that used in the Agénor et al. (2018) model described in Box 7.2. Note that Dagher et al. (2012) measure aggregate welfare directly in the model surveyed in Box 7.3, by summing consumers' lifetime expected utilities.

[23] See our discussion in Box 4.2.

and Montoro (2012) model the interaction between formal and informal labour markets, with its effects on wage-setting, unemployment, transmission of monetary policy, and the dynamics of inflation. Batini et al. (2011) use a two-sector DSGE model in which the informal sector is highly credit-constrained but operates in a flexible labour market, while the formal sector faces rigidities in its labour market, as well as financial frictions.

Standard open-economy DSGE models are used to assess policy issues especially relevant for LICs. Benes et al. (2018), for example, study the effects and desirability of sterilized foreign-exchange market interventions for inflation targeting LICs. Limited capital mobility and financial frictions that introduce balance sheet effects of monetary policy are the model's main ingredients to portray the specific environment of LICs. Baldini et al. (2018) study the effects of the global financial crisis on a monetary aggregate targeting LIC. Their DSGE model is calibrated to match relevant available data for Zambia. The crisis is modelled as a combination of shocks—of terms of trade, of banks' risk aversion, and of the country risk premium. The shocks are identified by setting their path in such a way that the model replicates Zambian data during the crisis for selected key variables. The model is then used to analyse how these shocks are transmitted through the economy, and to explore counterfactual monetary policy responses to the crisis.

The six DSGE models for LICs mentioned in this section feature a structure that is already rather complex, although each model integrates only a limited number of characteristics among all those that describe a typical LFDC. For each model, the LFDC characteristics embedded are mostly selected in view of the study's main research question, while others are sidelined in favour of those of the standard model. The lessons these studies offer are very valuable, as they shed light on issues that are very important for LFDCs. However, these lessons would be enhanced if it could be shown that they are robust within a model that encompassed *all* the essential features of LFDCs.[24] This is a demanding task, especially so when these models need to rely on calibration in order to allow meaningful numerical policy simulations and experiments.[25]

7.3.4 Limits of DSGE models

Despite the considerable popularity of the DSGE approach to macroeconomic modelling, and the significant place it has acquired in policy discussions in many central

---

[24] Senbeta (2011) provides an extensive discussion of the applicability of the New Keynesian DSGE models to the environment of low-income countries.

[25] Estimated structural DSGE models for LICs are rare, because of low availability of quality data. Some studies, however, have used Bayesian estimation to bring their model to the data. Examples are Peiris and Saxegaard (2007), who study monetary policy rules for Mozambique and use a mix of calibration and estimation. This is also the case for Houssa et al. (2010), who estimate for Ghana a subset of their model's parameters, including those of the Taylor rule.

banks, and also despite the continuing efforts to progressively address its short-comings, some strong criticisms continue to be voiced. Recurrent criticisms are:

(i) Full-scale DSGE models are complex systems of nonlinear simultaneous equations. Interpreting simulation results, capturing the intuition of the mechanisms at work is often difficult, significantly more so than with simpler models, where insights can be better grasped. This weak transparency makes them a bad tool for communication, and they are often seen as a 'black Box'. Their complexity also means that adapting them to changes in the policy environment involves hard and time-consuming work. They lack the flexibility that is necessary to adapt policy to rapidly changing events. All these reasons are probably behind the scepticism with which DSGE models are often considered by monetary policy decision-makers (Gerlach, 2017).

(ii) The strong constraints imposed on DSGE models—microeconomic foundations and general-equilibrium approach—makes their confrontation with the data, through a mix of calibration and estimation, difficult and sometimes questionable (Blanchard 2018: 45–6). This may represent a significant handicap if the model is used to explore country-specific monetary issues for which closeness to the data is of key importance.

(iii) Most DSGE models still adhere to the paradigm of rational, emotionless utility-maximizing agents, neglecting behavioural factors that may guide decisions by households and firms. Not taking those into account may entail, not only different effects of shocks and policies on aggregate demand and on its dynamics, but also quite different policy implications, as indicated by the behavioural approach to macroeconomics (De Grauwe and Ji 2019: 1–2).[26]

One can expect these general criticisms to apply with even greater force to DSGE modelling for LFDCs, the first two ones in particular. In LFDCs' central banks, the staff trained to elaborate, develop, maintain, and operate structural DSGE models for policy purposes is often small. Also, the empirical validation of

---

[26] The behavioural approach to macroeconomics offers an alternative to DSGE modelling, as shown by De Grauwe and Ji (2019). They consider a basic behavioural macroeconomic model in which agents have cognitive limitations ('bounded rationality'), in choosing among simple, fundamentalist or extrapolative, decision rules for forecasting output and inflation. Agents are heterogeneous and influence each other, creating optimistic or pessimistic market sentiment ('animal spirits'). With this model, De Grauwe and Ji explore the consequences of these behavioural assumptions for the analysis of business cycles and the transmission of shocks, for optimal monetary policies, for the sustainability of public debt, etc. As a main message of their approach, they 'stress that the responsibility of the central bank is to stabilize an otherwise unstable system' (p. 2). Jump and Levine (2019) provide a survey of this relatively new literature. They note in their conclusions that progress has to be made in estimating the behavioural models, given that 'without a considerably improved empirical basis […] it is unclear why central banks, or any other policy institutions, should replace the standard NK framework in their forecasting and policy analyses' (pp. 73–4).

a DSGE model in a LFDC context is even more prone to a considerable impreci-
sion, given the low quality of macroeconomic data or even the unavailability of
crucial data.[27]

The many criticisms of DSGE models do not imply that they are useless.
However, they suggest that large-scale, complex DSGE models should be principally used for exploration of longer-term monetary policy issues, such as the
trade-offs and coordination issues of monetary, fiscal, and prudential policies.
Their strong theoretical base—provided it is sufficiently realistic—and their
resistance to the 'Lucas critique' are in this case a definite advantage, and their
difficulty in fitting the data and taking into account the specificities of a country
are less of a disadvantage. They can thus find their place within the suite of models
deployed by a central bank. In particular, they can be used as robustness checks of
other approaches to policy exploration. Comparing results of DSGE models with
those of other models that are less theoretically articulated but closer to the data
can deliver useful lessons about how policies work. In any case, it should be kept
in mind that all models are simplified representations of reality—and DSGE
models are particularly stylized ones— whose output should be taken with more
than a grain of salt and above all confronted with policy-makers' insights and
judgement. Only then can they feed a policy debate in which the most important
issues can be discussed with an appropriate critical distance.

For the reasons mentioned in the preceding section, however, the use of fully-
fledged DSGE models by central banks in LFDCs can be expected to be relatively
limited. Other models that can be more easily fitted to available data and that take
into account in a flexible way the country's specific structural characteristics will
be preferred, even if they are more ad hoc and theory-wise less pure. These are
often small, semi-reduced-form macro-models. We briefly discuss in the next
section a particular semi-reduced-form modelling approach that is shared by a
number of LFDCs, especially those who have opted for inflation targeting.

7.4 Semi-structural models for policy analysis in LFDCs

Central banks in AEs that have developed fully-fledged structural DSGE models
also employ, in parallel, models built on less stringent theoretical requirements,
but that have plausible properties and, in particular, provide a better fit with
observed evidence about the economy's dynamic response to shocks. They are
also general-equilibrium models, but embody less theoretical restrictions across

---

[27] To estimate the model, sufficiently long series of consistent data are needed. This is a challenge in
many LICs given that national accounts data are often established only on a yearly basis and frequently
suffer from drastic revisions. The high degree of informality in economic activity also impinges on the
measurement of macroeconomic aggregates. Consequently, DSGE models for LICs usually rely on
calibrations.

their structural equations. This is why they are labelled '*semi*-structural'. Examples are the Federal Reserve Board's FRB/US or the ECB's ECB-BASE models, which have detailed sectoral blocks and are very large. They are mostly estimated equation by equation, with limited cross-equation restrictions, to guarantee a better empirical fit. Expectations play an explicit role, but the models are sufficiently flexible to allow choosing between model-consistent expectations on the one hand and exogenous expectations generated e.g. by a satellite VAR model on the other.[28]

Central banks of LFDCs do not have the resources or the databases that are necessary to build large-scale semi-structural models. Their modelling options for policy purpose are thus usually limited to small-scale semi-structural models that either describe the whole economy or address specific issues, like explaining and forecasting inflation or interest rates. Most of these models are internal to the central bank and are often not published.[29]

For LFDCs and EMEs, the IMF has proposed its Forecasting and Policy Analysis System (FPAS), already mentioned in section 7.2.1. The FPAS approach is intended to 'help monetary policy committee meetings focus squarely on the strategic, medium term outlook' (Al-Mashat et al. 2018: 45). To this end, it recommends that central banks set up the necessary infrastructure and procedures in data collection and treatment to develop a core quarterly forecasting model, together with a suite of ancillary models, as well as providing for a clear and transparent monetary policy decision process. The core quarterly forecasting model is a cornerstone of this approach. The model is to be pragmatic, conform to general macroeconomic principles, and plausibly describe how the economy works. It should be easily adaptable and exploit efficiently available data.

The proposed benchmark model, to be adapted and extended so as to reflect the country's specificities, is a semi-structural New Keynesian model, actually the reduced form of a small, open-economy New Keynesian model. As such, it is the open-economy equivalent of the reduced form of the closed-economy version of the basic NK model described in Box 7.1. The model is linear and consists of four key behavioural equations (Berg et al. 2006; Al-Mashat et al. 2018): the aggregate demand determines the output gap; the Phillips curve determines core inflation; the open-economy interest rate parity, combined with an exogenous country risk premium, determines the exchange rate; and the monetary policy reaction function determines the short-term nominal interest rate. The equations usually include persistence effects in inflation, gradualism in setting the policy rate, and additional exogenous factors that may affect aggregate demand or inflation such as, respectively, world demand and energy prices. The benchmark core model

---

[28] As is the case for the ECB-BASE model (Angelini et al. 2019)
[29] Some central banks of LFDCs publish the research output of their staff. See e.g. Bank of Zambia (2015), which inter alia presents the 'Zambian Quarterly Macroeconometric Model'.

largely neglects, for reasons of simplicity, the economy's supply side, including capital accumulation and the labour market. The stochastic process for potential output is modelled separately.[30] The fiscal side and public debt dynamics are also ignored. Expectations are in principle forward-looking and rational, but can easily be modelled as including an adaptive, backward-looking component.

The FPAS semi-structural models also rely on calibration. This is, however, somewhat easier to implement than for structural DSGE models, as the parameters to be calibrated are not the 'deep' parameters of the structural equations, such as those of the consumers' utility function, but the parameters of the reduced-form behavioural equations, like the slope of the Phillips curve. Calibration is used flexibly to match data and to let the model produce sensible results. Once calibrated and fed with data for the exogenous variables, the core model can be used for different purposes of monetary policy analysis (e.g. of the transmission mechanism or the dynamics of shocks) or of forecasting. As a forecast tool, it delivers the path to be expected for the four endogenous variables that matter most for monetary policy decisions —inflation, output, exchange rate, and interest rate. Conditional forecasts that take into account different scenarios are necessary to give a proper measure of the uncertainty surrounding the economy's outlook and to allow decision-makers to confront these with their own judgement (see section 7.2.2).

FPAS semi-structural models have been developed in several LFDCs by IMF staff, in consultation with the respective central banks. Berg and Portillo (2018a) present examples of FPAS models with their respective country specification (for Kenya, Zambia, Rwanda, and Ghana), and report on how these models are used to explore different monetary policy issues. Charry et al. (2018), for instance, adapt the benchmark model by adding to the core hybrid Phillips curve two similarly specified equations for food and oil inflation. Foreign output is included as a determinant of aggregate demand, and the open-economy interest parity is modified to introduce a crawling-peg mechanism for the exchange rate and to allow for low capital mobility. The authors use the model to decompose the observed dynamics of inflation and output into the contributions of the different shocks that have hit Rwanda over a given period—food, oil, exchange rate, and monetary policy shocks, among others. This provides insights into how policy and the economy adapted to the shocks. The authors also use the model to perform in- and out-of-sample forecasts.[31]

It is in general difficult, for outside observers, to assess to what extent these models play an active role in the preparation of actual monetary policy decisions.

---

[30] Potential output is assumed to grow at a given rate and to be subject to transitory or permanent shocks. The latter can be manipulated for simulation purposes (Berg et al. 2006: 16)

[31] Several IMF working papers also present FPAS models used to explore specific monetary issues for Belarus, Morocco, Sri Lanka, the Philippines, and Vietnam. The IMF also proposes central-bank staff training in 'Model-Based Monetary Policy Analysis and Forecasting'.

Evidence on central bank 'ownership' of such models is at best somewhat indirect.[32]

The use of models to assist decision-making in LFDC monetary policy is still in a development phase. One can be confident, however, that there is increasing awareness in LFDC central banks of the need to rely on various analytical tools, including models, to structure monetary-policy thinking.

7.5 Summary

This last chapter of the book deals with the toolbox that central banks use to choose their monetary-policy strategy, design their operating framework, and implement it effectively with the instruments at hand. The toolbox consists of various types of models that describe in a simplified way how the economy functions, how it reacts to the various types of shock, and how monetary policy can be used to mitigate the effects of these shocks. The available tools allow a central bank to develop, with sufficient scope and depth, an analytical approach to monetary policy on which it can rely to take its decisions in the best-informed way. The overview provided in this chapter points out several aspects that may be usefully recalled.

(i) All models are a drastic simplification of the actual, complex workings of an economy. This is both their force and their limit. Their force is that they can provide useful and clear insights into the policy issue that is to be explored, as they abstract from aspects that are secondary to the analysis. Their limit is that the many simplifications and strong hypotheses that characterize them may generate large discrepancies with observed behaviours and outcomes, undermining the relevance of the analyses carried out with them. Model-users need to be aware of the trade-off between a model's strengths and its limitations, and hence exercise the necessary prudence in interpreting the model's results.

(ii) Models are used by central banks for two different aims: forecasting and policy analysis. Short-term forecasting usually relies on time-series models. A typical model is a VAR. For longer-term forecasting, it is necessary to impose structure on the economic interactions that determine the

---

[32] The model for Rwanda by Charry et al. (2018) mentioned above is, with slight modifications and extensions, presented in a publication of the Central Bank of Rwanda as the 'forecasting and policy analysis systems (FPAS) macro-model for Rwanda', with the indication that the model is used to inform the Monetary Policy Committee of the projections for inflation and the output gap (Karangwa and Mwenese 2015). The Central Bank of Indonesia has also adopted the FPAS approach and developed its own, extended 'semi general equilibrium macroeconomic model', which is reported as playing a dominant role in the modelling approach to policy-making (Warjiyo and Juhro 2019: 288).

variables to be forecasted. This is what structural models are for. They also allow the exploration of monetary policy issues of interest for decision-making, such as analysis of the monetary transmission mechanism, and identification of shocks and their role in key macroeconomic episodes in the past. They are also used to perform counterfactual monetary policy exercises and to simulate different forecast scenarios.

(iii) Structural models for monetary policy mainly fall into two categories. DSGE models emphasize the rigorous consistency with a set of micro-founded hypotheses about agents' behaviour, and semi-structural models aim to capture what is observed in the data, even if this is done at the cost of somewhat weaker theoretical foundations. The force of DSGE models lies in their theoretical rigour. They can be exploited principally to explore fundamental monetary policy issues. The richer their description of agents' behaviour, of the economy's constraints, and of policy environments, the more significant and pertinent will be their lessons. However, matching them with empirical data is, for methodological reasons, an often challenging exercise—particularly in LFDCs, where low quality or lack of data compound the problem. Their use as tools for policy-forecasting purposes is therefore much less manifest. This task can be more conveniently delegated to semi-structural models, which, though theoretically less pure, are intended to provide a better fit with the observed dynamics of the country's economy.

(iv) Central banks in LFDCs adopted later than in AEs and EMEs the modelling approach to monetary policy, but several of them have taken decisive steps in this direction. Financial deepening, diversification of monetary policy instruments, awareness of the significant role monetary policy can play, and the move to inflation targeting are factors that have emphasized the need for an analytical approach to monetary policy. The forecasting and policy analysis system (FPAS) of the IMF, which includes a modelling tool, has also played an important role. Several LFDCs now use small semi-structural FPAS models that are tailored to their country's specific characteristics.

(v) While models to assist monetary policy-making have become quite generalized, their use needs to be carefully monitored. They provide only one of the many elements on which to base monetary policy. Monetary policy committees take their decision according to their judgement, after having taken into consideration all available information about the economy's actual and future outlook. Models are to be viewed as a complement to judgement, not as a substitute.

Afterword

While we were finalizing this book, the corona virus pandemic struck. It affected all countries around the world, causing heavy human suffering everywhere. Its economic consequences can probably be expected to be dire for many LFDCs, of which most are low-income countries. At the time of writing, the severity of the longer-term consequences of the pandemic for these countries is difficult to gauge. We nevertheless feel it necessary to briefly assess how the environment in which monetary policy is deployed in LFDCs could be affected, and discuss the new challenges that are raised.

LFDCs, like almost all economies, are suffering a double shock: a supply shock and a demand shock of unprecedented levels. The lockdowns followed in many countries, necessary to contain the pandemic, entailed a sharp drop in aggregate working hours. According to CCSA (2020: 18) the drop for LICs was 2.4% in the first quarter of 2020 and increased to 11.1% in the second. For the LM countries the drops are even larger, 3.0% for the first quarter and 16.1% for the second. This extracted a heavy cost from workers, in the formal and informal labour markets, in terms of foregone income. The self-employed and those in family employment have very instable incomes, earned on a day-to-day basis. With the lockdown, their survival was at stake. This domestic shock was compounded by the pandemic-induced international recession, especially for the many LFDCs that are either oil and natural gas exporters or dependent on the receipts of tourism and of remittances. As a result of this double shock, GDP growth was strongly impacted in all LFDCs and was predicted to be negative for 2020 in 71% of our set, from −13.5% for Belize, −5.9% for Bolivia, −3.2% for Nigeria to −0.2% for Chad (World Bank 2020: 208–9).

The burden of assisting the most vulnerable populations has fallen on governments. Fiscal balances of affected countries have sharply deteriorated as a result of the recession-induced fall in fiscal revenues and the huge additional costs for health infrastructure and personnel, as well as for social programs and support to enterprises to avoid permanent closing and destruction of production activities. As fiscal conditions were already weak or very weak in many LICs before the onset of the pandemic, their sustainability may soon become a worrisome issue, especially if health risks continue to weight on economic activities and thus on budgetary receipts and expenditures. For instance, in sub-Saharan African countries, the gap between the actual and debt-stabilizing overall fiscal balance was projected to widen from −0.5% of GDP in 2019 to −4.2% in 2020 (World Bank 2020: fig. 1.21, p. 52). The fiscal burden of many LFDCs may reach huge dimensions, possibly at unprecedented levels.

Monetary policy is accompanying the fiscal effort, and central banks carry an important load. The main burden is fiscal, but monetary policy is being subordinated temporarily to it. Central banks in LFDCs have lowered their policy short-term interest rate, sometimes aggressively so, as in Paraguay and Bolivia. More importantly, central banks have been lending to governments in relatively large amounts.

The fiscal space has thus been enlarged with seigniorage. The latter has its limits, however, especially for countries with fixed exchange rates and low inter-national reserves. Overly large increases in the monetary base in order to finance government deficits can produce a run on the domestic currency and cause a cur-rency crisis. The probability of such exchange rate runs is, however, currently somewhat reduced, as capital outflows from LFDCs are discouraged by the low level reached by international asset returns in AEs, following their exceptionally expansionary monetary policies.

Large monetary financing always raises the risk of inflation coupled with exchange rate depreciations. However, the current outlook does not appear to be particularly worrying in this respect. Some countries with flexible exchange rates initially experienced an unwarranted rate of depreciation of their domestic cur-rencies, but depreciation has slowed. Inflation has to a large extent remained sub-dued because of the collapse in output and, for oil-importing LFDCs, because of the sharp drop in international oil prices.

Central banks have seen their missions significantly enlarged, in support of the financial sector but also of the economy at large. Ample liquidity and liquidity guarantees have been provided to financial intermediaries, either through open-market operations or, more rarely, through direct loans. The set of assets eligible for open-market operations has been considerably enlarged, as well as their maturity tenors. Interventions in the foreign exchange market have also been more frequent. Central banks in AEs and EMEs have purchased long-term gov-ernment and corporate bonds owned by financial institutions, with the aims of stabilizing financial markets, increase their liquidity and give a backstop for the government securities market (Arslan et al. 2020). Similar asset purchase pro-grammes have been initiated with local currency government securities by sev-eral LFDC central banks, as in Bolivia, Ghana, Guatemala, Indonesia, Philippines, and Rwanda. These purchases were intended to enhance the attractiveness of these securities to domestic and foreign investors, in order to avoid an unwel-come increase in sovereign and corporate spreads, and relieve pressures on the foreign exchange market.

Credit policies have complemented monetary policies. The monetary and supervision authorities have been requesting banks to reschedule the payments of their debtors, firms, and even households. Forbearance in the banking regulations on provisioning has accompanied rescheduling. Also, many LFDCs have eased the provision of credit by providing a government guarantee for bank loans. These measures have been especially (but not only) targeted to alleviate the credit conditions for small and medium-size enterprises.

Central banks in LFDCs have taken very seriously their output stability mandate, by making use of the traditional instruments, decreasing policy rates and required reserves, but also by providing in some cases more direct support to economic activity by, for instance, participating in government sponsored loan guarantee schemes.

These requests have diverted central banks from their customary tasks and obligations. However, financial stability continues to be of utmost concern to them. Because the recession rooted in the health crisis may cause deterioration of bank assets that could lead to a banking crisis, central banks have been behaving supportively. In most LFDCs, central banks have been keen to preserve the soundness of the banks within their purview, and have invested time and effort in avoiding credit crunches which would obstruct recovery of the economy once the health crisis subsides.

It is too early to pass judgement on the additions to the usual range of policies and interventions of central banks brought about by the pandemic. Uncertainties loom large. Fiscal dominance and financial repression may once again become a structural constraint for the pursuit by central banks of their price stability mandate, if the exit strategy from the pandemic does not include the restoration of a credible and sustainable fiscal framework. Achieving such fiscal consolidation without jeopardizing long term growth will be a key, though difficult, challenge for policy-makers. The exit strategy has also to include progressive dismantling of the exceptional support given by the central bank to the financial sector. If not, moral-hazard effects in bank lending would transform an exceptional recourse to the central bank into a permanent one, entailing major efficiency costs and derailing the central bank from its proper mission of financial stability.

The exit strategy needs also to prepare for the (as yet unlikely, but still possible) flaring up of inflation. Central banks would in this case be faced with the well-known but in this case very acute trade-off between striving to tame inflation and avoiding nipping output recovery in the bud. Central banks endowed with a large credibility asset may have the best chances of achieving an acceptable trade-off.

Finally, it appears that domestic efforts to contain the economic disarray caused by the health crisis need to be complemented by ample foreign aid. The IMF's Rapid Credit Facility and debt service relief measures as well as the G20's suspension of official bilateral debt service for poor countries partially meet this need. They are steps forward but insufficient. Much more direct aid is required. Substantial reductions of the external debt for the most heavily burdened poor countries should be part of that aid. If foreign aid is not forthcoming, the economies of low-income countries will not recover and suffer major damages to their long term growth prospects, with major negative effects beyond the afflicted countries.

September 2020

References

Abuka, C., R. Alinda, C. Minoiu, J. L. Peydróc, and A. F. Presbitero (2019), 'Monetary Policy and Bank Lending in Developing Countries: Loan Applications, Rates, and Real Effects'. *Journal of Development Economics* 139: 185–202.

Acemoglu D., S. Johnson, P. Querubín, and J. A. Robinson (2008), 'When Does Policy Reform Work? The Case of Central Bank Independence'. *Brookings Papers on Economic Activity* (Spring): 351–429.

Acosta-Ormachea, S., and D. Coble (2011), 'The Monetary Transmission in Dollarized and Non-Dollarized Economies: The Cases of Chile, New Zealand, Peru and Uruguay'. IMF, WP 11/87.

Adler, G., and C. E. Tovar (2014), 'Foreign Exchange Interventions and their Impact on Exchange Rate Levels'. *Monetaria*, Centro de Estudios Monetarios Latinoamericanos, CEMLA 0(1): 1–48.

Adrian, T., D. Laxton, and M. Obstfeld (2018), 'An Overview of Inflation-Forecast Targeting'. In T. Adrian, D. Laxton and M. Obstfeld (eds), *Advancing the Frontiers of Monetary Policy*, 3–14. IMF.

African Development Bank (2019), *African Economic Outlook 2019*.

Agénor, P. R., K. Alper, and L.A. Pereira da Silva (2018), 'External Shocks, Financial Volatility and Reserve Requirements in an Open Economy'. *Journal of International Money and Finance* 83: 23–43.

Agénor, P. R., and P. Montiel (1999), *Development Macroeconomics*, 2nd edn. Princeton University Press.

Agénor, P. R., and P. Montiel (2015), *Development Macroeconomics*, 4th edn. Princeton University Press.

Agénor, P. R., and L.A. Pereira da Silva (2013), 'Inflation Targeting and Financial Stability: A Perspective from the Developing World'. Banco Central do Brasil, WP 324.

Agénor, P. R., and L. A. Pereira da Silva (2019), *Integrated Inflation Targeting: Another Perspective from the Developing World*. Bank of International Settlements (Feb.).

Agoba, A. M., J. Abora, K. A. Oseia, and J. Sa-Aadu (2017), 'Central Bank Independence and Inflation in Africa: The Role of Financial Systems and Institutional Quality'. *Central Bank Review* 17: 131–46.

Alesina, A., and L. H. Summers. (1993), 'Central Bank Independence and Macroeconomic Performance: Some Comparative Evidence'. *Journal of Money, Credit, and Banking* 25(2): 151–62.

Alexander, W., T. Baliño, and C. Enoch (1995), 'The Adoption of Indirect Instruments of Monetary Policy'. IMF, Occasional Paper 126.

Alidou, S. (2014), 'Degree of Price Rigidity in Low Income Countries: Implications for Monetary Policy'. Munich Personal RePEc Archive, no. 59844 (Nov.).

Al-Mashat, R., K. Clinton, D. Laxton, and H. Wang (2018), 'Nuts and Bolts of a Forecasting and Policy Analysis System'. In In T. Adrian, D. Laxton, and M. Obstfeld (eds), *Advancing the Frontiers of Monetary Policy*, 45–52. IMF.

Alonso, P. (2018), 'Creation and Evolution of Inflation Expectations in Paraguay'. Inter-American Development Bank WP 900.

Alper, C. E., B. Clements, N. Hobdari, and R. Moyà Porce (2019), 'Do Interest Rate Controls Work? Evidence from Kenya'. IMF, WP 19/119 (May).

Anand, R., A. Berg, and R. Portillo (2018), 'Low-Income Countries'. In T. Adrian, D. Laxton, and M. Obstfeld (eds), *Advancing the Frontiers of Monetary Policy*, ch. 13. IMF.

Anderson-Reid, K. (2011), 'Excess Reserves in Jamaican Commercial Banks: The Implications for Monetary Policy'. Bank of Jamaica Working Paper.

Andrle, M., A. Berg, R. A. Morales, R. Portillo, and J. Vlcek (2015), 'On the Sources of Inflation in Kenya: A Model-Based Approach'. *South African Journal of Economics* 83(4).

Andrle, M., A. Berg, E. Berkes, R. A. Morales, R. Portillo, and J. Vlcek (2018), 'Do Monetary Targets Matter for Monetary Policy in Kenya?' In A. Berg and R. Portillo (eds), *Monetary Policy in Sub-Saharan Africa*, ch. 16. Oxford University Press.

Angelini, E., N. Bokan, K. Christoffel, M. Ciccarelli, and S. Zimic (2019), 'Introducing ECB-BASE: The Blueprint of the New ECB Semi-structural Model for the Euro Area'. ECB Working Paper no. 2315.

Arbatli, E., and K. Moriyama (2011), 'Estimating a Small Open-Economy Model for Egypt: Spillovers, Inflation Dynamics, and Implications for Monetary Policy'. IMF, WP 11/108.

Armas, A., P. Castillo, and M. Vega (2014), 'Inflation Targeting and Quantitative Tightening: Effects of Reserve Requirements in Peru'. WP No 2014–03, Banco Central de Reserva del Perú (Feb.).

Armas, A., and F. Grippa (2005), 'Targeting Inflation in a Dollarized Economy: The Peruvian Experience'. Inter-American Development Bank WP 538 (Sept.).

Armas, A., A. Ize, and E. Levy Yeyati (2006), 'Financial Dollarization: An Overview'. In A. Armas, A. Ize, and E. Levy Yeyati (eds), *Financial Dollarization*, 1–12. New York: Palgrave Macmillan.

Arnone, M., and D. Romelli (2013), 'Dynamic Central Bank Indepedence Indices and Inflation Rate: A New Empirical Exploration'. *Journal of Financial Stability* 9(3): 385–98.

Arnone, M. B., B. J. Laurens, J. F. Segalotto, and M. Sommer (2007), 'Central Bank Autonomy: Lessons from Global Trends'. IMF, WP 07/88.

Aron, J., R. Macdonald, and J. Muellbauer (2014), 'Exchange Rate Pass-Through in Developing and Emerging Markets: A Survey of Conceptual, Methodological and Policy Issues, and Selected Empirical Findings'. *Journal of Development Studies* 50(1): 101–43.

Arrow, K., and G. Debreu (1954), 'Existence of an Equilibrium for a Competitive Economy'. *Econometrica* 22(3): 265–90.

Arslan Y., M. Drehmann, and B. Hofmann (2020), 'Central Bank Bond Purchases in Emerging Market Economies'. BIS Bulletin no. 20. Basel: Bank for International Settlements.

Assenmacher, K. (2017), 'Bridging the Gap between Structural VAR and DSGE Models'. In R. S. Gürkaynak and C. Tille (eds), *DSGE Models in the Conduct of Policy: Use As Intended*, ch. 2. A VoxEU.org eBook, CEPR Press.

Baldini, A., J. Benes, A. Berg, M. Dao, and R. Portillo (2018), 'Monetary Policy in Low-Income Countries in the Face of the Global Crisis'. In A. Berg and R. Portillo (eds), *Monetary Policy in Sub-Saharan Africa*, ch. 17. Oxford University Press.

Baldini, A., and M. Poplawski-Ribeiro (2011), 'Fiscal and Monetary Determinants of Inflation in Low-Income Countries: Theory and Evidence from Sub-Saharan Africa'. *Journal of African Economies*, Centre for the Study of African Economies (CSAE) 20(3): 419–62.

Balima, H., E. Kilama, and R. Tapsoba (2017), 'Settling the Inflation Targeting Debate: Lights from a Meta-Regression Analysis'. IMF, WP 17/213.

Baliño, T., A. Bennett, and E. Borensztein (1999), 'Monetary Policy in Dollarized Economies'. IMF Occasional Paper no. 171.

Ball, L., A. Chari, and P. Mishra (2016), 'Understanding Inflation in India'. National Bureau of Economic Research, WP 22948 (Dec.).

Bank Indonesia (2005), 'Foreign Exchange Intervention and Policy: Bank Indonesia Experiences'. In Bank for International Settlements, *Foreign Exchange Market Intervention in Emerging Markets: Motives, Techniques and Implications*, 177–87 BIS Papers no. 24.

Bank Indonesia (2018), Economic Report on Indonesia 2018.

Bank of England (2019), 'Future of Finance, Review on the Outlook for the UK Financial System: What it Means for the Bank of England'. Chaired by H. van Steenis. www.bankofengland.co.uk/report/2019/future-of-finance.

Bank of Nigeria (2018), 'Monetary Policy Review' (Aug.).

Bank of Zambia (2015), 'Issues on the Zambian Economy'. Working Papers, The BOZ Reader 2(1).

Bannister, G., M. Gardberg, and J. Turunen (2018), 'Dollarization and Financial Development'. IMF, WP 18/200.

Banque de France (2015), 'La Zone Franc'. Note d'information (Aug.).

Barajas A., R. Chami, C. Ebeke, and A. Oeking (2016), 'What's Different about Monetary Policy Transmission in Remittance-Dependent Countries?' IMF, WP 16/44.

Barja Daza, G., J. Monterrey Arce, and S. Villarroel Böhrt (2005), 'The Elasticity of Substitution in Demand for Non-Tradable Goods in Bolivia'. Inter-American Development Bank, WP R–488.

Barnichon, R., and S. Peiris (2008), 'Sources of Inflation in Sub-Saharan Africa'. *Journal of African Economies*, Centre for the Study of African Economies (CSAE) 17(5): 729–46.

Barro, R., and D. Gordon (1983), 'A Positive Theory of Monetary Policy in a Natural Rate Model'. *Journal of Political Economy* 91: 589–610.

Barro, R., and V. Grilli (1994), *European Macroeconomics*. Macmillan.

Barth, M., and V. Ramey (2001), 'The Cost Channel of Monetary Transmission'. National Bureau of Economic Research *Macroeconomics Annual* 16: 199–240. DOI: 10.1086/654443.

Basu, K., and A. Varoudakis (2013), 'How to Move the Exchange Rate if you Must: The Diverse Practice of Exchange Intervention by Central Banks and a Proposal for Doing It Better'. The World Bank, Policy Research Working Paper, WPS 6460.

Batini, N., B. Jackson, and S. Nickell (2005), 'An Open-Economy New Keynesian Phillips Curve for the U.K.'. *Journal of Monetary Economics* 52: 1061–71.

Batini, N., Y. B. Kim, P. Levine, and E. Lotti (2010), 'Informal Labour and Credit Markets: A Survey'. IMF, WP 10/42.

Batini, N., P. Levine, E. Lotti, and B. Yang (2011), 'Monetary and Fiscal Policy in the Presence of Informal Labor Markets'. University of Surrey Working Paper (May).

BCEAO (Banque Centrale des États de l'Afrique de l'Ouest) (2018), 'Annual Report 2017, Summarized Version'. Dakar.

Beauregard, P. (2003), 'Overshooting and Dollarization in the Democratic Republic of the Congo'. IMF, WP 03/105.

Beetsma, R., and M. Giulodori (2010) 'The Macroeconomic Costs and Benefits of the EMU and Other Monetary Unions: An Overview of Recent Research'. *Journal of Economic Literature* 48: 603–41.

Benes, J., A. Berg, R. Portillo, and D. Vavra (2018), 'Modelling Sterilized Interventions and Balance Sheet Effects of Monetary Policy in a New Keynesian Framework'. In A. Berg and R. Portillo (eds), *Monetary Policy in Sub-Saharan Africa*, ch. 13. Oxford University Press.

Berg, A., P. Karam, and D. Laxton (2006), 'Practical Model-Based Approach to Monetary Policy Analysis: Overview'. IMF, WP 06/80.

Berg, A., T. Mirzoev, R. Portillo, and L.F. Zanna (2018a), 'The Short-Run Macroeconomics of Aid Inflows: Understanding the Interaction of Fiscal and International Reserve Policy'. In A. Berg and R. Portillo (eds), *Monetary Policy in Sub-Saharan Africa*, ch. 12. Oxford University Press.

Berg, A., J. Vlcek, L. Charry, and R. Portillo (2018b), 'The Monetary Transmission Mechanism: Lessons from a Dramatic Event'. In A. Berg and R. Portillo (eds), *Monetary Policy in Sub-Saharan Africa*, ch. 5. Oxford University Press.

Berg, A., and R. Portillo (eds) (2018a), *Monetary Policy in Sub-Saharan Africa*, Oxford University Press.

Berg, A., and R. Portillo (2018b), 'Monetary Policy in Sub-Saharan Africa'. In A. Berg and R. Portillo (eds), *Monetary Policy in Sub-Saharan Africa*, ch. 1. Oxford University Press.

Berg, A., R. Portillo, and F. Unsal (2010), 'On the Optimal Adherence to Money Targets in a New-Keynesian Framework: An Application to Low-Income Countries'. IMF, WP/10/134

Berg, A., R. Portillo, and F. Unsal (2018c), 'On the Role of Money Target in the Monetary Framework in SSA'. In A. Berg and R. Portillo (eds), *Monetary Policy in Sub-Saharan Africa*, ch. 8. Oxford University Press.

Bernanke, B. S. (2004), 'The Great Moderation'. Remarks at the Meetings of the Eastern Economic Association, Washington DC (20 Feb.). www.federalreserve.gov/BOARDDOCS/SPEECHES2004/20040220/default.htm

Bernanke, B. S. (2006) 'Monetary Aggregates and Monetary Policy at the Federal Reserve: A Historical Perspective'. Speech at the Fourth ECB Central Banking Conference, Frankfurt, Germany (Nov.).

Bernanke, B. S., and S. A. Blinder (1988), 'Credit, Money and Aggregate Demand'. National Bureau of Economic Research, WP 2534.

Bernanke, B. S., J. Boivin, and P. Eliasz (2004), 'Measuring the Effects of Monetary Policy: a Factor-Augmented Vector Autoregressive (FAVAR) Approach'. National Bureau of Economic Research, WP 10220.

Bernanke, B. S., and M. Gertler (1995), 'Inside the Black Box: The Credit Channel of Monetary Policy Transmission'. *Journal of Economic Perspectives* 9(4): 27–48.

Bernanke, B. S., M. Gertler, and S. Gilchrist (1999), 'The Financial Accelerator in a Quantitative Business Cycle Framework'. *Handbook of Macroeconomics* 1: 1341–93.

Bernanke, B. S., and F. S. Mishkin (1997), 'Inflation Targeting: A New Framework for Monetary Policy'. *Journal of Economic Perspectives* 11(2): 97–116.

Blanchard, O. (2018), 'On the Future of Macroeconomic Models'. *Oxford Review of Economic Policy* 34(1–2): 43–54.

Blanchard O., G. Adler, and I. de Carvalho Filho (2015), 'Can Foreign Exchange Intervention Stem Exchange Rate Pressures from Global Capital Flow Shocks?' Peterson Institute for International Economics WP, 15–8.

Blanchard, O., and J. Galí (2007), 'Real Wage Rigidities and the New Keynesian Model'. *Journal of Money, Credit and Banking* 39, supplement 1: 35–65.

Blanchard, O., and J. Galí (2010), 'Labor Markets and Monetary Policy: A New Keynesian Model with Unemployment'. *American Economic Journal: Macroeconomics* 2: 1–30.

Bleaney, M., and M. Francisco (2017), 'Is the Phillips Curve Different in Poor Countries?' *Bulletin of Economic Research* 70(1): 1–11.

Bleaney, M., A. Morozumi, and Z. Mumuni (2020a), 'Inflation Targeting in Low Income Countries: Does It Work?' Research Paper 20/01, Centre for Research in Economic Development and International Trade, University of Nottingham.

Bleaney, M., A. Morozumi, and Z. Mumuni (2020b), 'Inflation Targeting and Monetary Policy in Ghana'. *Journal of African Economies*, Centre for the Study of African Economies (CSAE) 29(2): 121–45.

Bofinger, P. (2001), *Monetary Policy. Goals, Institutions, Strategies, and Instruments*. Oxford University Press.

Boivin, J., M.T. Kiley and F.S. Mishkin (2010), 'How has the Monetary Transmission Mechanism Evolved over Time?'. In B. M. Friedman and M. Woodford (eds), *Handbook of Monetary Economics*, vol. 3, 369–422. Elsevier.

Bordo, M. D. (2007), 'A Brief History of Central Banks'. Federal Reserve Bank of Cleveland(Dec.).www.clevelandfed.org/en/newsroom-and-events/publications/economic-commentary/economic-commentary-archives/2007-economic-commentaries/ec-20, 071, 201-a-brief-history-of-central-banks.aspx

Bordo, M. D., and L. Jonung (1999), 'The Future of EMU: What Does the History of Monetary Unions Tell Us?' National Bureau of Economic Research, WP 7365.

Bordo, M. D., and P. L. Siklos (2017), 'Central Banks: Evolution and Innovation in Historical Perspective'. National Bureau of Economic Research, WP 23847.

Boughrara, A., and S. Ghazouani (2009), 'Is There a Bank Lending Channel of Monetary Policy in Selected MENA Countries? A Comparative Analysis'. Economic Research Forum, Cairo, WP 471.

Brownbridge, M., and L. Kasekende (2018), 'Inflation Targeting in Uganda: What Lessons Can We Learn from Five Years of Experience?' In A. Berg and R. Portillo (eds), *Monetary Policy in Sub-Saharan Africa*, ch. 2. Oxford University Press.

Brunner, K., and A. H. Meltzer (1968), 'Liquidity Traps for Money, Bank Credit, and Interest Rates'. *Journal of Political Economy* 76(1): 1–37.

Brunner, K., and A. H. Meltzer (1972), 'Money, Debt, and Economic Activity'. *Journal of Political Economy* 80(5): 951–77.

Buiter, W. (2008), 'Can Central Banks Go Broke?' Center for Economic Policy Research, Policy Insight 24.

Buzeneca, I., and R. Maino (2007), 'Monetary Policy Implementation: Results from a Survey'. IMF, WP 07/7.

Cagan, P. (1956), 'The Monetary Dynamics of Hyperinflation'. In M. Friedman (ed.), *Studies in the Quantity Theory of Money*. University of Chicago Press.

Calvo, G. (1983), 'Staggered Prices in a Utility-Maximizing Framework'. *Journal of Monetary Economics* 12(3): 383–98.

Canzoneri, M. B., R. E. Cumbi, and B. E. Diba (2001), 'Is the Price Level Determined by the Needs of Fiscal Solvency?' *American Economic Review* 91(5): 1221–38.

Caporale, G. M., A. Çatık, M. Helmi, F. Ali, and M. Tajik (2020), 'The Bank Lending Channel in the Malaysian Islamic and Conventional Banking System'. *Global Finance Journal* 45: 1–26. Elsevier.

Carlstrom, C. T., and T. S. Fuerst (2000), 'The Fiscal Theory of the Price Level'. *Federal Reserve Bank of Cleveland Economic Review* 56(1): 22–32.

Carrera, C. (2010), 'The Bank Lending Channel in Peru: Evidence and Transmission Mechanism'. Banco Central de Reserva del Perù, WP 2010/21 (Dec.).

Castillo, P., and C. Montoro (2012), 'Inflation Dynamics in the Presence of Informal Labour Markets'. Bank for International Settlements, WP 372.

Castillo, P., H. Vega, E. Serrano, and C. Burga (2016), 'De-dollarization of Credit in Peru: The Role of Unconventional Monetary Policy Tools'. Banco Central de Reserva del Perú, WP (Apr.).

Catao, L., and R. Chang (2010), 'World Food Prices and Monetary Policy'. National Bureau of Economic Research, WP 16563 (Dec.).

CCSA (Committee for the Coordination of Statistical Activities) (2020), 'How Covid-19 Is Changing the World: A Statistical Perspective'. Vol. II. https://unstats.un.org/unsd/ccsa/documents/covid19-report-ccsa_vol2.pdf. (Sept.).

Cecchetti, S. G., and E. Kharroubi (2012), 'Reassessing the Impact of Finance on Growth'. Bank for International Settlements, WP 381.

CEMLA (Center for Latin American Monetary Studies) (2018), 'Central Banking Market Operations Framework in Latin America and the Caribbean, Compendium of Practices'. Available on *www.cemla.org*

Central Bank of Armenia (2019), 'Indirect Instruments of Monetary Policy and Mechanisms of Use'. www.cba.am/Storage/AM/downloads/karger/Indirect%20instruments_eng.pdf

Central Bank of Bangladesh (2019), 'Annual Report 2017–2018'. Available on www. bb.org.bdl

Central Bank of Cambodia (2018), 'Annual Report 2017'. Available on *www.nbc.org. kh/english*

Central Bank of Costa Rica. https://www.bccr.fi.cr/seccion-inversiones-bccr

Central Bank of Kazakhstan (2018), 'Financial Stability Report of Kazakhstan 2015–2017'. https://nationalbank.kz/cont/Financial%20Stability%20Report%20of%20Kazakhstan%202,015–2017.pdf

Central Bank of Kenya. https://www.centralbank.go.ke/monetary-policy/

Central Bank of Nicaragua (2019), 'Informe Anual 2018'. Available on *www.bcn.gob.ni*

Central Bank of Paraguay (2016) 'Guía de Instrumentos de Política Monetaria'. Available on www.bcp.gov.py/notas-metodologicas-y-articulos-de-interes-i540

Cerutti, E., S. Claessens, and L. Laeven (2017), 'The Use and Effectiveness of Macroprudential Policies: New Evidence'. *Journal of Financial Stability* 28: 203–24.

Céspedes, L. F., R. Chang, and A. Velasco (2004), 'Balance Sheets and Exchange Rate Policy'. *American Economic Review* 94(4): 1183–93.

Céspedes, L. F., R. Chang, and A. Velasco (2012), 'Is Inflation Targeting Still on Target?' National Bureau of Economic Research, WP 18570.

Chang, R., and A. Velasco (2001), 'A Model of Financial Crises in Emerging Markets'. *Quarterly Journal of Economics* 116(2): 489–517.

Céspedes, L. F., and A. Velasco (2012), 'Macroeconomic Performance during Commodity Price Booms and Busts'. National Bureau of Economic Research, WP 18569.

Charry, L., P. Gupta, and V. Thakoor (2018), 'Introducing a Semi-structural Macroeconomic Model for Rwanda'. In A. Berg and R. Portillo (eds), *Monetary Policy in Sub-Saharan Africa*, ch. 18. Oxford University Press.

Christensen, B. V. (2011), 'Have Monetary Transmission Mechanisms in Africa Changed?' In Bank for International Settlements (ed.), *Central Banking in Africa: Prospects in a Changing World*, BIS Paper 56, 37–61. Bank for International Settlements.

Christiano, L. J., M. S. Eichenbaum, and C. Evans (2005), 'Nominal Rigidities and the Dynamic Effects of a Shock to Monetary Policy'. *Journal of Political Economy* 113(1): 1–45.

Christiano, L. J., M. S. Eichenbaum, and M. Trabandt (2018), 'On DSGE Models'. *Journal of Economic Perspectives* 32(3): 113–40.

Christiano, L., and T. Fitzgerald (2000), 'Understanding the Fiscal Theory of the Price Level'. *Federal Reserve Bank of Cleveland Economic Review* 36(2): 2–38.

Christiano, L, H. Dalgic and A. Nurbekyan (2019) "Financial Dollarization in Emerging Markets: Efficient Risk Sharing or Prescription for Disaster?" Slides Presentation. Available on *www.minneapolisfed.org*

Čihák, M., A. Demirgüç-Kunt, M. S. Martínez Pería, and A. Mohseni-Cheraghlou (2012), 'Bank Regulation and Supervision around the World: A Crisis Update'. World Bank Policy Research, WP 6286.

Clarida, R., J. Galí, and M. Gertler (1999), 'The Science of Monetary Policy: A New Keynesian Perspective'. *Journal of Economic Literature* 37(4): 1661–707.

Cochrane, J. H. (2011), 'Understanding Policy in the Great Recession: Some Unpleasant Fiscal Arithmetic'. *European Economic Review* (Jan.): 2–30.

Coibion, O., Y. Gorodnichenko, and R. Kamdar (2017), 'The Formation of Expectations, Inflation and the Phillips Curve'. National Bureau of Economic Research, WP 23304.

Collier, P., and J. W. Gunning (1999), 'Trade Shocks. Theory and Evidence'. In P. Collier and J. W. Gunning (eds)., *Trade Shocks in Developing Countries*, vol. 1: *Africa*, 1–63. Oxford University Press.

Commission of the European Communities (1990), 'One Market, One Money: An Evaluation of the Potential Benefits and Costs of Forming an Economic and Monetary Union'. *European Economy* 44.

Cooper, R. N. (1971), 'An Assessment of Currency Devaluation in Developing Countries'. In G. Ranis (ed.), *Government and Economic Development*, 472–515. Yale University Press.

Corsetti, G., L. Dedola, and F. Viani (2011), 'Traded and Nontraded Goods Prices, and International Risk-Sharing: An Empirical Investigation'. In J. Frankel and C. Pissarides (eds), National Bureau of Economic Research *International Seminar on Macroeconomics*, 403–66. University of Chicago Press.

Creamer K., G. Farrell, and N. Rankin (2012), 'What Price-Level Data Can Tell Us about Pricing Conduct in South Africa'. South African Reserve Bank, WP 12/4.

Crispolti, V., E. Dabla-Norris, K. Jun, K. Shirono, and G. Tsibouris (2013), 'Assessing Reserve Adequacy in Low-Income Countries'. IMF, Occasional Paper 276.

Crowe, C., and E. Meade (2008), 'Central Bank Independence and Transparency: Evolution and Effectiveness'. *European Journal of Political Economy* 24(4): 763–77.

Cukierman, A., S. B. Webb, and B. Neyapti (1992), 'Measuring the Independence of Central Banks and Its Effect on Policy Outcomes'. *World Bank Economic Review* 6: 353–98.

Cull, R., and J. Morduch (2017), 'Microfinance and Economic Development'. World Bank Policy Research WP 8252.

Dagher, J., J. Gottschalk, and R. Portillo (2012), 'The Short-Run Impact of Oil Windfalls in Low-Income Countries: A DSGE Approach'. *Journal of African Economies*, Centre for the Study of African Economies (CSAE), 21(3): 343–72.

De Grauwe, P. (1994), *The Economics of Monetary Integration*, 2nd rev. edn. Oxford University Press.

De Grauwe, P., and Y. Ji (2019), *Behavioural Macroeconomics: Theory and Policy*. Oxford University Press.

De Grauwe, P., and M. Polan (2005), 'Is Inflation Always and Everywhere a Monetary Phenomenon?' *Scandinavian Journal of Economics* 107(2): 239–59.

De Gregorio, J. (2019), 'Inflation Targets in Latin America'. Peterson Institute for International Economics, WP 19/19.

de Haan, J., and S. Eijffinger (2016), 'The Politics of Central Bank Independence'. De Nederlandsche Bank, WP 539.

de la Torre, A., E. Levy Yeyati, and S. Schmukler (2003), 'Living and Dying with Hard Pegs: The Rise and Fall of Argentina's Currency Board'. *Economia* 3(2): 43–107.

de la Torre A., E. Levy Yeyati, and S. Schmukler (2010), 'Varieties of Internal Devaluation: Peripheral Europe in the Argentine mirror'. VOX CEPR Policy Portal (6 Mar.).

Debelle, G., and S. Fischer (1994), 'How Independent Should a Central Bank Be?' Proceedings of a Conference Sponsored by the Federal Reserve Bank of Boston, Falmouth, MA, June, 195–221. www.bostonfed.org/economic/conf/conf38/conf38f.pdf.

Debrun, X., P. R. Masson, and C. Pattillo (2011), 'Should African Monetary Unions Be Expanded? An Empirical Investigation of the Scope for Monetary Integration in Sub-Saharan Africa'. *Journal of African Economies*, Centre for the Study of African Economies (CSAE) 20 (suppl. 2) (May).

della Valle, G., V. Kota, R. Veyrune, E. Cabezon, and S. Guo (2018), 'Euroization Drivers and Effective Policy Response: An Application to the Case of Albania'. IMF WP 18/21

Devereux, M., and J. Yetman (2014), 'Globalisation, Pass-Through and the Optimal Policy Response to Exchange Rates'. Bank for International Settlements WP 450.

Di Bella, G. (2011), 'The Impact of the Global Financial Crisis on Microfinance and Policy Implications'. IMF, WP 11/175.

Dincer, N., and B. Eichengreen (2014), 'Central Bank Transparency and Independence: Updates and New Measures'. *International Journal of Central Banking* (Mar.): 189–253.

Dincer, N., and B. Eichengreen (2015), *Central Bank Transparency Data for 1998–2014* (new figures and tables, posted Sept. 2015).

Domanski, D., E. Kohlscheen, and R. Moreno (2016), 'Foreign Exchange Market Intervention in EMEs: What Has Changed?' *Bank for International Settlements Quarterly Review* (Sept.).

Dornbusch, R. (1976), 'Expectations and Exchange Rate Dynamics'. *Journal of Political Economy* 84: 1161–76.

Dunne, J. P., and E. Kasekende (2016), 'Financial Innovation and Money Demand: Evidence from Sub-Saharan Africa'. Economic Research Southern Africa (ERSA), WP 583.

Eagleton, C., and J. Williams (2007), *Money: A History*, 2nd edn. British Museum Press.

Easterly, W. (2004), *An Identity Crisis? Examining IMF Financial Programming*. New York University.

Economist, The (2019), https://www.economist.com/finance-and-economics/2019/09/02/argentinas-beleaguered-government-imposes-capital-controls.

Edwards, S. (1989), *Real Exchange Rates, Devaluation, and Adjustment: Exchange Rate Policy in Developing Countries*. MIT Press.

El Hamiani Khatat, M. (2016), 'Monetary Policy in the Presence of Islamic Banking'. IMF, WP 16/72.

European Central Bank (2011), 'The Implementation of Monetary Policy in the Euro-Area, General Documentation on Eurosystem Monetary Policy Instruments and Procedures' (Feb.).

Federico, P., C. A. Vegh, and G. Vuletin (2014), 'Reserve Requirement Policy over the Business Cycle'. National Bureau of Economic Research, WP 20612 updated dataset on www.guillermovuletin.com/data.

Fernández, A., M. Klein, A. Rebucci, M. Schindler, and M. Uribe (2016), 'Capital Control Measures: A New Dataset'. *IMF Economic Review* 64(3): 548–74. Database update on http://www.columbia.edu/~mu2166/fkrsu/, consulted on 3 June 2019.

Fielding, D. (2005a), 'Introduction'. In D. Fielding (ed.), *Macroeconomic Policy in the Franc Zone*, ch. 1. Palgrave Macmillan.

Fielding, D. (2005b), 'What Can the European Central Bank Learn from Africa?' UNU Policy Brief 4 (website www.wider.unu.edu).

Fiess, N., M. Fugazza, and W. Maloney (2010), 'Informal Self-Employment and Macroeconomic Fluctuations'. *Journal of Development Economics* 91 (2010): 211–26.

Financial Stability Institute (2015), FSI Survey Basel II, 2.5 and III Implementation. Bank for International Settlements.

Fischer, S. (1993), 'The Role of Macroeconomic Factors in Growth'. *Journal of Monetary Economics* 32(3): 485–512.

Fischer, S. (2001), 'Exchange Rate Regimes: Is the Bipolar View Correct?' *Journal of Economic Perspectives* 15(2): 3–24.

Fischer, S. (2015), 'Central Bank Independence'. Speech delivered at the 2015 Herbert Stein Memorial Lecture, National Economists Club, Washington, DC, 4 Nov. www.federal-reserve.gov/newsevents/speech/fischer20151104a.htm

Fisher, I. (1933), 'The Debt Deflation Theory of Great Depressions'. *Econometrica* 1(4): 337–57.

FLAR (Fondo Latinoamerico de Reservas) (2015), *Building a Latin American Reserve Fund: 35 Years of FLAR*. Bogotá: Latin American Reserve Fund.

Frankel, J. (2010), 'Monetary Policy in Emerging Markets: A Survey'. National Bureau of Economic Research, WP 16125

Frankel, J. (2012), 'The Death of Inflation Targeting'. *Project Syndicate* (16 May).

Frankel, J., X. Ma, and D. Xie (2019), 'The Impact of Exchange Rate Regimes on Economic Growth with Continuous Classification of *De Facto* Regimes'. WP, Kennedy School, Harvard University.

Frankel, J., D. Parsley, and S. J. Wei (2005), 'Slow Pass-Through around the World: A New Import for Developing Countries?' National Bureau of Economic Research, WP 11199.

Freixas, X. (1999), 'Optimal Bail-out Policy, Conditionality and Constructive Ambiguity'. Universitat Pompeu Fabra, Economic WP 400.

Friedman, M. (1968), 'The Role of Monetary Policy'. *American Economic Review* 58(1): 1–17.

Friedman, M. (1970), 'The Counter-Revolution in Monetary Theory'. Institute of Economic Affairs, Occasional Paper 33.

Friedman, M., and A. Schwartz (1963), *A Monetary History of the United States, 1867–1960*. Princeton University Press.

Fry, M. (1995), *Money, Interest, and Banking in Economic Development*, 2nd edn. Johns Hopkins University Press.

Gagnon, E. (2007), 'Price Setting During Low and High Inflation: Evidence from Mexico'. Federal Reserve Board, International Finance Discussion Paper 896.

Galí, J. (2008), *Monetary Policy, Inflation and the Business Cycle: An Introduction to the New Keynesian Framework*. Princeton University Press.

Galí, J. (2018), 'The State of New Keynesian Economics: A Partial Assessment'. *Journal of Economic Perspectives* 32(3): 87–112.

Galí, J., M. Gertler, and D. Lopez-Salido (2005), 'Robustness of the Estimates of the Hybrid New Keynesian Phillips Curve'. *Journal of Monetary Economics* 52: 1107–18.

García-Escribano, M., and S. Sosa (2011) 'What Is Driving Financial De-dollarization in Latin America?' IMF, WP 11/10.

Garriga, A. C. (2016), 'Central Bank Independence in the World: A New Dataset'. *International Interactions* 42(5): 849–68. DOI: 10.1080/03050629.2016.1188813

Gerlach, S. (2017), 'DSGE Models in Monetary Policy Committees'. In R. S. Gürkaynak and C. Tille (eds), *DSGE Models in the Conduct of Policy: Use as Intended*, ch. 3. A VoxEU.org eBook, CEPR Press.

Goldfeld, S. M. (1976), 'The Case of the Missing Money'. *Brookings Papers on Economic Activity* 7(3): 683–740.

Gonzalez-Vega, C., and M. Villafani-Ibarnegaray (2011), 'Microfinance in Bolivia: Foundation of the Growth, Outreach and Stability of the Financial System'. In B. Armendáriz and M. Labie (eds), *The Handbook of Microfinance*. World Scientific 203–50.

Goodhart, C. A. E (1989a), 'Central Banking'. In J. Eatwell, M. Milgate, and P. Newman (eds), *The New Palgrave: Money*. Macmillan.

Goodhart, C. A. E. (1989b), *Money, Information and Uncertainty*, 2d ed. MacMillan.

Gray, S. (2008), *Liquidity Forecasting*. Centre for Central Banking Studies, Bank of England.

Gray, S., P. Karam, V. Meeyam, and M. Stubbe (2013), *Monetary Issues in the Middle East and North Africa Region: A Policy Implementation Handbook for Central Bankers*. Institute for Capacity Development and Monetary and Capital Markets Department, IMF.

Gray, S., and R. Pongsaparn (2015), 'Issuance of Central Bank Securities: International Experiences and Guidelines'. IMF, WP 15/106.

Grilli, V., D. Masciandaro, G. Tabellini, E. Malinvaud, and M. Pagano (1991), 'Political and Monetary Institutions and Public Financial Policies in the Industrial Countries'. *Economic Policy* 13: 341–92.

Gulde, A. M., D. Hoelscher, A. Ize, D. Marston, and G. De Nicoló (2004), 'Financial Stability in Dollarized Economies'. IMF, Occasional Paper 230.

Guyer, J. I., and K. Pallaver (2018), 'Money and Currency in African History'. *Oxford Research Encyclopedia, African History*. DOI: 10.1093/acrefore/9780190277734.013.144

Ha, J., M. Stocker, and H. Yilmazkuday (2019), 'Inflation and Exchange Rate Pass-Through'. In J. Ha, M. Kose, and F. Ohnsorge (eds), *Inflation in Emerging and Developing Economies: Evolution, Drivers, and Policies*, ch. 5. World Bank.

Hammond, G. (2012), *State of the Art Inflation Targeting*. Bank of England Centre for Central Banking Studies.

Hanke, S., and N. Krus (2012), 'World Hyperinflations'. Cato Institute, WP (Aug.).

Hauner, D., and G. Di Bella (2005), 'How Useful Is Monetary Econometrics in Low-Income Countries? The Case of Money Demand and the Multipliers in Rwanda'. IMF, WP 05/178.

Heng, D. (2015), 'Impact of the New Financial Services Law in Bolivia on Financial Stability and Inclusion'. IMF, WP 15/267.

Hofman, D., M. Chamon, P. Deb, T. Harjes, U. Rawat, I. Yamamoto (2020), 'Intervention under Inflation Targeting: When Could It Make Sense?' IMF, WP 20/09.

Houssa, R. (2008), 'Monetary Union in West Africa and Asymmetric Shocks: A Dynamic Structural Factor Model Approach'. *Journal of Development Economics* 85(1–2): 319–47.

Houssa, R., C. Otrok, and R. Puslenghea (2010), 'A Model for Monetary Policy Analysis for Sub-Saharan Africa'. *Open Economies Review* 21: 127–45.

IMF (International Monetary Fund) (2004), 'Monetary Policy Implementation at Different Stages of Market Development'. IMF.

IMF (2009), *Balance of Payments and International Investment Position Manual*, 6th edn. IMF.

IMF (2010), 'Monetary Policy Effectiveness in Sub-Saharan Africa; Regional Economic Outlook, Sub-Saharan Africa'. *World Economic and Financial Surveys*, ch. 2. IMF.

IMF (2011), 'Target What You Can Hit: Commodity Price Swings and Monetary Policy'. *World Economic Outlook* (Sept.), ch. 3. IMF.

IMF (2012), 'Why Do LIC Banks Not Lend?' In *Enhancing Financial Sector Surveillance in Low-Income Countries*, Background paper, ch. 7. IMF.

IMF (2013), 'Energy Subsidy Reform in Sub-Saharan Africa: Experiences and Lessons'. IMF African Department 13/2.

IMF (2014), 'Conditionality in Evolving Monetary Policy Regimes'. IMF (Mar.).

IMF (2015a), 'Monetary Policy and Financial Stability'. Staff Report, IMF (Aug.).

IMF (2015b), 'Evolving Monetary Policy Frameworks in Low-Income and Other Developing Countries'. IMF Policy Paper (Oct.).

IMF (2016a), 'Guidance Note on the Assessment of Reserve Adequacy and Related Considerations'. IMF (June).

IMF (2016b), 'Benin, Country Report'. IMF, 16/7.

IMF (2017), 'Egypt, Article IV Consultations, Staff Report'. IMF, Country Report 17/290.

IMF (2018a), 'Indonesia: Selected Issues'. IMF, Country Report 18/33.

IMF (2018b), 'Bolivia Article IV Consultation'. IMF, Country Report 18/379.

IMF (2019a), 'Annual Report on Exchange Arrangements and Exchange Restrictions 2018'. IMF (Oct.).

IMF (2019b), 'Uruguay'. 22. IMF, Country Report 19/64.

IMF (2019c), 'Nigeria, Staff Report'. IMF, Country Report 19/92.

IMF (2019d), 'Myanmar, Technical Assistance Report, Monetary Operations'. IMF, Country Report 19/87.

IMF (2019e), 'West African Monetary Union, Article IV Consultation: Staff Report on Common Policies for Member Countries'. IMF, Country Report 19/90.

IMF (2019f), 'Paraguay, Article IV Consultation'. IMF, Country Report 19/111.

IMF (2019g), 'Vietnam: Article IV Consultation'. IMF, Country Report 19/235.

IMF (2019h), 'Central African Economic and Monetary Community'. IMF, Country Report 19/383.

Islamic Financial Services Board (2019), 'Islamic Financial Services Industry Stability Report 2019'. IFSB.

Ize, A., and E. Levy Yeyati (2003), 'Financial Dollarization'. *Journal of International Economics* 59: 323–47.

Jácome, L. I. (2015), 'Central Banking in Latin America: From the Gold Standard to the Golden Years'. IMF, WP 15/60.

Jahan, S. (2018), 'Inflation Targeting: Holding the Line', *Finance and Development* (June). www.imf.org/external/pubs/ft/fandd/basics/target.htm

Julio, J. M., H. Zárate, and D. Hernández (2009), 'The Stickiness of Colombian Consumer Prices'. Banco de la República, Colombia, Borradores de Economía 578.

Jump, R. C., and P. Levine (2019), 'Behavioural New Keynesian Models'. *Journal of Macroeconomics* 59: 59–77.

Kaplan, G., B. Moll, and G. L. Violante (2018), 'Monetary Policy According to HANK'. *American Economic Review* 108(3): 697–743.

Karangwa, M., and B. Mwenese (2015), 'The Forecasting and Policy Analysis Systems (FPAS) Macro-model for Rwanda'. *BNR Economic Review* 7: 101–31.

Kashyap, A., and J. Stein (1995), 'The Impact of Monetary Policy on Bank Balance Sheets'. Carnegie–Rochester Conference Series on Public Policy 42: 151–95.

Kawai, M. (2015), 'From the Chiang Mai Initiative to an Asian Monetary Fund'. Asian Development Bank Institute, WP 527 (May).

King, D., and T. Mancini-Griffoli (2018), 'Monetary Operations'. In T. Adrian, D. Laxton, and M. Obstfeld (eds), *Advancing the Frontiers of Monetary Policy*, ch. 5. IMF.

King, M. (2004) 'The Institutions of Monetary Policy'. National Bureau of Economic Research, WP 10400.

Kireyev, A. (2015), 'How to Improve the Effectiveness of Monetary Policy in the West African Economic and Monetary Union'. IMF, WP 15/99.

Klomp J. and J. de Haan (2010), 'Inflation and Central Bank Independence: A Meta-Regression Analysis'. *Journal of Economic Surveys* 24(4): 593–621.

Kose, M. A., and R. Riezman (2001) 'Trade Shocks and Macroeconomic Fluctuations in Africa'. *Journal of Development Economics* 65: 55–80.

Kovanen, A. (2006), 'Why Do Prices in Sierra Leone Change So Often? A Case Study Using Micro-Level Price Data'. IMF, WP 6/53.

Krugman, P. (1979), 'A Model of Balance-of-Payments Crises'. *Journal of Money, Credit and Banking* 11(3): 311–25.

Krugman, P. (1999). 'Balance Sheets, the Transfer Problem, and Financial Crises'. In P. Isard, A. Razin, and A. Rose (eds), *International Finance and Financial Crises: Essays in Honor of Robert Flood,* 31–55. Kluwer Academic.

Krugman, P., and M. Obstfeld (2009), *International Economics: Theory and Policy*, 8th edn. Pearson International.

Krugman, P., and L. Taylor (1978), 'Contractionary Effects of Devaluation'. *Journal of International Economies* 8(14): 445–56.

Kydland, F., and E. C. Prescott (1977), 'Rules Rather than Discretion: The Inconsistency of Optimal Plans'. *Journal of Political Economy* 85: 473–91.

Laeven, L., and F. Valencia (2018), 'Systemic Banking Crises Revisited'. IMF, WP 18/206.

Lane, P. R., and G. M. Milesi-Ferretti (2017), 'International Financial Integration in the Aftermath of the Global Financial Crisis'. IMF, WP 17/115.

Laskaridis, C., and J. Toporowski (2016), 'Financial Sector Development in the Context of the Franc Zone'. Financialisation, Economy, Society and Sustainable Development (FESSUD), WP 158.

Laurens, B. J., K. Eckhold, D. King, N. Maehle, A. Naseer, and A. Durré (2015) 'The Journey to Inflation Targeting: Easier Said than Done. The Case for Transitional Arrangements along the Road'. IMF, WP 15/136.

Leeper, E. M. (1991), 'Equilibria under Active and Passive Monetary and Fiscal Policies'. *Journal of Monetary Economics* 27: 129–47.

Leeper, E. M. (2009), 'Anchors Away: How Fiscal Policy Can Undermine the Taylor Principle'. National Bureau of Economic Research, WP 15514.

Leeper, E. M. (2013), 'Fiscal Limits and Monetary Policy'. National Bureau of Economic Research, WP 18877.

Lendele, K., and J. Kamanda Kimona-Mbinga (2005), 'Nature et Spécificité de la Dollarisation de l'Économie Congolaise (RDC)', *Mondes en Développement* 2005/2(130): 41–62. www.cairn.info/revue-mondes-en-developpement-2005-2-page-41.htm

Levy Yeyati, E. (2006), 'Financial Dollarization: Evaluating the Consequences'. *Economic Policy* 21(45): 61, 63–118.

Levy Yeyati, E., and F. Sturzenegger (2002), *Dollarization*. MIT Press.

Lewis, M., and L. Algaoud (2001), *Islamic Banking*. Edward Elgar.

Li, B., C. Adam, A. Berg, P. Montiel, and S. O'Connell (2018), 'Identifying the Monetary Transmission Mechanism in Sub-Saharan Africa'. In A. Berg and R. Portillo (eds), *Monetary Policy in Sub-Saharan Africa*, 112–32. Oxford University Press.

Loayza, N. V. (2016), 'Informality in the Process of Development and Growth'. World Bank, WPS 7858.

Loyo E. (1999), 'Tight Money Paradox on the Loose: A Fiscalist Hyperinflation'. John F. Kennedy School of Government, Harvard University, June.

Lucas, R. E. (1976), 'Econometric Policy Evaluation: A Critique'. In K. Brunner and A. Meltzer (eds), *The Phillips Curve and Labor Markets*, 19–46. Carnegie–Rochester Conference Series on Public Policy. North-Holland.

Maehle, N. (2020), 'Monetary Policy Implementation: Operational Issues for Countries with Evolving Monetary Policy Frameworks'. IMF, WP 20/26.

Marchettini, D., and R. Maino (2015), 'Systemic Risk Assessment in Low Income Countries: Balancing Financial Stability and Development'. IMF, WP 15/190.

McCallum, B. T., and E. Nelson (2006), 'Monetary and Fiscal Theories of the Price Level: The Irreconciliable Differences'. National Bureau of Economic Research, WP 12089.

McCallum, B. T., and E. Nelson (2010), 'Money and Inflation: Some Critical Issues'. In B. M. Friedman and M. Woodford (eds), *Handbook of Monetary Economics*, vol. 3, 97–153. Elsevier.

McKinnon, R. I. (1973), *Money and Capital in Economic Development*. Brookings Institution.

Medina, J., D. Rappoport, and C. Soto (2007). Dinámica de Ajuste de los Precios: Evidencia de Datos Microeconómicos para Chile. *Economía Chilena* 10: 5–26.

Mehrota, A., and J. Yetman, J. (2015), 'Financial Inclusion: Issues for Central Banks'. *Bank for International Settlements Quarterly Review* (Mar.): 83–96.

Milgrom, P. (1989), 'Auctions and Bidding: A Primer'. *Journal of Economic Perspectives* 3(3): 3–22.

Mishkin, F. S. (1995), The Economics of Money, Banking and Financial Markets. New York: Pearson, fourth edition.

Mishkin, F. S. (1996), 'The Channels of Monetary Transmission: Lessons for Monetary Policy'. National Bureau of Economic Research, WP 5464.

Mishkin, F. S. (1999), International Experiences with Different Monetary Policy Regimes. *Journal of Monetary Economics* 43(3): 579–605.

Mishkin, F. S. (2011), 'Monetary Policy Strategy: Lessons from the Crisis'. National Bureau of Economic Research, WP 16755.

Mishra, P., and P. Montiel (2012), 'How Effective Is Monetary Transmission in Low-Income Countries? A Survey of the Empirical Evidence'. IMF, WP 12/143.

Mishra, P., P. Montiel, P. Pedroni, and A. Spilimbergo (2014), 'Monetary Policy and Bank Lending Rates in Low Income Countries: Heterogeneous Panel Estimates'. *Journal of Development Economics* 111: 117–31.

Mishra, P., P. Montiel, and A. Spilimbergo (2012), 'Monetary Transmission in Low Income Countries'. *IMF Economic Review* 60(2): 270–302.

MIX (2019), MIX Market Database, Microfinance Information Exchange, Inc., www.themix.org/mix-market

Monet, E., and M. Vari (2019), 'Liquidity Ratios as Monetary Policy Tools: Some Historical Lessons for Macroprudential Policy'. IMF, WP 19/176.

Monroe, H., A. Carvajal, and C. Pattillo (2010), 'Perils of Ponzis'. *IMF Finance and Development* (Mar.).

Morales, J.A (2012), 'La Política Económica Boliviana 1982–2010'. Plural Editores.

Moreno, R. (2003), 'Fiscal Issues and Central Banking in Emerging Economies: An Overview'. Bank for International Settlements, Paper 201–9.

Muellbauer, J. (2016), 'Macroeconomics and Consumption: Why Central Bank Models Failed and How to Repair Them'. VOX–CEPR Policy Portal (21 Dec.).

Mwase, N., and F. Kumah (2015), 'Revisiting the Concept of Dollarization: The Global Financial Crisis and Dollarization in Low-Income Countries'. IMF, WP 15/12.

Nchake, M., L. Edwards, and N. Rankin (2015), 'Price-Setting Behaviour in Lesotho: Stylised Facts from Consumer Retail Prices'. *South African Journal of Economics* 83(2): 199–219.

Nugent, J., and C. Glezakos (1982), 'Phillips Curves in Developing Countries: The Latin American Case'. *Economic Development and Cultural Change* 30: 321–34.

O'Connell, S. A. (2011), 'Towards a Rule-Based Approach to Monetary Policy in Sub-Saharan Africa'. *Journal of African Economies*, Centre for the Study of African Economies (CSAE), 20 (suppl. 2): ii1–ii66.

Obstfeld, M. (1994), 'The Logic of Currency Crises'. *Cahiers Économiques et Monétaires* 43: 189–213.

Obstfeld, M., and K. Rogoff (1996), *Foundations of International Macroeconomics*. MIT Press.

OECD (2008), 'Economic Surveys: Indonesia 2008, Economic Assessment'. OECD.

Opolot, J. (2013), 'Bank Lending Channel of the Monetary Transmission Mechanism in Uganda: Evidence from Panel Data Analysis'. Bank of Uganda, WP 01/2013.

Ostry, J. D., A. R. Ghosh, and M. Chamon (2012), 'Two Targets, Two Instruments: Monetary and Exchange Rate Policies in Emerging Market Economies'. IMF Staff Discussion Note.

Owoundi, F. (2016), 'Do Exchange Rate Misalignments Really Affect Economic Growth? The Case of Sub-Saharan African Countries'. *International Economics* 145: 92–110.

Patel, N., and P. Cavallino (2019), 'FX Intervention: Goals, Strategies and Tactics'. In Bank of International Settlements, Reserve Management and FX Intervention, *BIS Papers* 104: 25–44.

Peiris, S. J., and M. Saxegaard (2007), 'An Estimated DSGE Model for Monetary Policy Analysis in Low-Income Countries'. IMF, WP 07/282.

Pereira da Silva, L. A. (2018), 'In Defense of Central Bank DSGE Modelling'. Opening Speech, Bank for International Settlements Research Network meeting, Basel (8 Mar.).

Perrault III, Nicolas (2020), https://commons.wikimedia.org/wiki/File:Venezuela_inflation_on_the_blackmarket_(DolarToday)_on_a_logarithmic_scale.png

Phillips, A. W. (1958), 'The Relation between Unemployment and the Rate of Change of Money Wage Rates in the United Kingdom, 1861–1957'. *Economica* 25(100): 283–99.

Polillo, S., and M. Guillén (2005), 'Globalization Pressures and the State: The Worldwide Spread of Central Bank Independence', *American Journal of Sociology* 110(6): 1764–1802.

Poole, W. (1970), 'Optimal Choice of Monetary Policy Instruments in a Simple Stochastic Macro Model'. *Quarterly Journal of Economics* 84(2): 197–216.

Portillo, R., and Y. Ustyugova (2015), 'A Model for Monetary Policy Analysis in Uruguay'. IMF, WP 15/170.

Ramayandi, A., and A. Rosario (2010), 'Monetary Policy Discipline and Macroeconomic Performance: The Case of Indonesia'. Asian Development Bank Economics, WP 238.

Ramey, V. (1993), 'How Important Is the Credit Channel in the Transmission of Monetary Policy?' Carnegie–Rochester Conference Series on Public Policy 39: 1–45. North-Holland.

Reding, P., and J. A. Morales (2014), 'Currency Substitution and Network Externalities'. PDF, University of Namur, Belgium. Also in SSRN Electronic Journal. DOI: 10.2139/ssrn.549061

Reinhart, C. (2016), 'The Return of Dollar Shortages'. *Project Syndicate* (14 Oct.).

Reinhart, C., and K. Rogoff (2009), *This Time is Different*. Princeton University Press.

Reserve Bank of Fiji (2013), 'Monetary Policy in Fiji'. www.rbf.gov.fj/getattachment/Publications-(1)/Booklet/RBF%E2%80%A2MPB%E2%80%A2for-Web.pdf.aspx.

Rey, H. (2018), 'Dilemma Not Trilemma: The Global Financial Cycle and Monetary Policy Independence'. National Bureau of Economic Research, WP 21162.

Rodriguez, G. (2010), 'Using a Forward-Looking Phillips Curve to Estimate the Output Gap in Peru'. *Review of Applied Economics* 6: 85–97.

Rogoff, K. (1985), 'The Optimal Degree of Commitment to an Intermediate Monetary Target'. *Quarterly Journal of Economics* 100: 1169–90.

Romer, C., and D. Romer (1989), 'Does Monetary Policy Matter? A New Test in the Spirit of Friedman and Schwartz'. In O. Blanchard and S. Fischer (eds), *National Bureau of Economic Research Macroecononomics Annual* 4, 121–70. MIT Press.

Rosenberg, R., S. Gaul, W. Ford, and O. Tomilova (2013), 'Microcredit Interest Rates and Their Determinants 2004–2011'. In D. Köhn (ed.) *Microfinance 3.0*. Berlin, Heidelberg: Springer. DOI: 10.1007/978-3-642-41704-7_4

Rusuhuzwa T. K. (2019), 'Moving from Monetary Targeting Framework to Price Based Monetary Policy: The Experience of the National Bank of Rwanda'. *BNR Economic Review* 14: 1–17.

Rusuhuzwa T. K., and J. Irankunda (2012), 'Assessing the Stability of the Money Multiplier'. *BNR Economic Review* 5: 41–55.

Rusuhuzwa T. K., and J. P. Mutuyimana (2016), 'Financial Innovations and Monetary Policy in Rwanda'. *BNR Economic Review* 9: 1–29.

Sachs, J. D. (1987). 'The Bolivian Hyperinflation and Stabilization'. *American Economic Review* 77: 279–83.

S&P Global Ratings (2020), 'The Eco Era: What Will West Africa's New Currency Mean for the Region?' (17 Feb.).

Salter, W. E. (1959), 'Internal and External Balance: The Role of Price and Expenditure Effects'. *Economic Record* 35: 226–38.

Samarina A., M. Terpstra, and J. de Haan (2014), 'Inflation Targeting and Inflation Performance: A Comparative Analysis'. *Applied Economics* 46(1): 41–56.

Sargent, T. J., and N. Wallace (1981), 'Some Unpleasant Monetarist Arithmetic'. *Quarterly Review*, Federal Reserve Bank of Minneapolis (Fall).

Sarker, A. (2016), 'An Evaluation of Islamic Monetary Policy Instruments Introduced in Some Selected OIC Member Countries'. *Islamic Economic Studies* 24(1): 1–47.

Saxegaard, M. (2006), 'Excess Liquidity and Effectiveness of Monetary Policy: Evidence for Sub-Saharan Africa'. IMF, WP 06/115.

Saz, G. (2011), 'The Turkish Phillips Curve Experience and the New Keynesian Phillips Curve: A Conceptualization and Application of a Novel Measure for Marginal Costs'. *International Research Journal of Finance and Economics* 63: 8–45.

Schaechter, A. (2001), 'Implementation of Monetary Policy and the Central Bank's Balance Sheet'. IMF, WP 01/149.

Schaechter, A., T. Kinda, N. Budina, and A. Weber (2012), 'Fiscal Rules in Response to the Crisis: Toward the "Next-Generation" Rules. A New Dataset'. IMF, WP 12/187.

Schanz, J. (2019), 'Foreign Exchange Reserves in Africa: Benefits, Costs and Political Economy Considerations'. Bank for International Settlements, Paper 105.

Schuler, K. (2005), 'Ignorance and Influence: U.S. Economists on Argentina's Depression of 1998–2002'. *Econ Journal Watch* 2(2): 234–78.

Seidel, R. N. (1972), 'American Reformers Abroad: The Kemmerer Missions in South America, 1923–1931'. *Journal of Economic History* 32(2): 520–45.

Senbeta, S. (2011), 'How Applicable Are the New Keynesian DSGE Models to a Typical Low-Income Economy?' Munich Personal RePEc Archive (MPRA) Paper 30,931, University Library of Munich.

Shaw, E. S. (1973), *Financial Deepening in Economic Development*. Oxford University Press.

Stiglitz, J., and A. Weiss (1981), 'Credit Rationing in Markets with Imperfect Information'. *American Economic Review* 71: 393–410.

Svensson, L. E. O. (2005), 'Monetary Policy with Judgment: Forecast Targeting', *International Journal of Central Banking* 1(1): 1–54.

Svensson, L. E. O. (2010), 'Inflation Targeting'. In B. M. Friedman and M. Woodford (eds), *Handbook of Monetary Economics*, 1237–302. Elsevier.

Svirydzenka, K. (2016), 'Introducing a New Broad-Based Index of Financial Development'. IMF, WP 16/5.

Swan, T. (1960), 'Economic Control in a Dependent Economy'. *Economic Record* 36: 51–66.

Taylor, J. B. (1993), 'Discretion versus Policy Rules in Practice'. *Carnegie–Rochester Conference Series on Public Policy* 39: 195–214. North-Holland.

Taylor, J. B. (2016), 'Central Bank Models: Lessons from the Past and Ideas for the Future'. Keynote presentation, Workshop 'Central Bank Models: the Next Generation', Bank of Canada (17 Nov.).

Tobin, J. (1969), 'A General Equilibrium Approach to Monetary Theory'. *Journal of Money, Credit and Banking* 1(1): 15–29.

Torvik, R. (2018), 'Oil Prices and the Exchange Rate: Optimal Monetary Policy for Oil Exporting Countries'. In R. Arezki, R. Boucekkine, J. Frankel, M. Laksaci, and R. van der Ploeg (eds), *Rethinking the Macroeconomics of Resource-Rich Countries*: 65–74. VoxEU. org eBook.

Tucker, P. (2014), 'The Lender of Last Resort and Modern Central Banking: Principles and Reconstruction'. In *Re-thinking the Lender of Last Resort*, Bank for International Settlements Papers, vol. 79: 10–42.

Valdivia, D. (2008), '¿Es Importante la Fijación de Precios para Entender la Dinámica de la Inflación en Bolivia?' Instituto de Estudios Avanzados en Desarrollo, WP 02/2008.

Van Wijnbergen, S. (1986), 'Exchange Rate Management and Stabilization Policies in Developing Countries'. *Journal of Development Economics* 23(2): 227–47.

Van't dack, J. (1999), 'Implementing Monetary Policy in Emerging Market Economies: An Overview of Issues'. Bank for International Settlements Policy, Paper 5: 3–72.

Varian, H. (2004), 'Why Is That Dollar Bill in Your Pocket Worth Anything?' *New York Times* (15 Jan.).

Vegh, C. A. (2013), *Open Economy Macroeconomics in Developing Countries*. MIT Press.

Velasco, A. (2013), 'Monetary Regime Transition in the Emerging World'. *Project Syndicate* (7 Jan.).

Walsh, C. E. (2000), 'Teaching Inflation Targeting: An Analysis for Intermediate Macro'. *Journal of Economic Education* 33(4).

Walsh, C. E. (2003), *Monetary Theory and Policy*, 2nd edn. MIT Press.

Walsh, C. E. (2010), *Monetary Theory and Policy*, 3rd edn. MIT Press.

Warjiyo, P., and S. Juhro (2019), *Central Bank Policy: Theory and Practice*. Emerald Publishing.

Wicker, E. (1986), 'Terminating Hyperinflation in the Dismembered Habsburg Monarchy'. *American Economic Review* 76(3): 350–64.

Woodford, M. (1995), 'Price Level Determinacy Without Control of a Monetary Aggregate'. *Carnegie–Rochester Conference Series on Public Policy* 43 (1): 1–46. North-Holland.

Woodford, M. (2001), 'Fiscal Requirements for Price Stability'. *Journal of Money, Credit and Banking* 33(3): 669–728.

Woodford, M. (2012), 'Inflation Targeting and Financial Stability'. National Bureau of Economic Research, WP 17967.

World Bank (2018), 'Global Financial Development Data Base, July 2018 version', available on *www.worldbank.org*

World Bank (2019), 'Inaugural RAMP Survey on the Reserve Management Practices of Central Banks, Results and Observations'. World Bank.

World Bank (2020), 'Global Economic Prospects'. World Bank (June).

World Economic Forum (2012), *The Financial Development Report 2012*. World Economic Forum.

Zaheer, S., S. Ongena, and S. J. G. van Wijnbergen (2013), 'The Transmission of Monetary Policy through Conventional and Islamic Banks'. *International Journal of Central Banking* 9(4): 175–224.

Zoli, E. (2005), 'How Does Fiscal Policy Affect Monetary Policy in Emerging Market Economies?' Bank for International Settlements, WP 174.

Name Index

Subject Index